AF179542

Wicked Ladies

Wicked Ladies: Provincial Women, Crime and the Eighteenth-Century English Justice System

By

Gregory J. Durston

CAMBRIDGE
SCHOLARS
PUBLISHING

Wicked Ladies:
Provincial Women, Crime and the Eighteenth-Century English Justice System,
by Gregory J. Durston

This book first published 2013

Cambridge Scholars Publishing

12 Back Chapman Street, Newcastle upon Tyne, NE6 2XX, UK

British Library Cataloguing in Publication Data
A catalogue record for this book is available from the British Library

Copyright © 2013 by Gregory J. Durston

All rights for this book reserved. No part of this book may be reproduced, stored in a retrieval system, or transmitted, in any form or by any means, electronic, mechanical, photocopying, recording or otherwise, without the prior permission of the copyright owner.

ISBN (10): 1-4438-4269-9, ISBN (13): 978-1-4438-4269-3

CONTENTS

ACKNOWLEDGEMENTS

I would like to acknowledge the invaluable assistance provided by the staff of Kingston University Library, the British Library, Kingston Local History Room, and the National Archives in Kew. I am extremely grateful for assistance and advice from a wide variety of people on many different aspects of this book and, in particular, Judge Nicholas Philpot and Esther Snell. I would also like to thank Philippa Russell for help with the preparation of the manuscript. In a work with a large element of synthesis, a huge debt is owed to the many scholars who have worked in the same field and whose work is cited. Nevertheless, all mistakes are, needless to say, purely those of the author. Readers should note that abbreviated titles are often used in footnotes, especially for the Assizes reports; the full versions of these sources can be found in the bibliography.

—Gregory J. Durston.
London, All Saints Day, 2012.

CHAPTER ONE

INTRODUCTION: WOMEN AND CRIME IN PROVINCIAL ENGLAND

Introduction

This book will consider the experiences of eighteenth-century women in provincial England as both the perpetrators of various crimes and as suspects and defendants in the era's criminal justice process. In this context, 'provincial' is taken to refer to all parts of the country outside London and Middlesex; that is, all areas that did not send their serious crimes to the Old Bailey court for trial, whether they were in the Home Counties, West Country, Midlands, East Anglia, or the North. The period under consideration is what is sometimes termed the 'long' eighteenth century, that is the years from the Glorious Revolution of 1688 to the Battle of Waterloo in 1815. Of course, such delineations, though necessary, are inherently artificial; the era witnessed enormous social, political, cultural, and economic changes. Indeed, these years straddle two further conventional divisions, that between early modern and modern history. Wherever the line that separates these two periods is drawn, almost all scholars would place the era's first 12 years in the former, and last 15 in the latter.

A justification for such a study and its parameters is necessary, if only because, in recent years, there has been a considerable amount of work on female crime during this period, not least by the present author. It can no longer necessarily be said that historians universalise the male experience. However, many of these studies have had an overwhelmingly or specifically Metropolitan focus. This is for two reasons. Firstly, the eighteenth-century Metropolis was and is (to modern observers) an eye-catching phenomenon. Based on the neighbouring cities of London and Westminster, and incorporating urban Middlesex, it was, according to one contemporary estimate, a city of almost 631,000 souls in 1716.[1] It

[1] *The Gentleman's Magazine*, 1735, vol.5, p.355.

continued to grow exponentially, so that at the end of the century the Metropolitan area contained about a million people, many of them attracted from the provinces, Ireland, Scotland, the Continent, or even further afield. As a result, it was also characterised by an unprecedented degree of change. Social cohesion could, and sometimes did, become attenuated in such an environment, something that was manifest in a lack of family ties, participation in communal activities, and transient accommodation arrangements. By 1700, London was grappling with many of the problems posed by urbanisation that have become so important around the Globe in the last three centuries.

Moral conformity was harder to enforce in the capital, which was the epicentre for novel social trends, such as the unprecedented popular consumption of large quantities of cheap gin and brandy. This vice extended to women, who participated in the vogue for "dram-drinking", which was quickly addictive, not least because spirits were so easily ingested. For example, Martha Tracey, capitally convicted in 1744 at the Old Bailey for picking pockets, had been addicted to alcohol for some time before her death, although less than twenty years old when she was hanged. She could not remember the offence for which she was executed, or many others that she had perpetrated, because she was "always dead drunk when they were committed".[2] This was shocking to respectable people. Excessive drinking was a sin in either sex: "…but in women it is still more abominable".[3] One woman who became an alcoholic allegedly found that her eyes grew dull and languid, her complexion pale and: "…her mind stupid and regardless of every avocation befitting her sex and station".[4]

The Metropolis also attracted more than its fair share of the most dramatic and so 'interesting' female crimes, even if they were unrepresentative of the whole. Amongst them was the case of Maria Phipoe. Helped by her maid, Maria seized the wealthy John Courtoy at knifepoint, held him prisoner, and tried to make him sign over his fortune to her, while also asking him how he would like to be killed (gun, dagger or poison) when he had done so![5]

However, even more importantly than this, the Metropolis is enormously attractive to criminal justice historians because of the sheer number, detail, and ready availability of its sources, especially printed materials, many of which are now accessible on searchable online databases. Research that in

[2] *Ordinary's Account*, 15th March 1744: OA17440315.
[3] Broughton, Thomas (1800) *Serious Advice and Warning to Servants*, p.21.
[4] Anon ('Mira'), (1756) *The Wife*, pp.165-166.
[5] OBSP, Trial of Maria Theresa Phipoe, 20th May 1795: t17950520-27.

the 1990s would have taken months can be done in a matter of hours. For example, the most complete collection of the *Old Bailey Sessions Proceedings* available (a unique printed and published account of nearly all serious Metropolitan trials) has been digitalised and placed online (at www.oldbaileyonline.org). This superb facility has been supplemented by several others, which are almost as valuable. Thus, the Newgate Prison chaplain's biographies of those awaiting execution are also available, as are details of 240,000 manuscripts from eight different archives and fifteen datasets relating to eighteenth-century London, with a particular focus on its poorer citizens (at www.londonlives.org). Some of these will be cited in this book where they illustrate points of national or legal significance.

By contrast, provincial records are often poor or missing, usually available only in handwritten manuscript form, and frequently confined to court or jail registers and calendars. There is no provincial equivalent of the Old Bailey *Proceedings*, though there are individual published tracts on specific Assizes Sessions, many of which are used in this study. This is particularly unfortunate, given the very limited records produced by the English criminal justice system of the era, especially when compared to the Roman law countries of Continental Europe, with their heavy reliance on deposition evidence. Only the bare details (name, gender, employment, plea and verdict etc.) are normally given of defendants and trials, and even some of these, such as employment, can be unreliable.

Nevertheless, despite the huge importance of the London area to the wider nation, most eighteenth-century Englishwomen did not live in the Metropolis or in an environment that was remotely like it. London (broadly construed) contained only an eighth of England's population in 1800. The country's largest provincial cities were tiny by comparison. For example, when Norwich, England's second largest city during the first half of the era, was overtaken by its third, Bristol, in about 1750, the West Country city still only had about 50,000 inhabitants. As a result, London was *sui generis*. When it comes to crime and justice, women's experiences in the capital cannot be taken as representative of the wider country, though there were, inevitably, many similarities.

Frequently, the Metropolis had different types of police, magistrate, and court to those found in the provinces. Its justice system also worked under considerable pressure, as a result of the huge number of suspects being processed through it. This affected how criminal cases were dealt with. Most importantly for this book, the proportion of Metropolitan women committing, and being prosecuted for, property crime appears to have been extremely high by both its own previous and later standards and by those of most contemporary English counties, especially during the early decades of the eighteenth century.[6] It declined gradually thereafter, but was still a third higher than the national average in 1800, although by the mid-1840s the proportion of female offenders (compared to the whole) who were indicted in the Metropolis was almost the same as that for counties such as Devon and Cornwall.[7]

Contemporary observers were vaguely aware of this discrepancy, and occasionally sought to explain it. Some suggested that rural areas were inherently less corrupting for women. As a lawyer noted of the murderer Mary Edmondson, she originally came from the Yorkshire countryside, where there were: "...few or no temptations to debauchery or extravagance, these rocks upon which so many of the female sex split, especially in and about London and Westminster".[8] Some of the modern work done to explain the reduction in female offending after the early 1700s has, perhaps, not fully appreciated that its very high incidence at that time was largely a localised and Metropolitan, rather than national, phenomenon.

The level of female offending elsewhere in the country was usually more modest, and also more stable over the course of the century, albeit subject to short-term fluctuations, especially during wartime. A sustained *national* decrease in the proportion of female offenders and, arguably, an attendant 'masculinisation' of crime, did eventually occur, but not until well into the 1800s. As a result, women would fall as a total of those who were prosecuted for indictable offences from 25 per cent in 1860 to 12 per cent in 1960, while for summary matters their proportion fell from 21 per cent in England and Wales in 1860, to six per cent in 1960.[9] (Both categories have increased since then). There was a particularly marked national decline in the proportion of women prosecuted on indictment between the 1850s and 1890s.

This book is primarily about Englishwomen. However, there will be some consideration of females and their experiences from other parts of the British Isles and even further afield. Obviously, England and Wales shared a legal system, and also uncertain legal boundaries (Monmouth was on the Oxford Circuit, Cheshire linked with Welsh counties), so that women from the Principality will also be discussed in considerable detail, and some of the most important statistics used include Wales. Ireland was

---

6 Feeley, Malcolm and Little, Deborah (1991) "The Vanishing Female: The Decline of Women in the Criminal Process, 1687-1912", p.721 and p.736.

7 King, Peter (2006) *Crime and Law in England, 1750-1840,* p.218.

8 Anon (By a gentleman of the law), (1759) *The Case of Mary Edmondson*, p.4.

9 D'Cruze, Shani and Jackson, Louise A. (2009) *Women, Crime and Justice in England since 1660*, p.18.

also governed by common law (albeit often somewhat more loosely) and applied many of the same legal doctrines to women as the English courts, frequently using the same books on criminal procedure. At the end of the period, in 1800, the two islands experienced political union. Scotland had a separate legal system, but formed part of the same state after 1707. Women from both countries merit consideration, as do those from other parts of the English speaking world, particularly the Americas, and even those from Continental Europe and beyond, if only for comparison. Additionally, there will be some reference to women's experiences in other historical periods, to put those from the eighteenth century into chronological perspective.

This study is about provincial not just rural women. This means that as well as considering females in the countryside it will also examine women in the nation's towns and small cities. Although about a third of the British workforce was still engaged in agriculture at the end of the eighteenth century, the number of English people outside the Metropolis who lived in places with at least 5,000 inhabitants had increased from 275,000 in about 1700 to 1,420 000 in 1801.[10] England was slowly becoming urbanised.

Such towns, though tiny by Metropolitan comparison, and having little in common with the capital, were often very different in character to rural areas. They absorbed much of the country's generally increasing population during the period. This growth, which slowly set in at the end of the 1720s and accelerated after the middle of the century, was the result of both increased fertility and declining mortality rates. The presence of growing towns also encouraged internal migration, with its attendant loss of social control. Women were heavily involved in such movement, as urban environments often offered female employment opportunities. For a very specific example can be considered the new spas in places such as Bath and Buxton, which provided much work for washerwomen.

Although this book is confined to provincial England, it must always be remembered that the country differed greatly by region and county and such variation was often manifest in penal and prosecution strategies, and even the *apparent* incidence of female offending. This can make generalisations inherently very difficult, if not positively dangerous. For any assertion made, an exception can usually be found, if a sufficiently diligent search is conducted. Nevertheless, although all parts of the country were quite distinctive, there was also a significant degree of homogeneity throughout the land. Even the supposedly 'wild' North East,

---

[10] Borsay, Peter (Ed.) (1990) *The eighteenth-century town: a reader in English urban history, 1688-1820*, p.45.

which was influenced by its proximity to the Scottish border, sparse population, hilly topography, and distance from the capital, produced a crime rate and offending profile that was broadly similar to that for other parts of England, with numerous minor property offences interspersed with occasional serious offences, such as robbery or murder.[11]

The presence of the centrally based Westminster judges at provincial Assizes encouraged a degree of procedural uniformity. The rapid growth in legal publishing and printing, especially of standard forms, meant that this increased steadily during the period. Additionally, the country 'shrank' over the course of the century. Roads improved enormously after the 1730s as a result of the establishment of turnpike trusts, which took responsibility for maintaining some arterial routes from the parishes that bordered them. A growing network of canals encouraged the movement of freight in the era's latter decades. Journeys from London to major provincial centres such as Exeter and Manchester, which would have taken over three days at the start of the century, could be made in little more than 24 hours by its end. This also encouraged the transmission of Metropolitan fashions and trends. As a result, in 1761, the dramatist George Colman could observe that there was a growing similarity between Metropolitan and provincial manners. Fifty years earlier, they had been so different that the: "…inhabitants of the distant counties were regarded as a species, almost as different from those of the Metropolis, as the natives of the Cape of Good Hope".[12]

It should be noted that, even though it was unique, it is not possible to completely and tidily distinguish the Metropolitan area from the rest of the country. Most importantly, although the Borough of Southwark was an integral part of Surrey, and its serious crimes were heard at that county's Assizes (whether held there, at Kingston on Thames, or Croydon), it was firmly within the Metropolitan orbit by 1700. It even had its own 'Rotation magistrates' in the 1760s, to deal with the pressure of criminal work produced by its large population (over 66,000 people at the end of the period).[13] Southwark was a: "…borough [that was] not the best regulated, though the biggest in Britain".[14] Effectively, it was in some ways an across river extension of the capital, as were some of its adjacent or nearby parishes, such as Lambeth.

---

[11] Morgan, Gwenda and Rushton, Peter (1998) *Rogues, Thieves and the Rule of Law,* pp.9-11 and p.216.

[12] Langford, Paul (2000) *Eighteenth-Century Britain*, p.65.

[13] *Public Advertiser*, June 4, 1768.

[14] Anon, (1786) *An Authentic Narrative of the Most Remarkable Adventures, and Curious Intrigues, Exhibited in the Life of Miss Fanny Davies*, p.7.

Other parts of the Home Circuit, such as North Kent and West Essex, were also heavily affected by their proximity to the capital, which cast a very long shadow. London's presence drove up crime rates, prosecutions and executions in its collar counties, though not necessarily those involving women (who usually made up a smaller proportion of prosecuted offenders on the Home Circuit than elsewhere in the country). Conversely, rural parishes on the fringes of Middlesex had far more in common with other villages in the Home Counties than they did with the Metropolis, but their serious cases were still heard at the Old Bailey, and their lesser matters went to the Quarter Sessions held at Hick's Hall in Clerkenwell, like those from urban parts of the county. Many of their crimes were of a decidedly bucolic type, such as the theft of farm animals and the burning of haystacks.

Additionally, there was not a hermetic seal between the capital and other parts of the country. The Metropolis served as a place to flee to for provincial criminals, including women. In 1727, when Elizabeth Archer was suspected of murdering her newborn illegitimate baby by burying it alive near Burton in Staffordshire, she immediately made her escape to London. She was ultimately arrested in a house near the Tyburn Road, before being sent back to her native county for trial.[15] Many of those who ended their days at Tyburn had drifted into crime while still in the provinces, before moving to the city and resuming their criminal careers. Other nefarious individuals could be forced to go there by local pressure in their own areas, as the capital served as a receptacle for (perceived) ne'er do wells. London was the general receiver of: "…fugitives and vagabonds from all the nations in the universe". They included the ill-fated Ann Sharp, a Norfolk woman from a respectable and well-to-do background, who went there after being deflowered by an army officer in her native county, losing her reputation for chastity as a result and so embarrassing her prosperous friends.[16] Lower down the social scale, Mary Taylor, who had been born in Worcestershire of "mean" parents who gave her very little education, "came to Town" without even telling her mother. After she had been in domestic service in the capital for a few years she grew tired of such work and "fell to whoring and stealing".[17]

Furthermore, the proceeds of crimes that were committed far outside the Metropolis might be liquidated in the capital. In an extreme illustration, from 1726, John Murrel, a Yorkshire man, stole a mare worth

---

[15] *The British Journal,* June 17, 1727.

[16] Anon (By a Lover of Justice), (1760) *An Answer to the Pamphlet Wrote by the Juryman, Touching the Death of Ann Sharp*, p.13.

[17] Ordinary's Account, 20th May 1728: OA17280520.

eight pounds from Jonathan Wood at a fair in Newcastle upon Tyne. He bargained for the horse, and then asked for a test ride, from which he failed to return. The loser "traced him all over Yorkshire", but eventually sent a letter to a friend in London who made enquiries and found the missing animal.[18] More typically, George Robertson lost a gelding from a field in Essex and found him pulling a cart in Fleet Street a month later.[19]

Sources of Information

To an extent, and even after decades of scholarship on women, crime, and the eighteenth-century justice system, we still see through a glass, darkly. Much important information has been permanently lost, and some was never recorded. This is unfortunate, especially when it comes to studying gender and crime. Sometimes, it has allowed the development of accounts of the phenomenon that are not properly grounded in reliable evidence. However, as with most such studies, this book is based on a mixture of primary and secondary sources. The former straddle both quantitative analysis (usually statistics for indictments and recognisances) and qualitative material, each with their respective strengths and flaws.

The (often rather sparse) surviving records of the era's Assizes are preserved at the National Archives, while many of those for Quarter and Borough Sessions can be found in local record offices, though some records from almost all of these forums have been completely lost. For an example of such resources can be considered those of the Borough Sessions for Kingston on Thames. These were held four times a year, just like the Surrey Quarter Sessions. Indeed, within the town, the County's Quarter Sessions had an overlapping jurisdiction with those for the Borough, albeit that more serious matters gravitated to the former. The records from these sessions are available from 1668 to 1748, while the files of presentments and recognizances are present from 1676 to 1762.[20] Both series have gaps in the sequence, but can be considered for specific sessions and years during the eighteenth century, and provide valuable information for this study. Kingston was located less than 20 miles from the Metropolis, but unlike Southwark it was in no way part of the capital, though influenced by its proximity to London.

Most importantly, it must always be remembered that a majority of criminal accusations at this time (albeit not of the most serious matters)

---

[18] OBSP, Trial of John Murrel, 20th April 1726: t17260420-5.
[19] OBSP, Trial of David Davis, 15th September 1756: t17560915-53.
[20] At KE2/2/1-66 and KE2/3/1-10 in the Kingston Local History Room.

were resolved without any type of formal prosecution, and do not show up in the official records at all. Relatively few offences came for jury trial. Between 1660 and 1730, for example, indictment levels averaged 4.2 per annum at the Great Sessions for Denbighshire, and only 2.4 a year at the same county's Quarter Sessions. Admittedly, this sparsely populated Welsh shire had a relatively low prosecution rate compared to many English counties, especially those in the South East. Its annual rate of indicted theft was only about 1.8 cases per 10,000 people during the late seventeenth century, whereas in Restoration Essex they ran at about 3.7.[21] Nevertheless, this is still a very small total, vastly smaller than the number of crimes that must have been committed there. Even a large majority of thefts did not result in formal prosecutions. For example, the habitual Yorkshire criminal and eventual murderer, Mary Bateman (born in 1768), had been caught stealing and pilfering on several occasions while still a young woman, but had "compromised" matters by returning or paying for stolen items, without the authorities becoming involved.[22] Similarly, all nine women suspected of committing such a crime and identified in a selection of eighteenth-century diaries (taken at random) escaped formal proceedings.[23]

Other deviant acts might be dealt with by community action. Many areas still had a considerable ability to police themselves, without requiring recourse to formal methods of law enforcement. This was sometimes lacking in the Metropolis, especially after the early years of the century, and was another distinguishing feature of provincial England. For example, various types of charivari, often termed 'rough music', 'skimmingtons', and 'stang ridings', depending on where in the country they occurred, still operated to punish those who broke community norms, including (though it was not limited to) the criminal law. Large numbers of villagers might assemble, sometimes blacked up or disguised, and bang pots and pans outside the home of erring neighbours. Thus, in 1769, ten men and eleven women rioted outside the home of Mary Jones, in Braunton, Devon. Mary may have been committing adultery, as the crowd carried a ram's horns and a "mock child made of rags".[24] Despite the apparent jocularity (to modern eyes), such events were no light matter. In

[21] Howard, Sharon (2004) "Investigating responses to theft in early modern Wales: communities, thieves and the courts", p.411

[22] Anon, (1809) *Extraordinary Life and Character of Mary Bateman, the Yorkshire Witch*, 9th edn., p.15.

[23] King, Peter (2000) *Crime, Justice and Discretion in England 1740-1820*, p.200.

[24] Williams, Amy (2000) *The Criminality Of Women In The 18th Century In The South West Of England*, pp.160-161.

1736, a stang riding aimed at shaming an Edinburgh blacksmith who had beaten his wife excessively was so humiliating that he committed suicide the following day.[25] Although in decline by 1700, and universally accepted as illegal by that time, they continued until late in the century. Even where the authorities *were* involved, they themselves sometimes acted informally and left no record or, at the very most, their actions were recorded in the notebooks kept by contemporary justices of the peace (see below). Few of these survive, though this study will refer extensively to the handful that do.

Another major source of information, one heavily mined in this book, can be found in the crime reports published in contemporary newspapers, journals and periodicals. The eighteenth century was an era of mass (but far from universal) literacy.[26] Wealth and gender greatly influenced the ability to read and write. In late eighteenth-century Essex, only six per cent of the mainly poor females who tried to glean from post-harvest fields could sign their names, while all of the prosperous male farmers who owned those fields were literate.[27] Nevertheless, by the latter part of the century there was enough female demand for reading matter that a specialist journal like the monthly *The Lady's Magazine*, founded in 1770 and sold for six pence a copy, could draw a large number of subscribers to its mixture of pieces on fashion, domestic economy, advice for wives and mothers, news, geography and history.

The newspaper became the dominant manifestation of the country's popular print culture during the early 1700s, replacing chapbooks in this role. Although it was an industry that was centred on London, and many newspapers had a Metropolitan focus, especially when it came to reporting crime, there was also a significant provincial press.[28] As a result of this expansion, newspapers became the main source of popular information about crime, selling for about 2 1/2d in the middle of the century, each copy usually having multiple readerships, if only via barber shops, taverns and coffee-houses. Typically, accounts of crime made up an average of over 30 per cent of all reports in *The Kentish Post* in most years between 1729 and 1767, only falling below this figure in times of war, when stories of battles

---

[25] *Daily Gazetteer (London Edition)*, April 6, 1736.

[26] Hay, Douglas and Rogers, Nicholas (1987) *Eighteenth-century English Society*, p.9.

[27] King, Peter (1989) "Gleaners, Farmers and the Failure of Legal Sanctions in England 1750-1850", p.122.

[28] Snell, Esther (2007) "Changing Discourses of Crime: Representations of Criminality in the Eighteenth-Century Newspaper Press", pp.13-47. Snell, Esther (2005) "Representations of Criminality and Victimisation in Provincial Newspapers: The Kentish Post 1717 to 1768", pp.48-75.

competed for attention.[29] Although this was a little higher than some other newspapers, all devoted a very significant proportion of their news to crime coverage. Of course, their reports were usually very short when compared to pamphlets. The medium was also more interested in dramatic offences than in mundane 'everyday' crimes, though still vastly superior to chapbooks when it came to coverage of the latter; *The Kentish Post*, for example, always reported a few misdemeanours. Although less likely to focus on crimes that did not produce suspects they are also infinitely superior to court records in this respect (by definition official records exclude such offenders).

Some journals were also quite casual about checking the accounts that they reported. Nevertheless, as Horace Walpole observed, the papers: "…though always full of lies, seldom fail to reach the outline at least of incidents".[30] The basic facts were usually correct, even if some of the incidental details might be mistaken or exaggerated. Indeed, some modern historians have suggested that, where criminal cases were not notorious, most of the information provided by the era's newspapers was reliable.[31]

It has sometimes been argued that eighteenth-century newspapers exaggerated the importance of crime for their readers and made them more fearful of the phenomenon than it properly deserved. However, this assertion has been questioned in its turn. Crime was a regular feature of eighteenth-century life. Collating newspaper and Old Bailey reports (including advertisements of reward) for Metropolitan J.P.s who had been personally victimised suggests that it was a far more serious phenomenon in the 1700s, at least in the London area, especially in its East End, than it is for professional people today. Statistics don't hint at the 'dark figure' of unreported crime. This is still very substantial in the modern era, when it is merely based on those crimes that are not reported to the police. For the eighteenth century, it is necessarily based on crimes that were not indicted, rendering it far greater. For example, at least five of 65 Justices personally became the victims of street or highway robbery between 1768 and 1793. Several of these cases were not even considered newsworthy and reported,

[29] Snell, Esther (2007) "Changing Discourses of Crime: Representations of Criminality in the Eighteenth-Century Newpaper Press", pp.20-21.
[30] King, Peter (2007) "Newspaper reporting and attitudes to crime and justice in late-eighteenth-and early-nineteenth-century London", pp.73-112.
[31] Oldham, James (1987) "Law Reporting in the London Newspapers, 1756-1786", pp.177-178.

so 'routine' were they deemed to be.[32] Crime was also a major problem in provincial England, if not on quite the same scale.

The Role of Women in Provincial Society

In theory, female autonomy had little place in the eighteenth century, especially outside London. Women were widely seen as not just physically but also psychologically and intellectually weaker than men, while also being more superstitious.[33] It was argued that members of the "delicate" part of the human species were so fragile that they would: "...frequently die with frights, which to our [male] robust constitutions the same objects are only diversions".[34] Even women from prosperous backgrounds had very inferior educations when compared to their male equivalents. For example, it was noted of the well-to-do poisoner Mary Channing that she had been taught to read and write: "...to a proficiency suitable enough to one of her sex".[35] Daniel Defoe, who believed strongly in female education, thought it barbarous that men denied the advantages of learning to women: "We reproach the sex every day with folly and impertinence, while I am confident, had they the advantages of education equal to us, they would be guilty of less than ourselves".[36] An intelligent and well informed woman might be advised, in the words of Lady Mary Montagu Wortley, to: "...conceal whatever learning she attains, with as much solicitude as she would hide crookedness or lameness". It was not something that would endear her to many members of the opposite sex.[37]

Throughout the period under consideration, and as in all previous eras, men dominated English society, and this was rarely challenged. As late as 1810, in an introduction to her *Epistles on Women,* Lucy Aikin, a well-educated female author of the time, was careful not to question the essentially patriarchal character of her society, although seeking more recognition for female achievements and merits: "Let me in the first place

---

[32] Landau, Norma (2010) "Gauging crime in late eighteenth-century London", pp.396-417.

[33] Hanway, Jonas (1758) *A Plan for establishing a Charity-House or Charity Houses for the reception of repenting prostitutes*, p.xiii.

[34] Anon (By a Lover of Justice), (1760) *An Answer to the Pamphlet Wrote by the Juryman, Touching the Death of Ann Sharp*, p.4.

[35] Anon, (1706) *Serious admonitions to youth, in a short account of the life, trial, condemnation and execution of Mrs Mary Channing,* pp.1-4.

[36] Defoe, Daniel (1697) *An Essay Upon Projects,* p.282.

[37] Porter, Roy (1991) *English Society in the Eighteenth Century,* p.23.

disclaim entirely the absurd idea that the two sexes ever can be, or ever ought to be, placed in all respects on a footing of equality. … As long as the bodily constitution of the species shall remain the same, man must in general assume those public and active offices of life which confer authority, whilst to woman will usually be allotted such domestic and private ones as imply a certain degree of subordination".[38] Even Mary Wollstonecraft wanted fairness, not equality, for women. Nevertheless, the intellectual basis for male domination changed slightly during the era. At the start of the period, a scriptural foundation was often cited. By its end, although this had certainly not disappeared, accounts that relied on historical and anthropological theories about gender relations, or which stressed biological 'facts', had become more common.[39]

As a result of these (and similar) attitudes, it was quite normal to believe that females should live under the control of their fathers, masters, or husbands, to use a typical succession for the first few decades of a woman's life. Unlike London, with its many new, unattached, female arrivals, these could readily be found for most provincial women. As a result, it is not difficult to find evidence of the power that men exerted over their lives, and the subservience that this often engendered. For example, in breach of promise actions, counsel for female plaintiffs who had been jilted by their fiancées could openly declare that they were, effectively, 'shop-soiled' and call evidence from men who had been potential suitors but withdrawn their attentions on learning that the object of their affections was already engaged.

However, English society did not, and never had, fully matched the 'ideal typical' model of normative literature, especially that found in conduct books, which was aimed at setting out what was 'desirable' rather than reflecting reality. In theory, the patriarch's role within the family was supreme; it was analogous, if only as a faint echo, to that of the monarch in the wider state and the Deity in creation. In reality, such an interpretation was often not remotely compatible with day-to-day life. It is vital to remember that much writing on gender relations and roles was not an accurate description of normal existence and common experience, especially for the poor. Taken literally, it can produce a highly caricatured view of contemporary expectations of women's behaviour, and ignore numerous ambiguities. It did not allow for women like Elizabeth Hook who, although married, was presented at Kingston Borough Sessions in

---

[38] Aikin, Lucy (1810) *Epistles on Women, Exemplifying Their Character and Condition,* p.v.

[39] Dabhoiwala, Faramerz (2012) *The Origins of Sex: A History of the First Sexual Revolution*, p.188.

1746 for: "…calling of Murder and fire & other disturbing noises & c. in the night".[40] Still less did it provide for a Liverpool corn-factor's wife who, on a visit to London in 1784, got into a heated argument with two other women over opera seats at Covent Garden. When constables attended to break up the disturbance, she gave two of them black eyes.[41]

In the modern era, the concept of 'agency', the degree to which people can influence the course of their own lives and, perhaps, of those around them, has become a central theme in academic discourse. No eighteenth-century Englishwomen were free agents, though they were *comparatively* free by much international comparison (something that is often overlooked in modern discourse). There was *some* foundation to Robert Burton's seventeenth-century comment that, when compared to Italy, England was a "Paradise for women and hell for horses". Women could certainly influence their fates via a variety of stratagems.

More importantly, gender relations frequently departed from the tenets of a patriarchal society, even in rural areas. The hen-pecked husband was a recurring cultural trope, and the era possessed many observers who feared that there had been an erosion in the traditional distinctions between the genders and male and female behaviour: "Their peculiar and characteristic manners are confounded and lost: The one sex having advanced into boldness, as the other have sunk into effeminancy".[42] For a glaring example can be considered the regular cases of eighteenth-century women who dressed as men, such as the notorious criminal Fanny Davies, who often passed as a beardless youth when engaged in nefarious activities.[43] Some went further, and engaged full-time in the most 'masculine' of professions. The low level of ablution amongst many sections of the population, and a corresponding lack of physical exposure, combined with rudimentary medical tests for recruits to many of the era's institutions, facilitated this. Nevertheless, there was probably more awareness (and tolerance) of the reality to such cases than was sometimes publicly acknowledged.

In 1759, for example, a woman became known as the 'Female Shipwright' after it was revealed that as a sixteen-year-old she had left her parents, dressed herself in man's apparel, and gone down to Chatham, where the carpenter of H.M.S. *Sandwich* employed 'him' as a personal

---

[40] Sessions for 6th October 1746, Kingston Local History Room, KE 2/2/1-14.

[41] *Whitehall Evening Post (1770),* December 21-December 23, 1784.

[42] Brown, John (1757) *An Estimate of the Manners and Principles of the Times*, p.51.

[43] Anon, (1786) *An Authentic Narrative of the Most Remarkable Adventures, and Curious Intrigues, Exhibited in the Life of Miss Fanny Davies*, p.32.

servant. After working some time in this capacity, she bound herself as an apprentice to a shipwright, served the whole term of her indentures, and then worked as a qualified artisan for two more years, (allegedly) without raising suspicion.[44] Barbara Hill, from York, was of a more martial turn, and enlisted as an infantry soldier under the name of John Brown; she would have gone undiscovered had not someone informed her platoon sergeant. She then became a stonecutter.[45] Hannah Snell, from Worcester, went one better, and not only successfully enlisted in the army but was flogged and saw active service in India, where she was wounded several times.[46] According to Parson James Woodforde, who later met her, she retired after 21 years service, on a government pension, and then worked as a peddler with the "liberty of wearing men's cloaths".[47]

Some of these women sought partners. (Unlike 'sodomy', lesbianism was not a crime). In 1764, a woman died in Middlesex who had gone by the name of John Chivy, passed as a man for decades, and spent 20 years 'married' to another female.[48] In one of the most extreme illustrations, at the Quarter Sessions held at Taunton in Somerset, in 1746, Mary Hamilton was accused of marrying 14 women according to the rites of the Church of England, while dressed as a man. It was hard to find an offence to charge her with (as none of the marriages were valid she could not be guilty of bigamy). Mary Price, the fourteenth wife, gave evidence for the Crown. She swore that she was lawfully married to the prisoner, and that they bedded and lived together as man and wife for more than three months. During this time, Hamilton assumed the behaviour of a man: "...using certain vile and deceitful practices, not fit to be mentioned".[49] Hamilton was found guilty of being a common cheat and sentenced to six months in prison and to be publicly whipped in Taunton, Glastonbury, Wells and Shepton Mallet.

Society, and the position of females, also changed significantly during the course of the eighteenth century, which witnessed a major shift in attitudes towards femininity and the role of women. This can clearly be seen in the very changed official approach to their physical punishment, especially in public, between 1700 and 1799 (discussed in chapter two). However, exactly why and how society changed in this regard is rather

---

[44] *London Evening Post,* August 2, 1773.

[45] *London Chronicle*, 31 January – 2 February, 1760.

[46] Anon, (1750) *The Female Soldier; Or, The Surprising Life and Adventures of Hannah Snell*, pp.1-30.

[47] Woodforde, James (1999) *The Diary of a Country Parson, 1758-1802,* at p.100.

[48] *London Chronicle*, 16-18 February, 1764.

[49] *London Evening Post*, November 6, 1746 - November 8, 1746.

more difficult to say, and has been the subject of considerable debate. Certainly, it was a time of transition, but so are most historical periods, especially in the last 500 years. Furthermore, it was not just the position of women that changed during the era. In 1819, it could be noted in parliament that, apart from cases of murder, treason, or arson, both juries and prosecutors were averse to prosecuting and condemning convicts when they knew the likely penalty to be a death sentence.[50] This was a squeamishness that their predecessors a century earlier had not shared. It is important not to attribute changes in the position of women to developments in gender relations when, in reality, they were the result of more widespread trends.

Separate Spheres?

According to one popular modern analysis, the sexes, which in the early decades of the century had often worked alongside each other, became increasingly separated into different 'spheres' during its second half. One of these was private and domestic, which was the province of women, and the other was public and work-oriented, and the preserve of men. Women's lives increasingly revolved around the home and domesticity, rather than employment, so that marriage and children were the most important things in them. By the end of the century, female craftsmen engaged in trades like carpentry and bricklaying were very rare, these occupations having become masculinised.

Women were also gradually excluded, or at least discouraged, from certain other, less physical, occupations and activities. For example, and perhaps surprisingly, there was a considerable decline in their participation in retailing and shop work. Trial transcripts of witnesses who were present during cases of Metropolitan shoplifting reveal a major move from the employment of female staff in favour of men between the 1740s and 1770s. The proportion of premises staffed entirely by women fell from 35 per cent to just 12 per cent. By the 1770s, three quarters of shops were staffed purely by men.[51]

Women had also played a major role as small traders in market towns and villages, selling meat, candles, bread, fish, cheese and ale, and being legally recognized as *feme sole merchant.* The number of such women declined during the course of the century. Thus, Oxford market saw a

---

[50] *The Times*, July 7, 1819, p.3.

[51] Tickell, Shelley (2010) "The prevention of shoplifting in eighteenth-century London", p.300.

steady fall in female stallholders during the 1700s.[52] Similarly, a large number of female retailers and alehouse keepers were presented at Kingston Borough Sessions in the late seventeenth and the first half of the eighteenth centuries for regulatory offences, such as using defective balances or, in the case of the Widow Clark in 1744: "...for using a pint mugg wanting a quarter of a pint of the just measure".[53] Their numbers had also fallen by the end of the century. The work that was still open to women became less varied, increasingly tedious and the preserve of females or (even more significantly) 'women and children'.

However, in recent years the generality of this paradigm has, at the least, been questioned. Women entered several new occupations during the period, such as working in spas, even if their presence in others declined. It should also be remembered that many of these developments were centered on, or initiated in, the London area. Things moved more slowly in the provinces, especially in the early decades of the century, rippling out from the capital over time. Change occurred at very different rates. Even rural Surrey was a radically different society to the more remote parts of Lancashire. In the modern era, an examination of social trends suggests that for many British people the '1960s' only arrived in the 1970s. The same can be said of some aspects of sexual relations and gendered behaviour during the 1700s, albeit that change was measured in decades rather than years. Many features of the previous century lingered long into the following era, particularly in isolated parts. As a result, linear histories can be unsatisfactory when applied to the whole country.

Courts and Policing

During the eighteenth century, most criminal offences were, in theory, triable on indictment before a jury. More serious crimes of this type, such as murder, robbery, and burglary, were classified as felonies, and normally determined by juries at the Assizes. Less serious crimes, including most assaults and some lesser offences of dishonesty, were termed misdemeanours and usually heard by juries at county Quarter Sessions or (their equivalent in some towns) Borough Sessions.

However, most indicted cases of petty theft (less than a shilling in value), the only felony not to carry a potential death penalty, were also tried at Quarter Sessions. Furthermore, some lesser examples of those felonies that were 'clergyable' (see below) were determined at this forum,

---

[52] Laurence, Anne (1996) *Women In England 1500-1760: A Social History*, p.170.
[53] Sessions 26th April 1742, Kingston Local History Room, KE 2/2/15-56.

especially in the provinces, and particularly after the middle of the century, although the willingness of these courts to hear such cases varied greatly. For example, the Surrey Quarter Sessions tried many cases of grand larceny after a sudden change in policy in 1748, possibly linked to an increase in prosecutions and prison overcrowding. Initially, this was done by nominally valuing stolen items at 10d (petty theft), whatever their true worth. Subsequently, the Justices were quite open about trying the more serious form of larceny.[54] This entailed no legal problems, as Quarter Sessions had always been empowered to hear such cases, and in centuries gone by had done so. These developments were matched elsewhere. In the North East, for example, Justices appear to have been particularly willing to hear minor clergyable felonies at Quarter Sessions, especially when women were involved, not least as a way of preserving local control over their fates and limiting the consequences of conviction.[55]

Some Quarter Sessions went further, and tried a few quite serious matters, that really ought to have gone to Assizes, particularly where women were involved. They included the occasional female-perpetrated case of horse-theft, as occurred twice in Devon between 1735 and 1782. On three other occasions women who stole sheep were also tried at that county's Quarter Sessions, as was one female who took a pig (though this was a 'clergyable' animal throughout the era).[56] Indeed, a handful of special City and Town Sessions, including those at Berwick, Exeter, Bristol, King's Lynn, Oxford, and Yarmouth, had full power of gaol delivery and continued to try tiny numbers of potentially capital matters during the eighteenth century. Margaret Dryden, for example, was executed after her trial for infanticide at the Berwick Sessions in May 1758.[57] Against this, some Quarter Sessions would not determine anything more serious than petty larceny, leaving all other felonies to the Assizes as a matter of course, especially early in the century.

Conversely, misdemeanours and petty thefts could be tried at Assizes if the felonies had been disposed of and time allowed (frequently not the case). For example, at the Northampton Assizes in 1797 Judith Mills was

---

[54] Beattie, John (1986) *Crime and the Courts in England 1660-1800,* pp.283-284 and p.512.

[55] Morgan, Gwenda and Rushton, Peter (1998) *Rogues, Thieves and the Rule of Law,* p.123. It should be noted that only about a fifth of Quarter Sessions' time was devoted to criminal matters. Much civil and administrative work was also dealt with, a considerable amount of it in open court.

[56] Williams, Amy (2000) *The Criminality Of Women In The 18th Century In The South West Of England*, p.121.

[57] *Lloyd's Evening Post and British Chronicle*, May 17, 1758 - May 19, 1758.

tried for stealing a flax sheet initially valued at only 10d.[58] It was also possible, and quite common, for prosecutors to artificially down-value goods to ensure that they were indicted as petty, or at least a clergyable form of, theft. In an extreme example of this phenomenon, at the Warwick Quarter Sessions in 1690, three sheep were initially valued together at only 11d, although their real value was well over 12 shillings.[59] Other crimes could be indicted as misdemeanours, even though they involved allegations that, in reality, amounted to serious felonies.

As their name suggests, Quarter Sessions sat four times a year. Frequently, they would move on a regular cycle through a county's major towns. Thus, for much of the eighteenth century, the Hilary sessions for Wiltshire would meet in Salisbury, the county's Easter sessions at Devizes, the Trinity sessions at Warminster and those for Michaelmas in Marlborough. Assize Courts were held just twice a year, during Lent and Michaelmas in one or more major towns. The former were presided over by a bench of county magistrates (usually between four and a dozen of them). These were the unpaid, part-time, (usually) legally untrained, Justices of the Peace, albeit that they were often aided by a legally qualified, part-time, Recorder (normally a professional barrister). The latter were the province of the itinerant Westminster judges, a pair of which rode each of the six clusters of adjacent English counties known as 'circuits' ('Home', 'Midland', 'Norfolk', 'Northern', 'Western' and 'Oxford'). Wales (and Cheshire) had their own system of four circuits, known as the Great Sessions.

By the eighteenth century, there were also a number of minor offences that did not require a jury trial at all, but which could be formally determined by J.P.s, either when sitting alone or with colleagues on a bench of two or more magistrates. The latter frequently sat in a local public house at what were termed 'petty sessions'. These often had greater powers than a single J.P. For example, in 1748, Hannah Beard was convicted before the magistrate William Hunt (sitting alone) for the summary offence of cursing in public. She had been caught "swearing six oaths" in Lavington market, and found guilty on the evidence of a local clergyman who had been present at the time. (The offence could be established by a magistrate 'viewing' it, the evidence of one reliable witness, as in this case, or by a confession made by the suspect).[60] Beard

---

[58] *Oracle and Daily Advertiser*, July 9, 1799.

[59] Johnson, H.C. (1964) *Warwick County Records, vol.IX: Quarter session records; Easter, 1690 to Michaelmas, 1696*, p.23.

[60] Blackerby, Samuel (1715) *The Justice of Peace His Companion*, 3rd edn., p.3.

was unable or unwilling to pay the fine and, as a result, was committed to ten days' imprisonment in the Devizes Bridewell.[61]

The number of such summary offences gradually expanded during the era, though their use varied greatly. Thus, it appears to have been quite low in rural Lincolnshire during the middle of the century, but higher in some other parts of the country. This variation is unsurprising. In some respects, the growth in formal summary powers, like the expansion in informal settlements supervised by magistrates, replaced earlier processes that were based on more active popular engagement in the justice system and, in particular, the use of Quarter Sessions to deal with interpersonal quarrels.[62] Unfortunately, calculating the incidence of summary prosecutions is extremely difficult. Magistrates were supposed to return details of all convictions that they made to the ensuing Quarter Sessions. In practice, this was often not done.

Some very specific forms of minor theft (stealing vegetables etc.) could be, and were, prosecuted summarily. In 1809, for example, Elizabeth Bishop was sent to the House of Correction in Hereford for a month after a local J.P. convicted her of stealing turnips. The following year, two sisters received the same disposal for a similar crime. In 1811, two more Herefordshire women were summarily fined 2s 6d each for stealing kindling "out of Riggs Wood".[63] However, as Hannah Beard's case suggests, the procedure was most commonly employed to deal with bad language, especially amongst females. Three quarters of the women in mid-eighteenth-century Devon who were convicted using this mechanism, and whose records of conviction were returned to Quarter Sessions (142 of them), had been prosecuted for cursing and swearing. In just over a quarter of these cases, the allegation was confined to one oath. A similar number had been convicted of uttering ten or more curses, with the rest in-between.[64] The more curses charged (and proved), the greater the fine that could be imposed. Sometimes it also provided a mechanism by which assaults and disturbances could be dealt with summarily. Few blows were struck without bad language being used.

---

[61] Crittall, Elizabeth (Ed.) (1982) *The Justicing Notebook of William Hunt, 1744-1749*, p.85.
[62] Lemmings, David (2011) *Law and Government in England during the Long Eighteenth Century: From Consent to Command,* p.173
[63] Shakesheff, Tim (2003) *Rural Conflict, Crime and Protest: Herefordshire 1800-1860*, p.115.
[64] Williams, Amy (2000) *The Criminality Of Women In The 18th Century In The South West Of England*, p.170.

Many other misdemeanours (not felonies) were 'prosecuted' by magistrates issuing recognisances (rather than indictments) against suspects binding them over to appear at the next Quarter Sessions, on pain of forfeiting a sum of money (often £20) if they failed to do so. These were usually issued at the behest of their alleged victims.[65] The complainant could then attend at the same time as the defendant and ask for him/her to be indicted for the relevant misdemeanour. If he (or she) did so, the matter would be considered by the Quarter Sessions' Grand Jury with a view to going before a trial jury at the same sessions. Nevertheless, the complainant was not *required* to attend sessions and prosecute. He would not forfeit anything if he failed to appear and the matter was then dismissed. In *practice*, complainants would often not attend and the defendant would simply be discharged after paying a small fee to the Quarter Sessions' clerk and court crier. The procedure served as a cheap warning and minor punishment for erring individuals. It was used fairly regularly until the latter decades of the century. For example, women accused of assault in Devon and Dorset between 1736 and 1741, or Somerset between 1775 and 1785, were almost as likely to go through such a process as to be indicted.[66]

Additionally, J.P.s had the power to commit to a House of Correction for vagrancy. Early in the century, this power was sometimes construed very generously to address a range of nefarious behaviour. For an example can be considered a case from Thorpe, in Surrey, in which Ann Hart appears to have been gratuitously attacked by another single woman, Mary Dodsworth. She was beaten with a stick and, at the same time, Dodsworth set a large dog on her, which "tore her in several parts of her body". Dodsworth was committed to the House of Correction at Kingston on Thames.[67] As the era advanced, the courts became more nervous about invoking this power too loosely. Nevertheless, as late as 1730, a major *Habeas Corpus* action was unsuccessful on this issue when brought by the notorious Moll Freeman in the Court of King's Bench. She had been committed to the Bridewell as an "idle and disorderly" person for picking up a 15-year-old youth and taking him to a disorderly house, where he spent large amounts of his father's money. Although represented by several expensive lawyers, who objected to her incarceration on this basis,

---

[65] Shoemaker, Robert (1991) *Prosecution and Punishment,* p.25.

[66] Williams, Amy (2000) *The Criminality Of Women In The 18th Century In The South West Of England*, p.150

[67] Silverthorne, Elizabeth (Ed.) (1978) *The Deposition Book of Richard Wyatt JP, 1767-1776*, p.5.

the Lord Chief Justice concluded that the Justices' decision was "just and legal" and commended their action in punishing such a vile woman.[68]

Irrespective of either this power or formally established summary offences, magistrates were the entry point to the entire criminal justice system, and would often deal informally with as much of the business that came before them as possible, even if they did not always have a sound legal basis for their actions (see below). The initial decision to use such a procedure was unlikely to have been entirely gender neutral.

It is a crude generalisation, but one that is normally (but not quite invariably) accurate, that more women are to be found in the lower jury court than its senior counterpart. For example, in County Durham, Newcastle and Northumberland, in the North East (admittedly an extreme case), women made up 22.43 per cent of defendants at Assizes, but fully 46.18 per cent at Quarter Sessions. In the North West (Cumberland, Westmorland and Lancashire) the respective figures were 12.94 per cent and 22.04 per cent. In Devon, on the Western Circuit, they were 17.30 per cent and 31.21 per cent.[69] Going across the Welsh border to Denbighshire, the difference was smaller, but still present; less than one-fifth (19.2 per cent) of those indicted at the county's Great Sessions (the Welsh equivalent of Assizes) between 1660 and 1730 were female, while just over one-quarter indicted at Quarter Sessions (25.7 per cent) were women.[70] Bristol, however, showed little difference, turning in figures of 32.85 per cent and 34.67 per cent respectively.[71] More generally, its (partly) surrounding county of Somerset also appears to have been something of an exception at several points during the eighteenth century.

However, and perhaps confusingly, going even further down the judicial pyramid it seems that women were often in a clear minority of defendants who were formally tried for summary offences, without a jury. For example, in Essex between 1748 and 1804 only 10.4 per cent of those summarily convicted of stealing wood or vegetables were female. Nevertheless, a majority of those convicted of stealing yarn in this fashion *were* women, making up 61 per cent of the total (and fractionally more in absolute numbers than females who were summarily convicted of wood

[68] *Grub-street Journal*, December 3, 1730.
[69] Morgan, Gwenda and Rushton, Peter (2004) *Eighteenth-Century Criminal Transportation: The Formation of the Criminal Atlantic*, p.48.
[70] Howard, Sharon (2003) *Crime, Communities And Authority In Early Modern Wales: Denbighshire, 1660-1730*, p.44.
[71] Morgan, Gwenda and Rushton, Peter (2004) *Eighteenth-Century Criminal Transportation: The Formation of the Criminal Atlantic*, p.48.

and vegetable theft).[72] How typical the county was in this regard is, of course, open to debate. Women also featured heavily in Justices' notebooks, having been dealt with informally, rather than being sent for trial on indictment or even tried summarily under a formal legal power (see below).

Policing

Eighteenth-century policing was largely parish-based and organised, with a major input coming from amateur rather than professional officers. Parish constables were normally unpaid men fulfilling a part-time, year-long, local office for healthy, moderately well to do, male ratepayers. They were usually selected by rota. In provincial towns and cities watchmen (often householders at the start of the period, paid men later on) might also patrol the nocturnal streets. For example, Newcastle had a fairly elaborate system of daily and nightly watchmen, who were placed under the supervision of a salaried officer. Women had no active involvement in this process, something that could create problems on those occasions when law enforcement agencies had to search female suspects intimately. Thus, when the killer Anne Broderick was suspected of carrying a (second) loaded pistol, after her arrest by an Essex constable, the peace officer had to send for a female servant to search her.[73] Interestingly, the Kingston on Thames Borough Sessions from about 1690 to 1750 contain numerous presentments of women, usually widows, who had failed to keep watch "having been warned". Presumably, these individuals were householders, on the watching rota because of their ownership of property, who had failed to provide a male substitute or to compound for the duty with a money payment.

Females and Crime

Most criminologists agree that a gender gap in the commission of crime, especially serious crime, is widespread, being almost (but not quite) universal in human experience. Women are nearly always, and almost everywhere, significantly less likely than men to offend, though the gap between male and female crime rates is not entirely stable. It changes over time and place, and varies greatly with offence type. Given this, it is unsurprising that during the eighteenth century crime in provincial

---

[72] King, Peter (2000) *Crime, Justice and Discretion in England 1740-1820*, p.209.
[73] *True Briton (1793)* July 20, 1795.

England was, ostensibly, a predominantly male phenomenon, and serious crime was overwhelmingly masculine.

By way of illustration, at the Summer Assizes for Hertfordshire in 1780 all four convicts sentenced to death were men: one for stealing a lamb, one for horse-theft, and two for robbery.[74] Similarly, at the Lent Assizes for Stafford, in March 1787, six men received death sentences (some would later have been reprieved) while a man and a woman, Mary Cooksey, were sentenced to transportation for various burglaries.[75] A week later, at the Shropshire Assizes, all eight people who were capitally convicted (six were reprieved by the judge) were men, found guilty of stealing 'large' animals, highway robbery, burglary, and being at large while under sentence of transportation.[76] Thus, only one woman was found guilty of a serious felony at the three sessions and none was sentenced to death. This was a slightly but not especially unusual profile.

Occasionally, of course, even the higher criminal courts saw much greater numbers of female defendants and convicts. Thus, at the Assizes held at Maidstone in March 1797 two sisters were convicted of burglary from a man's house, another woman of a housebreaking, during which three gowns and a silver watch were taken, yet another female for petty treason (the murder of her husband), and one more for taking furniture from a dwelling house with a male accomplice. On this occasion, they made up a majority of the sessions convicts.[77] However, this profile was extremely rare.

As a very rough generalization, it seems that, historically (at least in western societies), women commit between eight per cent and 25 per cent of prosecuted 'serious' crime (itself an inherently very loose concept). For example, they made up less than 15 per cent of all those prosecuted on indictment in late sixteenth and early seventeenth-century Hertfordshire, at the county's Assizes and Quarter Sessions, taken together.[78] During the eighteenth century there were some remarkable similarities between the low incidence of female prosecution for property offences at the Assizes held for County Armagh in Ireland, between 1735 and 1796 (9.7 per cent of cases), and their (rough) equivalent in eighteenth-century Sussex (10.8 per cent). They made up an even smaller, but again similar, proportion of those prosecuted for assault and murder at these forums: 6.5 per cent and

---

[74] *Whitehall Evening Post (1770)* August 1, 1780 - August 3, 1780.
[75] *The Times*, March 21, 1787, p.3.
[76] *The Times*, March 28, 1787, p.3.
[77] *True Briton (1793)* March 21, 1797.
[78] Anon, (1659) *The Caterpillars of this Nation Anatomised,* p.4.

7.6 per cent respectively of the male total in the two jurisdictions.[79]

Across the Atlantic, the figures returned are sometimes a little higher, depending on legal definition, though this variation precludes very much, if any, significance being placed on the national differences. Thus, a modern observer has concluded that women made up 15.4 per cent of prosecutions for 'serious' crimes (a set of offences in which "some real harm was done to a specific victim"), ranging from homicide to theft, that were committed in Halifax, Nova Scotia, from its foundation in 1749 to 1803. The Halifax figures are slightly exceeded by those found in New France at this time, where the proportion was 19.7 per cent, and a similar representation has been noted for colonial America.[80] In lowland Scotland, women made up 23 per cent of those indicted at the Justiciary Court between 1750 and 1815.[81] In the same country, they constituted 20 per cent of those investigated by the Lord Advocate's Department for all forms of serious crime in 1828.[82]

A generalization that can be made about female offending during the eighteenth century, and one that also holds good for most societies and eras, is that the gender gap is greatest for more serious crimes, whether directed against property or (even more so) persons, and smallest for lesser forms of lawbreaking, such as minor property offences. In the modern era, this has been confirmed by self-report and victimisation surveys, not just the official arrest and prosecution records available for earlier times.[83] This, in part, explains why the proportion of women tried at Quarter Sessions was usually greater than that at Assizes.

In provincial England women were nearly always a minority of indicted offenders, particularly for violent offences and those property crimes that either used or threatened violence (such as robbery), or which carried an inherent risk of violent confrontation (such as burglary). However, even when it came to 'routine' property offences, such as larceny (the most

---

[79] Garnham, Neil (1996) *Courts, Crime and the Criminal Law in Ireland, 1692-1760*, p.216.

[80] Phillips, Jim, and May, Allyson N. (2002) "Female Criminality in 18th-Century Halifax", pp.38-71.

[81] Kilday, Anne-Marie (2007) *Women and Violent Crime in Enlightenment Scotland*, p.147.

[82] Symonds, Deborah A. (2006) *Notorious Murders, Black Lanterns, & Moveable Goods: The Transformation of Edinburgh's Underworld in the Early Nineteenth Century*, p.13.

[83] Steffensmeier, Darrel and Allan, Emilie (1996) "Gender and Crime: Toward a Gendered Theory of Female Offending", pp.460-463.

common eighteenth-century crime), women were usually in a minority, albeit a very much more substantial one than for most other offences.

An assessment of female indictment rates at both Assizes and Quarter Sessions, when taken together for the eighteenth and early nineteenth centuries, shows a remarkable amount of variation between English counties. For example, in the years from 1805 to 1807 women made up 12.82 per cent of all indictments in Buckingham. In Kent, over the same period, it was 19.32 per cent. In Gloucestershire, it was 23.99 per cent, while both Durham and Cornwall posted rates of 25 per cent or more, and in Shropshire it reached 28.9 per cent.[84] Such figures raise serious questions, if not outright doubts. Were women really more than twice as likely to offend in Shropshire as in Buckingham, or is it simply a localised reflection of differences in the reporting and processing of their crimes? Most circuits, counties, and sometimes even individual courts, had their own distinct legal cultures that could well have affected the incidence of female prosecution and conviction. Indeed, it is at least questionable whether it is possible, centuries later, to measure the era's crime levels with any degree of reliability using official statistics, especially those for indictments, which were several steps removed from the original offence (arrest, prosecution, examining magistrate, Grand Jury, etc.).

Putting reservations about their value to one side, outside the Metropolitan area the figures show a measure of consistency, and a clear trend, between 1688 and 1815, even if individual courts and counties varied significantly from each other. Women are consistently in a minority for most parts of the country, particularly when it comes to serious crimes. However, there were periodic short-term increases in the proportion of females who offended, especially when wartime took away potential male offenders, though not normally enough to put them close to being a majority. These then usually declined to the period's 'norm' with the return of peacetime. Indeed, it has been plausibly suggested that it is unlikely that the proportion of women prosecuted showed great change outside the London area between 1650 and 1850. (It declined significantly shortly thereafter).[85]

The discrepancy between male and female indictment totals in eighteenth-century England (and other eras) and in the courts in which they were likely to be tried can be interpreted in different ways. Most obviously, it could be argued that women were simply much less likely than men to commit serious crimes, and somewhat less likely to commit

---

[84] King, Peter (2006) *Crime and Law in England, 1750-1840,* p.221.
[85] King, Peter (2006) *Crime and Law in England, 1750-1840,* p.220

minor offences. Alternatively, females might have been less likely to be prosecuted when they offended. Furthermore, women who committed relatively serious crimes might have been more likely to be prosecuted in a lower level forum than their exact male counterparts. Inevitably, a cautious historian is likely to settle on all three as having some role to play in the process. However, this still leaves the question of relative degrees of importance.

It is probably safe to say that eighteenth-century women in provincial England were much less likely to commit serious crimes than their male counterparts, and somewhat less likely to commit lesser offences, and this was the most important factor in their lower indictment levels. Nevertheless, it is also probable that fewer women who committed offences were prosecuted and that where they were, they were more likely to be tried in a lower forum than their exact male counterparts.

'Female' Felonies

There were a few offence specific exceptions to the general trend of male dominance, even for 'serious' crimes. Amongst them were the traditionally "feminine" offences of witchcraft and infanticide. Ostensibly, the latter continued to be an overwhelmingly female crime during the eighteenth century (see chapter four). Formal allegations of the former quickly dwindled to near non-existence in the 30 years before formal abolition of the felony in 1736 (a development that was linked to major changes in élite attitudes). This was partly because of an increased recognition of the evidential problems attendant on establishing the offence, even amongst those who believed in its reality. In 1669, this had reduced a judge at the Surrey Assizes, presiding over the trial of a woman where "nothing appeared sufficient to convict her of witchcraft", to ask the court chaplain to administer the popular (but legally very frowned upon) test of asking her to repeat the *Lords Prayer* in full, in court, without making an error or missing part of it out (she eventually did this successfully).[86] As was noted after the trial and acquittal of Joan Butts at the same forum in 1682, although many thought her guilty of witchcraft: "...others who consider the great difficulty in proving a witch, thought the jury could do no less than acquit her".[87]

---

[86] Anon, (1670) *Inquest after blood, being a relation of the several inquisitions of all that have died by any violent death ...*, p.14.

[87] Anon, (1682) *An Account of the tryal and examination of Joan Buts, for being a common witch and inchantress,* pp.1-2.

Nevertheless, formal allegations of witchcraft were still occasionally being made against provincial women in the early 1700s, albeit that it seems that no women were executed in England (unlike Scotland) for the crime during the 'long' eighteenth century (the first half of the 1680s saw three or four hangings for witchcraft). Rural allegations of witchcraft continued for longer than they did in the Metropolis, as the process of urbanization appears to have influenced the incidence of such claims. For example, it was reported that Ellinor Shaw from Oundle in Northamptonshire became a witch at the start of the century to be revenged on neighbourhood children who taunted her about her debauched and sluttish lifestyle. She could: "...hardly peep out of her door, but the children would point at her in a scoffing manner, saying, *There goes a whore, there's Nell the strumpet, &c*".[88] Much more reliably, in 1712, Jane Wenham, from Walkerne in Hertfordshire, was formally accused of the crime, following many years of suspicion. It was claimed that she had bewitched a servant maid as part of a dispute with a local farmer. Even at the time, most educated observers, including a local doctor, felt that she was, in reality, nothing more than a poor, ignorant, wretch, who had been: "...harassed out of her senses, threatened by all the parish, [and] Brow-beaten by the Justice".[89] Although capitally convicted at Assizes, she was subsequently reprieved. Even so, arrests and (much more rarely) prosecutions for witchcraft continued in England for a few years after the Wenham case. It was popularly, if wholly inaccurately, believed that Mary Hickes and her nine-year-old daughter Elizabeth had been condemned to death and executed at the Huntingdon Assizes for raising a storm in July 1716. (This mistake was the result of an entirely fabricated pamphlet account of the case published in the same year).[90] Much more reliably, a trial that did not result in a conviction appears to have taken place in Leicester in 1717, and as late as the early 1720s magistrates seem to have examined several provincial women over formal allegations of witchcraft, even if they did not eventually go for trial.

Even so, by then, a much more common *legal* accusation was that females were claiming to be 'cunning women' simply as a way of fraudulently earning a few shillings by, for example, telling disappointed young ladies why their lovers had forsaken them.[91] Thus, in 1727, Elizabeth Esquire, a gypsy fortuneteller, was convicted at the Gloucester

---

[88] Anon, (1705) *The Northamptonshire Witches*, p.14.
[89] Anon, (1712) *A Full Confutation of Witchcraft,* p.11 and p.33.
[90] Cooke, George Alexander (1802) *The modern British traveller: or, Tourist's pocket directory: Huntingdon*, pp.92-93.
[91] *Telegraph*, February 21, 1797.

Assizes for cheating Elizabeth Cox out of clothes and some silver: "…under pretence of telling her that there was 150l. hid in her master's cellar". In her defence, Elizabeth unavailingly claimed that it had been payment for the normal cunning-woman services of: "…telling her [Cox] when she should enjoy her sweetheart, and the like".[92] At the end of the eighteenth century, the fraudster Mary Bateman extracted large sums of money by pretending to provide charms and other magical services to young women in Yorkshire. It was often claimed that credulous females, especially servant maids, were most prone to becoming the "dupes of fortune-tellers".[93]

At a popular level, 'mob' action (albeit only rarely lethal) against suspected witches continued throughout the era, despite occasional efforts by the authorities to stamp it out, and many cases probably went entirely unreported or recorded. Thus, there was an outbreak of forced 'swimming' of suspected witches in millponds near Frome in Somerset in 1731. As in the previous century, those who 'floated' were deemed to be guilty. At least three cases occurred, the last of which resulted in an old woman dying an hour after she was pulled out of the water, in front of 200 spectators.[94] In the same year that the criminal offence of witchcraft was abolished (1736), the vicar of Twyford in Gloucestershire was moved to condemn the 'swimming' of an elderly woman in his parish who was popularly reputed to be a witch. Fifteen years later, in 1751, Thomas Colley, a chimney sweep, was hanged for the murder of the septuagenarian Ruth Osborne in Tring, Hertfordshire. He had led a huge mob, organised in advance, that seized Ruth and her husband John from a local workhouse, claiming that they were witches. They then tied up and 'swam' the pair in Marlstone Mere. Ruth was also beaten and dragged through the shallow water until she drowned. Perhaps significantly, her spouse survived, and later gave evidence at Colley's trial. Colley was hanged in chains near the mere, after his execution, to set a deterrent example to others who might be considering such vigilante action. He appears to have had very considerable local support, and his execution had to be well guarded to prevent rescue attempts.[95] Despite this punishment, the Tring case did not bring an end to popular action against suspected witches. There was another major outbreak of forced swimming near

---

[92] *Gloucester Journal*, August 1, 1727.

[93] Anon, (1809) *Extraordinary Life and Character of Mary Bateman, the Yorkshire Witch*, 9th edn., p.18.

[94] *Daily Journal*, January 15, 1731.

[95] *Old England or The National Gazette*, August 3, 1751; *Read's Weekly Journal Or British Gazetteer*, August 10, 1751.

Leicester in the summer of 1760, during which several elderly women were tied up and thrown into gravel pits, albeit that none died. Only a handful of local people were eventually punished for their involvement in the incident; they received small fines or were bound over to Quarter Sessions.[96]

There was no sustained official attempt to deal with the problem of vigilante action over the remaining decades of the century. This led to the strange situation whereby some women accused of witchcraft actually volunteered to be 'swum' to clear their names, because their local justices could not protect them from their neighbours. As late as 1792, an elderly woman from Stanningfield in Suffolk pleaded with two J.P.s (one of them a cleric) to protect her against local allegations of witchcraft. The two men were unable or unwilling to help, so she decided to let herself be swum in front of her community so as to clear her name. Her husband and brother went along with this proposal, as they feared that otherwise she would kill herself, and they even participated in the process to ensure that she was not mistreated. Fortunately she 'sank', and so was cleared of being a witch, although she was pulled from the water "almost lifeless".[97]

Communal action against witches, whether swimming or mob 'scratching' (believed to break a witch's power) lingered into the nineteenth century. In 1808, for example, a group of villagers from Great Paxton in Huntingdonshire were indicted at the Court of King's Bench for attacking a suspected witch, Ann Izzard, who was thought to have caused several local women to fall ill and experience fits. They cut Ann with pins and other sharp instruments, inflicting numerous lacerations to her neck, shoulders, breasts and other parts of her body, in the process.[98] It appears that such incidents only finally disappeared with the advent of a police force, in all parts of the provinces, as a result of the Police Act of 1856.[99]

'Female' Misdemeanours

At a less serious level, a few minor but gender specific crimes (classified as misdemeanours) were still prosecuted during the era. Foremost amongst them was 'scolding', which was a purely female offence by 1700, just as barratry (a roughly similar crime) was a male one. In Blackstone's words, the law and legal terminology "confines it [scolding] to the feminine

---

[96] *Read's Weekly Journal Or British Gazetteer*, June 28, 1760.

[97] Davies, Owen (1999) "Witchcraft: The Spell that Didn't Break", pp.7-9.

[98] Mitchell, Stephen (2000) "Witchcraft Persecutions in the Post-Craze Era: The Case of Ann Izzard of Great Paxton, 1808", pp.304-305.

[99] Davies, Owen (1999) *Witchcraft, Magic and Culture, 1736-1951*, pp.117-118.

gender".[100] The crime was committed by an obstreperous, brawling woman who damaged and disturbed the social harmony of those around her. Her prosecution would often be preceded by a petition from her neighbours, and needed evidence of repeated disturbance and of the woman behaving in a disorderly or "turbulent" manner. Mere verbal assertiveness was not enough. The offence required insult, abuse, harassment, indiscriminate slander, or tale-bearing.[101] Thus, in April 1690, two women were presented at the Borough Sessions for Kingston on Thames for the offence. One of them, the wife of John Mazlow, was accused of being: "...a common scold and disturber of her neighbours".[102] Sometimes, the charge was appended as a makeweight to another, such as assault.

Scolding was comparatively rarely prosecuted by the start of the eighteenth century, even in the provinces.[103] Nevertheless, it remained in the calendar of offences for most of the era. Its legality, and punishment, was upheld in a case from 1704, in which the defendant had been convicted at Quarter Sessions for being a scold and sentenced to a ducking. She brought a writ of error (with leave of the Attorney General) in the Court of Queen's Bench to prevent this. However, when counsel for the woman stated that he knew of no law that allowed the ducking of scolds, Lord Chief Justice Holt appears to have rejected his analysis although he was, apparently, somewhat amused by the case. He declared that it was better to be ducked in the Trinity rather than Michaelmas law term (the former being warmer). Even so, judgment was arrested on a technicality.[104]

There are other mentions of scolding during the eighteenth century, especially its first half. In July 1732, Mary Millicent pleaded guilty to being a common scold at the Quarter Sessions for Westminster. Because she had been in prison for ten weeks, the court merely fined her a shilling and ordered her to be discharged.[105] However, in 1738, an elderly woman, "notorious for her vociferation", was convicted at the Surrey Quarter Sessions for being a common scold and: "...sentenced to receive the old punishment of being duck'd". The court's officers then carried this out,

---

[100] Blackstone, William (1769) *Commentaries on the Laws of England*, vol.4, p.169.

[101] Ingram, Martin J. (1994) "'Scolding Women Cucked or Washed': A Crisis in Gender Relations in Early Modern England", pp.66-69.

[102] Sessions 22nd April 1690, Kingston Local History Room, KE 2/2/1-14.

[103] Walker, Garthine (2003) *Crime, Gender and Social Order in Early Modern England*, p.104.

[104] *The Queen v Foxby* (1704) 1 Salkeld 266.

[105] *Daily Post*, July 4, 1732.

using a chair that had been expressly preserved for just this purpose. True to her character, as soon as she was released from the apparatus, the woman attacked one of her acquaintances with "tongue, tooth, and nail".[106] Whether there was something special to Surrey or Kingston in this regard is unclear, but seven years later, in April 1745, a woman who kept the *Queen's Head* alehouse in the county town was: "…ordered by the court there to be duck'd for scolding, and was accordingly placed in the chair, and duck'd in the river Thames, under Kingston Bridge, in the presence of 2 or 3,000 people".[107] This was unusual enough to be reported in a large group of newspapers. Later that year, a woman was convicted on an indictment for being a scold at the Court of King's Bench, though sentence was deferred to the following term.[108]

Parish records, especially those for places at a distance from London, also refer to ducking stools until late in the century. For example, the accounts of Barnsley, in Yorkshire, mention regular payments relating to their town's apparatus, such as one of ten shillings made to Thomas Moorhouse in 1731 for "mending ye ducking-stool". As late as 1768, the parish of Skipton in the same county paid: "John Brown for new ducking-stool L1 0s. 11-1/2d". However, its use seems to have been abandoned about two years later. The Scarborough ducking stool lasted longer and was last employed in about 1795, when a Mrs. Gamble was ducked.[109] There were very belated reports of ducking having been employed against a notorious scold named Jenny Pipes, who was immersed in the River Kenwater in Leominster, Herefordshire, for using foul and abusive language in 1809 (if true, its last recorded use in England). Nevertheless, although this disposal was, allegedly, ordered by local magistrates, the case was very little reported at the time.[110]

An analogous, but even more arcane form of female punishment was imposed in Morpeth in 1741, when a married woman was punished for using "opprobrious language" by being put in the 'branks'. These were the northern version of the ancient, and largely vanished (in other parts of eighteenth-century England) 'scold's bridle', which muzzled a woman by forcing a piece of steel, set in a head-enclosing metal framework, into her mouth.[111] In England, branking had been imposed quite commonly in

---

106 *London Evening Post*, October 7, 1738 - October 10, 1738.

107 *General Advertiser (1744)* April 30, 1745.

108 *St. James's Evening Post*, December 5, 1745 - December 7, 1745.

109 Andrews, William (1899) *Bygone Punishments*, p.81.

110 *The Morning Post,* August 5, 1867, p.6.

111 Morgan, Gwenda and Rushton, Peter (1998) *Rogues, Thieves and the Rule of Law,* p.127.

northern towns (such as Morpeth), during the middle of the seventeenth century, being seen as an alternative to the ducking stool for local scolds. However, it was only rarely used after the early 1700s. (It also lingered in Scotland, as a punishment for insulting women).[112] Far more commonly, by the eighteenth century, women were simply prosecuted for disturbing the peace and behaving in a disorderly manner, even if not positively identified as scolds.

In any event, taken together, and ignoring the problematic issue of prostitution (the most common female 'crime') but including offences in which there could be peripheral male involvement, such as abortion, specifically 'female' offences made up only a tiny minority of crimes perpetrated by women, the vast majority of which were for conventional offences such as theft. Conversely, there were only a few inherently male crimes, such as rape, in which women were *largely* unrepresented, and even there they could be charged as accessories to an offence.

Explaining the Gender Difference

The normally low level of female crime compared to male offending rates is particularly remarkable because more women than men usually live in poverty and they are often the chief (sometimes the only) providers for dependent children. Unsurprisingly, many attempts to explain this gender difference have been made over the past century. In the modern era, the 'gender equality' hypothesis has been popular. According to this theory, the gender gap in crime narrows in those social environments where female roles differ less from those of men.[113] Although this analysis has been strongly challenged, in the context of eighteenth-century London, where the 'equalizing effect' of the capital appears to have had a significant effect on female offending rates, the paradigm has considerable mileage. Nevertheless, when it comes to provincial England, several of the more 'traditional' criminological theories that have attempted to explain lower levels of female deviance probably have greater value, provided they are not given mono-causal status or exaggerated importance.

Thus, women might offend less frequently than men because they are/were: less subject to a cultural emphasis on material success (anomie); less likely to get involved with gangs (cultural transmission); less exposed

---

[112] Harrison, John G., (1998) "Women and the Branks in Stirling, c.1600 to c.1730", p.114.

[113] Steffensmeier, Darrel and Allan, Emilie (1996) "Gender and Crime: Toward a Gendered Theory of Female Offending", pp.467-468.

to the influence of delinquent peers (differential association); subject to greater supervision and possessed of stronger social bonds (social control). The last, of course, was an inherent feature of the era's form of patriarchy. It has also been argued that women were often excluded from criminal opportunities because of the nature of their employment and the routine of their daily lives. For example, almost no eighteenth-century females worked in provincial docks. This deprived them of one opportunity for lucrative pilfering. Furthermore, stereotypes of eighteenth-century femininity, such as submissiveness, nurturance, domestication, and other 'ladylike' behavior, were often the antithesis of those qualities valued in the criminal underworld, unlike many approved male virtues. The separation between desirable 'masculine' traits such as boldness and repugnant 'criminal' traits was sometimes quite thin. For many men, drifting into crime did not require so radical a change in their outlook on the world.[114]

In the nineteenth century, rather speculative if not entirely fanciful biological theories based on women's physical constitutions were often advanced to explain their lower involvement in crime. In recent years, a reaction to such biological determinism has threatened to go to the opposite extreme, and deny any role at all to physical differences between the sexes. However, an examination of eighteenth-century graveyards, a fair number of which have been excavated due to modern redevelopment, reveals that men were usually significantly larger than the women of the era. Thus, the *average* stature of eighteenth-century skeletons from the Farringdon Street excavation in London, carried out during the 1990s, was about 5' 6" for males and 5' ½" for females (urban reared people tended to be slightly smaller than their rural counterparts until the twentieth century). This discrepancy was helped by gender-based differences in the biological standard of living. For example, women appear to have seen a greater deterioration in diet during the early 1800s than did men.[115]

A perusal of eighteenth-century fashion also quickly shows that men were more suitably dressed for certain activities. They were likely to be wearing knee breeches or trousers and to be shod in boots, rather than wearing petticoats, skirts, and flimsier shoes. It was easier to run and fight in male attire. It does not need a discussion of relative testosterone levels and muscle-mass to appreciate that these differences were likely to make *some* difference to crime levels.

---

[114] Steffensmeier, Darrel and Allan, Emilie (1996) "Gender and Crime: Toward a Gendered Theory of Female Offending", pp.472-473 and p.476.

[115] Komlos, John (Ed.) (1994) *Stature, Living Standards, and Economic Development*, p.217.

For example, if there is any truth to the notion that "big people hit little people", size and strength are likely to be factors that potential aggressors weigh up before resorting to violence. As a result, simple differences in physical strength may go *some* way toward explaining gender differences in cases of assault.[116] Indeed, it has been suggested that the move towards male dominance of retailing in eighteenth-century London, as clearly occurred, may have been *partly* linked to a belief, on the part of both retailers and thieves, that women made 'softer' targets. Case transcripts suggest that shoplifters sometimes deliberately chose premises that were staffed by women because they thought they were more easily intimidated. Certainly, female shopkeepers regularly testified to their fear when being victimised.[117]

Of course, it is all a matter of degree and statistical probability. Women who carried out hard manual labour, as many did during the eighteenth century, were often very strong. Men who were chronically ill, injured, or maimed (as was not uncommon at this time) were frequently weak and vulnerable. Some females were extremely aggressive, some men very passive. It is important not to argue from the general to the particular, or vice versa.

The capital also saw the development of criminal families and sub-cultures, in which deviant values appear to have been transmitted from parents to children, including girls. This *may* have encouraged female offending in the Metropolis. For example, within months of Mary Haycock being burned at Tyburn for coining, one of her daughters had been arrested for shoplifting and another for picking pockets. One of them (Ann) had earlier stood trial with Mary, but been acquitted and so escaped sharing her fate.[118] There was less scope for this to happen in the provinces. Nevertheless, it was certainly not entirely absent. Female offenders there were often associated with male criminals. For example, Iphemia Barnes was capitally convicted at the Norfolk Assizes held at Thetford in 1727, but respited from execution for further consideration. At the very same Sessions, her husband Andrew was found guilty of a separate offence of housebreaking and ordered for immediate execution.[119] Doubtless the offspring of such unions, male or female, were also likely to become offenders.

---

[116] Warner, Jessica et al (2005) "Women Behaving Badly: Gender and Aggression in a Military Town, 1653–1781", pp.289-298.

[117] Tickell, Shelley (2010) "The prevention of shoplifting in eighteenth-century London", p.300.

[118] *Old Whig or The Consistent Protestant*, April 10, 1735. OBSP, Trial of Mary and Ann Haycock, 10th July 1734: t17340710-17.

[119] *Weekly Journal or British Gazetteer*, April 1, 1727.

Contemporary Explanations for Female Crime

To the eighteenth-century mind there were many similarities in the way in which both men and women entered criminal life. Very importantly, small sins were thought to beget bigger ones in a process that might start by ignoring the Sabbath and finish at the gallows. However, in women, early indications of personal indiscipline and a reluctance to be 'ruled' were considered to be particularly significant. Thus, Mary Edmondson, who would go on to be convicted at the Surrey Assizes for murdering her aunt, had shown herself to be "self-willed, uncontroulable and unadviseable" when very young. She became even more headstrong after she turned seventeen. On one occasion, she stabbed her mother with a penknife after being rebuked. Shortly afterwards, her parents arranged for Mary to leave their native Yorkshire and become a maid to her ill-fated aunt.[120]

Women were thought to be especially susceptible to a number of character defects; in the wrong circumstances, these could lead them into crime. For example, Mary Channing began her journey to the gallows by manifesting "sluttishness", allegedly brought about by her mother's frequent absence from the family home (and so her female duties), as well as "pride and affected gaudiness".[121] As this comment suggests, it was feared that women were prone to vanity, being inherently given to extravagance and constantly craving fine clothes.[122] Indeed, some thought that: "Vanity is so imprinted in the minds of women, that nothing less than a super-natural hand can totally efface it".[123] Some women of the poorer sort would accuse their husbands of being a "niggard" if they were not prodigal with their money, regularly demanding gowns of the "newest fashioned silk". They would also spend large amounts of their time: "...painting themselves, and frizzling their hairs, and prying in their [looking] glass like apes, to prank up themselves in their finery".[124] Even

---

[120] Anon, (1759) *A genuine narrative of the trial and condemnation of Mary Edmondson, for the murder of Mrs. Susannah Walker, her aunt. At the Assizes held at Kingston ... county of Surrey, on Saturday, March 31, 1759,* pp.4-5.

[121] Anon, (1706) *Serious admonitions to youth, in a short account of the life, trial, condemnation and execution of Mrs Mary Channing,* p.5

[122] Wilkes, Wettenhall (1751) *A Letter of Genteel and Moral Advice to a Young Lady*, p.194; and Gisborne, Thomas (1797) *An Enquiry into the Duties of the Female Sex*, p.34.

[123] Brown, Thomas (1705) *A Legacy for the Ladies Or, Characters of the Women of the Age*, p.3.

[124] Swetman, Joseph (1733) *The Arraignment of Lewde, Idle, Froward and Unconstant Women,* p.15 and p.38.

apparent female strengths could lead to potentially criminogenic weaknesses. For example, the vivacity and imagination of women, qualities that were in themselves quite good, could also result in: "…unsteadiness of mind; to fondness of novelty; to habits of frivolousness and trifling employments; to repugnance of graver studies".[125] Any female attempt to subvert the proper gender order might also lead to disaster. Ann Williams, for example, who was executed at Gloucester in April 1753 for poisoning her kindly but weak husband, had "ruled him with a rod of iron". He had feebly yielded to her in all things, but this merely served to nurse her opposition and violence.[126]

---

[125] Anon, (1798) *The Female Aegis; or, The Duties of Women from Childhood to Old Age and in most Situations of Life, Exemplified*, p.13.
[126] *Public Advertiser*, April 19, 1753.

CHAPTER TWO

PROSECUTION AND PUNISHMENT

Introduction

This chapter will consider the experiences of female offenders within the eighteenth-century provincial justice system, as suspects, defendants, and convicts. It should be noted immediately that it was a male world. Nearly all of the permanent personnel found in the era's pre-trial process, courts and prisons, whether they were judges, attending dignitaries, examining magistrates, jurors, clerks, lawyers, ushers, or executioners were male. Other than as the accused or members of the 'jury of matrons' (see below), women were largely confined to giving evidence or, occasionally, being spectators, though interestingly, a handful of women ran or assisted in the running of jails during the course of the century, even if they were the widows of men who had first held such positions. As early as 1660, the gaoler at Fisherton in Wiltshire had been removed in favour of Mary Thorpe, the widow of a royalist who had been killed during the Interregnum. She was commended for preferment in a letter sent from the King to local magistrates. Her descendants (she remarried) ran the prison for the ensuing 70 years.[1] Women also played a significant, if not official, role as informers when it came to minor and regulatory matters. For example, after the advent of the 1736 Gin Act they were often active wherever spirits were distributed, seeking the rewards that were available for revealing such activity to the authorities. Thus, two women in Norwich, described as "very expert in their Business", entrapped several distillers and a large number of "petty Traders in Spirituous Liquors".[2]

At every stage in the eighteenth-century criminal process, cultural expectations as to how women should behave helped determine forensic and penal responses to their crimes. In general terms, this resulted in an apparently widespread, though certainly not universal, leniency towards

---

[1] Pugh, R.B. and Crittall, Elizabeth (Eds) (1953) *A History of the County of Wiltshire*, vol. 5, pp.170-194.
[2] Warner, Jessica (1999) "Damn you, you informing Bitch", p.299.

female suspects and defendants.[3] Sometimes, this was even expressly alluded to by both private and judicial figures. For example, on one occasion, the notorious Fanny Davies escaped prosecution for theft at Quarter Sessions when her male victim did not proceed with his indictment because he: "…did not like to prosecute a poor weak woman, lest he should meet the contempt of the crowd, and the laughter of the lawyers". Later, when she was convicted at the Essex Assizes in 1786 of stealing an enormous amount of money (*allegedly* £1,250 when banknotes were included) from a country grazier, while he slept at an inn, she was warned by the trial judge, Mr. Justice Ashurst, not to anticipate a pardon or to: "…expect that her sex would protect her from the hand of justice on this occasion". (Suggesting that on others it might have done). Even so, and significantly, she was later reprieved on condition of transportation.[4]

It is extremely difficult to factor in (or exclude) the many variables *other* than their sex that might have contributed to this phenomenon. It is certainly possible that this apparent leniency is illusory. For example, eighteenth-century women may have received higher acquittal rates because fewer of them were "old offenders" in a system where previous bad character was routinely revealed at trial until late in the century. Similarly, they may have received milder sentences because they were not as 'hardened' as their male equivalents or because they had committed less serious examples of the crimes for which they were convicted. There are some examples of this from other eras. Thus, it appears that the lower conviction rates for female assault defendants in English summary trials at the turn of the twentieth century *can* be explained by such contextual factors.[5] To take another comparator, it has been argued (although not totally accepted) that continuing disparities in modern sentencing between male and female offenders are due to such gender related factors, rather than bias.[6]

There is *some* (albeit very limited) support for such an analysis to be applied in the eighteenth century. For example, female crime in the eighteenth-century North East of England was largely based on the small-

---

[3] Garland, David (1990) *Punishment and Modern Society: A Study in Social Theory,* p.202.

[4] Anon, (1786) *An Authentic Narrative of the Most Remarkable Adventures, and Curious Intrigues, Exhibited in the Life of Miss Fanny Davies*, p.35 and pp.50-53.

[5] Davies, Andrew (1999) "'These viragoes are no less cruel than the lads': young women, gangs and violence in late Victorian Manchester and Salford", pp.72-89.

[6] Godfrey, Barry et al (2005) "Explaining Gendered Sentencing Patterns for Violent Men and Women in the Late-Victorian and Edwardian Period", pp.696-697.

scale theft of goods that appeared attractive and which were readily available to steal, exchange, or sell. Nevertheless, such explanations do not appear to be supported by much of the other available evidence.[7] Thus, it seems that female defendants at the Old Bailey were no more likely than men to be of previous good character.[8] Similarly, a nationwide examination of defendants' offences and previous convictions does not suggest a sufficiently large divergence to account for different male and female outcomes. Indeed, while 61 per cent of all male transports to Australia had previous convictions, the figure was 65 per cent for women.[9] That the average female crime *might* have been of slightly less gravity than that of the average male in the same 'class' of offenders could have been a factor in their better treatment, but on its own it does not fully explain the more benign approach taken by courts and officials towards women.

In reality, it seems that male 'sympathy' (broadly construed) for accused women helped produce beneficial outcomes in a criminal process that contained a huge degree of discretion.[10] This discretion could be, and regularly was, exercised in favour of women. However, it should be noted that this phenomenon was certainly not without parallel in other times, both before and after the eighteenth century. Indeed, historically, it seems to have been almost the 'norm'. In medieval England, for example, women appear to have been denounced less frequently, arrested less often, and punished less severely than their male counterparts.[11] Female acquittal rates were also significantly higher than they were for men.[12]

Similarly, leniency was even more marked in the Victorian era than it had been in the eighteenth century.[13] An analysis of cases in the summary courts in the early twentieth century also suggests that women received fewer custodial sentences than men for assaults of similar gravity.[14] On a more specific basis, although the small number of young women convicted of gang-related crimes of violence in the Manchester conurbation in the

---

[7] King, Peter (1999) "Gender, crime and justice in late eighteenth-and early nineteenth-century England", p.46 and pp.62-64.
[8] See generally, King, Peter (1998) "The rise of juvenile delinquency in England".
[9] King, Peter (2006) *Crime and Law in England, 1750-1840,* p.188.
[10] King, Peter (2000) *Crime, Justice and Discretion in England 1740-1820,* p.355.
[11] Dean, Trevor (2001) *Crime in Medieval Europe 1200-1550*, p.78,
[12] Bellamy, John (1998) *The Criminal Trial in Later Medieval England: Felony Before the Courts From Edward I to the Sixteenth Century*, p.124.
[13] Zedner, Lucia (1991) *Women, Crime and Custody in Victorian England*, p.26.
[14] Godfrey, Barry et al (2005) "Explaining gendered sentencing patterns for violent men and women in the late-Victorian and Edwardian period", p.718.

last three decades of the nineteenth century were loudly condemned as 'vixens', 'viragoes' and 'Amazons' in the local press, and subjected to stern lectures by magistrates about their 'unwomanly' behaviour, they generally received less stringent sentences than disorderly young males. Magistrates appear to have shared a broader Victorian perception of women as more malleable and easily led than men.[15]

Nor was such gendered lenience confined to England. It was found in much of Western Europe during the eighteenth century. Thus, in France, prior to the Revolution, the punishment of women might be harsh in the small number of cases that were thought to undermine vital family values (such as husband killing). However, it was relatively lenient when compared to men in cases deemed to pose little threat to society. As in England, this was especially likely with regard to female thieves who were in personally precarious economic circumstances. The French courts were increasingly reluctant to execute women where they could reasonably be imprisoned instead. French women also normally enjoyed significantly higher acquittal rates at trial, like their English counterparts.[16]

Whatever its historical roots, descendants, and cousins, it must be asked why eighteenth-century justices, judges, jurors, and prosecutors were more sympathetic towards female offenders than to those of their own gender? One answer is that women were increasingly seen as weak, emotional, passive, sometimes even pathetic individuals, who were likely to have been led astray by others (who were often men). This meant that they were less culpable and so “less entitled to severity”.[17] Offending women often became ‘disturbed’ individuals.

A general belief that women were inherently more chaste and honest than men also took root during the 1700s, replacing older views that had seen them as the lineal successors of Eve, and so responsible for man’s original fall from grace. The portrayal of female thieves in the popular crime literature that was available at the start of the eighteenth century often followed the tradition of the previous era. Women were depicted as fundamentally untrustworthy, devious, and even ruled by an ungovernable sexuality.[18] As late as 1750, one observer, keen to enhance the punishment available for convicted felons, suggested that women should suffer transportation for their very first offence, however trivial. He felt that there

---

[15] Davies, Andrew (1999) "‘These viragoes are no less cruel than the lads’: young women, gangs and violence in late Victorian Manchester and Salford”, pp.72-89.
[16] Castan, Nicole (1993) “Criminals”, pp.486-489.
[17] *The Times*, June 27, 1788, p.3.
[18] Shoemaker, Robert (2010) “Print and the Female Voice: Representations of Women’s Crime in London, 1690–1735”, p.80.

could be no better punishment for their crimes, which usually sprang from "idleness and lust", than to be forced to labour. Put to work, they would no longer live in "laziness, filth, dishonesty and wickedness".[19]

Such attitudes were increasingly rare by the late 1700s. Women came to be seen as the victims of men in sexual matters, rather than as predators. In the early eighteenth-century, Daniel Defoe could produce a novel, *Moll Flanders* (perhaps the first true English novel), in which the heroine was a sexually adventurous/promiscuous, socially marginal, habitual thief. By the end of the century, this would have been almost unthinkable.[20] Eve increasingly became the first seduced woman, one who had been followed by many other female victims of male lust, rather than a corrupter of men.[21] Published accounts of female crime, while not absolving women of culpability, placed a growing stress on economic deprivation and the malign influence of the men who misled and abused them.[22]

Of course, this change in outlook was not entirely advantageous to women, who were, to an extent, 'infantalised' by it. Towards the end of the century, in 1792, Mary Wollestonecraft lamented a situation in which one-half of the human race was encouraged to passive: "…listless inactivity and stupid acquiescence? Kind instructors [men]! What were we created for? To remain, it may be said, innocent; they mean in a state of childhood". It was the same mentality that prompted men to perform exaggerated acts of 'gallantry', such as picking up dropped handkerchiefs, that treated women as if they were physically incapable of the least movement.[23] Nevertheless, it encouraged beneficial outcomes for women in the forensic process.

More rationally, there was also a growing acceptance that women were often in material distress, particularly if they were raising children, for reasons that were beyond their control. It was recognised that they were greatly disadvantaged on the labour market, both as to wage levels (much inferior to those of men even when doing similar work) and employment

---

[19] *Gentleman's Magazine,* vol.20, 1750, p.533. It should be noted that the same observer also thought that male convicts ought to be castrated.

[20] Lacey, Nicola (2007) *From Moll Flanders to Tess of the D'Urbervilles: Women, Autonomy and Criminal Responsibility in Eighteenth and Nineteenth Century England,* p.28.

[21] Dabhoiwala, Faramerz (2012) *The Origins of Sex: A History of the First Sexual Revolution*, pp.152-153.

[22] Shoemaker, Robert (2010) "Print and the Female Voice: Representations of Women's Crime in London, 1690–1735", p.84.

[23] Wollestonecraft, Mary (1792) *A Vindication of the Rights of Women,* 2nd edn., p.121.

prospects, and frequently abandoned by their partners, in an increasingly mobile society, even if they had dependant children. This awareness was reflected in the popular literature of the period. For example, in Defoe's novel of 1724, *Roxana*: *The Fortunate Mistress,* the eponymous heroine is abandoned by her first husband, when his business fails, leaving her "in rags and dirt" to look after their five small children alone. Roxana is forced into a life of prostitution to support herself. Women often had more excuse for offending than did men.

Eighteenth-century judges and jurors *could* be compassionate, if they chose, even to other males. For example, on one occasion, when a man was tried at the Surrey Assizes for stealing a leg of mutton to support his hungry family, his trial jury made a collection for him. They were much more willing to extend such compassion to women. However, sympathy was certainly not unqualified or lightly dispensed, even for females. It usually required a low level, non-violent, property crime, ideally for food, that was committed to meet pressing need, preferably outright hunger, before it became operative. The latter feature, in particular, was not enormously common, even though food constituted up to 70 per cent of working-class family budgets as late as the early nineteenth century.

For example, samples of female convictions for property offences on the Western Circuit Assizes suggest that food was the predominant item of value (even if mixed in with other items) in only 16 per cent of cases in 1740-43, five per cent in 1755-1759, and six per cent in 1780-1784, even though many of these years were economically difficult. Of course, most such thefts would have been valued at less than a shilling, and so classified as petty theft, or were viewed as minor clergyable felonies, and heard at Quarter Sessions as a result. Nevertheless, although the percentage of 'true bills' for female-perpetrated property offences involving the (predominant) taking of food, drink or fuel (the last not included in the Western Circuit figure) returned at the Dorset Quarter Sessions was higher than at Assizes, it was still in a clear minority. Between 1735 and 1745, it constituted 35.29 per cent of offences, while in the years from 1780 to 1785 the figure was only 30.3 per cent.[24] Indeed, at the Oxfordshire Quarter Sessions during the late eighteenth century, men were more likely to steal food or fuel, items that could meet pressing 'need', than were women.[25]

---

[24] Williams, Amy (2000) *The Criminality Of Women In The 18th Century In The South West Of England*, p.100.

[25] Kilday, Anne-Marie (2005) "Women and Crime in Britain, 1700-1850", at p.179. Of course, it should be noted that men were sometimes more exposed to the opportunity to steal foodstuffs, especially when at work.

In the Metropolis (where attitudes on this issue were similar to those in the provinces), pleas of hardship did not avail Mary Billingsby, a totally uneducated eighteen-year-old from Norwich, who had come up to London three years before her execution. She was accused of coshing an infant in Hoxton in 1714. She had then stripped the child of its clothes and valuables. After being capitally convicted she claimed that poverty had driven her to act as she did. The Reverend Paul Lorrain, the Newgate Ordinary, swiftly rejected this suggestion, and pointed out that: "…if she had been an honest and diligent person, she might have supply'd her wants otherwise than by such unlawful means, and such too as were most base and cruel".[26] Even much less serious crimes could produce similar forensic outcomes. For example, the following year, Mary Nichols was capitally condemned and executed for a housebreaking, during which she had taken just one pair of flaxen sheets, even though she blamed her downfall on her acute domestic situation. The pressure of: "…providing for her small children as well as for her self, being great, she was reduc'd to extream poverty, and by that driven to stealing".[27]

Nevertheless, other women in this situation, especially those accused of simple grand larceny, were more fortunate. For example, at the Surrey Assizes in 1740, Rose Pluckrose was tried for stealing 5s 6d from Joseph Stone, who "fully prov'd the fact". Rose does not appear to have disputed the allegation, merely telling the court: "I have a bad husband, and three children ready to starve with hunger". She was convicted of petty larceny to the value of 10d, rather than grand larceny (for which she would probably have been transported).[28]

On a practical basis, of course, if women with small children were executed, transported, or imprisoned for long periods of time, family breakdown would ensue and their infants might be forced onto the parish. This would occasion considerable expense for local ratepayers. It could also add to the number of youthful thieves wandering the streets. In such circumstances, acquittals or less drastic punishments might appear attractive.[29] Furthermore, the era's criminal trials were moral theatre. Women *may* have been more adept than men at publicly "humbling

---

[26] Ordinary's Account, 16th July 1714: OA17140716

[27] Ordinary's Account, 21st September 1715: OA17150921

[28] Anon, (1740) *The Proceedings at the Assizes of Peace, Oyer and Terminer, for the County of Surrey, Held at the Town-Hall of Kingston Upon Thames, in the 14th Year of His Majesty's Reign ... To Which is Added the Genuine Proceedings at the Assizes for the County of Essex*, p.15.

[29] King, Peter (1999) "Gender, crime and justice in late eighteenth-and early nineteenth-century England", p.46 and pp.62-64.

themselves", to use a contemporary phrase, encouraging pity from judges and juries.

Perhaps the most important factor was that male crime was perceived as inherently more 'threatening' than that committed by women, and so more likely to be prosecuted to conviction and condign punishment. Men were usually much more violent, and there were many more male than female offenders. They were considered to be more of a social menace. Any indulgence when it came to verdict or sentencing males might send out a dangerous message and undermine deterrence, the primary aim of the period's criminal justice system.

Married Offenders and *Feme Covert*

Irrespective of any male 'sympathy', there was one legal doctrine, *feme covert,* that in theory greatly helped the prospects of married female defendants, both at and before trial, and which made a contribution to their favourable results. It was certainly not enough to fully, or even largely, explain the discrepancy in trial outcomes between the genders. A substantial majority of formally prosecuted female offenders throughout the eighteenth century were always single women, whether spinsters or widows, and so unaffected by the concept.[30] For example, at the Essex Assizes between 1776 and 1804, just under 30 per cent of female defendants were married, and the figure was even smaller at the county's Quarter Sessions.[31] (Of course, this does not preclude the doctrine influencing the initial decision to indict married women). Significantly, the gradual abandonment of *feme covert*, and its growing absence from legal textbooks, did not coincide with any increase in female prosecution and conviction rates. Nevertheless, it warrants detailed consideration.

When eighteenth-century women married, and until their husbands died, they acquired the status at common law of *feme covert,* unlike spinsters and widows (who were *feme sole*). In theory, a woman's legal existence largely became merged with that of her husband by dint of his "subsumption" of her into himself. She was figuratively veiled although, supposedly, the two became one legal person for many purposes, rather than being (male) owner and (female) property.[32] In William Blackstone's words, albeit made with slight exaggeration: "By marriage, the husband

---

[30] King, Peter (2006) *Crime and Law in England, 1750-1840,* p.191.
[31] King, Peter (2000) *Crime, Justice and Discretion in England: 1740-1820,* p.203.
[32] Dolan, Frances E. (2003) "Battered women, petty traitors, and the legacy of coverture", pp.255-256.

and wife are one person in law: that is, the very being or legal existence of the woman is suspended during the marriage".[33] Although a woman lost many of her rights to personal property, her husband became responsible for most of her civil liabilities.[34]

However, coverture also had potentially important consequences in criminal matters. On a procedural basis, for example, a *feme covert* could not be bound by recognisance on her own to appear at Sessions, although this was not always appreciated by J.P.s: "Sometimes Justices' Clerks are so stupid to take their recognizances only; but such recognizances cannot be estreated".[35] Much more importantly, the law was, ostensibly, often reluctant to find that a married woman who offended with, and in the presence of, her husband - unless it was in an overtly active role - was implicated in 'his' crime, even as an accessory. Instead, it was assumed that she had committed it by the "coercion of her husband", not least because obedience to her spouse was a fundamental female duty.[36] (Although the doctrine did not extend to a man's daughters or female servants).[37]

When John and Jane Graham were indicted for forgery at the Old Bailey in 1782, accused of altering a bank note for £15 to one of £50, prosecuting counsel openly considered how coverture might affect Jane's position, if advanced as a defence, giving an exegesis on its operation in the process. He noted that if a married woman stole in the company of her spouse it was assumed that she had committed the offence: "…under the dominion and authority of her husband; but that, as well as any other presumption, can only stand till there is a proof to the contrary; for I take it to be equally clear, that if from the evidence it should appear, that the married woman was the active person, and acted without the control or interference of the husband, it would be clear in point of law, that she was involved in the same degree of guilt; if it should appear that it was not in the presence of the husband but distinct from him, I take it to be clear, that a woman in that situation has no privilege whatever". Both defendants were convicted in this case, although, perhaps significantly, the jury recommended Jane to mercy.[38]

---

[33] Blackstone, William (1765) *Commentaries on the Laws of England*, vol.1, pp.442-445.

[34] Anon, (1738) *Baron and Feme: A treatise of Law and Equity Concerning Husbands and Wives*, 3rd edn., p.29.

[35] Stubbs, W. and Talmarsh, G. (1749) *The Crown circuit companion,* p.59.

[36] Anon, (1632) *The Laws Resolutions of Womens Rights,* p.6 and p.206.

[37] Blackstone, William (1769) *Commentaries on the Laws of England*, vol.4, p.28.

[38] OBSP, Trial of Jane and John Graham, 11th September 1782: t17820911-12

As this extract suggests, *feme covert* did not apply if a woman stole at her husband's command but in his absence or, very importantly, if she offended of her "own voluntary act", even in his presence. Additionally, it did not extend to a few very serious felonies, such as robbery and murder (though women who concealed or assisted their husbands *after* a killing escaped being accessories to their spouse's crime).[39] At the other end of the offence calendar, a variety of lesser, sometimes fairly arcane crimes were specifically exempt from its reach. For example, a woman could be indicted for managing a brothel with her husband, and in his presence. An even more recondite example involved the enforcement of legislation prohibiting the wearing of foreign fabrics against married women. An Act from 1748 (and an earlier statute that it replaced) forbidding the wearing and importation of "cambricks and French lawns" had occasioned problems. If a woman was *feme covert* she couldn't be punished, even though wearing foreign cloth or clothes. (Her husband might have bought them for her). However, the husband did not wear them, and it was his assets from which any fine would have to be paid. An amendment, introduced in 1750, made it clear that, in these situations, if the: "…person convicted be a feme covert, [enforcement could] be levied by law on the goods and chattels of her husband".[40] Some contemporary observers felt that the doctrine should not extend to misdemeanours generally.

During the 1600s, coverture appears to have played a fairly significant role in at least some criminal trials.[41] Nevertheless, by the eighteenth century, its day-to-day application in the courts did not *necessarily* reflect the apparently unequivocal endorsement of the doctrine made by William Blackstone and some other contemporary legal writers, many of whom were not specialists in criminal law. It seems that its criminal implications were increasingly questioned during the 1700s, and its operation gradually restricted. Although, quite exceptionally, coverture was being claimed as late as the early nineteenth century, its publicly acknowledged use at trial became increasingly uncommon after 1700, and rare after about 1750. The doctrine could be restricted without being entirely rejected because it created a rebuttable presumption, not a rule of law. A woman who offended in the presence of her husband could be deemed to have done so quite voluntarily, rather than as a result of his pressure, and so to be outside its protection.[42]

---

[39] Anon, (1777) *The Laws Respecting Women*, pp.70-71.
[40] *General Advertiser (1744),* August 9, 1750.
[41] Walker, Garthine (2003) *Crime, Gender and Social Order in Early Modern England*, pp.202-203.
[42] Bingham, Peregrine (1816) *The Law of Infancy and Coverture*, p.228.

By the late eighteenth century, even the courts were reluctant to give unqualified and overt support to coverture. In 1787, for example, the distinguished barrister Newman Knowlys sought to argue that in a case of receiving stolen goods a co-habiting woman, even if not legally married, was covered by the doctrine. He also suggested that she had no right, if asked to assist her partner in such nefarious activity, to question the actions of the: "…person to whom she looks up for assistance; on whom she depends; whose servant she is; who has power to compel her to do things at times from fear, she cannot resist his commands". However, the court was more circumspect, pointing out (uncontroversially) that coverture did not extend to concubines, and (more significantly) that: "…even in the case of a wife, she must be under the immediate coercion of her husband". (The female defendant was still acquitted).[43] Throughout the period, some women who committed property crimes with their husbands were convicted. For example, in 1739, when Henry and Margaret Cole ("his wife") broke into a dwelling house together, and stole eleven shirts and ten tablecloths inside, they were both swiftly convicted of the felony at the Kingston Assizes.[44]

This increasingly strict approach towards the doctrine was not confined to England. In eighteenth-century Pennsylvania, for example, it also seems that prosecutors did not routinely dismiss charges against married women and juries did not acquit those coming before the courts in circumstances where, in theory, they should have been able to rely on coverture.[45] Similarly, in Ireland, *feme covert* did not *necessarily* prevent women being prosecuted, although it was, in theory, as applicable there as in England. Of 180 females indicted at the County Armagh Assizes for felony, in a sample taken from the years 1736 to 1795, 81 were indicted as part of a gender mixed group. It appears that 61 of these groups contained men of the same family name, suggesting that a significant number of married women were put on trial with their husbands.[46]

Nevertheless, in provincial (just as in Metropolitan) England, the doctrine may still have influenced the initial decision to prosecute, and

---

[43] OBSP, Trial of Darcy Wentworth and Mary Wilkinson, 12th December 1787: t17871212-7

[44] Anon, (1739) *The Genuine Proceedings at the Assizes on the Home Circuit, Held in March, 1739. … at Hertford, for the County of Hertford; Chelmsford, for the County of Essex,* p.15.

[45] Rowe, G. S. (1988) "Femes Covert and Criminal Prosecution in Eighteenth-Century Pennsylvania", p.154.

[46] Garnham, Neil (1996) *Courts, Crime and the Criminal Law in Ireland, 1692-1760,* p.217.

then whether to convict, married women, even if it was not expressly referred to in magistrates' examinations and trial reports. Certainly, far more wives were acquitted when tried with husbands who were convicted than vice versa. It has been claimed that a close examination of a variety of English sources for trial on indictment, taken from about 1640 to 1760, reveal that assumptions about coverture allowed many married women to walk free when involved in crime with their spouses. Indeed, some of these sources suggest that the acquittal rate amongst married women accused of a theft related offence, but acting alone, was only 48.48 per cent compared to one of 81.63 per cent for wives caught stealing with their husbands.[47] At a more localised level, it can be noted that between 1776 and 1800, nearly all female co-defendants in Essex whose husbands were convicted were found 'not guilty'.[48]

Occasionally, the doctrine was still expressly invoked to secure an acquittal. For example, in a comparatively rare example of the presumption being publicly mentioned, in 1745, Elizabeth Hood was indicted at the Surrey Assizes with her spouse John for stealing £30 worth of plate from a pewterer's warehouse in Rotherhithe. John was quickly convicted, as the matter was clearly proved. However: "…his wife was acquitted, as acting under the direction of her husband".[49] (John Hood was later sentenced to transportation).[50] What can be extrapolated from this brief report? Firstly, Elizabeth's relationship to her husband had not been enough to prevent her from being charged or her bill of indictment surviving scrutiny by the Assizes Grand Jury. The evidence is reported as clear-cut. Did this encourage John to throw his hands up at trial and absolve his wife, taking all the blame himself?[51]

Even at the very end of the period, the doctrine was still being openly referred to in court, albeit only rarely, particularly to deal with situations involving married female defendants that were considered 'unfair' in some

---

[47] Caswell, Marisha Christine (2012) *Married Women, Crime, And Questions Of Liability In England, 1640-1760*, pp.151-160.
[48] King, Peter (2000) *Crime, Justice and Discretion in England 1740-1820*, p.201.
[49] Anon, (1745) *The Proceedings at the assizes of the peace, oyer and terminer, and general gaol-delivery for the county of Surry, held at Croydon, on Friday the 22d, Saturday the 23d, Monday the 25th, Tuesday the 26th, and Wednesday the 27th Days of March*, pp.13-14.
[50] *Daily Gazetteer (London Edition)* March 29, 1745.
[51] A woman by the same name, in the same place, became a Crown witness against her husband, also called John, and other men, in a major housebreaking case in Rotherhithe some 19 years later: *Lloyd's Evening Post*, July 11, 1764 - July 13, 1764. John Hood was convicted at the Guildford Assizes for receiving stolen goods from the break-in and sentenced to 14 years transportation.

way. For example, as late as 1808, Emmia (possibly Emma) Adams, whose husband kept a broker's shop, was prosecuted on her own for receiving stolen copper, albeit that this had been done in the presence of her spouse. This astonished the Recorder of London. He directed the jury that if they accepted the evidence given at trial that the receiving: "...was done in the presence of the husband. It is not a strict felony because her husband was present; he is supposed to have a controul over her". Emmia was acquitted.[52]

More commonly, it seems that women were acquitted in these situations without the doctrine being publicly mentioned. Juries, then as now, did not have to explain their verdicts. As will be seen in the remainder of this book, when women offended with men, whether for crimes of violence or dishonesty, there was a tendency for them not to be prosecuted or to be acquitted if they were. This occurred even if coverture was not expressly referred to as a justification for such a course of action, and sometimes even if they were not married to the men involved or the doctrine did not apply for some other legal reason, *provided* the women concerned were on the periphery of what had happened. Such an indulgence was even shown to women on the fringes of homicide cases, although they were certainly not covered by *feme covert* (see chapter three). As a result, it is probably fair to say that the formal application of the doctrine was at the summit of a broader set of eighteenth-century social attitudes that could and did favour female criminals who were accompanied by men.

In the London area, as Knowlys's comment might suggest, the protection of *feme covert* was normally extended to 'common law' wives and even fairly short-term co-habitants, who were not legally married, *provided* this was not formally admitted by the parties. This greatly increased its significance.[53] This was partly because, prior to 1753, marriages could be contracted quite loosely. For example, Mary Baker, who came from Salisbury and finished her life at Tyburn in 1713, admitted before her death that she had married four men in as many years prior to her execution, all of whom were still living. She blamed them for: "...leaving her, as soon as she was marry'd to them".[54] Similarly, shortly before her execution at Tyburn in 1708, Mary Goddard acknowledged that she had "lived in fornication" for a decade with a man and: "...went all

---

[52] OBSP, Trial of Emmia Adams, 13th January 1808: t18080113-49.

[53] King, Peter (1996) "Female offenders, work and life-cycle change in late-eighteenth-century London", p.68. See also letters from an "English Crown Lawyer" *The Times*, January 27th 1785, p.2 and February 9th 1785, p.4.

[54] *Ordinary's Account*, 23rd December 1713: OA17131223

along for his wife, though they neither were, nor ever intended to be marry'd".[55] However, in provincial and especially rural areas, with their greater population stability, it was harder (though not impossible) to claim marriage where it was not properly warranted, somewhat reducing the importance of the doctrine.

Arrest and Prosecution

Women entered the eighteenth-century criminal process in much the same way as men. They were arrested and produced before a Justice of the Peace (or 'J.P.'). The arrest was often made at the crime scene, usually by the victim, albeit sometimes aided by local people or a parish constable. For example, one Sunday evening, a Mrs Jones returned to her apartment at St. Peter's Hill, near Doctors Commons. She found a woman inside, with stolen clothes bundled up ready to be taken away. With great presence of mind, Mrs Jones went out of the room and locked the thief in: "…and calling for the assistance of a constable, had her secured". (The arrested woman had 19 skeleton keys and a chisel in her possession).[56] If a woman was not caught red handed but was suspected of a crime an arrest warrant might have to be obtained from a J.P. and enforced by the complainant (again with assistance where necessary).

In homicide cases, friends, relatives, and neighbours of the victim might become involved in securing a suspect. For example, in Yorkshire, Anne Fogget killed her husband with an axe and threw his corpse down a well. However, her brother-in-law and some neighbours visited the next day, noticed bloodstains as well as the victim's absence, and remembered the former "jars and quarrels" between the couple. They quickly became suspicious and tied her to a tree while they searched for and discovered her husband's body. Anne made full admissions to an examining J.P. and was convicted and burned in York.[57]

A few women (not many) were caught by thief-takers seeking the rewards on their heads or, much more commonly, after being incriminated by a criminal associate seeking to turn Crown evidence to save their own skins. Such individuals could themselves be female. For example, Mary Burton, one of a gang of shoplifters: "…surrender'd herself in order to be made an evidence against her Confederates".[58] Very dramatically, in 1716

[55] *Ordinary's Account*, 3rd March 1708: OA17080303
[56] *General Evening Post*, August 16, 1783 - August 19, 1783.
[57] *St. James's Evening Post*, September 11, 1716 - September 13, 1716.
[58] *Weekly Journal, or The British Gazetteer*, July 9, 1726.

Sarah Richardson: "...impeach'd 38 persons concern'd in several burglaries".[59] At a more mundane level, in 1732, a woman who belonged to a gang that pawned or sold false plate (brass cutlery that had been silvered over) as solid silver was examined by a J.P. and then sent to Tothill Fields Bridewell, where it was expected that: "...to obtain her discharge from thence, she will discover her accomplices".[60]

A handful of women were caught by more active investigations, instigated by the authorities, rather than by private individuals. For example, Hannah Bromley, from the Borough, was connected to a burglary in 1798 because another woman remembered hearing an "unusual noise and bustle" on the night that it occurred. Learning about this, the Surrey J.P.s sent their own officers to search the courtyard in which she lived, where they discovered some of the stolen goods hidden.[61]

Even if aware that they were suspected of a serious crime and in danger of arrest, the practical options for women were often fairly limited. Fleeing most provincial areas at short notice posed many difficulties, especially for females, particularly as they could not provide employment references without the risk of compromising their whereabouts. In 1735, for example, Anne Verjon initially avoided arrest for infanticide after being publicly exposed, and immediately escaped from her native Bedford. She travelled considerable distances within England looking for a domestic 'live in' position, but without success. Eventually, she was: "...reduced by sickness and want to the last extremity". She asked to be 'passed back' to her parish of original settlement, pursuant to the 1662 Settlement Act. As she was going through Bedford in a cart, she was recognised, arrested, and committed to jail.[62] In a large city like London, things were slightly different. The capital's size and anonymity provided a real chance of escaping post-crime detection for those women who were familiar with the Metropolis.

The J.P. would conduct a formal examination of the suspected woman, pursuant to sixteenth-century statutes dating from the reign of Queen Mary. He would take down any confession she made, decide whether to commit the matter for trial and, if so, to what forum, Quarter Sessions or Assizes, and for what crime. He would also make a decision about bail in lesser matters. Thus, in 1768, when Susannah Lott (suspected of poisoning her husband) was examined by a J.P. in Hythe she made (and signed) a full

---

[59] *Weekly Journal or British Gazetteer*, September 8, 1716.
[60] *Fog's Weekly Journal*, August 19, 1732.
[61] Anon, (1798) *The Young and Thoughtless Criminal*, pp.4-5.
[62] *Daily Gazetteer (London Edition)*, August 15, 1735.

confession that was later adduced against her at trial.[63] Similarly, when Margaret Wickes was suspected of murdering an infant it was noted that: "...on examination before the Justice of Peace, she has confess'd".[64]

Most women in this situation were legally unrepresented, many were uneducated, and they often spoke when silence might have been more prudent for their future prospects. For example, Margaret Onions, who had poisoned her husband, was described as a "poor, ignorant, illiterate, creature". She quickly made admissions, even though poisoning cases could be very hard to establish in the absence of a confession.[65] (See chapter three). Nevertheless, some women stonewalled or denied everything. When the Mayor of Dorchester examined Mary Channing, in his capacity as an *ex officio* magistrate for that town (with several other local J.P.s in attendance), she declared her innocence and voluntarily offered to clear herself by touching her husband's dead body. According to popular (if rapidly fading) belief, it would bleed if she were guilty ('cruentation'). She then refused to answer any further questions.

The examining J.P. would also take statements from potential prosecution witnesses. Unlike those made by suspects, these were usually made on oath. He would also bind over complainants to ensure that they went ahead with the prosecutions that they had initiated. Some were reluctant to do this and abandoned their actions as a result. For example, in County Durham, Mary Cleghorn alleged that Ann Marley had stolen £2 10s from her personal chest. However, when she was summoned by the local J.P. to enter into a recognizance to prosecute, the matter was swiftly "dropped". Other prosecutions were abandoned after illegal (in the case of felonies) negotiations and settlements ('compounding') between complainant and defendant. For example, Isabel Robson had been arrested for stealing two silver teaspoons, handkerchiefs, and other items from George Delaval, who was a sailor from Shields. The case did not go to trial, the magistrate noting: "The man (as I believe) compounded, for her paying for them".[66]

The thoroughness of these pre-trial preparations could be very important to prosecution success when a matter came to trial at the Assizes, and varied considerably with the commitment, ability and efficiency of the

---

[63] Anon, (1769) *A Collection of Tracts, Relating to the Crimes, Examination, Trial, Sentence and Execution of Sussanah Lott and Benjamin Buss, for Poisoning Mr. Lott*, p.8.
[64] *London Evening Post*, June 2-4, 1737.
[65] *Read's Weekly Journal Or British Gazetteer*, August 16, 1735.
[66] Morgan, Gwenda and Rushton, Peter (Eds) (2000) *The Justicing Notebook (1750-64) of Edmund Tew*, p.61 and p.180.

relevant J.P. For example, those for the poisoner Ann Evans, conducted in Plymouth in 1675, were meticulous, with numerous witnesses being carefully examined, and their depositions recorded, to build the case against her.[67]

The Trial Process

The forensic advantages enjoyed by women often began before they were arraigned. They were more likely than men to avoid trial altogether, either because prosecutors failed to attend court to testify at their hearings (even if this meant that their recognisances were estreated) or because Grand Juries returned indictments marked 'ignoramus' or (after 1733) 'no true bill', having decided there was not a prima facie case against them. For example, Margaret Suthens was accused of stealing half a guinea and some silver coins from a house in Lambeth, but: "No evidence appearing, she was acquitted".[68] On a less anecdotal basis, on the Northern Circuit in 1804, 29 per cent of all women avoided trial at Assizes for these reasons (for all offences), compared to just 18 percent of men.[69]

However, although widespread, particularly in England, this was not a universal phenomenon, especially in other parts of the British Isles. For example, Grand Juries do not necessarily appear to have shown the same indulgence to female defendants at the Armagh Assizes in Ireland between 1736 and 1760, where murder was the only offence category in which men had a higher percentage of 'true bills' than women. For property offences, 52 per cent of women and just 49 per cent of men were in this category. (The comparison totals are very small, making it hard to draw firm conclusions).[70] Similarly, at the Welsh Great Sessions held between 1660 and 1730, the Grand Jury decisions on theft indictments for Denbighshire suggest that men received findings of 'ignoramus' or 'no true bill' (after 1733) 29.5 per cent of the time, while women did so in only 26.7 per cent of cases. In the same county, men accused of a homicide offence were twice as likely as women to have their bill found 'ignoramus', although (and as in Ireland) this probably reflects differences in the characteristics

---

[67] See generally, Quick, John (1676) *Hell open'd, or, The infernal sin of murther...* .

[68] Anon, (1739) *The Genuine Proceedings at the Assizes on the Home Circuit, Held in March, 1739 ... at Hertford, for the County of Hertford; Chelmsford, for the County of Essex*, p.8

[69] King, Peter (2006) *Crime and Law in England, 1750-1840,* p.177

[70] Garnham, Neil (1996) *Courts, Crime and the Criminal Law in Ireland, 1692-1760*, p.236.

of many male killings.[71]

Arraignment and Plea

The number of defendants (of both sexes) who formally admitted their felonies at eighteenth-century Assizes was tiny by modern comparison, and quite small even by the standards of the previous century. Edith Saunders, executed for murder after the Gloucester Assizes in 1759, having penitently "confessed herself guilty", was fairly unusual.[72] Sometimes, the judiciary were even reluctant to accept such pleas. For example, the elderly Margaret Ryan initially pleaded guilty to murdering her husband when arraigned at the Maidstone Assizes in 1776: "…but at the desire of the court she put herself on her country". She was subsequently convicted of the full offence.[73] Guilty pleas were slightly more common for clergyable felonies than for capital offences (especially before the advent of mass transportation for such crimes in 1718), and very much more common for misdemeanours and cases of petty larceny tried at Quarter Sessions. In a typical example of the latter from 1681, Deborah Haynes pleaded guilty to stealing a cheese worth 4d (petty theft), at the Warwickshire Quarter Sessions, and was flogged.[74] At provincial Assizes, it also seems that women were slightly more likely than men to plead guilty.[75]

Standing 'mute of malice', that is deliberately refusing to plead, would theoretically result in the imposition of the *peine forte et dure* prior to 1772. This entailed being pressed to death under a board holding progressively greater weights, unless a plea was forthcoming, which could then be accepted with permission from the court.[76] However, the full *peine* does not appear to have been used against women during the eighteenth century. They were much less likely to have heritable property than were males, reducing its attractions. Traditionally, this had been the main reason for refusing to plead, as it meant that the defendant was not formally

---

[71] Howard, Sharon (2003) *Crime, Communities And Authority In Early Modern Wales: Denbighshire, 1660-1730*, p.85 and p.133.

[72] *Universal Chronicle or Weekly Gazette*, April 21, 1759 - April 28, 1759.

[73] *General Evening Post*, March 16, 1776 - March 19, 1776.

[74] Ratcliff, S.C. and Johnson, H.C. (1946) *Warwick County Records Volume vii: Quarter Sessions records Easter, 1674, to Easter, 1682,* p.234.

[75] Beattie, John (2001) *Policing and Punishment in London, 1660-1750*, p.338.

[76] Blackstone, William (1769) *Commentaries on the Laws of England*, vol.4, p.320. See also Baker, John (1973) "Criminal Justice at Newgate 1616-1627", p.316.

convicted of a felony when he or she died, which could lead to confiscation. Even for men, it seems that use of the full *peine* was very rare after 1700. Nevertheless, a man accused of murder at the Sussex Assizes in 1735, who refused to enter a plea, although several witnesses had heard him speak, was "gradually pres'd to death" in Horsham Gaol.[77] The process was last used in Cambridge seven years later, and more than 30 years before formal abolition.

In 1772, a deliberate refusal to plead was made tantamount to a guilty plea.[78] As a result, when Sarah Chandler initially refused to enter a plea in the 1790s, hoping that she could use it to force the Crown to return some of her confiscated personal possessions, she was warned that if she persisted in such a course a death sentence would automatically be passed on her.[79] If it was unclear as to whether a defendant, such as Elizabeth Steele in 1787, was 'mute of malice' or by 'visitation of God', a jury would be empanelled to determine the issue. In Steele's case they heard from her jailers, who thought she was deaf. Accepting this, they returned a verdict of mute by visitation of God, which meant that a trial could proceed, the court supposedly taking care to conduct the case as: "...advantageously to a prisoner, as if they had the advantage of hearing the evidence adduced to prove the fact".[80]

Questioning and Testimony

Prosecuting counsel could present felony cases throughout the era, though they were only used in a minority of (normally grave) matters until late in the period. Before the 1730s, the use of defence counsel at felony trials was limited to arguing points of pure law. After this time, it became possible for defendants to be legally represented when it came to questioning witnesses, though it did not become widespread until the final two decades of the century. Advocates could still not directly address the jury on behalf of the accused and would not be allowed to do so until 1836.

Women who faced very serious charges, or who were possessed of significant financial resources, appreciated that a barrister could improve their prospects. In an exchange of letters between two wealthy female murderers, awaiting trial in a pair of unconnected but notorious cases, one

---

[77] *Gentleman's Magazine* vol.5, August 1735, unnumbered page.
[78] *Craftsman or Say's Weekly Journal*, May 9, 1772.
[79] Anon, (1796?) *The True and remarkable life and extraordinary adventures of that unfortunate woman, Sarah Chandler*, p.4.
[80] *World and Fashionable Advertiser*, May 30, 1787.

urged her correspondent to "spare no cost" when selecting counsel.[81] Of course, it was not a panacea. Although, and ridiculously, Elizabeth Branch and her daughter were represented by eight barristers at their murder hearing (the mother was a very wealthy woman), both were found guilty at the Somerset Assizes and sentenced to death.[82]

Even if represented, female defendants still had to give their own (unsworn) testimony as to what had occurred, while those who did not have counsel would have to question witnesses personally or with the assistance of the trial judge. Women may have found the forensic atmosphere more intimidating than men, if only because the latter dominated courts, possibly limiting their effectiveness in this regard. They also had very little time to make the right impression. The average Assizes trial lasted less than half an hour, some for just a few minutes, though cases that were both complicated and serious could take several hours.

At her trial for murder at the Surrey Assizes held in Croydon, in 1775, Elizabeth Scawen was too distressed to give her own version of events in person. Prudently, however, she had written it out in advance and asked the court clerk to read it aloud to the jury, which he duly did. Scawen was able to avoid active involvement in the hearing because she had counsel to conduct the questioning of witnesses. Mary Reed, accused of poisoning her spouse at the Gloucester Assizes 20 years later, followed a similar course, preparing a statement in advance to be read out in which she solemnly declared her innocence and stated that she had "really loved" her late husband. As with Scawen, after retiring for more than an hour, the jury acquitted her.[83] In 1800, the well-to-do Jane Leigh Perrot started to address the jury at her theft trial, but: "…after speaking a few sentences she became so much agitated that her voice failed her". Fortunately, she had counsel, and was able to dictate her comments on the Crown's case, which he then repeated to the court![84]

Some women, like some men, were naturally good at giving evidence, questioning witnesses, and raising defences, even if legally unrepresented,

---

[81] Blandy, Mary (1752) *Genuine letters that pass'd between Miss Blandy and Miss Jeffries, before and after conviction*, p.23

[82] Anon, (1767) *An Appeal to humanity: in an account of the life and cruel actions of Elizabeth Brownrigg…To which is added the Trial of Elizabeth Branch and her Daughter, for the murder of their Servant Maid, &c.*, pp.27-64. *Country Journal or The Craftsman*, April 19, 1740.

[83] Anon, (1795) *The Trial of Mrs. Mary Reed, Upon the Charge of Poisoning Her Husband, At Berkeley, in Gloucestershire, in April, 1794,* p.26.

[84] Pinchard, John (Attorney) (1800) *The Trial of Jane Leigh Perrot, wife of James Leigh Perrot*, p.30.

being more eloquent in a forensic environment than their more tongue-tied sisters. For example, Charlotte Walker, a habitual Metropolitan criminal in the late eighteenth century, was notorious for her abilities in this regard. She survived numerous trials at the Old Bailey as a result, producing convincing defences when most needed.[85] The same situation applied in the provinces. In 1736, such adroitness almost saved Elizabeth Thompson, early in the criminal process. She was accused of murdering a Dutchman in Yarmouth, but: "Her behaviour, on her examination by the Coroner, was insolent, and tho' confronted by circumstantial evidences, as the blood on the floor, curtains and bed, yet she braved all the evidences, and it was with some difficulty the Coroner could be brought to commit her to gaol".[86] Of course, even forensic ability required that the situation was not hopeless to produce a result. It was noted at Mary Channel's trial for petty treason at the Dorchester Assizes in 1703 that the defence she made: "…(whether it was real or pretended) was so full of wit and ingenuity, and uttered with such an extraordinary courage and humility, that it caused admiration in the judges". Even so, she was convicted, as the evidence against her was clear.[87]

As with men, many poor and legally unrepresented women, like Mary Richardson and Sarah Gibbs, indicted at the Essex Assizes in 1740, said little or nothing when given the opportunity to speak on their own behalf, despite pleading 'not guilty'. The two women were quickly convicted after: "Neither of them said any thing in their defence". At the Kingston Assizes in the same year, Mary Cooper was capitally convicted after she "made no defence".[88] But for the frequent reluctance of the courts to accept 'guilty pleas', and the presence of the death penalty, such cases would probably not have gone for a contested trial.

Insanity

In theory, insanity was the only exculpatory mental state allowed at common law.[89] It was a defence to all crimes, not just those involving

---

[85] Clayton, Mary (2008) "The Life and Crimes of Charlotte Walker, Prostitute and Pickpocket", pp.4-8.
[86] *Daily Gazetteer*, 22 June, 1736.
[87] Rayner, J. L. and Crook, G. T. (Eds) (1926) *The Complete Newgate Calendar*, vol.II, p.148.
[88] Anon, (1740) *The Proceedings at the Assizes of Peace, Oyer and Terminer, for the County of Surrey, Held at the Town-Hall of Kingston Upon Thames, in the 14th Year of His Majesty's Reign ... To Which is Added the Genuine Proceedings at the Assizes for the County of Essex*, p.11 and p.4.
[89] See generally, Brydall, J. (1700) *Non compos mentis: or, The law relating to*

violence. Thus, in 1726, Rebecca Gardner was accused of housebreaking but: "In consideration of her lunacy, the jury acquitted her".[90] Nevertheless, Anne Broderick was not alone in successfully using insanity as a defence in a murder case. In 1752, a woman in Surrey, accused of killing her husband with a poker, was not fit to be tried on her first appearance at Assizes because she manifested "plain signs of lunacy". She was tried a few months later and acquitted, very possibly because of her mental condition.[91] In the North East, Ann Wilson successfully pleaded that she was insane when accused of petty treason after killing her husband with an axe in 1769.[92]

Although the legal definition of insanity was not very precise during the eighteenth century, and there was a great reluctance to use technical terms in court throughout the period, the ability to distinguish between good and evil in the quality of the act committed appears to have been vital. As William Blackstone noted, an "unwarrantable act without a vicious will [was] no crime at all". The consequences of acquittal on this ground could be very benign, even for those accused of the most serious offences. It was only in 1800, after a brain-damaged former soldier who had attempted to assassinate King George III was found 'not guilty' by reason of insanity, that the Criminal Lunatics Act authorized courts to keep those acquitted for this reason in custody, if they constituted a danger to the public. (Within a few years there would be complaints in parliament about the number of lunatics being held for this reason). Prior to this date, they would often be released to their families, unless incarcerated in a House of Correction as vagrants or sent to a private mad hospital.[93] For example, in 1794, the Suffolk Assizes ordered the child-killing Ann Gosling's parish officers to "keep and treat her as an insane person". The following year, it seems that the murderer Anne Broderick was released into the custody of her family after the Essex Assizes.

Nationally, about a dozen such claims were made each year during the 1750s. Approximately a third of these were successful. However, both the number and success-rate of insanity defences appear to have increased in subsequent decades. Women made, proportionately, more use of the defence than did men, especially after the middle of the century.[94] As

---

natural fools, mad-folks, and lunatick persons.

[90] OBSP, Trial of Rebecca Gardner, 7 December 1726: t17261207-59

[91] Beattie, John (1986) *Crime and the Courts in England 1660-1800,* p.85.

[92] Morgan, Gwenda and Rushton, Peter (1998) *Rogues, Thieves and the Rule of Law,* p.113.

[93] Goddard, K. S. (2004) "A Case of Injustice? The Trial of John Bellingham", p.2.

[94] Walker, Nigel (1969) *Crime and Insanity in England*, vol.1, p.70.

mental illness was considered to be a disproportionately female malady, this is not very surprising. In eighteenth-century England, men with mental disturbances were more likely to have their conditions ascribed to physical trauma, such as a blow or other injury to the head. For women, the root causes of madness were more likely to be attributed to innate constitutional weaknesses, linked to the female body or psyche, and so was thought inherently more likely to occur.[95]

It has been suggested (albeit mainly from Old Bailey sources) that 38 per cent of insanity claims made during the 1750s and 1760s were advanced by women. This was an increase on the 26 per cent found earlier in the century, and far greater than the proportion of trial defendants who were female.[96] Nevertheless, although they may have made such a claim much more readily than men, assessments as to the degree of female advantage when they did so are fairly modest. According to one analysis, the data on successful insanity pleas assembled for the years between 1760 and 1843 suggests that women making these claims persuaded juries in 60 per cent of cases, while men were only slightly less successful at about 50 per cent.[97] (A huge amount turns on defining when such a claim was being seriously advanced at a trial).

However, the courts often rejected insanity claims, even when made by women. In theory, the onus of proof was, very roughly, on the defendant to prove that they were not *compos mentis*, although, where the court was sympathetic to a claim, this might be quietly ignored.[98] Thus, Lord Chief Baron Macdonald, summing up in the trial of Anne Broderick, directed the jury that if any doubt remained as to her sanity: "...common charity required that the balance should turn in the prisoner's favour". Nevertheless, until the end of the period, the courts usually needed some prior history of eccentric behaviour, or a seriously abnormal reputation, before they would accept such claims. For example, at the Kingston Assizes in 1681, Margaret Osgoode, on trial for killing her husband with an axe while he slept: "...aledged she was not *Compes Mentis* but *Distracted* when she commited the horrid Fact". Unfortunately, the Crown called several witnesses who had seen her earlier on the day that the crime was committed, and who gave evidence that she behaved: "...as at other times and they saw no Distraction in her, whereupon not being able to

95 Eigen, Joel (1998) "Criminal Lunacy in Early Modern England. Did Gender Make a Difference?", p.414.
96 Walker, Nigel (1969) *Crime and Insanity in England*, vol.1, p.70.
97 Eigen, Joel (1998) "Criminal Lunacy in Early Modern England. Did Gender Make a Difference?", *International Journal of Law and Psychiatry*, p.414.
98 *Arnold's Case* (1724) 16 St Tr 694.

make any farther Defence the Jury after having received their charge, brought her in guilty of [petty] Treason and Murther".[99]

By contrast, over a century later at the Essex Assizes, Anne Broderick was helped by exhibiting a litany of strange behaviour prior to shooting her former lover, as well as by having a family history of derangement. Her brother-in-law gave evidence that Anne's mother had been considered to be insane for fifteen years and a sister had also been an inmate in Bedlam (the capital's psychiatric hospital). Her charwoman told the court that she had once thrown a saucepan of boiling water over her (the charwoman) at Christmas for failing to scour her doorsteps properly. A woman who sold china testified that Anne wanted to purchase some large flower–pots to kill men that she feared were trying to break into her rooms, and that she would frequently march in the road with arms folded and head back like a soldier. A baker stated that Anne would often buy a three-penny loaf and not expect any change from a shilling or even a half-crown. He had also seen her come up to his wife and talk to her in a manner that "convinced him that she was deranged in her mind". Anne was acquitted as insane after just two minutes of deliberations by the jury.[100]

Similarly, in 1794, Ann Gosling was known to have been "struggling with fits" before she killed a toddler grandson she loved with a razor. Her jailer had also come to the conclusion that she was "out of her mind". Furthermore, she had a sympathetic trial judge, who summed up the case in a helpful manner. Gosling was found to be insane at the Assizes held in Bury St. Edmunds.[101]

Without such supporting evidence, insanity claims were often given short shrift, and were sometimes not advanced very seriously, even if raised at trial. For example, Ann Goodson was quickly convicted and executed for petty treason, in April 1738, after stabbing her husband, even though a defence witness at trial had unavailingly floated the possibility that she was "at times out of her senses".[102]

---

[99] Anon, (1681) *The True narrative of the confession and execution of the prisoners at Kingstone-upon-Thames, on Wednesday the 16th of this instant March, 1681*, pp.1-2.

[100] Thurrock History Society, at www.thurrock-community.org.uk/historysoc/murder1.htm. Last accessed 28th June 2012.

[101] Anon, (1794) *The trials of Samuel Hammond, for the murder of Ann Avey; and Ann Gosling, for the murder of John Sage,* pp.12-16.

[102] Anon, (1738) *The Proceedings at the Assizes for the County of Surry, held at Guildford, ... On Thursday the 16th, Friday the 17th, Saturday the 18th, Monday the 20th, and Tuesday the 21st March, 1738*, p.16.

Verdicts

It is apparent that the verdicts passed by the major criminal courts were influenced by gender, at least to some extent. Arguably, acquittal rates are more valuable as indicators of systemic lenience towards women than are punishments, which might reflect the inherent gravity of an offence. By contrast, it is highly unlikely that the prosecutions of women involved inherently weaker cases than those of men. They would have survived scrutiny by an examining magistrate and then the Grand Jury, whether at Assizes or Quarter Sessions. Indeed, given that there appears to have been a greater reluctance to pursue females through the courts, it might be expected that they would be based on stronger evidence than their typical male counterparts.

Generally speaking, women secured more favourable verdicts than men. Thus, they were less likely to be convicted of the full offence for which they were tried and more likely to be acquitted outright. For example, in the County Palatine of Lancaster between 1798 and 1818, 64 per cent of men accused of burglary and theft in a dwelling house were convicted as charged, compared to just 39 per cent of women (though men enjoyed a small advantage when it came to pick-pocketing and shoplifting). On the Home Circuit between 1782 and 1827 just 27.7 per cent of all male property offenders were acquitted outright, compared to 38.9 per cent of females.[103]

However, the figures vary enormously with the crime charged and, to a smaller extent, where in the country trials took place. Significantly, simple grand larceny, one of the least serious and most common property offences (especially amongst women), often produced only a small advantage for females. On the Home Circuit in the years from 1782 to 1827, 62.9 per cent of men on trial for the crime were convicted of the full offence compared to 58 per cent of women. For robbery, by contrast, there was a huge difference between the genders. More than three times as many men as women were convicted of the full offence (58.8 per cent compared to 17.7 per cent).[104]

When it came to homicide, it seems that females were also often favoured in their trial outcomes. Men accused of murder in Lancashire during the late eighteenth century were six times more likely to be convicted of the full offence and executed than women (albeit that this was an extreme case). Even in Surrey, during the same period, women were 50

---

[103] King, Peter (2006) *Crime and Law in England, 1750-1840,* p.173.
[104] King, Peter (2006) *Crime and Law in England, 1750-1840,* pp.172-175.

per cent more likely to be acquitted outright than their male counterparts.[105] Between 1660 and 1800, 63.2 per cent of female murder defendants in the county were found 'not guilty' of any offence, compared to only 43.8 per cent of their male counterparts.[106]

Partial Verdicts

Even if not acquitted outright, women were much more likely than men to be convicted of a lesser offence than that initially charged. However, murder was a notable exception to this general pattern, as comparatively few women received findings of manslaughter, unlike many men accused of murder, for readily explicable reasons (see chapter three). Ignoring this offence, partial verdicts were a regular phenomenon amongst women charged with property crimes. Sometimes, they were based on a genuine lacuna in the evidence for the greater crime, or over-enthusiastic valuing of stolen property. Nevertheless, in many cases (probably the great majority) the lesser verdict was not the result of doubts about the commission of the offence indicted, but a deliberate attempt by the tribunal to mitigate the consequences for the defendant of being found guilty. This was especially likely where the offence initially charged was capital. Blackstone called this form of well-intentioned jury behaviour 'pious perjury'.

'Pious Perjury'

Pious perjury seems to have been almost institutionalised, and was sometimes actively encouraged by the judiciary, with verdicts to lesser offences being routinely returned in certain regularly recurring situations. In others, it would be defendant specific and depend on the individual characteristics of the accused person or the case for which they were being tried. In many cases, both factors came into play. Overt gestures of repentance and co-operation with the authorities might be vital.

For example, in appropriate cases, juries regularly downgraded items of relatively low value, that were still well above the shilling petty theft threshold, to an almost customary amount of 10d. Thus, Elizabeth Granger from Camberwell was indicted at the Surrey Assizes in 1743 for stealing a satin gown, a cloak, and several other items while in the house of

---

[105] King, Peter (1999) "Gender, crime and justice in late eighteenth-and early nineteenth-century England", p.55.

[106] Beattie, John (1986) *Crime and the Courts in England 1660-1800,* p.437.

Christopher Flynn (i.e. grand larceny). Perhaps because she had made swift admissions when examined by 'Squire Copeland' (a local J.P.), in a case that would otherwise have been very hard to prove, she was only convicted of petty theft (i.e. the jury valued the goods taken at less than a shilling).[107] Similarly, Elizabeth Randal had been the tenant of furnished lodgings in Surrey. She stole a feather bed, sheets, and other goods, valued by the landlord at £2 8s, from her room or apartment. (This was a fairly common form of female crime). She later admitted that she had pledged/sold these items on to various pawnbrokers, the bed going for seven shillings. Although the landlord tracked some of the stolen items down, including the bed, the pawnbrokers would not let him recover them. Nevertheless, Randal was only convicted of theft to the value of 10d (petty larceny) and whipped.[108]

It seems that jurors, some of whom nearly always had previous personal experience of jury service, were very conscious about where clergyable levels for more serious offences began and ended. Thus, in trials for stealing in a dwelling-house, valuables worth several pounds might be found by the jury to be worth only thirty-nine shillings. This was just below the 40s 'cut-off' point at which the crime became capital. A similar approach might be taken to the five-shilling limit for capital forms of pick-pocketing and non-clergyable housebreaking in an empty residence.

It appears that gender was a major consideration when it came to pious perjury. On the Home Circuit, during the late eighteenth and early nineteenth centuries, not only were female defendants in property crimes 40 per cent more likely than their male equivalents to secure an outright acquittal, but they were also 50 per cent more likely to gain a partial verdict.[109] On the Western Circuit, during the eighteenth century, 64 per cent of women convicted of simple theft had been the beneficiaries of partial verdicts where more serious offences (pick-pocketing, housebreaking, shoplifting, or robbery) had initially been charged.[110] However, at the Great Sessions for Denbighshire, in Wales, female advantage in this

---

[107] Anon, (1743) *The Proceedings at the Assizes of Peace, Oyer and Terminer, for the County of Surrey, Held at Kingston Upon Thames, on Friday the 15th, Saturday the 6th, Monday the 8th, and Tuesday the 9th Days of August*, p.9.

[108] Anon, (1738) *The Proceedings at the Assizes for the County of Surry[sic], held at Guildford, ... On Thursday the 16th, Friday the 17th, Saturday the 18th, Monday the 20th, and Tuesday the 21st March, 1738,* p.21.

[109] King, Peter (2006) *Crime and Law in England, 1750–1840*, pp.172-175.

[110] Morgan, Gwenda and Rushton, Peter (2004) *Eighteenth-Century Criminal Transportation: The Formation of the Criminal Atlantic*, p.47.

respect was more muted. Although women accused of theft between 1660 and 1730 were significantly more likely to be acquitted outright than men, they were only slightly more likely to receive a partial verdict; 17.3 per cent of them were convicted of a reduced value or charge, compared to 15.6 per cent of men. (The total includes cases thrown out by the grand jury).[111]

Leniency and the Lower Courts

The evidence for a degree of leniency being shown towards female defendants in the higher courts, whether at Assizes or the Old Bailey, appears strong; but what of women who were accused of assault, petty theft and even minor clergyable felonies at Quarter or Borough Sessions? The evidence here is rather more mixed. Taken as a whole, it seems that there *may,* occasionally, have been a modicum of extra 'compassion'. However, it was modest when compared to that found in the higher courts, although in the later decades of the century there was to be a much greater reluctance to order the flogging of females in the lower forums, especially if carried out in public (see below). There are obvious explanations for this: much less turned on a 'benevolent' result. Most Quarter Sessions' cases resulted in fiscal or corporal punishment, or, at the most, a short period of incarceration. A determination to avoid female death or transportation if it could reasonably be prevented was not usually needed. Men and women could be given similar penalties. This reduction in differentials between male and female defendants was also a logical continuation of the clear pattern at Assizes, where less serious crimes, such as simple grand larceny, attracted less 'relative leniency' for women than more serious matters, such as robbery.

Appeals

There was no general right to appeal a jury decision in eighteenth-century England. However, when a question of law arose during the course of a trial at Assizes it could be reserved for collective review by the twelve common law judges who presided over the three Westminster Courts (King's Bench, Common Pleas, and Exchequer). Their deliberations, often conducted in Serjeants' Inn, were informal and private, although counsel might be asked to address them with legal argument. Initially, the method

---

[111] Howard, Sharon (2003) *Crime, Communities And Authority In Early Modern Wales: Denbighshire, 1660-1730*, p.133.

used to put a matter in front of the judges was to take a special verdict, in which the jury would find certain facts established, then refer it to the court to say whether upon those facts the prisoner was guilty of the crime for which he had been indicted. This was an expensive and time-consuming process, so that during the eighteenth century the much simpler expedient developed of taking a general verdict ('guilty' or 'not guilty') but reserving the legal question for the twelve judges.[112]

Several provincial women had their cases considered in this fashion. For example, after Mary Norwood was convicted of petty treason in April 1765, having poisoned her 'husband', she was sentenced to death by burning. However, doubts appear to have arisen at trial as to the strength of her conjugal bonds, and so whether a conviction and hanging for murder might not have been more appropriate. The matter was referred to the 12 judges while sentence was respited for a month. Despite this, she was burned in early May: "...the judges being clearly of opinion that her marriage was sufficiently proved, and that she was convicted properly of petit treason".[113]

Women and Benefit of Clergy

Throughout the eighteenth century convicted women could claim 'benefit of clergy' or, more accurately, its statutory equivalent, on equal terms to men. This historic privilege was a relic of the Church-State struggles of the medieval era. Originally, it had allowed clerics who committed secular offences to escape temporal trial and punishment. However, after 1575, the benefit was not pleaded before trial, so that a case was transferred to an ecclesiastical court for hearing, but used after conviction in front of a common law court and prior to sentencing. It affected punishment rather than forum.

During the early modern period, clergy was also extended by a series of legal fictions to include most men and, by two seventeenth century Acts, women (technically, they claimed 'benefit of statute'), though the number of offences for which it could be claimed was simultaneously reduced. Thus, women were allowed clergy for minor thefts in 1623. In 1692, another statute granted them clergy on the same basis as men, so that, for example, they could be clergied for manslaughter. Indeed, in one respect they were in a slightly better situation as, until 1706, men had to be

---

[112] Oldham, James (2011) "Informal Lawmaking in England by the Twelve Judges in the Late Eighteenth and Early Nineteenth Centuries", pp.181-220.

[113] *Lloyd's Evening Post*, May 6-8, 1765.

able to read to claim the privilege (at least in theory), while under the two statutes women were not required to prove literacy.[114]

Laymen, and all women, who were clergied would be branded on the thumb until 1779 -on the face between 1699 and 1706- and then released, rather than being sentenced to death for what would otherwise be a capital felony. For example, in 1709, when Jane Locker of Wrexham Regis was convicted in the town for stealing five flaxen sheets, valued at 20s, she pleaded benefit of statute, was branded and discharged.[115]

By the early 1700s, branding was often a fairly perfunctory and ineffectual process, frequently done 'gently' or even with a purely symbolic cold iron, rather than one that had been rendered red-hot.[116] Sometimes, the mark it left was not visible or could readily be disguised. In 1716 for example, Deborah Stent, a female member of a gang of burglars, was described as being a tall woman who had been previously: "…burnt in the left cheek, over which gun powder is drawn, so that it is now a blue spot".[117] Presumably, she had tried to camouflage her mark. As a result, some provincial women, just like some men, appear to have received clergy more than once, sometimes on several occasions, even though, in theory, only one claim was allowed (it was one of the reasons that branding had been introduced centuries earlier). For example, Elizabeth Brightman, who was executed for burglary at York in 1716, was an 'old offender' who, although just 25 years of age, had already "been twice burnt in the hand".[118]

Pleading the Belly

A woman who was convicted of an unclergyable felony, even murder, and so facing an automatic death penalty could 'postpone' her execution if pregnant. After conviction, she would be asked if there was any reason why sentence should not be passed upon her or, in the words of Mary Blandy's clerk of arraigns: "What have you now to say for yourself". She could then "plead her belly". (Occasionally, late applications were entertained, as with Sophia Pringle in 1787, who claimed that she was

---

114 Blackstone, William (1769) *Commentaries on the Laws of England*, vol.4, pp.362-363.

115 National Library of Wales, Great Sessions gaol files 4/39/8 (unfoliated file) Examinations before Peter Ellice JP, 3 February 1709.

116 Quarrell, W. H. and More, Margaret (Eds) (1934) *London in 1710 From the Travels of Zacharias Conrad Von Uffenbach*, p.124.

117 *Weekly Journal or British Gazetteer*, September 8, 1716.

118 *St. James's Evening Post*, September 11, 1716 - September 13, 1716.

pregnant just two days before she was due to be hanged and was brought back to court from prison to make her plea).[119] It was for this reason that Elizabeth Hughes, who had been capitally convicted of horse-theft at the Oxford Assizes in 1726, was viewed as extremely unfortunate when she miscarried, just after the jury found her guilty, and: "…thereby lost the benefit of pleading her belly".[120]

Such a doctrine, aimed at sparing an innocent life, was widely found in other parts of the British Isles and Europe. For example, Elizabeth Robertson, convicted of infanticide in Edinburgh in 1729, unavailingly pleaded her belly to avoid execution in the Scottish capital.[121] Indeed, it was not even confined to the West. In 1752, a higher court judgment in Japan held that a pregnant woman who had been sentenced to death should have a reprieve until she came to term, as the "child had nothing to do with either parent's crime".[122]

In England, once she made such a claim, the Sheriff would have to return a jury of "matrons" to try the issue. This body dated back to the fourteenth century and was only formally abolished in 1931, albeit not used for many years prior to that time. (It was last employed by the child-murderer Ada Annie Williams in December 1913). The judge would direct the matrons to determine whether the convict was "quick with child". (Supposedly, the movement of the foetus could be felt *in utero*). Carrying a dead or newly conceived child was not sufficient, though this limitation was occasionally ignored.[123]

Quickening, an inherently vague concept that was also vital in cases of abortion (see chapter four), was normally thought to occur at some point during (or just after) the fourth month of pregnancy. The law had originally been influenced by the ancient theory that human life began at the point of 'animation'. Timing was usually vital. Thus, when a woman, about to be sentenced to death at the Plymouth Assizes in 1675, pleaded her belly, she was examined but: "…after their strictest Scrutiny and Inquest, they [the Matrons] find her a Lyar, to have troubled the Court needlesly, she is not quick … if she have at all conceived".[124] For this same reason, Ann Giles failed in her claim when capitally convicted of

[119] *Whitehall Evening Post*, February 27, 1787.
[120] *Mist's Weekly Journal*, July 30, 1726.
[121] *Fog's Weekly Journal*, January 4, 1729.
[122] Wright, Diana (2004) "Female Crime and State Punishment in Early Modern Japan", p.17.
[123] Blackstone, William (1769) *Commentaries on the Laws of England*, vol.4, p.388.
[124] Quick, John, (1676) *Hell open'd, or, The infernal sin of murther...* p.25.

setting fire to a barn in Berkshire in 1761. The jury of matrons: "…found her pregnant, but not quick, upon which she was left for execution".[125] Mary Parker, a housebreaker, received a similar result at the Kingston Assizes in 1728.[126]

Courts used the all-female jury for reasons of decency and because they viewed the women concerned (if sometimes rather optimistically) as experts in identifying the signs of pregnancy.[127] Ideally, the matrons would be midwives. More commonly, most were women with personal experience of pregnancy, perhaps assisted by one or two midwives if they were fortunate. For an example, can be considered the jury of matrons assembled by a trial judge when a woman convicted at the Plymouth Assizes (see above) cried out: "I am with Child, do not kill two Innocents. If I must die, let my Child live!" This jury included just one midwife, called in from outside the court, presumably to provide a modicum of expert assistance to her less qualified sisters.[128]

Frequently, the matrons included the wives of court personnel and even female spectators who were simply watching trials. In 1714, this practice led Alexander Smith to complain, albeit with considerable exaggeration, that female thieves would sometimes have: "Matrons of [their] own Profession ready at hand, who, right or wrong, bring their wicked Companions quick with Child to the great Impediment of Justice".[129] Nevertheless, Smith's allegation was not entirely unfounded. Almost a century later, in 1809, after Mary Bateman was convicted of murder at the Yorkshire Assizes, she claimed to be twenty-two weeks pregnant. The presiding judge then ordered the Sheriff to empanel a jury of matrons. This apparently caused consternation amongst the ladies present: "…who hastened to quit the court, to prevent the execution of so painful an office being imposed upon them". However, the judge ordered that the court's doors be closed, to prevent this. Within half-an-hour, twelve married women had been empanelled and sworn in. The jury of matrons then retired with the prisoner and on their return to court delivered

---

[125] *Public Advertiser*, March 10, 1761.

[126] *Weekly Journal or British Gazetteer*, August 31, 1728.

[127] Cornett, Judy M. (1997) "Hoodwink'd by custom: The exclusion of women from juries in Eighteenth-Century English Law and Literature", pp.18-28.

[128] Quick, John (1676) *Hell open'd, or, The infernal sin of murther…* p.25.

[129] Smith, Alexander (1719) *A Complete History of the Lives and Robberies of the Most Notorious Highwaymen, Footpads, Shoplifts, & Cheats of Both Sexes*, 2nd edn., p.185.

a negative verdict.[130] Odd though it appears, sealing the doors of the court so that any women present could not 'escape' this unpleasant duty seems to have been standard practice in such cases, as was noted as late as 1838.[131]

Unlike a trial jury, the jury of matrons received their evidence in private, normally conducting an intimate physical inspection of the convicted woman after being led by the court bailiff to a closed room. Several tests were employed, though most were not conclusive. For example, the convict's belly might be felt and her breasts squeezed for signs of lactation.[132] Exactly how reliable these tests were, like the matrons' degree of expertise, is debatable. When Martha Allen was hanged for horse-theft at Heavytree (Heavitree) gallows in Devon, in 1740, she insisted that she was five months pregnant.[133] In a very rare and late example of the claim being made, in 1847, a jury of matrons was asked to investigate whether the convicted murderer Mary Ann Nunt was pregnant. They declined the offer of a surgeon's assistance and returned with a negative answer half an hour later. However, the Secretary of State intervened, and ordered a further examination by experienced doctors who concluded that she was indeed 'quick with child'. The medical press of the time deplored a law that left the decision in the hands of "ignorant and incompetent persons".[134]

Nevertheless, as this case indicates, and perhaps because of such criticism, a practice developed towards the end of the eighteenth century of allowing doctors to assist the matrons, although the Nunt case also suggests that they could reject such an offer of help. Thus, when Margaret Hughes pleaded her belly after being found guilty of murder, in 1798, the matrons were "assisted by some gentlemen of the Faculty". After two hours of examination they produced a positive verdict.[135]

The matrons would act publicly only when they took a special oath to enquire into whether a woman was pregnant and, if so, was quick with child, and later when returning their verdict. Their jury could be the same size as that for a trial. Thus, the jury of matrons assembled at the Court of Queen's Bench that considered whether Sarah Baynton was pregnant, after

---

130 Anon, (1809) *Extraordinary Life and Character of Mary Bateman, the Yorkshire Witch*, p.19

131 *R v Anne Wycherley (*1838) 8 Car. & P. 262.

132 Gowing, Laura (1997) "Secret Birth and Infanticide in Seventeenth-Century England", pp.157-187.

133 *London Evening Post*, August 30, 1740 - September 2, 1740.

134 Forbes, Thomas R. (1988) "A jury of matrons", p.30.

135 *London Packet or New Lloyd's Evening Post*, July 13, 1798 - July 16, 1798.

she was convicted of assisting in a case of abduction, had a dozen women. (It took them half an hour to reach a positive verdict).[136] However, it was sometimes much smaller, perhaps six or even three women. In the rare cases where they disagreed, the matrons decided by a simple majority, unlike trial juries which had to be unanimous. Normally, the matrons were also unanimous in their decisions, even if it took some debate. For example, when Elizabeth Wade was convicted and pleaded pregnancy, the jury of matrons: "…could not agree upon their verdict for a considerable period of time".[137]

In theory, if the jury gave an affirmative answer, execution would be delayed until the baby's delivery, or until it became apparent that the woman was not pregnant. Until 1848, pregnancy merely postponed her hanging or burning; it did not commute the punishment.[138] As a Newgate inmate tells Moll Flanders, in Defoe's eponymous work of 1721: "…'I am under sentence, only I pleaded my belly, but I am no more with child than the judge that tried me, and I expect to be called down next sessions.' This 'calling down' is calling down to their former judgment, when a woman has been respited for her belly, but proves not to be with child, or if she has been with child, and has been brought to bed".[139] Thus, when Susan Sciffel was found guilty of murdering her female apprentice at the Salisbury Assizes in March 1766, she escaped being hanged with her husband (also found guilty of the crime) by pleading pregnancy, so that her execution was respited for two months.[140] She did slightly better, but was still hanged in July of the same year.

If their executions were not permanently commuted, women were supposed to go to the gallows on the next 'hanging day' after their delivery. In practice, as the Sciffel case suggests, there was often some slippage on timings. In theory, the conditions of detention for such women could be quite grim. Until her sentence was carried out, Sciffel, although very pregnant, was subjected to the: "…usual restraint of close confinement, and to be fed with nothing but bread and water".[141] (Not an

---

[136] Anon, (1703) *The tryals of Haagen Swendsen, Sarah Baynton, John Hartwell and John Spurr: for feloniously stealing Mrs Pleasant Rawlins, a virgin and heiress of a considerable fortune*, p.30.

[137] *Daily Post*, May 19, 1727.

[138] Anon, (1632) *The Laws Resolutions of Womens Rights: or, the Lawes Provision for Women*, p.207.

[139] Defoe, Daniel (1721) *The Fortunes and Misfortunes of the Famous Moll Flanders*, p.55

[140] *St James's Chronicle or the British Evening Post*, March 18-20, 1766.

[141] *London Evening Post*, March 18, 1766 - March 20, 1766.

ideal diet for a woman in her condition). However, it is probable that those convicted of less heinous offences received better treatment.

Irrespective of her conditions of detention, after a female felon had been temporarily reprieved for pregnancy a warrant for her execution had to be issued by the Sheriff before she could be hanged. In practice, this often did not happen, especially for less serious capital offences and/or where a woman had made a genuine claim and subsequently given birth. This was particularly likely later in the eighteenth century. In many cases, after the child was born, or the woman proved not to be pregnant, she would spend a few months in jail and then be permanently reprieved and released although, after 1718, this might be on condition of transportation.

For example, in March 1731 it was noted that Constance Buckle, who had been capitally convicted the previous December for a street robbery and pleaded her belly: "...being since deliver'd, is to be transported".[142] Similarly, Anne Hoar was capitally convicted (presumably under the 1699 Shoplifting Act) at the Bristol Assizes in April 1737 for stealing some money (which she swallowed) and nutmegs from a baker's shop. However, she successfully pleaded her belly and was temporarily reprieved.[143] The following September she too was permanently reprieved and transported for 14 years.[144] Ann Lucas was even more fortunate, over forty years later. She had been capitally convicted at the Summer Assizes at Kingston for coining and successfully pleaded her belly. After being kept in custody at the New Gaol in Southwark she gave birth (in the prison) to two healthy boys. Three months later she received a free pardon and was released. The American War, which prevented transportation, may have helped produce this decision, while no parish would wish to take on the expense of two infants if they could possibly help it.[145]

Of course, in particularly serious cases, such as murder, such an outcome was extremely unlikely, even at the end of the century. In 1715, for example, Anne Fogget gained an extra few months of life, having been impregnated by her husband shortly before she killed him! However, having been "brought to bed" in the castle in York where she was being held, she was duly executed.[146] In like manner, when Margaret Williams was sentenced to death for the murder of her six-year-old stepson, in August 1774, she was reprieved for pregnancy but hanged at Caernarfon at the end of the year. Similarly, in 1798, after Margaret Hughes successfully

---

142 *Daily Journal*, March 8, 1731.
143 *Country Journal or The Craftsman*, April 2, 1737.
144 *Daily Gazetteer (London Edition)*, September 5, 1738.
145 *Morning Post and Daily Advertiser*, August 3, 1781.
146 *St. James's Evening Post*, September 11, 1716 - September 13, 1716.

pleaded her belly at the Canterbury gaol delivery, where she had been convicted of poisoning her militia soldier husband, and initially reprieved for three months, she was: "…desired not to indulge the most distant idea of mercy on this side of the grave".[147] Her execution was delayed for nine months, but she was duly hanged in July 1799.

Given its obvious benefits, it is unsurprising that many women who were capitally convicted should have had recourse to pleading their bellies. Of course, it was not too difficult for women of childbearing age to become pregnant in many of the relatively poorly segregated eighteenth-century prisons, whether it was by male visitors, turnkeys, or fellow inmates. This sometimes happened, though some women were unsuccessful in this direction. It was said of Margaret Osgood, who was indicted at the Surrey Assizes for killing her husband, that: "…during her Imprisonment she did what she could to be got with Child, thereby to respite her Execution, but her expectation failed her, for she proved not pregnant". Osgood was convicted and burnt (possibly, and unusually, while still alive).[148] Other women met more success.

However, many females, like Defoe's character, would make such a claim as a matter of course, even if well aware that it was unfounded, especially early in the century. For example, Sarah Metyard, convicted of murdering a maid, unsuccessfully pleaded her belly in 1762, despite being a virgin. She later told the Newgate Ordinary that she had been advised to: "…use this plea, tho' without foundation, to gain a respite". Unfortunately, she was unaware of the examination conducted by the matrons, who swiftly found her not to be with child.[149] The plea was particularly common with capitally convicted women who knew that a reprieve was unlikely, such as the twice previously convicted horse-thief Elizabeth Bing. She unavailingly pleaded her belly when the death penalty was passed on her, on a third occasion, at the Oxford Assizes.[150] The majority of women who sought the privilege were probably not pregnant.

Historically, the right to 'plead the belly' had mitigated some of the harshness of the criminal law for women, particularly the death for felony rule. As a result, before women could claim clergy on the same terms as men (in 1692) and when, as in the late seventeenth century, reprieves for those who were capitally convicted were more unusual than a century

---

[147] *London Packet or New Lloyd's Evening Post*, July 13, 1798 - July 16, 1798.

[148] Anon, (1681) *The True narrative of the confession and execution of the prisoners at Kingstone-upon-Thames, on Wednesday the 16th of this instant March,* pp.1-2.

[149] Anon, (1762) *God's Revenge against Murder*, p.24.

[150] *Universal Spectator and Weekly Journal*, July 26, 1729.

later, the matrons were sometimes very generous when conducting the test. For example, of the three women sentenced to death at the Lent Assizes held in Surrey in 1683, two pleaded their bellies and: "Juries of Women being thereupon Impannelled; they brought them in to be Quick with Child".[151] In 1696, there were reports of a woman of almost 60 being found to be pregnant by the matrons.[152] On some counts, up to half of all capitally convicted women at this time claimed to be pregnant, and a majority of such claims were accepted. More precisely, at the Old Bailey, it seems that 38 per cent of women who were sentenced to death during the first quarter of the eighteenth century made such a plea.[153] On one occasion, four women found guilty at the Old Bailey in a single trial all claimed pregnancy.

During the course of the eighteenth century the matrons employed at Assizes appear to have become increasingly strict when applying the test, and claims were made less frequently. This was particularly marked after 1718, when capitally convicted women could be reprieved on condition of transportation, encouraging clemency from the Crown for capital convicts, and further reducing any need to use the fiction of pregnancy to circumvent draconian laws. As a result, there was a steady reduction in the number of women who succeeded with such a plea.[154] This, combined with a fall in the proportion of capital convictions at the end of the period, also seems to have influenced the number of claims that were initially made. At the Old Bailey, it appears that by the final quarter of the century only one in fifty women sentenced to death followed this course, and only a quarter of these claims were being accepted by the matrons.[155] This decline continued in the following century, greatly aided by the end of the 'Bloody Code'. Only three of the 155 women who were capitally convicted at the same court between 1825 and 1834 entered such a plea. The Assizes courts show a broadly similar pattern amongst provincial women.

---

[151] Anon, (1683) *A true account of the proceedings at the assizes, held for the county of Surrey at Croydon, begun on Wednesday the 28th. of February, 1683. and there continued for several days With a relation of the prisoners tryed and condemned at the said assizes*, p.4 .

[152] *Post Man and the Historical Account*, December 26, 1696 - December 29, 1696.

[153] D'Cruze, Shani and Jackson, Louise (2009) *Women, Crime and Justice in England since 1660*, p.125.

[154] King, Peter (2000) *Crime, Justice and Discretion in England 1740-1820*, p.28.

[155] Oldham, James (1985) "On Pleading the Belly: A History of the Jury of Matrons", p.17, p.23, and pp.33-37.

The Death Penalty and the Bloody Code

The proliferation of theoretically capital offences in the eighteenth-century 'Bloody Code' is highly misleading, particularly when it comes to women. Most of its more recondite crimes, such as destroying "trees planted in any avenue" (under the 1723 'Black Act') rarely (if ever) produced hangings. Indeed, of female executions (nationwide) during the entire period, about half were for various forms of homicide, whether murder, infanticide, or petty treason. Such cases made up a majority of executions after the first half of the century.[156] Thus, it seems that nationally 187 of the 355 confirmed executions of women between 1735 and 1799 were for killings (making up 52.7 per cent of the total). On one assessment, 80 of these women were hanged for murdering illegitimate (usually newborn) babies. About 76 women were executed for other types of murder, and 31 for petty treason (the murder by a woman of her husband or employer). Although detailed scrutiny of the sub-division might produce slightly different interpretations (one or two of the 'babies' seem to have been somewhat older children) the total number and broad thrust of the division is accurate.[157]

The remaining women were hanged for a variety of offences including, in descending order of importance, burglary, arson, housebreaking, coining, forgery, riot, shoplifting, horse or sheep theft, pick-pocketing, and returning from transportation. Mary Tilley became the sole English woman to be executed for sacrilege (usually theft from a church) after being convicted at the Hertford Assizes in 1786, though several others were tried for the offence during the century. Tilley had broken into the church at Hartingfordbury, with a male companion, and stolen the pulpit cloth and two surplices.[158] Nearly all of the cases of riot related to the aftermath of the Metropolitan Gordon Riots of 1780. Only one provincial woman, Margaret Boulker, hanged after the Warwick Assizes in August 1795, was executed for the crime. She had been convicted of rioting at the steam-mill in Birmingham.[159] The political overtones of her offence, in a city that had

---

[156] King, Peter (1999) "Gender, crime and justice in late eighteenth-and early nineteenth-century England", p.46 and pp.62-64.

[157] www.capitalpunishmentuk.org. Last consulted 30th March 2012. This very well researched site is authored by Mr Richard Clark and the statistics for the eighteenth century are largely based on the extremely detailed work of Mr David Mossop. The present author has managed to confirm the vast majority of the executions identified using contemporary newspaper reports.

[158] *Public Advertiser*, March 20, 1786.

[159] *True Briton (1793),* August 14, 1795.

seen previous riots of this type (perhaps a form of proto-Luddism), might explain this result.

Reprieves

Even if not clergied or pregnant, capitally convicted women (like men) could be reprieved and so avoid execution. Women who were sentenced to death were usually executed several weeks after their sentence had been passed, unless convicted of murder in the years following 1752, when the strict time constraints imposed by the Murder Act of that year applied, although even these could be (and often were) suspended by the court. Those sentenced to die at the Assizes normally had a report on their case forwarded by the trial judge in a letter sent to the Secretary of State, containing his recommendation as to whether the convict(s) should be "left for execution". Although the final decision was for the Crown, the judge's advice was almost invariably followed if he recommended a reprieve. Indeed, so routine was this that judges would openly announce their decisions on this issue before leaving an Assizes town. These have sometimes been termed "administrative pardons" as a result. Cynics thought that some criminals bribed Assizes Clerks to encourage their judges to make a favourable recommendation at this stage in the process. Clerks were often quite influential due to their detailed understanding of criminal procedure, something that was often not shared by the Westminster judiciary when first appointed.[160]

In making their recommendation, a judge would be influenced by the gravity of the offence, and the age, previous history, degree of involvement, motivation and, it seems, gender of the convict, as well as any need to set a deterrent example in a particular locality or at a certain time. For example, at the Oxford Assizes in July 1729, two women were capitally convicted for stealing horses together. The judge reprieved one of them. However, the other, an "old offender", who had survived previous death sentences, was left for execution.[161]

The normal delay between conviction and execution also gave individual women (like men) with friends and contacts (especially influential ones) the opportunity to petition for a reprieve, even if the Assizes judge had not initially recommended it. Women could benefit from this, but also in some cases instigated such a process. For example, the notorious Fanny Davies managed to get an aristocratic and influential

---

160 Anon (Lover of his country), (1752) *Villain'y Unmask'd …*, p.7.

161 *Country Journal or The Craftsman*, July 26, 1729.

lover to make representations on behalf of a capitally convicted former boyfriend, as a result of which his death sentence was commuted to transportation.[162] In these situations, the judge might be asked to make further observations on a case that was the subject of petition.[163] Thus, at the Bristol Assizes in 1737, Elizabeth Smith was capitally convicted of stealing five gold rings, two silver spoons, and a considerable sum of money from out of a dwelling house. She was not initially recommended for a reprieve by the trial judge.[164] Nevertheless, she was not subsequently executed, suggesting a successful intercession.

Sometimes, judges would themselves grant a temporary respite specifically to allow further consideration of a capital case or, alternatively, to permit those with influence a chance to petition for clemency. For example, in 1816, Elizabeth Ward was capitally convicted of attempted murder under Lord Ellenborough's Act of 1803, after she attempted to poison her older sister. The trial judge, Mr Justice Bayley, sentenced her to death and did not recommend a reprieve because of the deliberation behind the crime, which appears to have been motivated by jealousy. However, Ward was the subject of a vigorous campaign for mercy. Her supporters included the influential Lord Lascelles, who persuaded Bayley to postpone Ward's execution for a couple of weeks. This allowed him time to write to the Home Secretary, Viscount Sidmouth, supporting a reprieve. The Lord Mayor of York and other prominent citizens of that city also petitioned the Prince Regent for mercy, stressing the convict's penitence and the wish of her family, including her intended victim, that she be spared from death. Ward was eventually reprieved.[165]

Most reprieves, if granted, were conditional rather than free. As Lord Justice Gould observed in 1785, the King could grant a pardon "upon any condition he pleases".[166] After 1718, this was most commonly on condition of transportation. Normally, this would be for 14 or more years, though it could be less, and seven years was sometimes stipulated towards the end of the century. A reprieve could also be on condition of enlisting in the military. Obviously, this option was not open to female convicts,

---

[162] Anon, (1786) *An Authentic Narrative of the Most Remarkable Adventures, and Curious Intrigues, Exhibited in the Life of Miss Fanny Davies*, p.17.
[163] Hay, Douglas (2010) "Hanging and the English Judges: The Judicial Politics of Retention and Abolition", p.132.
[164] *Country Journal or The Craftsman*, April 2, 1737.
[165] Watson, Katherine (2004) *Poisoned Lives: English Poisoners and Their Victims*, pp.178-179.
[166] *The King v Aickles* (1785) 1 Leach 390.

perhaps putting them at a slight disadvantage in time of war, at least in this respect.

The vast majority of reprieves were granted for offences against property, though there were occasional instances of women being pardoned for more serious crimes. Murderers nearly, but not quite always, hanged. For a rare exception to this general rule can be considered the cases of Mary Dagger, Ann Hazard, and James Day, who were convicted of murder at the Kingston Assizes, after the three of them threw Simon Pottell out of a window in Southwark.[167] Unlike Ann and James (who were hanged), Mary was reprieved on condition of transportation for 14 years. Presumably, her role in the killing was peripheral.[168] Three years earlier, Susannah Houchin had also escaped death in similar circumstances (see below).

Rather more commonly, several women, such as Sarah Tolly in 1735, were reprieved after being convicted of infanticide. This was especially likely where there was special mitigation.[169] Thus, in Wiltshire in 1779, a servant named Katherine Hill murdered her newborn bastard by throwing it down a well. The brother of her mistress, who was strongly suspected of involvement in the crime, was also the man who had impregnated her, but had fled to avoid arrest. However, Hill's employer, Mary Smart (the genitor's sister), was accused of being an accessory to the killing and stood trial with Katherine at the Salisbury Assizes. Mary was acquitted but Katherine was found guilty and sentenced to death in March 1780. Nevertheless, she was initially reprieved and then granted a free pardon by warrant in April.[170] It may be that it was thought unfair that she should hang when others, perhaps more heavily involved or responsible for what had occurred, escaped.

This was not a new phenomenon. Even in the previous century, reprieves had been granted to some women convicted of infanticide, unlike the female murderers of adults.[171] However, during the 1700s, many quite ordinary cases of infanticide also received clemency. For example, at the Surrey Assizes in 1740, a servant, Mary Curtis, was accused of strangling and hiding her newborn baby and convicted under the 1624 Act (see chapter four), although she claimed that the child was born dead and that she was: "…in great pain, and knew not what I did".

---

[167] *London Daily Post and General Advertiser*, August 11, 1743.
[168] *London Evening Post*, March 31, 1744 - April 3, 1744.
[169] *Country Journal or The Craftsman*, August 23, 1735.
[170] Hunnisett, R.F. (Ed.) (1981) *Wiltshire Coroners' Bills 1752–1796*, p.71.
[171] Walker, Garthine (2003) *Crime, Gender and Social Order in Early Modern England*, pp.155-156.

The trial jury that convicted her "recommended her to the Court for mercy".[172] She was not subsequently executed. (The case is also, perhaps, indicative of 'new' attitudes in such cases towards mental conditions that did not amount to insanity; this is discussed in chapter four).

A pair of cases from the Shrewsbury Assizes in 1782 were much more typical of situations in which reprieves were granted. Hannah Jones was capitally convicted of horse-theft and Anne Smith was sentenced to death at the same time for shoplifting under the 1699 Act. Both received reprieves.[173] Similarly, at the Warwick Assizes in 1758, Margaret Jones was capitally convicted of picking a woman's pocket of three pounds but reprieved.[174] Mary Pearce, convicted and sentenced to death at the Lent Assizes in 1739 for housebreaking, in which she had stolen "wearing apparel", was also granted clemency.[175]

As these cases suggest, women did fairly well out of the reprieve system, often slightly better than men, even if it was on condition of transportation. In Surrey, between 1660 and 1800, only about 40 per cent of those (both men and women) who were convicted of capital felonies were actually executed, most of the rest (over 50%) being reprieved. (The figure for reprieves would be higher if confined to the eighteenth century). However, nationally, it seems that at least 1,230 of the females who were capitally convicted between 1735 and 1799, that is about 78 per cent of the total, received clemency. (A few others died in prison before execution or reprieve, while several cases are uncertain as to outcome).[176]

However, despite this general pattern, in some specific areas at least, it seems that the *proportion* of reprieves issued to women was smaller than that granted to men, even allowing for their reduced involvement in crime. For example, it was: just under ten per cent of the total in the North East; just over four per cent in the North West, and just over nine per cent on the Western Circuit. The explanation for this discrepancy probably lies in the small number of women who were capitally convicted in these areas. Jurors appear to have avoided the need to leave the lives of women to the mercy of the reprieve process by convicting of lesser, non-capital, offences via partial verdicts (which were far more common than with men), so that

---

172 Anon, (1740) *The Proceedings at the Assizes of Peace, Oyer and Terminer, for the County of Surrey, Held at the Town-Hall of Kingston Upon Thames, in the 14th Year of His Majesty's Reign ... To Which is Added the Genuine Proceedings at the Assizes for the County of Essex*, p.15.

173 *Gazetteer and New Daily Advertiser*, July 31, 1782.

174 *London Chronicle (Semi-Annual)*, August 1, 1758 - August 3, 1758.

175 *Daily Gazetteer (London Edition)*, March 16, 1739.

176 www.capitalpunishmentuk.org/fem1735.html. Last accessed 19th March 2012.

many females who were sentenced to death were fairly 'hard core' cases.[177]

The proportion of capitally convicted women who were reprieved varied considerably over time. For example, in the years around 1760, it was as low as 63 per cent but by the end of the century it had risen to 86 per cent. Partly as a result, and allowing for the country's growth in population after the middle of the era, the number of females executed in England and Wales relative to population fell, though not dramatically. Thus, 57 women died in the decade 1755-1764, compared to 46 in the years 1785-1794.[178]

Despite the use of reprieves, in the early years of the century, numerous capitally convicted female property offenders were hanged. For example, of the 11 women executed after the Surrey Assizes, in a selection of 19 years taken from between 1722 and 1748, only two died for murder, with nine being executed for property offences: two for robbery; three for burglary; and four for picking pockets.[179] By contrast, in the late eighteenth century, when reprieves were being granted more willingly, very few female property offenders were executed. Thus, in Essex (admittedly an extreme case) between 1740 and 1804, 271 men went to the gallows for property offences. Only one woman, Clare Montford, who was hanged in 1790 for burglary, experienced a similar fate, and her case had involved a particularly heinous breach of trust at a time when there was acute local concern about this form of crime.[180] In the North East, too, women were much less likely than men to be hanged if convicted of such crimes.[181]

As a result, in the last two decades of the eighteenth century, only 27 women in England and Wales outside the Metropolis were executed for property offences, and several of these had participated in robberies while others had worked with male accomplices. In September 1816, when Dinah Riddiford was hanged for burglary at Gloucester, she became the last provincial woman to die for a conventional property offence committed on its own, *other* than robbery.[182] (The following year,

---

[177] Morgan, Gwenda and Rushton, Peter (2004) *Eighteenth-Century Criminal Transportation: The Formation of the Criminal Atlantic*, at p.47.

[178] www.capitalpunishmentuk.org/fem1735.html. Last accessed 19th March 2012.

[179] Beattie, John (1986) *Crime and the Courts in England 1660-1800*, pp.514-515.

[180] King, Peter (2000) *Crime, Justice and Discretion in England 1740-1820*, p.282, *Whitehall Evening Post (1770)*, March 20, 1790 - March 23, 1790.

[181] Morgan, Gwenda and Rushton, Peter (1998) *Rogues, Thieves and the Rule of Law*, p.118.

[182] *The Morning Post*, September 2, 1816.

Elizabeth Fricker, in the Metropolis, became the last Englishwoman anywhere to hang for such an offence). More typically, all three of the women who were hanged in Northamptonshire between 1780 and 1834 were executed for murder.[183]

Even by the middle decades of the eighteenth century, the few exceptions to this general pattern, cases where female property offenders went to the gallows, normally had seriously aggravating features. For example, Mary Williams, who was convicted and executed in 1757 for housebreaking in Portsmouth, had taken the large sum of £60.[184] Even worse, Margaret Clarke, hanged at Coventry in August 1763 for stealing in a dwelling house, had been part of the notorious "Coventry gang" and engaged in large-scale crimes in the company of several others, including her husband. The offence that brought her to the gallows had involved taking the enormous sum of £186, along with several valuable pieces of plate.[185] Further aggravating her situation, Margaret was thought to be a doubly returned transport.[186] A combination of her history, her involvement in professional crime, and the very high value of her takings ensured that she was executed with other members of her gang, including her niece.

Less obviously, Elizabeth Wright was convicted and executed at the Hereford Assizes in 1784 for burglary. Her crime, though serious, was not especially grave. She had taken the head of a clock, two loaves, a gammon and part of a flitch of bacon.[187] However, she appears to have been a mature woman, perhaps 49 years of age, and so may well have been an "old offender". The case of Margaret Dunn, a soldier's wife, who was hanged at Morpeth in August 1793 for burglary, had more obviously aggravating features. Although she had not had recourse to violence, her crime had involved a breach of trust, as she had stolen from a widow in whose house she had lodged. Most importantly, she had stolen £120 in cash, and some clothes, just when a feeling of general crisis was encouraging judicial severity. At these times, the government, via the Lord

---

[183] Dyndor, Zoe (2008) "Death Recorded: Capital Punishment and the Press in Northampton, 1780–1834", p.185.

[184] *Lloyd's Evening Post and British Chronicle*, July 25, 1757 - July 27, 1757.

[185] *St. James's Chronicle or the British Evening Post,* April 17-19 1763, *Lloyds Evening Post*, August 5th-8th, 1763

[186] *Lloyds Evening Post*, August 8th-10th, 1763

[187] *London Chronicle*, August 7, 1784 - August 10, 1784.

Chancellor, would emphasize to the Westminster judges before they went on circuit that they should be economical with administrative reprieves.[188]

Female Executions

The number of women who were executed was dwarfed by the male total, and the discrepancy grew as the century advanced and the courts became increasingly reluctant to hang or burn females. On a local basis, for example, in a selection of 19 years taken from between 1722 and 1748, 11 women were executed after the Surrey Assizes, compared to 100 men (making them about nine per cent of the total).[189] According to one national assessment, between 1735 and 1799, there were 6,233 confirmed executions (and another 241 possible or probable ones) of both genders in England (including London) and Wales. During these 65 years, about 1,600 females were initially sentenced to death, having been convicted of a non-clergyable felony. However, just 355 women were certainly executed (the true figure may have been nearer to 375), making the female component of confirmed executions less than six per cent of the national total. Of the 355 who were certainly executed, 323 died by hanging and 32 by burning at the stake for petty treason.[190]

This general execution profile was certainly not unique to England. In Dublin, for example, only 13 women were hanged out of a total of 242 executions between 1780 and 1798 (a little over five per cent).[191] Across the Atlantic, between 1750 and 1800, only 8.7 per cent of executions in Boston were of women, while in Philadelphia, during the same period, it was just two per cent (two out of 101 cases).[192]

Inevitably, given its location, size and higher than average female offending rate, a significant proportion of executed women came from London and Middlesex. Approaching (but less than) 200 women were hanged/burned in the Metropolitan area during the whole of the eighteenth

---

[188] Hay, Douglas (2010) “Hanging and the English Judges: The Judicial Politics of Retention and Abolition”, p.137.
[189] Beattie, John (1986) *Crime and the Courts in England 1660-1800,* pp.514-515.
[190] www.capitalpunishmentuk.org. Last consulted 25th March 2012. The present author has confirmed the vast majority of the executions listed using contemporary newspaper reports.
[191] Henry, Brian (1993) *Dublin Hanged: Crime, Law Enforcement and Punishment in Late 18th-century Dublin*, p.59.
[192] Gottlieb, Gabriele (2005) *Theater Of Death: Capital Punishment In Early America, 1750-1800*, p.101, p.109, and p.121.

century.[193] Of these, 91 executions, just over a quarter of the national female total, took place between 1735 and 1799.[194]

Nevertheless, as this figure suggests, throughout the era, exceptional years apart, a considerable majority (about three quarters) of all executed females came from outside the Metropolis, albeit that this still meant that the ultimate sanction was used about twice as commonly for Metropolitan women on a per capita basis. Typically, in 1771, 28 women were sentenced to death; seven of them were eventually hanged (none were burned that year). Of these, only two were executed at Tyburn. Of the remainder, two came from Ipswich, two from Cornwall, and one from Shrewsbury. This is also consistent with the general eighteenth-century trend for both men and women. Between 1714 and 1830, judges at Assizes sentenced over three times as many people to death as did those at the Old Bailey, and almost three times as many were executed there as were hanged in the capital.[195]

Proximity to the London area appears to have driven up male execution rates in the Home Counties, especially in those shires that bordered the Metropolis, so that Kent, Essex, Hertfordshire and (most particularly) Surrey had relatively large numbers of hangings. However, this did not necessarily affect women, especially after the early years of the century. Just nine women were executed at all locations in Surrey (Kennington Common, Kingston, etc.) between 1735 and 1799. Kent saw 14 female executions during this period (at Maidstone and Canterbury), while Sussex witnessed just three or four. Six women hanged at Chelmsford in Essex. By contrast, Devonshire witnessed at least 22 female executions during this time (and probably several more that cannot be confirmed). More generally, there appears to have been a slight North South divide in favour of northern women. Only three, possibly four, women were executed in Newcastle over the same period.[196]

As with males, youth was not necessarily a bar to the execution of provincial women, though it might encourage the granting of a reprieve. Several teenage girls were hanged outside London during the course of the century. Among them was 15-year-old Elizabeth Morton (some accounts give her age as 16), the domestic maid to a farmer, who was hanged at Nottingham in April 1763 for the murder by strangling of her master's

[193] Gatrell, V.A.C., (1996) *The Hanging Tree: Execution and the English People 1770-1868*, p.616.

[194] www.capitalpunishmentuk.org

[195] Hay, Douglas (2010) "Hanging and the English Judges: The Judicial Politics of Retention and Abolition", p.132.

[196] www.capitalpunishmentuk.org

two-year-old daughter and the attempted murder of another of his small children (she twisted her neck so violently that blood issued from her nose and ears). Morton claimed that she was incited to the crime by a "gentleman in black", who came to her during the night. (Such a claim, placing the blame on the Devil's sudden intervention, had been common in the previous century, but was slightly 'old fashioned' by the 1760s). Perhaps more plausibly, other accounts suggest she did it because the infants "cried and were troublesome". Even Morton was given an initial three-week reprieve from execution at the Nottingham Assizes to allow her case to be considered more thoroughly (perhaps in view of her mental state).[197] Similarly, after the Dorchester Assizes in March 1794, Elizabeth Marsh, also 15 years of age, was hanged for the murder of her grandfather. She had struck the septuagenarian two vicious blows on the head with a hatchet while he was sleeping.[198] As these examples suggest, when females below the age of 18 were to be hanged, their crimes were always exceptionally serious. However, such cases were not quite confined to cases of murder. In September 1786, 17-year-old Susannah Minton was executed at Hereford for a non-fatal arson.

Execution Rituals

While awaiting execution, women would be ministered to by prison chaplains and other clerics, and encouraged to make their peace with God. Thus, while held in Oxford Castle, pending her hanging for infanticide, Mary Goodenough was attended by both the prison Ordinary and a non-conforming minister from the university city.[199] In 1736, the murderer Elizabeth Thompson proved less fertile ground for such ministrations. Her behaviour in jail was: "…all insolence and threats; nothing but oaths and execrations proceeded from her". However, when the death warrant came down to allow her execution, she modified this slightly and admitted to having led an immoral life, albeit still claiming that she was not guilty of the offence for which she was to die.[200]

The execution of provincial women was carried out in public (as it would be until 1868) and at the same time and place, usually the county gallows near an Assizes town, as their male counterparts. Thus, Elizabeth Morton was hanged on Gallows Hill, Nottingham, in April 1763. If the

---

[197] *Lloyd's Evening Post and British Chronicle*, March 21, 1763 - March 23, 1763. *London Chronicle (Semi-Annual)*, April 9, 1763 - April 12, 1763.
[198] *Sun*, April 22, 1794.
[199] Anon, (1692) *Fair warnings to murderers of infants ...*, pp.2-4.
[200] *Daily Gazetteer*, June 22 1736.

Assizes were held in a town a long way from where an offence had been committed, and an exemplary role for an ensuing execution was seen to be desirable, convicts might be returned to a gallows near their crime, even if it sometimes had to be improvised. For example, Philippa Cary and Anne Evans were sent back to Plymouth from Exeter for their executions.[201]

At the gallows, many women, like men, would die very 'penitent'. Among them was Mary Blandy, who was attended by the Reverend Swinton and chose to wear a: "...black crape sack, with her arms and hands ty'd with black paduasoy ribbons". Some would deliver a short homily from the scaffold on the justness of their sentences and the need to avoid falling into sin. Others left a written note containing similar sentiments. Women who failed to express suitable contrition could come under considerable pressure to conform. Elizabeth Thompson was "exhorted, in the strongest and most pathetick terms" by a Dr Macro and other ministers of religion to confess, when she refused to admit her guilt or take part in the singing of a pre-execution psalm.[202] Elizabeth Lavender, executed in Horsham at the end of the period for murdering her illegitimate baby, was thought to have behaved in a manner that was more appropriate to a woman in her unhappy situation: "She trembled and wept much ... and having expressed a hope that all other females would take warning by her untimely fate, she was turned off about half past twelve".[203]

As Thompson's case suggests, some women, like the murderer Margaret Palmer, would maintain their innocence to the end.[204] A few (not many) were openly defiant. In 1743, for example, Sarah Dodd, facing execution in Bristol for housebreaking, appeared quite intoxicated as she was carried to the gallows. She "behav'd very boldly" and toasted the hangman on the way with a bottle of liquor (probably gin). At the scaffold, she declared that she was innocent, despite having made pre-trial admissions, and: "...in token of her pretended innocence, call'd for water, and wash'd her hands before the spectators".[205] Elizabeth Boardingham, who was executed at York in 1776 for petty treason, also showed no contrition and behaved at the gallows with a: "...degree of boldness and unconcern, that shocked all who saw her". She shook hands with her male co-accused (her

---

201 Anon, (1687) *The poysoners rewarded, or, The most barbarous of murthers, directed and published...*, p.10.
202 *Daily Gazetteer*, June 22, 1736
203 *True Briton (1793),* August 2, 1799.
204 *Observer*, March 31, 1799.
205 *General Evening Post*, May 14, 1743.

lover) and saluted him prior to being 'turned off'.[206] Others were in a state of shock. Rebecca Downing, waiting to be strangled prior to immolation for murdering her master: "...appeared totally ignorant of her situation, and insensible to every kind of admonition".[207]

The Mechanics of Execution

Eighteenth-century execution was a grim process. As Lavender's case suggests, in the provinces, women (like men) would normally be turned off a ladder (which was suddenly twisted away) or the back of a horse-drawn cart (driven from under them), after being attached to the gallows by a noose. The lack of a 'drop' until the final years of the era meant that most women would strangle, a process that was slowed down by the thick hemp ropes usually employed. Thompson unavailingly tried to pre-empt this by asking to leap from her cart (which might have broken her neck), after the execution cap was pulled over her face, shouting "Let me jump, let me jump".[208] However, late in the period, a few women, like Margaret Hughes, who was executed at Canterbury in 1799, benefited from a 'short' drop, a lever releasing a platform under her feet and allowing her to fall six or eight inches. Unfortunately, unlike the 'long' drop of the late nineteenth century, even this was often not enough to ensure a broken neck, although it tightened the ligature and speeded up strangulation.

A few women, like Lavendar, "expired without any apparent agony". Others were less fortunate. When Elizabeth Jeffries and John Swan were hanged together John died in less than five minutes. Elizabeth, however, being much lighter, took over fifteen minutes to die, struggling to the end. As a result, it was very difficult for a woman to end her life with 'dignity', most writhing, and many spontaneously defecating and urinating. The public indecency that this created occasioned growing concern. Society was becoming increasingly squeamish about the public exposure of women's bodies and bodily functions. Illustrative of this change, the tiny number of females executed in Northamptonshire between 1780 and 1834 (three women convicted of murder on separate occasions) received very little coverage in the local *Northampton Mercury*, despite their rarity. It has even been suggested that, by this period, there was something of a 'taboo' surrounding women who were hanged.[209]

---

[206] *Morning Post and Daily Advertiser*, March 25, 1776.

[207] *Morning Herald and Daily Advertiser*, August 10, 1782.

[208] *Daily Gazetteer*, June 22, 1736.

[209] Dyndor, Zoe (2008) "Death Recorded: Capital Punishment and the Press in Northampton, 1780–1834", p.185.

To enhance the deterrent effect of execution, and to provide cadavers for medical schools, the Murder Act of 1752 provided that the bodies of those executed for murder should be dissected after they were cut down from the gallows. Prior to this time, they had normally been released to their families for burial, though a few were hung in chains or dissected for extra deterrent effect. The 1752 statute applied to women as much as to men. Agnes Cole, hanged in Exeter for the murder of her bastard child, became only the third person in the country to be anatomised pursuant to the Act, after it came into force.[210] Similarly, after Edith Saunders was executed for murder in Gloucester, in 1759, her body was sent to a local hospital for dissection.[211] In like manner, Elizabeth Morton's body was sent to a surgeon in Calverton. Unlike London, with its large number of teaching hospitals and college of surgeons, some provincial areas had little medical demand for bodies, and would carry out a somewhat cursory dissection to comply with the statute.

Execution for Treason/Petty Treason

Historically, women who were guilty of both high and petty treason were burnt 'alive'. In the case of high treason, where drawing and quartering was the set punishment for men, this was for reasons of public decency.[212] Thus, Lady Bulmer was burned alive after her involvement in the Pilgrimage of Grace in 1536. Such old cases apart, the punishment for this crime would have been of little more than academic interest to women during the 1700s if high treason had not encompassed coining or otherwise counterfeiting money, as well as plotting against the Crown. Coining was, traditionally, a crime with a high level of female involvement. Even so, such cases had a strong Metropolitan orientation (see chapter six). No women were actually burnt for this offence outside London after 1735, though one or two only very narrowly escaped such a fate.

Nevertheless, burning was not confined to women accused of high treason. It was also the punishment imposed on those who were convicted of the far more common crime of 'petty treason', an offence that dated back to 1351. This occurred in three situations: "Where a servant killeth his Master, the wife, the Husband, the Spirituall man his prelate". In a domestic environment, the protection afforded to employers was also

---

210 *Old England or The National Gazette*, August 15, 1752.

211 *Universal Chronicle or Weekly Gazette*, April 21, 1759 - April 28, 1759.

212 Blackstone, William (1769) *Commentaries on the Laws of England*, vol.4, p.93.

extended to their spouses.[213] It should be noted that a special execution regime for women in this situation was not unique to England. In some parts of continental Europe, at the start of the period, those who murdered their husbands were killed by being drowned or buried alive.[214]

However, it was not entirely disadvantageous to be accused of petty treason, as Sir Robert Peel pointed out to the House of Commons when Lord Lansdowne's Act of 1828 finally abolished the crime as a separate offence to murder. (This was 36 years after the Pennsylvania legislature had taken a similar step).[215] In *theory* those tried for the offence had a more generous right to challenge jurors peremptorily (without cause) than normal murderers; 35 challenges were allowed compared to the usual 20. In practice, such challenges were very rare, most defendants making none at all, but in a case from 1713, in which Mary Sayer was accused of killing her husband with the assistance of her lover and another woman (both of whom were accused of simple murder), Mary used her full 35 man allowance, while the other two were confined to their maximum of 20 challenges.[216]

In theory, like cases of high treason, petty treason required the evidence of two witnesses for a case to be proved, though this rule appears to have been applied a little loosely at times.[217] It was open to juries in such cases to convict of murder, if they had doubts about whether the legal or evidential prerequisites for the crime had been made out. For example, if they were not sure that an accused woman was actually married to her victim or there was a lack of corroboration. Additionally, juries in petty treason cases, like those determining murders, could convict of manslaughter where, for example, malice aforethought was not established.[218]

The great majority of cases of petty treason tried during the eighteenth century involved women who had murdered their husbands, although a few servants (both male and female) were indicted for killing their employers. In an example of the latter, from 1675, Philippa Cary, a nurse working in the Plymouth house of William Wicks, his wife and stepchildren, poisoned their evening broth with the assistance of a servant

---

[213] Coke, Edward (1644) *Institutes of the Lawes of England, Part Three, Concerning High Treason, and other Pleas of the Crown and Criminal causes*, p.20.
[214] Ruff, Julius (2001) *Violence in Early Modern Europe 1500-1800*, p.99.
[215] *Sun*, August 9, 1794.
[216] Anon, (1713) *A Full Account of the Case of John Sayer*, 2nd edn., p.24.
[217] *The Times*, May 6, 1828, p.2.
[218] Beville, Robert (1799) *A treatise on the law of homicide, and of larceny at common law*, p.213.

named Ann Evans. (The act seems to have been motivated by personal rancour). Two of the family died. Philippa was hanged for murder, while Ann was strangled and burnt for petty treason. The explanation for this apparent discrepancy was that Evans was a: "…covenanted servant, and had more immediately the lives of the family in her power".[219] Similarly, in March 1738, Mary Grote, aged just 16, was burned at Winchester for murdering her mistress who had, apparently, been a very harsh employer. More commonly, cases involved spousal murder. For example, in March 1757, Mary Ellah was burned at the York Tyburn for strangling her husband Thomas, in a fit of jealous excitement. (Other accounts suggest she struck him on the temples with an axe).[220] Almost twenty years further on again, Eliza Bordington became the last Yorkshire woman to be strangled and burned for killing her husband.[221]

The special execution regime for petty treason was intended to encourage deference to social and gender superiors. For the handful of men convicted of the crime (for murdering their masters) the punishment was much less draconian than that imposed for high treason, and almost the same as for a normal felony execution, merely involving the modicum of extra shame and discomfort attendant on being taken to the gallows while seated backwards on a flimsy wattle sledge or hurdle, drawn behind a horse, rather than riding in the customary cart. Once there, execution was by conventional hanging and there was no drawing and quartering. By contrast, women's punishment was (significantly) exactly the same as if they had committed high treason, i.e. they were burned after arriving at the gallows on a sledge.[222]

Both forms of petty treason were present in a murder case from 1762. Although only 21, Margaret Beddingfield had been married to a prosperous Suffolk farmer named John for four years. She began an affair with her husband's young farmhand, Richard Ringe, and resolved to murder her spouse with her new lover's assistance. After they failed to persuade a maid to poison John's food, Richard strangled him in his bed. The couple initially escaped detection, only being caught when the maid broke her silence. The pair were tried and convicted of petty treason at the Lent Assizes of 1763 held in Ipswich. Both were drawn on sledges to the gallows at a village just to the north of the town, where Richard was

---

[219] Anon, (1687) *The poysoners rewarded, or, The most barbarous of murthers, directed and published…*, pp.1-10.

[220] *London Evening Post*, February 10, 1757.

[221] Twyford, A. W., and Griffiths, Arthur (1880) *Records Of York Castle: Fortress, Court House, And Prison*, p.99.

[222] Bacon, Sir Francis (1641) *Cases of Treason*, pp.7-8.

hanged and Ann burned.[223]

The special punishment regime for women prompted growing concern as the century progressed, in part because of an increased sensitivity towards the public mutilation of female bodies, and partly because it was increasingly seen as 'unfair', given that it did not apply to men.[224] In light of the former consideration, by the 1780s, the strangled woman's body was normally completely covered in faggots prior to burning, to preserve public decency.[225] The final sentence of this type to be carried out for petty treason occurred in March 1784, when Mary Bailey, from Portsmouth, was burned after the Winchester Assizes, for killing her husband.[226] She was executed with her co-defendant, John Quin, who was hanged for beating their victim to death.[227] However, when Henrietta Radbourne was found guilty of killing her mistress, Hannah Morgan, in 1787, the Old Bailey jury conviction was for murder rather than petty treason. Their verdict was reserved for review by the 12 Westminster judges, as the lesser homicide (rather than the greater) did not seem to be justified on the facts of the case.[228] Nevertheless, Radbourne was ultimately hanged outside Newgate. Abolition of burning followed shortly afterwards.

William Wilberforce took a leading role in sponsoring a first, unsuccessful bill to abolish burning in 1786. Two years later, *The Times* referred to the punishment as a "barbarity".[229] (Some newspapers did not fully appreciate that women were never burned 'alive' by then). A statute of 1790 (30 George III c.48) finally substituted conventional hanging for women convicted of high and petty treason.[230] As a result, in 1797, when Rebecca Dunn was convicted at the Surrey Assizes for coining she was simply hanged on Kennington Common.[231] In the same year, Elizabeth Brockleby, found guilty of petty treason in Lincoln, became the first woman so convicted to hang. By 1814, Sir James Mackintosh, speaking in parliament, could cite the burning of women convicted of petty treason as

---

[223] Anon, (1763) *The genuine trial of Margery Beddingfield and Richard Ringe*, pp.3-43.
[224] Devereaux, Simon (2005) "The Abolition of the Burning of Women in England Reconsidered", p.78.
[225] Shoemaker, Robert (2004) *The London Mob*, p.94.
[226] *General Evening Post*, March 6, 1784 - March 9, 1784.
[227] *Bath Chronicle*, March 18, 1784.
[228] *World and Fashionable Advertiser*, July 16, 1787.
[229] *The Times*, June 27, 1788, p.3.
[230] Campbell, Ruth (1984) "Sentence of Death by Burning for Women", *Journal of Legal History*, pp.44-48.
[231] *Morning Post and Fashionable World*, August 22, 1797.

an example of the "disgraceful and oppressive statutes" that had been inherited from the feudal period.[232]

Execution by Burning

It was immolation on arrival that was terrifying, not the journey to the gallows. When Ann Evans, a poisoner who was executed at Plymouth in 1675, was drawn on a hurdle, it was noted that: "The posture she lay in was on her left side, her Face in her bosom, her Bible under her arm, seeming like one dead, rather than alive". It was a slow journey, as the streets were packed, it being estimated that 10,000 people (a large part of the city) had turned out for her execution.[233] Nevertheless, although the journey would have been very much more 'bumpy', and so less comfortable than in a cart, it was not a huge ordeal.

When women were burned, their executions would usually take place several minutes after any other condemned prisoners had been hanged, and they would normally be led past their suspended bodies to the stake. The women involved would often be draped in cloth or dressed in clothes that had been impregnated with tar, to facilitate swift combustion. Eleanor Elsom, who was burned at Lincoln in 1722, even had her legs, feet, and arms tarred, and she was wearing a tarred bonnet.[234] Traditionally, the women concerned were fastened to the stake by a set of irons.

After 1660, it became increasingly common for the executioner to strangle women before the flames reached them. For example, in 1675, it was noted that Ann Evans, about to die in Plymouth for petty treason, had mounted a box and been fastened to the post by her neck, and surrounded with kindling, at which point the: "…hangman would have set fire unto the fuze before she was strangled but some more charitable and tender-hearted, cryed to him to take away the Block from under her Feet; which having done, she soon fell down, and expired in a Trice".[235] Similarly, it was recorded of Esther Ives, who had assisted her lover to (ironically) strangle her husband, a Rumsey publican, in 1686, that: "…after the executioner had strangled her, the fire was kindled".[236] By the start of the

---

[232] HANSARD 1803–2005, HC Deb 25 April 1814 vol 27 cc527-38, c527.
[233] Quick, John (1676) *Hell open'd, or, The infernal sin of murther...* p.65.
[234] Davey, B.J. (1994) *Rural Crime in the Eighteenth Century: North Lincolnshire 1740 – 80*, p.53.
[235] Quick, John (1676) *Hell open'd, or, The infernal sin of murther...* p.55.
[236] Anon, (1687) *A Full and true account of a most barbarous and bloody murther, committed by Esther Ives,* p.8.

1700s, nearly all women burnt at the stake were granted this indulgence, which was normally effected using a pulley system.[237]

However, there appear to have been a few cases where this was either omitted, perhaps because executioners were not aware of the practice in remoter parts of the country or, more likely, because it failed as the flames took hold. For example, Mary Taylor, executed at Norwich in 1731 after killing her mistress: "…gave a few shrieks when the fire began to burn about her, and lifted up her hands amidst the flame, but was soon suffocated".[238]

Nevertheless, the practice of strangling women first had long been universal by the time of abolition in 1790.[239] Indeed, after the early decades of the century it was usually conducted *before* the fire was lit and, in the years immediately prior to 1790, women were, in effect, 'hanged' at the stake before being burnt. Thus, Margaret Beddingfield was chained up and a rope halter was then placed around her neck and threaded through a hole in the stake. The hangman strangled her by pulling on this apparatus, after which bundles of faggots were piled round Margaret and lit, the fire reducing her body to ashes. In a slight variation, four years later, when Susannah Lott was executed for poisoning her husband she was fastened with a rope by the neck to a post seven feet high, while standing on a stool. This was then taken away, and she hanged for a quarter of an hour until "quite dead". Her body was then reattached to the stake by a chain and burned.[240] Any surviving ashes or fragments of bone identifiable as being of human origin (very few if any) *may* have been buried afterwards. Certainly, Elizabeth Boardingham, awaiting execution by burning with her (apparent) lover, who was to be hanged for killing Elizabeth's husband, asked that she be buried with him.[241]

Much of the attendant ceremony was the same as for a hanging, though the wording of the death sentence was suitably altered, the judge informing the convicted woman that she would be: "…drawn on a hurdle to the place of execution; where you are to be burnt with fire until you are

---

[237] *London Journal*, May 14, 1726.

[238] *Read's Weekly Journal Or British Gazetteer*, April 3, 1731.

[239] Wenderborn, Frederick Augustus (1791) *A View of England Towards the Close of the 18th Century*, vol.1, p.80. See also Blackstone, William (1769) *Commentaries on the Laws of England*, vol.4, p.370.

[240] Anon, (1769) *A Collection of Tracts, Relating to the Crimes, Examination, Trial, Sentence and Execution of Sussanah Lott and Benjamin Buss, for Poisoning Mr. Lott*, p.11.

[241] *General Evening Post*, May 14, 1743.

dead". As with any other execution, there would be a clergyman present to the end.

Transportation

After execution, transportation was the most severe punishment in the penal repertoire, becoming especially common after the Transportation Act came into force in 1718. After this date, it was often imposed as a sentence (normally seven years) in its own right for what would previously have been clergyable thefts and sometimes, albeit very much less commonly, even for petty thefts of items worth under a shilling in value. For example, at the Worcester Assizes in July 1785, Sarah Bellamy was convicted of stealing fifteen and a half guineas (grand larceny) and sentenced to seven years' transportation, rather than being clergied and released.[242] At the end of the century, three unlucky women were sentenced to transportation to Australia for seven years, after being convicted of petty larceny at the Newcastle Quarter Sessions.[243] Quite exceptionally (at least in England), it was also used for vagrants who had not been tried on indictment; for example, in 1752, the female members of Northumberland's 'gang of the faws' were sent to the colonies by magistrates' order under the Settlement Act. After 1718, transportation was also used far more frequently than previously as a condition of reprieve for a convict sentenced to death; this was usually for 14 years or more. In the provinces, between a quarter and almost half of those transported appear to have been reprieved from execution.[244]

The use of transportation varied greatly within England. Women (and men) could still be clergied (and not transported) for theft, though this became very much less common after 1718. Nevertheless, Mary Pack was merely burnt in the hand and released for grand larceny in Northampton in 1736. Most women convicted of petty theft were still whipped, rather than being transported, even after 1718, albeit that some counties, such as Devonshire, imposed it fairly regularly at Quarter Sessions for the lesser form of larceny. In 1757, for example, Ann Lawson was sentenced there to transportation for a theft valued at just a penny.[245] More typically, however,

---

242 *The Times*, July 21, 1785, p.3.

243 *Courier and Evening Gazette*, July 23, 1799.

244 Morgan, Gwenda and Rushton, Peter (2004) *Eighteenth-Century Criminal Transportation: The Formation of the Criminal Atlantic*, pp.38-44.

245 Williams, Amy (2000) *The Criminality Of Women In The 18th Century In The South West Of England*, p.105.

Mary Searles was whipped and released after being convicted of petty theft at the Northampton Assizes in August 1736.[246]

London and its collar counties used transportation most frequently, which was unsurprising, given that the City had actively pressed for its introduction prior to 1718. The Home Circuit's transports would often be sent to Newgate, as would some from counties that were further away, to join those being transported from the Metropolis. They would then be loaded on board ship in the Thames for the voyage across the Atlantic. For example, in October 1719, 90 convicts were sent from Newgate to America, including fourteen sent for 14 years who had been reprieved from execution on condition of transportation, and another 76 for seven years, after conviction for clergyable offences.[247]

The Metropolitan bias towards transportation continued to the end of the century. Of the 178 women on the 'First Fleet' that sailed to Australia, 106 had been sentenced at the Old Bailey. However, 71 had received their disposals in the provinces (the origin of one woman is unknown). Most provincial Assizes locations provided between one and four women for the fleet. Unsurprisingly, given the Metropolitan influence, those conducted at Kingston on Thames provided seven. Nevertheless, the Assizes held at Exeter also sent seven women, and the Worcester Assizes provided eight.[248]

Given the number of times that transportation was imposed in England, compared to the death penalty, and its impact on the wider society, it can be argued that it was the country's most important punishment for the majority of the eighteenth century.[249] The most plausible estimate suggests that 36,000 convicts were transported from England and Wales between the advent of the 1718 Act and the American Revolution, though a few estimates place it higher, perhaps as many as 50,000. Several thousand others went between 1660 and 1718. However, in July 1775, a shipload of transported felons were refused admittance to America and turned back to Britain, marking the beginning of the end of this penal option.[250] (Another vessel did manage to unload convicts successfully the following year). After a hiatus in which those sentenced to transportation were held in 'hulks' in harbours and on the Thames, thousands more went to Australia after 1788. Nevertheless, prior to 1815, the great majority of prisoners

---

[246] *Daily Gazetteer (London Edition)*, August 14, 1736.
[247] *Post Boy (1695)*, October 22, 1719 - October 24, 1719.
[248] Ferguson, Reay (2008) *Female Felons of the First Fleet,* p.106.
[249] Willis, J. (2005) "Transportation versus Imprisonment in Eighteenth-and Nineteenth-Century Britain", p.174.
[250] *Gazetteer and New Daily Advertiser*, July 6, 1775.

finished their sentences of transportation in the hulks and were released (or died) without setting sail for the Antipodes.

Unsurprisingly, given the smaller numbers being convicted, fewer women than men were sentenced to transportation to America during the eighteenth century. About 20 per cent of all British transports were female.[251] In London, with its higher female offending rates, the discrepancy was much smaller than this; about a third of all transports from the Metropolis were women. Outside London, the use and gender distribution of the punishment varied greatly. As in the capital, a third of those sent to America from the Assizes and Quarter Sessions held for the major port of Bristol between 1727 and 1776 were women. By contrast, only one in nine of those transported from rural Gloucestershire were female. The North East was relatively slow to adopt transportation for either men or women before the 1750s, and particularly reluctant to send the latter to America before the middle of the century. Only 13 convicts (just over 12 per cent of the total) who were transported from Northumberland prior to 1750 were female. After 1751, the rate increased to 26 per cent of the total. However, in the same region, and reflecting its raised incidence of female crime, Newcastle sent an unusually high proportion of women to America, just over a quarter before the mid-century, and a little over half afterwards. In Devon, it was between a fifth and a quarter for the whole period.[252]

During the years from 1793 to 1810, 1,810 females went from England and Ireland to Australia, compared to 5,263 men. This was a larger proportion of women than would go to the Antipodes at any other time before 1846, albeit an annual average that was still only slightly over a hundred.[253]

Even if sentenced to transportation, some women from peripheral parts of England and Wales might wait up to several years before they could be shipped, and sometimes went in boats carrying general freight.[254] This situation was made worse by the relatively low price that their forced labour fetched in America when compared to that of men. Although most male convicts were sold as artisans (if they had a trade) or plantation workers (if they did not) on arrival, most female convicts served as

---

[251] Monkkonen, Eric (1991) "Bound for America: A Profile of British Convicts Transported to the Colonies, 1718-1775", p.99.

[252] Morgan, Gwenda and Rushton, Peter (2004) *Eighteenth-Century Criminal Transportation: The Formation of the Criminal Atlantic*, pp.51-53.

[253] Shaw, A.G.L. (1977) *Convicts and the Colonies,* p.147.

[254] Morgan, Gwenda and Rushton, Peter (2004) *Eighteenth-Century Criminal Transportation: The Formation of the Criminal Atlantic*, pp.51-53.

household servants or cooks after they reached America. As a result, they normally fetched considerably less money than their male counterparts. For example, the men sold by the convict firm Stevenson, Randolph, and Cheston, usually brought in between £10 and £14 a head, while most women sold for between five and nine pounds. James Cheston even offered partial refunds if felons were found to have flaws unknown at the time of sale. Buyers returned four of the 48 female convicts sold by his firm during the years from 1767 to 1775, claiming that the women had venereal disease. This may have been because they had been purchased to work as cooks, and it was feared that they would infect the food that they prepared.[255]

Even with the government paid subsidy for their passage, specialist contractors might anticipate little profit in carrying women, and could neglect to do so where possible. For example, in August 1723, the Common Council of Bristol was forced to pay 10 guineas to secure the pardons of a group of women who had been languishing in the city's jail, at public expense, because a contractor could not be found to take them across the Atlantic. Exactly the same situation arose 20 years later, when a local contractor refused to accept female convicts.[256]

The voyage to America was extremely unpleasant, especially for women. In the early and middle decades of the century some contractors even used slave ships to carry convicts across the Atlantic. About a seventh of them (both men and women) died of disease during the weeks immediately before sailing or on the journey itself. However, mortality rates appear to have been lower amongst females, perhaps just half of the male rate. One experienced merchant-shipper, Duncan Campbell, looking back on his career, attributed this to "their constitutions being less impaired, and to their sobriety".[257] Convicts crossing the Atlantic could expect to be at sea for between six and eight weeks, and would normally be kept in the lower part of the ship, even if it was not a specialist slaver. Many women were reduced or forced into providing sexual services for their ship's crew. Goronwy Owen, a schoolteacher bound for Virginia who traveled on a convict vessel in 1757, noted that every member of the crew had "taken to himself a strumpet from amongst the she-thieves".[258]

---

[255] Lodine-Chaffey, Jennifer (2010) "From Newgate to the New World: A Study of London's Transported Female Convicts, 1718-1775", at www.earlyamerica.com/review.

[256] Coldham, Peter Wilson (1992) *Emigrants in chains,* p.63.

[257] Morgan, Gwenda and Rushton, Peter (2004) *Eighteenth-Century Criminal Transportation: The Formation of the Criminal Atlantic*, p.34.

[258] Lodine-Chaffey, Jennifer (2010) "From Newgate to the New World: A Study

The journey to Australia would be even more arduous than that to America, although government contracts normally stipulated that the ships involved were to be clean and ventilated. The first of them took almost 13 months (over half of which was spent at sea) to reach the island continent.[259] Unfortunately, once out of sight of land, masters often ignored regulations, although the situation was aided, after the disastrous mortality rates experienced by the Second Fleet, by providing that the shipping contractors would receive an extra payment for every convict embarked who also reached Sydney alive. Women continued to enjoy an advantage in mortality rates during the long voyage. For example, of the 568 men on the First Fleet in 1788, 20 died. However, only three of the 191 females making the voyage failed to reach Australia. In 1790 and 1791, the divergence in survival rates was to be very much greater, although men enjoyed a small advantage in 1792.[260]

Conditions for women going to the Antipodes also varied enormously with the ship involved. In one of the most eye-catching voyages, in July 1789, the *Lady Julian,* a three-masted, two-decked, transport sailed from Plymouth for New South Wales, with up to 240 female convicts onboard, their ages ranging from 11 to 68. It was specifically intended that they help populate the new, and overwhelmingly male, colony. Some had infants with them, up to a maximum age of six years. However, as with the Atlantic journey, shortly after the ship departed, most of its crew (about 30 men) took a "wife" from among the convicts. More babies were born during the long journey, including one to 14 year-old Jane Forbes.[261] When it came to harsh conditions, the 1796 voyage of the *Britannia* was particularly bad. Its female convicts were often neck-yoked and kept in chains below decks, a few brief interludes apart, while many were punished for disciplinary infractions by being caned and having their heads shaved. Jenny Blacke was personally beaten by the ship's captain, on her head and shoulders, after she attempted suicide.[262]

---

of London's Transported Female Convicts, 1718-1775", at www.earlyamerica.com/review.

[259] *World (1787)*, March 26, 1789.

[260] Shaw, A.G.L. (1977) *Convicts and the Colonies,* pp.110-111 and p.363.

[261] Rees, Sian (2002) *The Floating Brothel,* pp.107-109.

[262] Campbell, Charles (2001) *The Intolerable Hulks,* p.66.

Premature Return

Few female convicts returned from America, and fewer still from Australia, even after their sentences were complete. Most who did so had outgrown crime. For example, Jean Grey was transported from Newcastle in 1766 for perjury and uttering false money, served her seven years in America, and then returned to her native city and previous occupation of making celebrated mutton pies.[263] Nevertheless, the notorious Jane (or Jenny) Voss, who had been transported for seven years in the middle of the 1670s, waited for her time to elapse before legally returning to England and resuming her criminal career, with fatal results.[264]

Very few women returned prematurely, before their terms had expired. This was a capital offence in its own right. Those who did, like the cross-dressing Sarah Knox from Cumberland, were nearly always highly resourceful individuals. Membership of a professional criminal gang also greatly increased their prospects. Indeed, some women, such as the pickpocket Eleanor Connor, who was convicted in Bristol in 1748, used money from this connection to bribe crewmen on their ship, so that they could flee before it even set sail for America.[265]

In the years between 1735 and 1799, only three females were executed for premature return, one at Tyburn and two in the provinces.[266] Some, of course, would have gone entirely undetected. (Sensible returnees kept away from their native counties, fearing that they would be recognised).[267] Interestingly, both of the provincial cases took place at Coventry, within eighteen months of each other. Thus, Margaret Clarke was hanged there in 1763. A career criminal of almost 60, connected to a gang, it was thought that she had already been transported and returned on two previous occasions (she used many aliases).[268] In December of the following year, Jane Smith met the same fate. She had been charged with several notorious robberies after her return, and was alleged to be a member of the same gang as Clarke.[269]

---

[263] Redfern, Barry (2003) *Shadow of the Gallows: Crime and Criminal Justice in and Around Newcastle Upon Tyne in the Eighteenth Century,* p.87.
[264] Ordinary's Account, 19th December 1684: OA16841219
[265] Morgan, G., and Rushton, P. (2003) "Running Away and Returning Home: The Fate of English Convicts in the Colonies", p.68 and p.75.
[266] www.capitalpunishmentuk.org
[267] Anon (Lover of his country), (1752) *Villain'y Unmask'd* … p.7
[268] *Lloyds Evening Post*, August 8th-10th, 1763.
[269] *St. James's Chronicle or the British Evening Post*, August 9, 1763 - August 11, 1763

Corporal Punishments

A few physical punishments that had been specifically associated with women lingered into the eighteenth century. By the early modern era, the cuckingstool, which allowed an offender to be dunked in a pond or river, was used almost exclusively for females, usually in cases where they had been convicted of 'scolding'. As Blackstone noted, if convicted of this offence, a woman could be placed in an engine of correction called a: "…cucking stool, which in the Saxon language signifies the scolding stool; though now it is frequently corrupted into ducking stool, because the residue of the judgement is, that, when she is so placed therein, she shall be plunged in the water for her punishment".[270] However, although discussed by Blackstone in the 1760s, prosecution for scolding, and use of the cuckingstool, seem to have *largely* (though not entirely) died out in the first half of the eighteenth century (see chapter one).

More significantly, the pillory and stocks were used for both sexes, punishing, *inter alia*, those who committed some lesser frauds, libelled the Crown, gave false testimony, blasphemed in the streets or, in some cases, could not pay minor fines. They involved detention in a public place, the first by the wrists and neck and the second by the ankles.[271] Parishes, like Malden in Surrey, in 1730, were regularly presented at Borough and Quarter Sessions during the first half of the century, for "not having a pair of stocks" in working order, and then inspected until they complied.[272]

A selection of cases is indicative as to how these punishments were used with regard to females. In 1754, for example, a woman sat in the stocks in St. James's, Westminster, for being drunk and using abusive language in public.[273] In 1727, a woman in Bath was pilloried, on the evidence of her maid, for both blasphemy and dancing naked in front of men for small sums of money.[274] In several cases of perjury, a pregnant woman was pilloried for swearing before a Justice that her condition had been occasioned by a man who was, in reality, entirely innocent of the matter.[275] The punishment was also sometimes used for women found guilty of keeping brothels. For example, two of the eight women who were

---

270 Blackstone, William (1769) *Commentaries on the Laws of England*, vol.4, p.169.
271 Misson, Henri (1719) *Memoirs and Observations in his Travels over England*, p.218.
272 Sessions August 19th 1730, Kingston Local History Room, KE 2/2/1-14.
273 *Read's Weekly Journal Or British Gazetteer*, March 9, 1754.
274 *Mist's Weekly Journal*, February 4, 1727.
275 *Flying Post or The Weekly Medley*, March 22, 1729.

convicted of this offence at Quarter Sessions in North Lincolnshire between 1740 and 1780 were sentenced to be pilloried, one for 30 minutes and the other for a full hour. This was only done in the county's towns and cities (in this case Lincoln and Gainsborough).[276] This may have been because public shame and popular hostility were often an implicit part of the punishment, and something that required a significant audience.

Crimes that were viewed harshly by the populace or 'mob' could produce an aggressive response with stones and rubbish being thrown at those being punished. Those that attracted less social opprobrium would usually result in more benign treatment from onlookers. For example, anticipating a harsh reception, the abortionist Eleanor Beare unavailingly tried to hide a specially shaped pewter plate under her headdress, to protect her skull from missiles, prior to undergoing her punishment.[277] By contrast, in 1758 it was noted that Susannah Fleming, who had been pilloried in Newcastle for fortune-telling, was "not molested by the populace". Unfortunately, she fainted in the apparatus and was almost strangled by the resulting pressure on her neck.[278]

Shaming punishments were found throughout eighteenth-century Europe. None in England matched the treatment meted out to Margaret Gibson in Edinburgh in 1728. She had been convicted of theft and was: "…drumm'd through the City in a most disgraceful manner". A board was fixed around her neck from which bells hung and rung as she walked. A false face was also attached to her head, over which a fox's tail was hung.[279]

By the 1760s, three times as many men as women were being pilloried, with the proportion of women falling to only 20 per cent in ensuing decades.[280] After 1816, use of the pillory was restricted to cases of perjury or subornation (persuading someone to commit perjury). It was not used at all after 1830, and the punishment was formally abolished in 1837. Fiscal penalties or short periods of imprisonment were used instead.

---

[276] Davey, B.J. (1994) *Rural Crime in the Eighteenth Century: North Lincolnshire 1740 – 80*, p.104.

[277] Knapp, Andrew and Baldwin, William (1825) *The Newgate Calendar: Comprising Interesting Memoirs of the Most Notorious Characters…*, vol.1, pp.315-316.

[278] Redfern, Barry (2003) *Shadow of the Gallows: Crime and Criminal Justice in and Around Newcastle Upon Tyne in the Eighteenth Century,* pp.86-87.

[279] *Weekly Journal or British Gazetteer*, November 16, 1728.

[280] Devereaux, Simon (2005) "The Abolition of the Burning of Women in England Reconsidered", p.85.

Flogging

Public flogging was the traditional punishment imposed for many offences against morality, some other misdemeanours and, most importantly, petty theft (the only felony not to carry a death sentence if unclergied). Historically, the whipping was carried out either with the convict tied to the back ('arse' or 'tail') of a cart and paraded through the streets while being beaten or, more commonly in rural areas, attached to a stationary post, whether in public or in jail. Of 153 people convicted of theft at the Quarter Sessions in North Lincolnshire between 1740 and 1783, 121 (about 79 per cent) were sentenced to be whipped "until the body be bloody". Only 14 cases resulted in fines. The keepers of the county's various houses of correction normally carried out these beatings, and a standard punishment was about 20 lashes. However, the magistrates varied this according to the gravity of the offence, sometimes specifying fewer lashes, or that the punishment be carried out in private and even, in the case of an elderly woman, that she be "whipp'd gently".[281] Given that women committed many cases of petty theft, they inevitably figured prominently amongst those who were flogged for the crime.

However, whipping was not just imposed after conviction on indictment. When Margaret Mattock from Great Chiverell in Wiltshire was summarily convicted of stealing turnips from an enclosure she was initially sentenced by a local J.P. to be "whipped publicly, not exceeding ten lashes". Fortunately, her victim was the local Rector and, perhaps uncomfortable with such a disposal as a man of the cloth, he forgave her and she escaped punishment. Anne Amor was not so lucky in 1744. Summarily convicted of hedge-breaking, she was ordered to pay a fine of five shillings or be whipped. Unable or unwilling to pay the money, she was flogged the same day.[282] In February 1764, the Reverend Edmund Tew, a Justice in County Durham, noted: "I ordered a woman rogue and vagrant from Shields to be whipped by West Boldon constable and sent her back with a pass".[283]

Until the middle of the eighteenth century, many of the women who received such a disposal were beaten in public. Indeed, this was the 'normal' location for such a punishment. Thus, at the Warwickshire

---

[281] Davey, B.J. (1994) *Rural Crime in the Eighteenth Century: North Lincolnshire 1740 – 80*, pp.101-102

[282] Crittall, Elizabeth (Ed.) (1982) *The Justicing Notebook of William Hunt, 1744-1749*, p.83 and p.32.

[283] Morgan, Gwenda and Rushton, Peter (Eds) (2000) *The Justicing Notebook (1750-64) of Edmund Tew*, p.190

Quarter Sessions in 1691, Margaret Jarrett was found guilty of petty larceny, to the sum of 10d, and was sentenced to be: "...openly whipped upon Saturday in Warwick till her body be bloody".[284] Mary Armsley received the same disposal for stealing a pewter chamber pot in Westminster in 1731.[285] When Elizabeth Rivett was convicted of petty larceny at the Norfolk Assizes in Norwich, in 1736, she, too, was sentenced to a public whipping.[286]

Public beatings, if not conducted at the 'cart's tail', were often carried out outside the door of the local House of Correction or, if a larger audience was desired, in a well-frequented place situated near to where an offence had been committed, such as a market place. For example, Ann Scoffin, who stole a pennyworth of wheat, was held in the House of Correction for a few days before being taken to Barton in Lincolnshire on market day and whipped there. Martha Hand was more fortunate; she was held overnight in a House of Correction and beaten in private for stealing a quantity of bacon. Elizabeth Leaning faired worst of all. She had stolen some cloth from a shop in Barton and was sentenced to be: "...whipped naked from the waiste upwards ty'd to a cart, and whipped publicly in time of full market from the sign of the George to the house of Thomas Sherlock in Barton till her body be bloody".[287] The potential for public indecency inherent in such a bare-breasted flogging, in an increasingly squeamish era, is obvious.

As Martha Hand's case suggests, even early in the century the court might order that a sentence be carried out in private if there were special considerations or circumstances. For example, Catherine Armstrong, who was convicted of petty larceny after stealing a book in 1731, was whipped privately, in prison, on the basis that it was thought to be her first offence and she was evidently a "woman of letters"![288] However, by the middle of the century there were signs that gender alone had a role to play in this decision. For example, at the Surrey Quarter Sessions held at Southwark in 1750, six people were convicted of petty larceny. All were sentenced to be whipped, still the normal penalty for this offence. It was specified that all five of the men involved be beaten in public, two of them on three separate

---

[284] Johnson, H.C. (1964) *Warwick County Records, vol.IX: Quarter session records; Easter, 1690 to Michaelmas, 1696*, p.23.
[285] *Daily Advertiser*, July 13, 1731.
[286] *Country Journal or The Craftsman*, September 4, 1736.
[287] Davey, B.J. (1994) *Rural Crime in the Eighteenth Century: North Lincolnshire 1740 – 80*, pp.101 -102.
[288] *Daily Journal*, January 12, 1731.

occasions. Nevertheless, the only woman so punished, Dorothy Rollings, was "ordered to be whipped privately".[289]

Both judges and magistrates became increasingly reluctant to sentence women to corporal punishment after the 1760s, particularly if it was to be administered in public.[290] Fewer such sentences were passed on women, and where they were, more were conducted in private. Of course, there were exceptions; for example, in January 1774, a woman was sentenced to a public whipping on St. Margaret's Hill.[291] Even so, a general trend can clearly be discerned. In the 1760s, it seems that men and women were still almost equally likely to be whipped through the streets of the capital. By the 1780s, a decade of crisis that saw a surge in male floggings, men were being beaten in public three times as often as a decade or two earlier, but women only a quarter as much. Only one London woman was whipped at the cart's tail in 1786. In 1793, only two women were whipped in the capital, both in private. The year after that, no woman was whipped there at all.[292]

This development was matched in the provinces. Fewer women were beaten and, when they were, it was increasingly done in private. Thus, Elizabeth Juggins, convicted of petty larceny at the Bedford Assizes in July 1788, without any special circumstances being present, was "ordered to be privately whipt".[293] However, the speed with which this process occurred varied across the country. Cornwall seems to have abandoned the public whipping of women in the decade after 1780 (the decline started even as that for men peaked), at about the same time that it largely ceased in the Metropolis, but rather later than was the case for Essex, and a little earlier than in some other counties.[294] When Anne Holdsworth was convicted of larceny at the York Assizes in 1783, she was still sentenced to a public whipping (and two years in a House of Correction).[295]

As a result of these developments, men were being whipped ten times more frequently than women during the 1790s and, by then, the flogging of a woman in public was exceptionally rare. Gender distinctions had

---

[289] *Whitehall Evening Post or London Intelligencer*, January 18, 1750 - January 20, 1750.

[290] Devereaux, Simon (2005) "The Abolition of the Burning of Women in England Reconsidered", pp.83-84.

[291] *Morning Chronicle and London Advertiser*, January 18, 1774.

[292] Devereaux, Simon (2005) "The Abolition Of The Burning Of Women In England Reconsidered", pp.73-98.

[293] *World (1787)*, July 14, 1788.

[294] King, Peter (2006) *Crime and Law in England, 1750-1840,* p.275.

[295] *Public Advertiser*, August 15, 1783.

become fundamental to the punishment. The public flogging of women had, effectively, been abandoned in England for over a decade before it was formally abolished in 1817, though it continued in active use in Scotland until that date. Indeed, the bill to abolish the public whipping of females was brought in by an M.P., General Thornton, who appears to have been motivated by an article in the *Inverness Journal* which described how a young and beautiful woman there had been beaten in the public streets. He felt that spectacles such as this were unlikely to improve public morals, and noted that the punishment had been "partially abolished in England". He proposed that it be ended entirely, by commuting it to a maximum of three months' hard labour in a workhouse.[296] Women were still being whipped in the streets of Dumfries and Perth as the bill received its third reading.[297]

The private flogging of women had also been effectively abandoned for several years before it was formally abolished in 1820. In that year, the M.P. Sir George Chetwynd introduced a bill to abolish the whipping of female offenders in "any case whatever". He thought that it was objectionable even behind closed doors, especially as it gave enormous scope to the jailer as to how vigorously to administer the punishment. However, public whipping continued to be employed against men for several years after this date, petering out in the 1830s, and only formally being abolished in 1868. This change in judicial attitudes reflected a wider change in popular mores with regard to women, their bodies, and their general role in society. Sir George Chetwynd was expressing almost universal 'educated' opinion when suggesting, in 1820, that "nothing could be more revolting to the feelings" than beating women in public.[298]

By the end of the eighteenth century, women normally received short custodial sentences for petty larceny, instead of being beaten. For example, when Mary Crack was convicted of the crime at the Bury Quarter Sessions in 1800 she was sentenced to three months' imprisonment in the local House of Correction.[299] At about the same time, at the Newcastle Quarter Sessions, three other women convicted of petty larceny were sentenced to three (one case) and six months (two cases) in a House of Correction.[300]

---

[296] HANSARD 1803–2005, HC Deb 10 June 1817 vol 36 c932.
[297] *The Times*, June 27, 1817, p.3
[298] HANSARD 1803–2005, HC Deb 29 June 1820 vol 2 cc105-6, c105
[299] *The Ipswich Journal*, January 25, 1800.
[300] *Courier and Evening Gazette*, July 23, 1799.

Women and Custody

Confinement in mainstream eighteenth-century prisons was primarily a means of securing those awaiting trial or, after conviction, holding those awaiting execution or transportation. It was not used very much as a punishment in its own right, in most of the country, until the second half of the era. However, the very early growth in imprisonment in the North of England, well before the publication of the classic Enlightenment treatises on punishment (Beccaria etc.), seems to have been something of an exception to this general pattern. It may have been partly linked to the large numbers of women convicted in some parts of the region, combined with a considerable reluctance to hang or transport them for a first offence, and a desire to keep their punishment under local control. Instead, Houses of Correction, which (in theory at least) put their prisoners to hard labour, were often used for the punishment of minor (especially female) thieves convicted at Quarter Sessions.[301] For a late example of this can be considered the case of Margaret Hill, who was convicted of stealing a piece of calico from a shop in Warrington, which was apparently charged as simple larceny (rather than under the 1699 Act), at the Lancaster Assizes in 1787. She was sentenced to six months in the local House of Correction.[302]

Nationally, the number of penal sentences of imprisonment increased steadily during the second half of the era, and quite quickly towards its end, especially for women. As a result, in the period from 1780 to 1840, more than three quarters of the women who were found guilty of property offences on the Home Circuit received some form of penal imprisonment.[303] In this, they often experienced better disposals than their male counterparts. For example, in 1797, at the Surrey Assizes, Jane Smith received a year's imprisonment for stealing a cotton gown.[304] Even so, long sentences of imprisonment remained uncommon.

Female prisoners made up a smaller proportion of inmates in provincial jails than they did in the Metropolis, not least because fewer women offended/were prosecuted outside London when compared to men, especially for serious offences that did not attract bail. In early 1784, for

---

[301] Morgan, Gwenda and Rushton, Peter (1998) *Rogues, Thieves and the Rule of Law,* p.173 and p.178.

[302] *World and Fashionable Advertiser*, September 1, 1787.

[303] King, Peter (1999) "Gender, crime and justice in late eighteenth-and early nineteenth-century England", pp.165-195, King, Peter (2006) *Crime and Law in England, 1750-1840,* pp.172-175.

[304] *True Briton (1793),* March 30, 1797.

example, Elizabeth Nokes, accused of infanticide, was the only woman amongst 32 prisoners held in Northampton jail pending the county's Assizes.[305] Outside London, with its large, often purpose-built jails, prisons were usually fairly improvised. Frequently, they might be accommodated in an old castle, such as those at Oxford and York, or a similar building. Conditions were normally cramped, uncomfortable, and extremely unhygienic; food was of very poor quality and the amount provided often inadequate; mortality rates were correspondingly high. Vermin and lice were endemic. The night before her execution, a turnkey advised Elizabeth Waldron to supplement her straw bed with that of another woman, who had just been sent to the Devonshire Bridewell. However: "She declined his advice, expressing her fears of catching the itch, knowing that woman to be infected with it".[306]

Towards the end of the period, attempts were made to improve the lot of incarcerated women. However, the British Ladies' Society for Promoting the Reformation of Female Prisoners was not established until 1821, albeit unifying several slightly earlier societies of a similar type. In its first year, it proposed the introduction of women prison officers to control female inmates, approving the appointment two years earlier of a woman as a turnkey in Liverpool Gaol. Their pressure led to the Gaols Act of 1823 (4th Geo. IV cap.64) requiring, *inter alia*, that female prisoners nationwide be attended by women. It was not, at first, universally followed, not least because there were no inspectors to enforce it.[307] Nevertheless, by the end of the period, female quarters in provincial prisons were slowly improving, in some areas at least. On a visit to the County Jail in York Castle in 1818, Elizabeth Fry and Joseph Gurney noticed that, whatever the prison's other problems, the women's area was (uniquely for the institution) kept in a "state of cleanliness and order". Bedding and work was provided and the female dayroom was comfortable if poorly lit.[308]

Although sometimes used to accommodate felons during the eighteenth century, and so serving as auxiliary jails, the country's Bridewells and Houses of Correction had originally been designed as short-term carceral institutions for minor offenders and prostitutes. As a result, and unlike

---

[305] Northampton Record Office Ref: X5402/27

[306] Anon, (1782) *Character and dying behaviour of the two murderers, executed at Heavitree gallows, Monday, March 25, 1782*, pp.1-2.

[307] Anon, (1840) *A Concise View of the Origin and Progress of the British Ladies: Society for Promoting the Reformation of Female Prisoners*, p.11.

[308] Gurney, Joseph (1819) *Notes on a visit made to some of the prisons in Scotland and the north of England*, p.5

other jails, traditionally a much higher proportion of their inmates were female, and this sometimes also influenced their use as stand-in prisons. Thus, Mary Barber, accused of stealing a loaf, was kept in the St. Albans House of Correction pending her trial at Quarter Sessions.[309] Even so, provincial Houses of Correction did not normally contain the proportion of females (often two thirds) that was found in their Middlesex counterparts. For example, in the Denbighshire establishment, the division of inmates seems to have been fairly even between men and women. In part, this was because of the markedly smaller number of prostitutes to be found in the area, compared to London, although in other respects the usual mixture of women accused of bastardy, vagrancy, etc., was present.[310]

Although they had reformist origins, most Houses of Correction were almost as run down as ordinary county jails by the early 1700s.[311] In the 1750s, Justices inspecting the establishment in Durham noted that there was very little segregation between the sexes and almost no work provided for the inmates.[312] However, a wave of rebuilding towards the end of the century saw a significant improvement in conditions. For example, the Bridewell for Kingston on Thames was rebuilt in 1775 as a generally commodious building, albeit lacking an infirmary. It had two wards, "quite distinct buildings", for men and women, allowing effective segregation of the sexes. Each had a separate court, workshops and pumps. Each ward had two main rooms. Those in the women's division were 15 feet square and nine feet high. Their windows were shuttered, but there was no glass in them, and bedding was still not provided by the authorities. Inmates received 14 or 15 ounces of bread a day.[313]

Whether they were jails or Bridewells, security was often not very high, encouraging the fettering of prisoners, including females, who were viewed as a high escape risk. Several women who were not fettered, and some who were, made successful breakouts. For example, the notorious criminal Moll Harvey (she went by many aliases) appears to have been an escapologist in the tradition of Jack Sheppard. In January 1731, she broke out of the King's Bench Prison, and was at liberty for three weeks before

---

[309] Dean, David (Ed.) (1991) *St. Albans Quarter Sessions rolls, 1784-1820,* p.5 and p.96.

[310] Howard, Sharon (2003) *Crime, Communities And Authority In Early Modern Wales: Denbighshire, 1660-1730*, p.45.

[311] Morris, N. and Rothman, D. J. (Eds) (1995) *The Oxford History of the Prison*, p.329.

[312] Morgan, Gwenda and Rushton, Peter (1998) *Rogues, Thieves and the Rule of Law,* p.183.

[313] Howard, John, (1777) *The state of the prisons in England and Wales*, p.237.

being recaptured by the jail's Marshal.[314] In June of the same year, she escaped from the New Gaol in Southwark, taking her imprisoned sister with her.[315] In Newcastle, in 1768, a woman confined in the city's Bridge Tower Gaol for minor crimes managed to get free from her irons, and crawled through a seven inch space in a window, from where she leapt into the River Tyne below, before surfacing and swimming until picked up by a prison boat.[316] In March 1800, the 38-year-old horse-thief Margaret Catchpole used a clothesline to escape from Ipswich Gaol by scaling a 22-foot wall. She was recaptured living rough on coastal marshes, dressed as a sailor in clothes that she had made from prison bed-sheets. So convincing were these that she "might be taken for a smart young man".[317]

Conclusion

During the eighteenth century women were normally favoured when it came to decisions to prosecute, as defendants when it came to trial outcomes, and as convicts when it came to punishment. This was more marked in provincial England than in the Metropolis. Overall, they were more likely to be acquitted outright, convicted of a lesser offence, and reprieved if they were capitally convicted, than were men. Their forensic advantage was most marked in draconian, potentially capital, property crimes, such as robbery, and least in evidence in routine, low level, offences, such as minor cases of theft. However, this was always purely a matter of statistical probability. Many women were dealt with very harshly and received no indulgence at all from the system.

The discrepancy between the genders occurred for a number of reasons, some of them entirely rational. In the provinces at least, they *may* have been slightly less hardened criminals on *average* than their male counterparts, committing less serious examples of the crimes for which they were convicted, taking more peripheral roles in such offences, and having superior previous characters. Frequently, and much more pertinently, they had far better mitigation than their male equivalents. Married women also enjoyed the declining legal benefits of *feme covert*, at least to some extent.

Nevertheless, these factors do not, on their own, fully account for the apparent leniency manifested by judges and juries. Women received

---

[314] *Daily Journal*, February 8, 1731.
[315] *Daily Journal*, June 17, 1731.
[316] Redfern, Barry (2003) *Shadow of the Gallows: Crime and Criminal Justice in and Around Newcastle Upon Tyne in the Eighteenth Century*, p.58.
[317] *The Ipswich Journal*, April 5, 1800.

benign outcomes because the male actors in the criminal justice process were predisposed to be sympathetic towards them. This was not primarily the result of 'chivalry' (though it may have played a role) but because they saw women as less of a threat. Female offenders were fewer in number and much less prone to serious violence. However, where they were seen to threaten the natural gender and social order, whether it was by murdering their husbands or simply by being obstreperous and uncouth, women might be subject to draconian and sometimes rather theatrical punishments, such as immolation or ducking.

Chapter Three

Homicide and Assault

Introduction

This chapter will consider the nature and incidence of female-perpetrated violence, both lethal and non-lethal, in provincial England. The former is easier to address than the latter, because murder is an offence with a historically high level of being reported and recorded. In eighteenth-century England, the prosecution process was greatly assisted by the coroner's active involvement in homicide investigations. It usually ensured a relatively thorough examination of obviously suspicious deaths. Where necessary, and unlike trial juries, if coroners' juries were initially unable to reach a verdict they could sit several times on a body and adjourn to hear fresh evidence, as they did with a woman whose corpse was found down a well in Southwark in 1736.[1] In 1780, Catherine Parker's trial in Salisbury for killing a child apprentice followed a particularly lengthy inquest presided over by the experienced coroner John Dexter, in which the jury unanimously found her (and her husband) responsible for murder.[2] The inquest lasted for three days and examined a "vast number of witnesses".[3]

Of course, institutional restraints and limited forensic abilities meant that coroners' inquests were not so effective at identifying very subtle killings, many of which must have passed entirely unnoticed. In 1780, for example, a sixty-year old woman from Bodmin in Cornwall was arrested after confessing to the previously unsuspected murder of her son, 30 years earlier.[4] Numerous suspicious deaths were probably never investigated. Even in the following century, a close examination of deaths reported in Victorian newspapers as 'mysterious' or 'suspicious' suggests that some,

---

[1] *Read's Weekly Journal Or British Gazetteer*, August 14, 1736.

[2] *Gazetteer and New Daily Advertiser*, March 2, 1780.

[3] *St. James's Chronicle or the British Evening Post*, March 4, 1780 - March 7, 1780.

[4] *Gazetteer and New Daily Advertiser*, March 1, 1780.

at least, were cases of murder, even though they did not produce formal investigations, let alone prosecutions. Deaths amongst certain groups, such as infants, foreigners, and female partners in violent heterosexual relationships, were particularly unlikely to be properly scrutinized by the authorities.[5]

Nevertheless, there is little reason to believe that in the eighteenth century killings perpetrated by women were more likely to be overlooked than those carried out by men, cases of poisoning, perhaps, apart. By the 1700s, government (whether national or local) was also prepared to fund prosecution by counsel in many murder cases, encouraging a modicum of professionalism when it came to bringing cases to court and preparing them for trial.[6] Thus, in 1738, a Surrey parish paid for the prosecution of one of its own (female) nurses who, it was alleged, had beaten a poor patient to death.[7]

Murder, legally the most heinous form of homicide, was also a crime for which a reprieve was only rarely granted, even to women (though a tiny number of individuals did receive clemency). As a result, executions are very roughly indicative of convictions, especially as, after 1752, there were strict time restraints on how long could elapse between conviction and death, reducing the risk of the condemned person dying in jail before execution. Additionally, executions were major events, and so can be calculated quite accurately due to their attendant publicity.

These factors, taken together, make counting homicide indictments, convictions and punishments greatly superior to measuring those for assault, a crime that was often ignored, even when quite serious, or dealt with informally. It was also indicted more frequently towards the end of the century than it had been at its start, as attitudes to non-lethal violence changed.

Women and Violence

Homicide (in all its forms) was (and is) at the apex of a much more broadly based pyramid of lesser offences of violence. It is hard not to coin what is now almost a cliché for the eighteenth century. It was a quick-

---

[5] Archer, John E. (2000) "Mysterious And Suspicious Deaths: Missing Homicides In North-West England (1850-1900)", pp.45-63.

[6] For the growth of prosecuting counsel generally see Langbein, John (2003) *The Origins of Adversary Criminal Trial*, pp.146-147.

[7] Anon, (1738) *The Proceedings at the Assizes for the County of Surry, held at Guildford, ... On Thursday the 16th, Friday the 17th, Saturday the 18th, Monday the 20th, and Tuesday the 21st March, 1738*, p.20.

tempered society, often characterised by a general 'prickliness', in which verbal abuse swiftly turned into violence, and where pursuing arguments with fists was a widely accepted method of conflict resolution. In 1782, a visiting German cleric, Charles Moritz, making a tour to Darbyshire, noted that when two Englishmen quarrelled the argument was often decided by actions rather than words: "Their anger seems to overpower their utterance, and can vent only by coming to blows".[8]

This culture affected women as well as men, at least to some degree. For example, nearly 20 per cent of wives who were assaulted by their husbands in Portsmouth between 1696 and 1781, and who took some form of action against their spouses in the local sessions, had themselves assaulted other people on one or more occasions and been the subject of legal proceedings of a similar description.[9]

Low-level violence in particular appears to have been a far more common form of social 'interaction' than it is today. Until late in the century, assaults of all but the most serious kind were frequently viewed as quasi-civil matters, rather than the province of deterrent criminal punishment. However, as this also suggests, recourse to violence was already in gradual decline, the era being a transitional period between early modern and modern attitudes to physical confrontation.

Inevitably, women were often the victims of this sort of behaviour, which could have tragic results. For example, at the Bristol Assizes in 1735, Captain James Newth, who ran an alehouse with his wife, was convicted of murdering her after she complained about customers creating a disturbance. He struck her with a cribbage board and then viciously stamped on her.[10] However, many women also perpetrated such violence, even though it was considered to be 'unfeminine'. Reality did not necessarily accord with social theory.[11] Thus, Isabel Turner, like Mrs Newth the wife of an alehouse-keeper, personally assaulted William Watson, a Sunderland constable, while he was attending her premises in the execution of his duty.[12] Indeed, this was a not uncommon scenario. Working women seem to have been particularly prone to using violence

---

[8] Moritz, Charles P. (1797) *Travels in England in 1782,* 2nd edn., p.242.

[9] Warner, Jessica, and Lunny, Allyson (2003) "Marital Violence In A Martial Town: Husbands And Wives In Early Modern Portsmouth, 1653-1781", pp.258-276.

[10] *General Evening Post*, September 13, 1735 - September 16, 1735.

[11] Walker, Garthine (2003) *Crime, Gender and Social Order in Early Modern England*, p.77.

[12] Morgan, Gwenda and Rushton, Peter (Eds) (2000) *The Justicing Notebook (1750-64) of Edmund Tew,* p.57.

against minor officials who sought to interfere in their (or their husbands') businesses.

In 1759, a lawyer claimed that the: "…spirit of an Amazon is not frequent among English women".[13] This was not entirely accurate. Certainly, bellicosity was less common than it was amongst men. This was an almost universal phenomenon in eighteenth-century Europe, as it has been in other ages. On a very generalised basis, women normally made up between 10 and 20 per cent of those people formally prosecuted for crimes of violence during the early modern era in Europe.[14] This is in keeping with longer historical trends. Thus, a series of estimates for the percentage of violent offenders who are female, taken from the eight centuries from 1200 to 2000, suggests that the proportion of women committing homicide (excluding infanticide), assault, or robbery has hardly ever risen above 15 per cent and typically ranged between 5 and 12 per cent. Interestingly, one glaring exception (completely out of step with most other places and times) was early eighteenth-century Stockholm, where 45 percent of homicide perpetrators and 41 percent of those who committed assault were women. These have been described as the highest female participation rates in serious violent crime found anywhere in the world. A number of possible explanations for this phenomenon have been advanced, including a serious demographic imbalance in the city at this time.[15]

Nevertheless, the figures for non-lethal violence amongst women probably underestimate its incidence. Throughout eighteenth-century Europe the judicial process appears to have been less concerned about low-level female violence, especially when it was intra-gender (as it often was), leading to it being under-reported.[16] This was not a new phenomenon. One English thirteenth-century court manual even noted that "mere squabbles amongst boys and old women" did not need to be sent to the Hundred Court. This equated some adult females with children.[17] Such violence could easily be dismissed as a manifestation of sexual pathology.

There were other factors behind the low figures returned for female defendants in cases of violence. Frequently, and as with some other crimes examined in this study, where husbands and wives were involved in an assault, only the men were prosecuted, even if the wife had taken a

---

[13] Anon (By a gentleman of the law), (1759) *The Case of Mary Edmondson*, p.23

[14] Walker, Garthine (2003) *Crime, Gender and Social Order in Early Modern England*, p.25 and p.75.

[15] Eisner, Manuel (2003) "Long-Term Historical Trends in Violent Crime", p.109 and p.112.

[16] Ruff, Julius (2001) *Violence in Early Modern Europe 1500-1800*, p.125.

[17] Dean, Trevor (2001) *Crime in Medieval Europe 1200-1550*, p.78.

moderately active role in the affair in support of her spouse. Where men were the victims of women -and five per cent of all assaults to come before the Portsmouth Borough Sessions in the eighteenth century involved this scenario- there must also have been acute embarrassment about taking formal action, encouraging matters to be quietly passed over or not pursued. For example, in 1727, at the Devon Assizes, Mary Hadden was released by proclamation (the normal procedure where no one appeared to prosecute), having been committed for "assaulting and beating her husband".[18] Certainly, in the domestic environment, many men who were themselves accused of using violence against their wives, whether in the Church or secular courts, would claim that it had been a restrained and proportionate response to their spouses' own aggression. For example, in 1737, John Head had a heated argument while in bed with his wife, over the treatment of one of their servants. She allegedly challenged him to a fight and then tried to throttle him, forcing him to respond by "gently throwing her on the floor".[19] Although many such claims were probably spurious, or greatly exaggerated, some, at least, were undoubtedly true.

The incidence of female involvement in non-lethal violence differs greatly across England, varying by area, court, and with what is taken as its measure. Very few assault cases (whether male or female) went to the Assizes during the eighteenth century. Until 1803, most assaults were classified as misdemeanours, even if extremely serious, a handful of rather recondite and technical crimes apart. This meant that, if prosecuted on indictment, assaults were usually heard at the lower jury court. Thus, at the Michaelmas Quarter Sessions for Warwickshire, in 1691, Mary Flewellen, the wife of a Warwick tailor, was convicted and fined for "assault and battery on Edward Mayo".[20]

However, using all cases that were prosecuted before a jury on indictment, whether as misdemeanours or (much more rarely) felonies and at *whatever* forum (Assizes or Quarter Sessions), as a measure of female violence still produces very small totals. In Essex, for example, women accounted for just eight per cent of defendants in assault trials indicted at that county's Quarter Sessions during four sample periods between 1748 and 1821.[21]

[18] *Parker's Penny Post*, April 10, 1727.

[19] Foyster, Elizabeth (2005) *Marital Violence: An English Family History, 1660-1857*, p.104.

[20] Johnson, H.C. (1964) *Warwick County Records, vol.IX: Quarter session records; Easter, 1690 to Michaelmas, 1696*, p.38.

[21] King, Peter (1996) "Punishing Assault: The Transformation of Attitudes in the English Courts", p.49.

Nevertheless, if all matters initially brought before the Borough Sessions in eighteenth-century Portsmouth, by any mechanism, are considered, rather than those that produced a jury trial, a somewhat different profile emerges. Portsmouth was a very violent town, far more so than most equivalent sized conurbations of the time, perhaps unsurprisingly given that it was an important port, contained a major naval dockyard, and was also possessed of a transient military garrison. More remarkably, its women seem to have been disproportionately prone to violence, albeit still firmly in a minority of offenders. Thus, at least 2,939 females were accused of assault, in whatever form, compared to 6,258 men, at Portsmouth's Sessions between 1653 and 1781. These are taken from 7,591 cases reported to the town's magistrates (most records are preserved after 1696, but there are significant gaps beforehand). As a result, just over 31 per cent of the total number of those accused of assault, of all types, were female. This is a significantly higher percentage than those reported for most other towns in eighteenth-century England and also by historical standards. Why this should have been the case is debatable, though it echoes Stockholm to some degree. Perhaps, in a very 'rough' town, some of the differences between the genders became blurred.[22]

Female assaults in Portsmouth covered a wide range of aggressive actions, from verbal threats or insults to using a potentially deadly weapon. Nevertheless, most of it was not at the trivial end of the scale. Nearly three-quarters of the women involved had physically kicked, punched, pushed or hit, rather than merely threatened, their adversaries, some of whom were left severely bloodied. For example, in 1749, Callaghan McCarty swore that Catherine Cody's assault had entailed giving him: "…several blows with her fist and tearing his clothes and striking his face so that it is bruised". A decade later, Michael Wade claimed that Elizabeth Brazeldene and Rose Lane beat him in a: "…violent manner and hurt and bruised him very much on his face and made his nose bleed". Both of these examples came from some 299 cases of female on male assault, although easily the most common scenario for violent women was female on female, with 1,690 cases recorded. (Participation in male and female combinations made up the balance). These must be compared to 2,666 cases of male-on-male assault, which was the most frequent single scenario found in the town. (Some assaults involved multiple participants).[23] It should be noted that the predominance

---

[22] Warner, Jessica et al (2005) "Women Behaving Badly: Gender and Aggression in a Military Town, 1653–1781", pp.289-298.

[23] Warner, Jessica et al (2005) "Women Behaving Badly: Gender and Aggression in a Military Town, 1653–1781", pp.289-298.

of female on female violence was also a normal pattern on indictment. Thus, at the Quarter Sessions for Denbighshire between 1660 and 1730, three-quarters of women indicted for assault had female victims; in those cases that were indicted at Great Sessions (the Welsh equivalent of the Assizes), the proportion dropped slightly, but was still 69 per cent.[24]

As the figures for Portsmouth suggest, the great majority of eighteenth-century assaults were resolved without going for trial on indictment, whether formally or informally, especially before the final decades of the era. This makes 'counting and comparing' indictment rates of limited value; indeed, most cases did not even result in the alleged perpetrator entering into a recognisance to appear at the next Quarter Sessions, let alone facing a jury trial there.[25]

Informal Settlements and Female Assault

Many provincial cases of assault left no formal record at all (unlike those considered for Portsmouth). Instead, the Justices' notebooks of the era suggest that magistrates would often supervise an informal settlement between complainant and suspect, sometimes involving a small payment of money in compensation and a verbal reprimand. Such resolutions were particularly common when it came to women. For example, when Hannah Gye, from Urchfont in Wiltshire, complained to her local magistrate that four other women, from the same parish, had assaulted her, he issued a warrant for their arrest. However: "Upon the parties appearing before me, they came to an agreement". No formal action was taken. When Sarah Oram accused Mary Jones of assault, it did not even reach the same magistrate. After he issued a warrant for Mary's arrest: "They agreed it before some neighbours without coming before me".[26]

Further north, in County Durham, the Reverend Edmund Tew, a local J.P., also dealt with numerous obstreperous women in this manner. In March 1764, for example, after he granted a special warrant against Isabel Haft from Shields for beating Ann Hall, the dispute was "agreed". The following month, Ann Adams of Monk Wearmouth, who had been arrested for assaulting Elizabeth Smith, also "agreed the matter". Some of these cases involved significant injury. Esther Woods agreed an assault in

---

[24] Howard, Sharon (2003) *Crime, Communities And Authority In Early Modern Wales: Denbighshire, 1660-1730*, p.83

[25] Morgan, Gwenda and Rushton, Peter (2003) "The Magistrate, the community and the maintenance of an orderly society in eighteenth-century England", p.68.

[26] Crittall, Elizabeth (Ed.) (1982) *The Justicing Notebook of William Hunt, 1744-1749*, p.41 and p.51.

which she had badly bruised Elizabeth Hayton and then knocked out one of her teeth. The sums paid over were usually quite modest, normally just a few shillings, and are often not recorded. However, in 1758, when Elizabeth Robson from Sunderland cut the nose and lip of Jane Newton, the matter was "agreed at 16s", a not insignificant sum.[27]

The Surrey J.P. Richard Wyatt, working in the 1770s, was, it *seems*, a little more cautious in this respect. There are far fewer mentions of settlements in his diary, although many assaults appear to go no further and *may* have been agreed in this manner but not recorded. Others resulted in low-level formal action. For example, in 1774 two labourers' wives attacked Ann Sussex, who complained to the J.P. Wyatt bound over two men, presumably friends or relatives of the women, in recognisances of £20 each for their "good behaviour" for a year. The money would be forfeit if they re-offended.[28] Attitudes towards informal settlements may have been slowly changing by then.

Female Fighting Styles

When it comes to non-lethal violence, some traditional stereotypes for combative female behaviour have an element of statistical support, provided it is always remembered that they are not representative of all such conflicts. There were 'styles' of fighting disproportionately associated with one or other gender. For example, an examination of assault cases in eighteenth-century Portsmouth suggests that scratching was a tactic that was primarily employed by women, especially when they were pitted against other females, perhaps in part because their nails were sometimes a little longer than those of men (most of whom were manual workers). Only seven of the 44 people accused of scratching in the court records were male, and only nine of their victims were men. An example of the latter situation occurred in 1763, when William Fosbrooke accused Anne Carrick of "scratching his face and making him bloody". Biting was another tactic favoured by women, and again this was especially the case when they were fighting other females. Of the 38 people accused of biting in the town, only 10 were men, and only 11 victims of biting were male. There were also differences between what parts of the anatomy the sexes bit. Women typically went for hands, while men bit faces.[29]

---

[27] Morgan, Gwenda and Rushton, Peter (Eds) (2000) *The Justicing Notebook (1750-64) of Edmund Tew,* p.92, and pp.192-197.

[28] Silverthorne, Elizabeth (Ed.) (1978) *The Deposition Book of Richard Wyatt JP, 1767-1776*, p.46.

[29] Warner, Jessica et al (2005) "Women Behaving Badly: Gender and Aggression

The throwing of excrement (usually the contents of a chamberpot) also seems to have been a 'weapon' that was primarily employed by women, and was normally used against other females. In Portsmouth, six assailants who threw human or dog excrement were women, and just three were men. Seven of the ten 'victims' of this sort of attack were women (two were children, and only one was an adult man). In no case did a man use excrement in a fight with another male.[30] Similarly, in Devon, in 1747, Katherine Atkey threw a pot full of urine and excrement at Jane Bond, while the following year Elizabeth Biley and another woman cast "great quantities of human excrements and other filth" over Miriam Banfield.[31]

Of course, excrement, though extremely unpleasant and humiliating, was unlikely to occasion injury, while scratching would rarely effect more than a minor wound. The use of implements as weapons was likely to make injuries very much worse. There were differences between the sexes in this regard as well. These were largely dependent on what was likely to come to hand. In Portsmouth, men were more associated with work tools, such as shovels, hammers and horsewhips, and women with household implements such as brooms. Similarly, when eighteenth-century women 'battered' their husbands, they often had recourse to domestic utensils, such as pokers, coal-shovels, ladles and even the proverbial rolling pin.[32]

The small female participation in homicide and indictable assaults, when compared to their more extensive involvement in the minor cases dealt with summarily or by recognizance (rather than on indictment) at Quarter Sessions, suggests that low-level female violence was less prone to escalating to lethal or very serious levels than that between men. Words may have turned into slaps and blows, but they more rarely led on to the use of heavy blunt instruments, let alone blades. There were probably numerous reasons for this, physical, cultural, and situational. Women were less likely than men to be intoxicated or carrying a knife, let alone a sword, in public space. Less turned on their public reputation for fighting prowess, though, as Portsmouth shows, this was certainly not entirely absent. Their smaller size meant they were more likely to be subjected to (often male) 'pacifiers' and physically separated before matters got 'out of hand' than were fighting men.

---

in a Military Town, 1653–1781", pp.289-298.

[30] Warner, Jessica et al (2005) "Women Behaving Badly: Gender and Aggression in a Military Town, 1653–1781", pp.289-298.

[31] Williams, Amy (2000) *The Criminality Of Women In The 18th Century In The South West Of England*, p.165.

[32] Foyster, Elizabeth (2005) *Marital Violence: An English Family History, 1660-1857*, p.103.

Homicide

As in many other eras, people in eighteenth-century England were fascinated by the murderess, the very idea exciting popular curiosity and figuring in much contemporary literature.[33] Then, as now, some women were capable of the most appalling violence and brutality. It would be easy to go through the records and literature, identify a dozen of the most egregious examples of female-perpetrated killings, in which ferocious or sadistic violence had been employed, and then to argue that contemporary (and modern) portrayals that suggest that the era's females were markedly less violent than men, were (and are) hugely exaggerated.

For an example of such women can be considered Margaret Osgood, who was executed at Kingston on Thames in 1681 for hacking her drunken, spendthrift, spouse to death with a hatchet while he slept. She first struck him on the forehead with a blow that: "…entered his skull half an inch; with that not being satisfied she gave him two mortal wounds, besides one which slit his nose, and another under the ears about an inch deep, nay so far was she transported with revenge and Hellish rage that whilst he extended his dying hands for mercy she slit one of them to the wrist". As he lay mortally wounded in a welter of blood she strangled him with a length of whipcord.[34] In a Metropolitan context can be considered the girlfriend of a married man who stuck red hot knitting-needles up his three year-old son's "fundament" until he died, so that a post-mortem revealed that the child's "Ureter were [sic] Cauteriz'd".[35]

However, everything turns on numbers. When these are 'crunched' it can be seen that women, both provincial and Metropolitan, were very much less likely to kill than men, provided that newborn babies (which would greatly boost their total) are ignored. This chapter will not consider neonatal infanticide, although this was the most common single form of homicide amongst women. For example, three of the six cases of murder heard at the Lincoln Assizes between 1771 and 1779 involved mothers killing their newborn babies.[36] Nevertheless, the crime was highly singular in its circumstances and often tried pursuant to special laws until 1803. It

---

[33] Saxton, Kirsten T. (2009) *Narratives of Women and Murder in England, 1680-1760,* p.1.

[34] Anon, (1681) *The True narrative of the confession and execution of the prisoners at Kingstone-upon-Thames, on Wednesday the 16th of this instant March*, pp.1-2.

[35] *The London Post,* July 3-5, 1700.

[36] Davey, B.J. (1994) *Rural Crime in the Eighteenth Century: North Lincolnshire 1740 – 80*, p.10.

is examined in the next chapter.

There were differences other than that of simple incidence between male and female homicides. As will be seen, women were not only much less likely than men to kill, but they were, *proportionately*, more likely to kill intimates, whether related by blood, marriage, or social bonds, and to do so in private rather than in public. When it came to killings perpetrated with a degree of premeditation, rather than in a heated quarrel, the disparity between male and female murders also falls significantly; the proportion of female homicides that were considered to be cases of manslaughter was very small when compared to that of men.

Incidence of Female Homicide

In Surrey, between 1660 and 1800, and ignoring cases of infanticide, just 19 women were prosecuted for murder as principals (rather than accessories) to a jury verdict, compared to 233 men (i.e. nine per cent of the total). Similarly, in Sussex, it seems that women constituted just 13 per cent of prosecuted perpetrators in homicide cases during the same period.[37] Outside the South East the pattern was the same. There were only 59 entries for female-perpetrated homicide in the gaol books in four counties of the Western Circuit (Devon, Somerset, Cornwall and Dorset) between 1735 and 1785. This constitutes an average of just one for each county every four years.[38] Similarly, although a quarter of the principals in homicide cases for Denbighshire in Wales at this time were women, more than half of these cases were for infanticide, again producing a female share of 'normal' murders of a little over ten per cent.

Outside the Metropolis, about 90 women were executed in the whole of England and Wales for murder and petty treason between 1735 and 1799. To put this into a local perspective, during the same period, 17 men were hanged for murder in Norfolk alone, while Rebecca Howard, a spinster who was executed for drowning her five-week-old baby, was the only woman in that county to meet the same fate.[39] Given that murder cases were investigated quite thoroughly, these figures are significant. They might suggest that there was not necessarily a 'dark figure' of unreported female crime for other serious violent offences that was vastly

---

[37] Beattie, John (1986) *Crime and the Courts in England 1660-1800,* p.437.

[38] Williams, Amy (2000) *The Criminality Of Women In The 18th Century In The South West Of England*, p.176.

[39] www.capitalpunishmentuk.org/norfolk.html; *True Briton (1793)*, September 12, 1796.

greater than the equivalent figure for men (both of them were undoubtedly very substantial by modern standards).

It should be noted that there was nothing new in this eighteenth-century divergence in male and female homicide rates, and it has been confirmed by subsequent experience. Historically, women rarely constitute more than 15 per cent of those who commit murder (ignoring infanticide), with an average of between seven and 12 per cent being fairly common. It has also been argued that this particular phenomenon has been: "...remarkably stable since the thirteenth century".[40] Certainly, in the 1200s, just 10 per cent of English homicide defendants were female.[41] Similarly, the number of women convicted for a homicide offence in modern England is about 10 per cent of all killings.[42]

However, such a pattern was not quite universal, even in the eighteenth-century British Isles. One recent study of violent women in lowland Scotland, based on the records of the Justiciary Court there between 1750 and 1815, suggests that they were "unusually bloodthirsty" by international comparison, and rather more aggressive than those found south of the border. During this period, 21 per cent of murder cases (broadly construed) conducted there, that is 57 out of 270 indictments, were brought against women. This is significantly (though not enormously) higher than most figures found in England.[43] Welsh women *may* have fallen between the English and Scottish female homicide rates, perhaps suggesting social or cultural factors that influenced homicide rates and that were operative in the 'Celtic fringe' at this time, though much more work is needed on this topic before firm conclusions can be drawn.[44]

The almost universal nature of women's relatively low involvement in serious violent crime, especially murder, suggests that biology (physical size, the presence of testosterone, etc.) plays a significant role in the process. Some modern psychologists have even identified an evolutionary process that has led to females being (on *average*) more risk averse than men. It is suggested that because, historically, a mother's presence was more critical to her offspring's survival, and so her own reproductive success, natural selection encouraged a genetic predilection to avoiding

[40] Muchembled, Robert (2012) *A History of Violence: From the End of the Middle Ages to the Present*, p.40.
[41] Dean, Trevor (2001) *Crime in Medieval Europe 1200-1550*, p.78.
[42] Cotton, J. (2003) "Homicide" in *Crime in England and Wales 2001/2002,* pp.1-23.
[43] Kilday, Anne-Marie (2007) *Women and Violent Crime in Enlightenment Scotland*, p.43
[44] Kilday, Anne-Marie (2005) "Women and Crime in Britain, 1700-1850", p.187.

risky confrontations and activities, whether these were manifest in dangerous sports or violent crime.[45]

Nevertheless, most modern historians have rejected any notion that 'biology is destiny' and attributed as much or greater importance to upbringing and cultural or social expectations when explaining the phenomenon. Such an analysis also explains why the amount of lethal violence in English society as a whole (both male and female) gradually and unevenly decreased from the medieval period until the middle of the twentieth century (though there were significant short-term Tudor and Stuart mini-peaks). This process was particularly marked during the 1700s. Thus, in England, there was an average of 2.3 homicides per 100,000 head of population during the first half of the eighteenth century, but only 1.4 in its second fifty years.[46] This change was first properly appreciated in 1819, when the Committee on Criminal Laws reported to Parliament on the *per capita* murder rate in various parts of England (including the Metropolis and the Home Circuit) since the Glorious Revolution of 1688. To considerable surprise, it was established that it had fallen greatly during this time. In the Home Circuit, over the previous 30 years, it was a third of what it had been in the first three decades of the period.[47]

In the modern era, John Beattie's study of criminal indictment rates for homicide for each 100,000 people in Surrey and Sussex between 1660 and 1800, confirms this development, and suggests that they declined steadily if unevenly in both urban and rural settings. For example, in Sussex there was a particularly sharp fall in the years around 1760, those between 1740 and 1759 producing a homicide rate of 1.9, while those from 1760 to 1779 suggest one of only 0.5.[48] In remote Denbighshire in North Wales, the same downward eighteenth-century trend (interrupted by short term fluctuations) can be identified.[49]

Many recent attempts to explain this phenomenon support the stress placed by the twentieth-century scholar Norbert Elias on the social effects of modernisation. As early modern states gained a monopoly of power and legitimate violence, and their societies became more complex and

---

45 Campbell, Anne et al (2001) "Women and crime. An Evolutionary Approach", pp.481-497.

46 Eisner, Manuel (2001) "Modernization, Self-control and Lethal violence", *British Journal of Criminology*, p.629.

47 *The Times*, July 7, 1819, p.2.

48 Beattie, John (1986) *Crime and the Courts in England 1660-1800,* p.109.

49 Howard, Sharon (2003) *Crime, Communities And Authority In Early Modern Wales: Denbighshire, 1660-1730*, p.58.

intertwined, they both encouraged and compelled their subjects to show higher levels of self-control. Enhanced levels of self-restraint were gradually internalised, and reflected in new standards governing violence and manners, with an attendant lowering of shame thresholds. Such 'learned' ways of behaviour seem to be more important in determining homicide levels than innate drives such as aggression (important though these undoubtedly are). This also explains why the process appears to have started in socially 'advanced' countries like England and Holland. It may have meant that England had the lowest homicide rate in Europe during the eighteenth century, something that could also have been influenced by the strength of the country's legal institutions and its freedom from war on its own territory.

Female-Perpetrated Murders

Between 1735 and 1799, about 107 women were executed in England and Wales for murder or petty treason (a few extra cases cannot be confirmed). Of these, about 76 cases were for murder and 31 for petty treason. Only 17 of the 107 were hanged or burned in the Metropolitan area.[50] The great majority of female-perpetrated cases of petty treason that resulted in execution involved the deaths of husbands, only a few the killing of employers by their maids. Most of them were, effectively, domestic murders. Of course, some cases, particularly successful poisonings, would have gone entirely undetected. Others did not produce a suspect or resulted in acquittals. A few women accused of murder (not many) were found 'not guilty', like Anne Broderick in 1795, because they were "lunatick".

It seems that, as with assaults and some property crimes, the courts were sometimes reluctant to prosecute women who, technically, could have been considered to be accessories to a murder, if they were with or assisting men when a killing occurred, unless they behaved in an overtly active role. Theoretically, women were subject to exactly the same rules on inciting, aiding, abetting, counselling or procuring as their male counterparts.[51] In *practice*, it appears that a widespread feeling that they were easily led astray meant that some indulgence was shown to women who had a peripheral role in killings, such as those who verbally encouraged their partners to lethal violence (although legally this was abetting the crime).

---

[50] www.capitalpunishmentuk.org

[51] Anon, (1777) *The Laws Respecting Women*, pp.70-71. This legal doctrine is discussed more fully in chapter two.

This was particularly important because, it seems, women who accompanied men in violent incidents often did take a peripheral role. Evidence from eighteenth-century Portsmouth suggests that although the presence of men emboldened women to confront people whom they might ordinarily avoid, it also had a dampening effect on their level of violence, which was normally lower than it was for women who fought on their own or alongside other women.[52] If present, men could be left to take the leading role.

Such leniency towards women who killed with men was not universal. For example, in only two of 14 cases of murder tried at the Assizes held for four of the counties on the Western Circuit between 1735 and 1785 did women secure a 'not guilty' verdict when their male co-defendants were convicted (whether of murder or manslaughter).[53] Nevertheless, it was a regularly occurring phenomenon. For a specific example of this indulgence can be considered the trial held at Kingston Assizes, in 1713, of Richard Noble, his married lover Mary Sayer, and Mary's mother, for the murder of John Sayer, Mary's estranged husband. John had been stabbed when he attended the trio at their lodgings accompanied by a constable. Noble was convicted, but the two women acquitted, it not "appearing sufficiently" that they were aiding in the murder, even though they had earlier hatched a plan to poison John, openly called for his killing, and tried to push him into a duel with an expert swordsman.[54] An appeal of felony appears to have been lodged against the two women after their acquittal. If granted this would have allowed a retrial, and suggests that many observers thought their verdict excessively lenient. However, like so many of these highly technical and legally moribund (by the eighteenth century) actions, it did not result in a fresh prosecution.[55]

Similarly, at the Winchester Assizes in 1749, Elizabeth Payne, a widow who ran a public house, and Mary Carter, another widow, were indicted as accessories to the killing of William Galley for inciting and counselling his murder. (One of the principals had already been convicted at an earlier Assizes). It appears that Galley and another man had threatened the smuggling venture to which they were linked. It was claimed that Carter had advised her male associates to "kill them, or hang them", and served drink at a meeting of those who carried out the crime.

---

[52] Warner, Jessica (2008) "Men and Women Fighting Side By Side: Examples From an English Town, 1653-1781", pp.156-172.

[53] Williams, Amy (2000) *The Criminality Of Women In The 18th Century In The South West Of England*, p.178.

[54] *Evening Post (1709)*, March 12, 1713 - March 14, 1713.

[55] *Post Boy (1695)*, March 14, 1713 - March 17, 1713.

However, both women were acquitted at the direction of the court, though convicted of a misdemeanour.[56] Also significantly, in 1787, William Rawby, a small farmer from Dogdyke in Lincolnshire, was hanged without his spouse, after being convicted at the Assizes of murdering Ann Leary, a thirteen-year old parish apprentice, even though: "...the girl's death was caused by ill-usage, [and] her mistress had also beaten her with great severity".[57]

Susannah Houchin, convicted at the Essex Assizes of aiding and abetting a murder in 1740, was only slightly less fortunate. She had been the lookout for her father and uncle during a burglary in which a man had been shot dead. Although under instructions to 'brain' anyone who interfered with the two men, it was Susannah's later crass behaviour, flashing money around in a pub after the crime and blabbing about where it came from, that led to the group's exposure. When questioned by J.P.s, she immediately made full admissions, assisted in finding the older men, and at trial "begg'd that the court would shew her mercy".[58] Although found guilty of murder, she was given a temporary reprieve from execution, unlike her father and uncle.[59] She was not subsequently hanged.

Background to Female Homicides

Much of the immediate background to female-perpetrated homicide was determined by women's lifestyles. Generally speaking, women killed people with whom they were intimate, or at least familiar. This was especially marked amongst those who lived outside the Metropolitan area. Even ignoring infanticide, over a third of female-perpetrated homicides in the eighteenth-century South West occurred in a specifically familial or domestic context (assuming killings perpetrated by 'live-in' servants against other household members are treated as domestic). The figure may well have been higher, as some cases are unclear.[60] If social relationships are added, the proportion becomes much greater still. In the North East,

---

[56] *Gentleman's Magazine*, vol.19, 1749, pp.358-359

[57] Davey, B.J. (1994) *Rural Crime in the Eighteenth Century: North Lincolnshire 1740 – 80*, pp.16-18.

[58] Anon, (1740) *The Proceedings at the Assizes of Peace, Oyer and Terminer, for the County of Surrey, Held at the Town-Hall of Kingston Upon Thames, in the 14th Year of His Majesty's Reign ... To Which is Added the Genuine Proceedings at the Assizes for the County of Essex*, pp.14-15.

[59] *London and Country Journal (1739 1st Thursday Edition)* August 7, 1740.

[60] Williams, Amy (2000) *The Criminality Of Women In The 18th Century In The South West Of England*, p.183 and p.189

for example, female-perpetrated homicides occurred almost entirely within the context of a breakdown in family or other relationships, rather than between strangers. Their victims were usually relatives, neighbours, or friends and associates. By contrast, a majority of homicides amongst men from the same area involved people who were, to *some* extent, strangers.[61] Men spent a higher proportion of their waking hours in 'public' spaces or away from home on work. As a result, it seems that more male killings took place outdoors or in taverns.[62]

This pattern can be found, to varying degrees, throughout Britain. For example, a very high proportion of women charged with homicide offences in Denbighshire, in Wales, were accused of killing members of their own families (again, broadly construed to include domestic servants) in 'private' circumstances. All but two of the twenty-four accused women from 1660 to 1730 for whom depositions survive fall into this category. Their victims included servants, in-laws, and an employer's young relative. (However, over half of the victims in this total were the newborn infants of unmarried women reducing the 'headline' proportion for 'conventional' murders considerably). By contrast, masculine homicide there has been described as "overwhelmingly a public occurrence".[63]

Unsurprisingly, in these circumstances, although the 'spark' for such female-perpetrated killings varied greatly, it was often of a domestic nature. For example, Elizabeth Barber, a middle-aged woman, was convicted at the Kent Assizes in 1805 of stabbing her long-term cohabiting lover to death. They had been having an argument over money "when a scuffle ensured". (Barber's trial prospects were not improved by her being found with the corpse, shortly afterwards, "coolly smoking her pipe").[64] Similarly, Ann Goodson was executed at Guildford in April 1738 for killing her husband Thomas with a knife, during a heated argument as to whether a friend of Ann (other accounts suggest her husband) could spend the night in their room in exchange for some gin.[65] Before her execution, Goodson, a 53 year-old woman who had been married for 23 years,

---

[61] Morgan, Gwenda and Rushton, Peter (1998) *Rogues, Thieves and the Rule of Law,* pp.112-113.

[62] Shoemaker, Robert (2001) "Male Honour and the decline of public violence in eighteenth-century London", p.200.

[63] Howard, Sharon (2003) *Crime, Communities And Authority In Early Modern Wales: Denbighshire, 1660-1730*, pp.84-85.

[64] *The Morning Post*, March 23, 1805.

[65] Anon, (1738), The Proceedings at the Assizes for the County of Surry, held at Guildford, … On Thursday the 16th, Friday the 17th, Saturday the 18th, Monday the 20th, and Tuesday the 21st March, 1738 p.16.

complained that her spouse was a very bad husband, took no care of his family, and would often beat and abuse her. Most seriously: "…when she had seven children living to provide for, he has not brought her seven pence in the week. He was a porter, but loved an idle life".[66]

Many of the murders perpetrated by female servants were also quasi-domestic killings. For example, in 1737, Margaret Wickes, a 22-year-old servant, was convicted of murdering an eighteen-month-old infant, Lydia Fagg, in Dover. Margaret had, apparently, become disgruntled with her mistress, who would not let her leave her employment, in breach of contract, when she became "uneasy in her service". Early one morning, at about four o'clock, Margaret, who had charge of Lydia, got up and took the infant down to the sea, where she threw her into the water. Local fishermen later recovered Lydia's corpse after it was swept into their nets.[67]

However, several female-perpetrated murders that involved intimates had more planning and these often became eighteenth-century *causes celebres*, even if they were not typical. Amongst the most notorious was that involving Elizabeth Jeffries in Essex, in 1751. Jeffries had been adopted by a childless but wealthy uncle, Joseph, at the age of five, though their relationship was very poor, and she subsequently claimed that he had seduced her when she was an adolescent. In due course, she began an affair with one of her uncle's servants, John Swan. When it seemed likely that her uncle would cut her out of his will, Elizabeth, who later admitted to having planned the murder for two years, decided to act, with John's assistance. They paid a man named Matthews for a pair of pistols and then shot Joseph, making it look like a botched robbery. Elizabeth was quickly questioned by magistrates, but initially released when no evidence incriminating her could be found. However, both Elizabeth and John were subsequently arrested and their trial delayed so that Matthews could be secured as a prosecution witness. Their hearing began eight months later, at the Assizes held in Chelmsford in March 1752. Both were convicted and sentenced to hang. Elizabeth was taken to the gallows in a cart, riding on her own coffin. (John was dragged there on a sledge for committing petty treason). As not infrequently occurs in such cases, their relationship

---

[66] Anon, (1738) *A Full, True, and Genuine Account of the Uncommon Behaviour of Mr. Gill Smith, ... Likewise the Confession, Behaviour, and Dying Words, of Anne Goodson, who was burnt for the murder of her husband*, p.13.

[67] *London Evening Post*, June 2-4, 1737. At this time, various Master and Servant Acts gave magistrates considerable power over employment relations including, in certain circumstances, the power to punish servants for breach of private contracts with their employers.

appears to have deteriorated immediately after the killing. Both bitterly blamed the other for their predicament.[68]

Manslaughter

Manslaughter covered a class of homicides that were seen as much less blameworthy than murder because they involved killings committed without 'malice aforethought', the mental intent needed for the graver crime. Most commonly, this was because the lethal incident developed out of a spontaneous quarrel and was committed in 'hot blood' or was one in which the victim had actively contributed to the fracas.[69] When Ann Schofield was tried for murdering her husband John, by stabbing him in the side with a fork, just *after* a physically violent quarrel, Lord Kenyon told the jury that: "...accidents arising from occasional quarrels, and the irascibility of human nature, did not amount to that sort of guilt necessary to constitute the crime of murder". A manslaughter verdict, followed by a shilling fine, was returned.[70] Similarly, to take a purely male case, when John Litchfield was accused of murdering Alexander West, he freely admitted that he had been "in liquor" when he stabbed West in a Rotherhithe tavern. Witnesses suggested that he had also behaved obnoxiously. However, and vitally, he did not stab his victim until West had given him two small hits across the back with a cord. This was crucial to securing a manslaughter verdict, as the court then directed the jury that in cases of this kind: "Blows were look'd on as provocation, but words were not".[71] Although the legal generality of this statement should, perhaps, be slightly qualified, it was particularly important where the victim had been stabbed, as the 'Statute of Stabbing' of 1604 (1 Jac 1 c 8) remained in force until 1828. This created a specially indicted form of capital manslaughter, where a killing was committed with a knife or other blade, the victim did not have a weapon drawn at the time, and had not first struck a blow before being stabbed.

Manslaughter was a 'clergyable' offence (unless specially indicted under the 1604 Act) for which the normal punishment, for much of the

---

[68] See generally, Anon, (1752) *The whole tryal of John Swann, and Elizabeth Jeffries, for the murder of her uncle Mr. Joseph Jeffryey: at Walthamstow ... at the assizes held at Chelmsford in Essex, on Wednesday the 11th of March, 1752.*

[69] Baker, John (1998) "The Three Languages of the Common Law", p.9.

[70] *True Briton (1793)*, July 20, 1795.

[71] Anon, (1739) *The Genuine Proceedings at the Assizes on the Home Circuit, Held in March, 1739. ... at Hertford, for the County of Hertford; Chelmsford, for the County of Essex,* p.9.

century, was branding (often very ineffectually) with the letter M on the brawn of the thumb, followed by discharge. Unlike property crimes, transportation was not used to supplement this minor penalty, even after 1718. As Ann Schofield's case suggests, when branding for clergyable offences was formally abolished in 1779, a small fine was usually imposed in its stead. Thus, when the wife of Thomas Hodges killed him in 1785, she was (unusually for the time) only charged with manslaughter, rather than being initially indicted for petty treason. When she was convicted at the Salisbury Assizes, she was fined just one shilling and discharged.[72] Indeed, in 1799, while presiding over a murder trial at the Maidstone Assizes, Sir Beaumont Hotham observed to a convict that a shilling fine was the "usual" disposal for manslaughter, albeit that because the instant case was of exceptional gravity, he would sentence him to the "utmost extremity the law allowed". He gave the man a year in jail.[73]

Most eighteenth-century homicides that came for trial were initially indicted as murder. Although manslaughter was occasionally prosecuted in its own right, as with Mrs Hodges, this was comparatively rare until the first half of the nineteenth century.[74] Indeed, some observers, such as Zachary Babbington, an Assizes Clerk who was active in the 1680s, felt that it was normally bad practice as such matters were for a trial jury to determine. This is important when it comes to considering statistics. Many homicides were indicted as murder or petty treason even though examining magistrates, Assizes clerks, and Grand juries, would have anticipated that, at most, a manslaughter verdict would be returned.

For example, in 1695, Elizabeth Flower was prosecuted for petty treason at the Old Bailey after killing her husband, Anthony, with a poker. She struck him a blow on the head, as a result of which he 'languished' and eventually died. It appeared that her spouse had been arrested for a debt contracted by Elizabeth's brother. This so enraged the deceased man that he threw a poker at his wife, which she threw back, occasioning his fatal wound: "But no premeditated Malice appearing, but on the contrary great Love betwixt them; and she being greatly provok'd, she was found guilty of Manslaughter only".[75] This verdict was probably foreseeable at the time. However, there were always a few exceptions to this general pattern, and these became much more common after the turn of the century. Thus, in 1803, when Mary Mullenger was convicted at the

---

[72] Hunnisett, R.F. (Ed.) (1981) *Wiltshire Coroners' Bills 1752–1796*, p.164.
[73] *Sun*, March 18, 1799.
[74] Wiener, Martin J. (1999) "Judges v Jurors: Courtroom Tensions in Murder Trials and the Law of Criminal Responsibility in Nineteenth-Century England", p.470.
[75] OBSP, 4th May 1698, Trial of Elizabeth Flower: t16980504-11.

Suffolk Assizes in Bury of the manslaughter of William Norman "in a scuffle" the offence was charged as manslaughter *ab initio*.[76]

In the Metropolitan area, cases where the lesser form of homicide was found included a significant number with female defendants, although still, proportionately, far fewer than amongst men. By contrast, in much of provincial England (and Wales) during the eighteenth century, manslaughter was a very rare verdict for women accused of murder. This appears to have been linked to their greatly reduced participation in what might loosely be termed 'brawling'.[77] This was typically male behaviour, motivated by concerns about reputation and status and sometimes linked to drink-fuelled tavern disputes. It also explains why a higher proportion of men (than women) being prosecuted for homicide were indicted in groups rather than as individuals.

For example, over a third of men (33.9 per cent) indicted for murder at the Surrey Assizes between 1660 and 1800 received a partial verdict, being found guilty of manslaughter. By contrast, little more than a tenth of women received such a finding. Only two females were among the 80 people, initially indicted for murder in the county, who obtained such a result.[78] This was a fairly typical pattern. Thus, in Denbighshire, in Wales, between 1660 and 1730, only tiny numbers of women being tried for murder received manslaughter verdicts, probably less than a fifth of the male proportion when infanticide is excluded from consideration.[79] Perhaps surprisingly, and certainly unusually, in four (of the six) counties of the Western Circuit between 1735 and 1785, although eight women were convicted of the full offence of murder, it seems that a further six were sentenced for manslaughter.[80]

Many male manslaughter verdicts arose from killings in which there had been a degree of voluntary participation in the fracas by both parties. For example, in 1790, two men, drinking together in a public house near Corsham: "…in the course of conversation, had some words, when one of them (a brazier) drew out his knife to stab the other". Although this case,

---

76 *The Bury and Norwich Post: Or, Suffolk, Norfolk, Essex, and Cambridge Advertiser*, August 3, 1803.

77 Walker, Garthine (2003) *Crime, Gender and Social Order in Early Modern England*, pp.124-125

78 Beattie, John (1986) *Crime and the Courts in England 1660-1800,* p.437 and p.97.

79 Howard, Sharon (2003) *Crime, Communities And Authority In Early Modern Wales: Denbighshire, 1660-1730*, p.85.

80 Williams, Amy (2000) *The Criminality Of Women In The 18th Century In The South West Of England*, p.178.

fortuitously, did not result in a fatality, it had the classic ingredients of many male killings: consumption of alcohol; the carrying of a weapon (whether purposely or for work); and a social occasion that suddenly turned sour.[81] Modern research indicates that, in the right environment and social context, with which it interacts, intoxication can be a major contributory factor to homicide. (In isolation it is much less potent).[82] Provincial women were less involved in such incidents, or even present in the places, such as alehouses, where they often occurred.[83] Furthermore, they were less likely to be carrying a blade. Unlike their Metropolitan sisters, who often participated in the era's 'gin craze', they were also less likely to be inebriated.[84]

Of course, this was purely a matter of degree, and there were numerous exceptions. Some women did carry a knife for work. Similarly, cheap spirits reached most parts of the country and many provincial women imbibed excessively. For example, in April 1690, Sarah Blathone, was presented at the Borough Sessions for Kingston on Thames as a "common drunkard and disturber of the peace".[85] Similarly, a married woman, Elizabeth Rawling from Monk Wearmouth, near Sunderland, agreed a matter in front of a J.P. after "getting drunk and assaulting Mrs Elizabeth Chambers".[86] Even so, outside 'unusual' towns such as Portsmouth, excessive alcohol consumption was less of a problem with provincial women.

Amongst men the incidence of brawling seems to have been greatly increased by an acute sensitivity to perceived slights to their honour, especially early in the century. Recourse to violence in these situations restored a man's status. Such notions of 'honour' were less common amongst females.[87] Indeed, this particular 'narrative' of violence was much less open to women who wished to put a positive interpretation on their aggressive behaviour. Female honour was usually to be found elsewhere, in areas such as in sexual reputation, and was not deemed to

---

81 *Whitehall Evening Post (1770)*, March 20, 1790 - March 23, 1790.

82 See generally, Miles, Caroline (2012) "Intoxication and Homicide: A Context-Specific Approach".

83 Hindle, Steve (2003) "Crime and Popular Protest", p.133.

84 Warner, Jessica and Ivis, Frank (2000) "Gin and Gender in Early Eighteenth-century London", p.86.

85 Sessions 22nd April 1690, Kingston Local History Room, KE 2/2/1-14.

86 Morgan, Gwenda and Rushton, Peter (Eds) (2000) *The Justicing Notebook (1750-64) of Edmund Tew,* p.52

87 Lacour, Eva (2001) "Faces of violence Revisited. A Typology of Violence in Early Modern Germany", pp.649-667.

warrant this sort of protection.[88]

Of course, differences between men and women in this regard can be exaggerated. An examination of the Sessions records for Portsmouth suggests that a lower-class woman's 'honour' did sometimes extend beyond preserving her reputation for chastity. Some even shared male notions of 'respect', and were willing to have recourse to violence to uphold it.[89] Nevertheless, this was comparatively uncommon.

Women were particularly unlikely to participate in the semi-regulated, organised fights that men used to settle quarrels, such as that between a butcher and another man over a consignment of pigs. After a formal challenge to fight from the butcher: "Both being stripped, they began to fight, and had three or four rounds". Any ensuing fatalities in these situations almost never produced verdicts more serious than manslaughter.[90]

In other situations, a lack of intent to murder could be extrapolated from the surrounding circumstances, such as the absence of prior threats towards the victim or the lack of a history of previous animosity between the two. Ann Goodson's defence at her trial for petty treason was greatly undermined for this reason. She claimed: "…how the knife stuck in his [her husband's] leg I don't know. I had no thoughts to kill him". She also suggested that she might have fallen over with the blade in her outstretched hand.[91] Unfortunately, she had earlier threatened her spouse of 23 years in front of a witness and, as he was dying, he stated that she had tried to stab him through the chest several times but that he had deflected the blows. The court also asked to hear from witnesses as to how amicably they had lived together before the fatal incident, something that did not assist Ann's case.[92]

---

[88] Walker, Garthine (2003) *Crime, Gender and Social Order in Early Modern England*, at p.271.

[89] Warner, Jessica et al (2005), "Women Behaving Badly: Gender and Aggression in a Military Town, 1653–1781", p.297.

[90] *Oracle and Public Advertiser*, February 18, 1797.

[91] Anon, (1738) *A Full, True, and Genuine Account of the Uncommon Behaviour of Mr. Gill Smith, ... Likewise the Confession, Behaviour, and Dying Words, of Anne Goodson, who was burnt for the murder of her husband*, p.13.

[92] Anon, (1738) *The Proceedings at the Assizes for the County of Surry, held at Guildford, ... On Thursday the 16th, Friday the 17th, Saturday the 18th, Monday the 20th, and Tuesday the 21st March, 1738*, p.16.

Methods of Killing

As with men, some of the women convicted of murder would have committed nothing more serious than an assault if a potentially lethal weapon had not come to hand during a heated confrontation. Poisoning apart, which was always premeditated and a hugely important part of provincial murders perpetrated by females (see below), stabbing or hacking was probably the most frequent method of killing employed by women, and a domestic blade or axe the most common weapon used. In 1759, a lawyer, considering whether Mary Edmondson would have stabbed her aunt to death, suggested that: "A woman seldom uses such desperate weapons as knives or swords".[93] He was correct about the second weapon. There was almost no female use of a purposely manufactured, bladed, weapon, such as a sword or dagger. Women never carried them. However, the lawyer was very wrong about knives, even if they nearly always had a domestic provenance. Edmondson was certainly not alone.

For example, and as already noted, Ann Goodson was executed at Guildford in April 1738 for stabbing her husband with a knife and severing an artery.[94] Similarly, in 1759, Edith Saunders and her suspected male accomplice, William Robinson, were committed to the county jail in Gloucestershire for wounding James Short with a penknife: "…in so desperate a manner, that he is since dead".[95] Saunders was the only person convicted of this crime at the Gloucester Assizes, suggesting that Robinson's role was very peripheral.[96] In like manner, the near-septuagenarian Margaret Ryan killed her husband in Kent in 1776 during another domestic argument. At trial, she merely noted that the: "…deceased and she had words, and she stabbed him with a penknife".[97] By their nature, it was much easier to inflict a lethal wound with such weapons than it was with a blunt instrument, especially when used by a person of more limited strength. Knives were readily available in a domestic environment, further encouraging the weighting of female-perpetrated killings towards the home.

---

[93] Anon (By a gentleman of the law), (1759) *The Case of Mary Edmondson*, p.23

[94] Anon, (1738) *The Proceedings at the Assizes for the County of Surry, held at Guildford, ... On Thursday the 16th, Friday the 17th, Saturday the 18th, Monday the 20th, and Tuesday the 21st March, 1738* p.16.

[95] *Public Advertiser*, February 22, 1759.

[96] *London Evening Post*, April 14, 1759 - April 17, 1759.

[97] *General Evening Post*, March 16, 1776 - March 19, 1776.

Unlike the Metropolis, a significant number of women had recourse to axes and hatchets; these were less needed as work-tools in an urban environment and so less readily to hand in the capital. For example, Anne Fogget, executed at York in 1716 for petty treason, had attacked her drunken husband as he went to bed with an axe she had "prepar'd on purpose". Although a Quaker, she clove his skull and, after hitting him several more blows: "...mangled his body in a very strange manner".[98] Similarly, 15-year-old Elizabeth Marsh killed her 70-year-old grandfather with two blows from a hatchet in 1794.[99] Ann Wilson used an axe to kill her husband in the North of England.[100]

The use of ligatures and blunt instruments also figured significantly in female-perpetrated homicides. For example, two women used a noose made from her own garters to strangle a Mrs. Pattison in her home, before escaping with her money (she was left for dead, but amazingly survived).[101] Margaret Osgood used a ligature to finish off her husband in Surrey in 1681. Blunt instruments were also quite popular, and easily found in most environments. However, they were less certain in outcome than blades. In 1748, Jonathan Coward giving evidence against a woman in front of the Portsmouth magistrates, noted that, during an argument: "Constance, wife of William Kitson, mariner, struck his head with a mug and his wrist with a candlestick".[102] This ended up as just a fairly routine assault; with more lethal weapons it could have been much more serious.

Unlike men, female killers very rarely used firearms, having reduced access to such weapons and, even more importantly, less familiarity with their fairly complicated flint-lock operation. Nevertheless, they were readily available in eighteenth-century society. Anne Broderick shot dead her former lover, and even had a spare pistol ready and loaded in her pocket when arrested.[103]

---

[98] *St. James's Evening Post*, September 11, 1716 - September 13, 1716.

[99] *Sun*, April 22, 1794.

[100] Morgan, Gwenda and Rushton, Peter (1998) *Rogues, Thieves and the Rule of Law,* p.113.

[101] *London Daily Post and General Advertiser*, December 29, 1735.

[102] Warner, Jessica et al (2005), "Women Behaving Badly: Gender and Aggression in a Military Town, 1653–1781", pp.289-298.

[103] *London Packet or New Lloyd's Evening Post*, July 17, 1795 - July 20, 1795.

Poisoning

Women apart, poisoning appears to have been *relatively* uncommon as a method of killing in Britain during the eighteenth century.[104] However, in the eighteenth-century mind, as in that of many other eras, females were particularly associated with this form of killing. It is sometimes suggested that this link was (and is) exaggerated, and that men were almost as likely to have recourse to this 'underhand' method of murder. Perhaps surprisingly, in the Metropolitan area, and despite occasional *causes celebres*, the strong association between women and poisoning does not appear to be supported by much of the evidence. Nevertheless, in the provinces, the link between female killers and poison was very real. Additionally, a much higher *proportion* of female killers (than male ones) had recourse to it.

Poisoning was by far the most important female *modus operandi* when it came to killing adults during the eighteenth century, in both England and other parts of Britain. For example, it accounts for 20 out of 48 female-perpetrated cases brought before the Justiciary Court in South West Scotland between 1750 and 1815, being only distantly followed by strangling (six cases). By contrast, it seems to have been used by just six out of 168 male killers there.[105] As will be seen, it was (proportionately) even more popular amongst Englishwomen. Indeed, it seems that female-perpetrated poisoning was a Europe-wide phenomenon and concern at this time, as increasingly powerful toxins became more readily available.

Indicative of its significance as a woman's weapon of choice, it often transpired that poison had initially been considered in female-instigated or perpetrated murders that were eventually carried out using a different *modus operandi*. For example, when Margery Beddingfield and her lover decided to kill Margery's husband they initially obtained arsenic from an apothecary in Aldburgh, Suffolk. It was only when the husband failed to ingest this poison, noticing something gritty in the bottom of his cup (but not suspecting its nature or provenance), that they had recourse to other methods.[106]

Additionally, cases that were exposed were almost certainly just the tip of a poisoning 'iceberg'. Numerous poisonings probably went entirely unnoticed, or at most were the subject of suspicious neighbourhood

---

[104] Burney, Ian (2006) *Poison, Detection, and the Victorian Imagination,* pp.1-20.

[105] Kilday, Anne-Marie (2007) *Women and Violent Crime in Enlightenment Scotland*, p.45.

[106] Anon, (1763) *The genuine trial of Margery Beddingfield and Richard Ringe*, p.40.

mutterings. Many of the symptoms of arsenic and some other forms of poisoning were very similar to those of three commonly occurring eighteenth-century bowel diseases: English cholera, dysentery, and ordinary diarrhea. All of these illnesses produced copious vomiting and purging.[107] This probably encouraged less obvious cases to be entirely overlooked. For example, when Elizabeth Mason poisoned the first of her two employers, in 1712, the mortally ill woman was not suspicious: "…without knowing the real Cause of her Illness, [she] said, She felt Death upon her". She died the following morning. Her death passed completely unnoticed until Mason went on to poison her other mistress.[108] This may well be significant. If, as certainly seems to have been the case, poisoning was disproportionately employed by women it might suggest that a somewhat higher proportion of murders were carried out by females than the Assizes records suggest, even if the women concerned were not subsequently prosecuted or even suspected.

Poisoning evinced a special horror throughout the eighteenth century, if only because of its stealthy and underhand nature, which made it difficult to guard against. At the trial of Mary Blandy at the Oxford Assizes, Serjeant Hayward, counsel for the Crown, noted that: "Of all kinds of murders, that by poison is the most dreadful". It was also usually a gruesome death, given the poisons available at the time. Victims would normally convulse and retch for some time before expiring. Mary Wittenback's dying husband had acute stomach cramps, terrible vomiting, and "perspiration bursting from every pore".[109] Mercury-based poisons gave their victims nauseatingly foul breath.

Poisons

Arsenic (usually white but sometimes yellow) was used in well over half of all eighteenth-century cases of poisoning, being almost tasteless. Its use as a toxin was only distantly followed by mercury. Nevertheless, Mary Channel employed mercury to kill her husband in 1703. Similarly, Jane Butterfield was accused of murdering William Scawen in 1775 by using mercury sublimate. A few more arcane poisons were also sometimes employed during the era. For example, Dorothy Longley appears to have

---

[107] Watson, Katherine D. (2003) *Poisoned Lives: English Poisoners and Their Victims*, p.7.
[108] Ordinary's Account, 18th June 1712: OA17120618
[109] *The Times*, September 17, 1827, p.2

used liquid laudanum to kill her husband, as did several other female killers. (Half an ounce was normally fatal).[110]

Poison was widely and freely available at this time, and in houses where there were constant problems with rats and mice there were many legitimate reasons to obtain it (though some thought traps a safer form of pest control). It was not until 1851 that the Arsenic Act would require purchasers of the poison to sign a register and sellers to ensure that it was mixed with indigo or soot so that it was harder to adulterate food without detection.[111] In 1800, Ann Mead simply purchased an ounce of arsenic from a grocer's shop in Royston.[112] Elizabeth Mason, who poisoned her female employers in 1712, having become convinced that she would inherit their fortune and being annoyed at their constant chastisement, merely went to a local druggist's shop while on an errand. There, she bought more than two ounces of yellow arsenic, on the pretence that it was to kill rats. The following morning she mixed this with her mistresses' coffee.[113] Mercury was widely employed to treat venereal disease (something that was used to explain its presence in Scawen's body), also making it readily available.

The improper use of poisons was a real enough risk that apothecaries would sometimes be cautious about selling them to strangers, or at least question them as to their reasons for purchasing such substances. For example, in 1802, the child-murderer Mary Voce was initially turned away when she attempted to obtain arsenic from a variety of outlets in Leicester, "under the pretence of destroying vermin".[114] Using a local apothecary was also potentially risky for women planning murder. In a Scottish case from 1773, a man's wife, intent on poisoning him, told a nearby druggist, who knew her spouse well, that she needed poison to deal with rats and mice. This immediately aroused suspicion, as the vendor also knew that her husband kept five cats![115] Mary Wittenback took precautions to avoid this danger, and purchased her arsenic from a chemist more than two miles from her Metropolitan home, so as to make subsequent identification

---

[110] *Universal Spectator and Weekly Journal*, April 15, 1732.

[111] Foyster, Elizabeth (2005) *Marital Violence: An English Family History, 1660-1857*, p.106.

[112] *Trewman's Exeter Flying Post*, August 7, 1800.

[113] *Ordinary's Account*, 18th June 1712: OA17120618

[114] Anon, (1802) *The last dying words and confession of Mary Vice* [sic], p.1.

[115] Kilday, Anne-Marie (2007) *Women and Violent Crime in Enlightenment Scotland*, p.46.

impossible. Again, she bought it on the grounds that she needed it to deal with rats.[116]

Proof

When brought to court, poisoning cases were often very hard to prove. As Serjeant Hayward noted, poisoning was: "…not like other murders, neither can it be proved with equal perspicuity".[117] Unusually for eighteenth-century trials, large amounts of expert medical evidence might be called. However, on its own this was often not sufficient to secure a conviction, as can be seen from a case in 1731, in which a cornfactor from Southwark died six weeks after marrying a widow named Dorothy Longley: "…under violent suspicions of being poison'd".[118] Longley was, apparently, vexed to find that her husband's financial circumstances were much poorer than she had expected. She sent out a maid to buy some poison (the girl being unaware of its intended use), and administered it to her spouse in a drink. Immediately after consuming it, he convulsed and his body "swell'd that it burst".[119] Some of the contents of the dead man's stomach (believed to contain remnants of the poison) were later tested on a dog. The animal immediately fell into a coma and died some eight hours later.[120] The use of dogs to test for poisons was not uncommon at this time. A medical witness who had been at the autopsy of another poisoning victim later recalled that: "…it was proposed to take the stomach out, to have an experiment tried upon a dog".[121] Although Longley's trial at the Surrey Assizes lasted 13 hours, largely because of the enormous amount of medical evidence called on behalf of both the Crown and defendant, it resulted in an acquittal.[122]

More successfully, the distinguished doctor Anthony Addington gave expert testimony for the prosecution on the effects of arsenic poisoning at the trial of Mary Blandy. His methods were quite innovative for the era. He compared particles of a white powder that had been recovered from the crime scene with arsenic, and declared that they were the same substance.

---

[116] *The Times*, September 17, 1827, p.2

[117] Anon, (1752) *The Tryal of Mary Blandy, Spinster; For the Murder of her Father, Francis Blandy, Gent.*, p.9.

[118] *Daily Journal*, September 9, 1731.

[119] *Daily Post*, September 6, 1731.

[120] *Universal Spectator and Weekly Journal*, April 15, 1732.

[121] OBSP, Trial of Jane Sibson, 26th May 1762: t17620526-18

[122] *The Gentleman's Magazine*, 1731, vol.1, p.454 and p.492, and 1732, vol.2, p.676.

Other doctors gave evidence that the dead man's organs had been unnaturally well preserved, suggesting that poison had been used.[123]

Even so, medical evidence on its own was necessarily of limited value, especially where no suspected poison had been recovered. In 1675, when two women fell violently ill in Plymouth, one of whom later died, a physician was called in and decided that they had been poisoned. However, it did not require great powers of diagnosis on his part. The evidence that: "…induced him the more readily to determine of the nature and manner of their Sickness, and her death, was a quantity of *Crude Arsenick,* presented him by a Neighbor of these Afflicted and Murthered Persons, which she had found in a Pot of Oatmeal in the Kitchin".[124] Unfortunately, most cases were rather more difficult to identify. There were no fully reliable tests for even the most common poisons until the nineteenth century.[125] For example, the English chemist James Marsh first developed an effective test for the presence of arsenic in 1836, while working at the Woolwich Arsenal. It was only such advances in forensic techniques that allowed the female 'Bluebeard' Sarah Dazley, who appears to have poisoned two young husbands and an infant, to be convicted at the Bedford Assizes in 1843, after local gossip came to the attention of the police.[126] Any eighteenth-century predecessors in the same situation would probably have escaped, even if her erstwhile spouses had been exhumed.

These forensic problems were evidenced in a notorious case from 1780, in which the twenty-year-old Sir Theodosius Boughton began convulsing and then died. His brother-in-law, who was set to inherit the young man's very considerable fortune, became a suspect. A Dr Rattray (a physician) and a Mr Powell (an apothecary) gave medical evidence for the prosecution, supporting the notion of poisoning. John Hunter, a distinguished surgeon and physician, appeared for the accused. When asked point blank by the presiding judge whether he could rule out poisoning, Hunter was unable to give a definite answer, one way or the other.[127]

Very few convictions were secured in poisoning cases without strong supporting evidence, in addition to any expert medical testimony that was called. Very commonly, this was in the form of admissions. Sometimes, it

---

[123] Bell, Suzanne (2008) *Crime and circumstance: investigating the history of forensic science*, p.57.

[124] Quick, John (1676) *Hell open'd, or, The infernal sin of murther...* p.1

[125] Kesselring, Krista (2006) "Detecting 'Death Disguised''', p.26.

[126] *Bedfordshire Mercury and Huntingdon Express*, July 22, 1843.

[127] *English Chronicle or Universal Evening Post*, March 29, 1781 - March 31, 1781; *Morning Chronicle and London Advertiser*, April 2, 1781.

came from eyewitnesses or physical evidence (such as the discovery of surplus poison), much more rarely, but as with Boughton, from particularly strong circumstantial evidence.

Admissions were often vital in poisoning cases. When Anne Whale and Sarah Pledge were arrested on suspicion of poisoning the former's husband, and carried before a magistrate, they both made and signed full confessions, which were read out in front of their trial juries. Pledge had hoped to give evidence for the Crown against her friend, and had probably (if fatally) made admissions quickly with the aim of pre-empting Anne from doing the same thing. At trial, both women were capitally convicted. Although there was some corroborative evidence, the case against them was largely based on their admissions. At the end of the period, when Ann Mead, aged just fifteen, was found guilty at the Hertford Assizes and executed for the murder by poisoning of an infant, her admissions played an important role. Mead had fed the child a spoonful of arsenic. A powder was found in the toddler's stomach, and: "…from some experiments that were made, was declared to be arsenic". However, and vitally, after a 'vigorous' examination by a J.P., Mead had also made a confession, something that she repeated to a coroner.[128] As late as 1827, it was candidly admitted that had Mary Wittenback, who poisoned her husband of many years with arsenic to escape a quietly unhappy marriage, and out of (concealed) jealousy for his apparent womanising, not made admissions to two beadles she would have escaped justice: "…it seems more than probable, that but for the confession made by the prisoner to them, the guilt of the miserable woman would not have been legally established".[129]

Circumstantial evidence was necessarily important in poisoning cases, even if not usually enough to secure a conviction in its own right, except in the very strongest cases. This explains why in allegations of spousal poisoning much store was placed on the pre-mortem quality of the marital relationship between husband and wife. Witnesses were regularly asked questions such as: "Do you in your conscience believe your mistress was not an affectionate good wife?"[130] Earlier suspicious behaviour would also be carefully examined. For example, in Denbighshire, in 1686, after Lettice Lloyd poisoned her son-in-law, several witnesses related how, on an earlier occasion, she had prevented her daughter from tasting a drink that she had prepared for her (the daughter's) husband and had quickly

[128] *The Derby Mercury*, June 26, 1800.
[129] *The Times*, September 17, 1827, p.2.
[130] OBSP, Trial of Jane Sibson, 26th May 1762: t17620526-18

emptied it out when he failed to consume it.[131]

Administering Poison

As women normally had responsibility for preparing and serving food and drink, and poisoners usually required close access to and trust from their victims, they were better placed than men to resort to this method of killing, at least when it came to domestic murders. As was noted of Jane Butterfield's alleged victim, he had: "…placed an unlimited confidence in the prisoner at the bar; she had the care and management of everything". It was claimed that she had used this opportunity to put poison in some of the quack medicine he consumed to deal with his rheumatism.[132]

Unsurprisingly, in these circumstances, when it came to husband-murder (by far the most common form of petty treason) a particularly large component of provincial women had recourse to poison. Indeed, a majority of those executed for the crime, such as Margaret Onion, who was convicted at the Chelmsford Assizes and burned, had used it as their *modus operandi*.[133] This was especially marked before the final 25 years of the century. Between 1735 and 1799, of the 27 provincial women executed for petty treason, where husbands rather than employers were their victims, over half (fifteen) clearly had recourse to this method of killing (and probably slightly more), and it was by far the most common *modus operandi* in the first half of the period. Why it should have become somewhat less 'fashionable' towards the end of the century is not immediately clear.

Some of these women acted alone. Others had assistance, often from a male lover, as with Lott, or a close female friend, as with Anne Whale. In 1752, when Whale was burned at Broadridge Heath in Sussex for poisoning her husband James, she died with her accomplice, Sarah Pledge, who was hanged for murder. Sarah had, initially, even tried to poison James' beer with spiders![134] He had earned Sarah's enmity when he banned her from his home, after concluding that her relationship with his wife was unhealthy. The murder was exposed when his neighbours became suspicious about the speed of his death, and called in a surgeon to examine the body.

---

[131] Howard, Sharon (2003) *Crime, Communities And Authority In Early Modern Wales: Denbighshire, 1660-1730*, p.67.
[132] Anon, (1775) *The Trial of Jane Butterfield for the Wilful Murder of William Scawen, Esq*., p.3.
[133] *Universal Spectator and Weekly Journal*, August 2, 1735.
[134] *General Advertiser (1744)*, August 22, 1752.

Motivation for Spousal Poisoning

Motivations for the crime varied. A common scenario involved a woman who wanted to be with a paramour while also enjoying her inheritance. For example, early in the eighteenth century, Mary Channing from Dorset poisoned her husband's morning milk to allow her to live with a lover.[135] In like manner, in 1767, Ann Sowerby of Whitby was burnt at York for lacing her husband's morning curds with arsenic, apparently with the assistance of a boyfriend.[136]

Other women simply wished to escape from unhappy or unfulfilling marriages, or to avoid difficult domestic situations in a society with almost non-existent access to divorce (except for the very rich) and only limited access to legal separation (*a mensa et thoro*). For example, Amy Hutchinson had formed a passionate sexual relationship with a man when she was only sixteen. Her father forbade its continuance, and she duly married another, who she did not love. She renewed her relationship with her former lover a few days after this wedding. Her new husband, aware of local gossip, became acutely jealous of his wife. A quarrel ensued, as a result of which he beat her and had recourse to the bottle to drown his sorrows. Amy then poisoned him by putting arsenic in his ale.[137]

Similarly, Mary Channel, who came from a small village near Dorchester, was a young woman of great beauty, high intelligence, and very good education who had been pressured by her socially ambitious parents into marrying the least attractive but richest of her suitors, a man that she personally detested. (Mr Channel was a wealthy but very ugly grocer, who was also possessed of a splayfoot). Mary eventually yielded to her parental wishes, but quickly set about escaping her fate by poisoning her spouse. The murder was extremely amateurish and she was immediately arrested, convicted and sentenced to death, being burned at the age of just 18, amid widespread popular sympathy.[138]

Ann Williams, who was burnt at Gloucester in April 1753 for poisoning her husband, was probably less romantically inclined. She had mixed white mercury (purchased by a servant at her behest) with her spouse's gruel. She apparently held her inoffensive husband in contempt,

---

[135] Anon, (1706) *Serious admonitions to youth, in a short account of the life, trial, condemnation and execution of Mrs Mary Channing,* pp.1-52.

[136] *Public Advertiser*, August 14, 1767.

[137] Knapp, Andrew and Baldwin, William (1825) *The Newgate Calendar; Comprising Interesting Memoirs of the Most Notorious Characters...*, vol.2, p.76.

[138] McLynn, Frank (1989) *Crime and punishment in eighteenth-century England*, pp.119-120.

and wished to 'rule' their household alone. (He guessed immediately what, and who, was the source of his fatal malady and alerted those who attended him).[139]

Although most commonly used by women to kill their husbands, some female domestic servants had recourse to poisoning to murder their employers (also petty treason) or members of his/her immediate family, if only by mistake in the latter case. For example, Rebecca Downing used arsenic to kill her master, Richard Jarvis, in 1782.[140] Jarvis was an elderly man who had been free with his criticism of the intellectually rather backward and overworked former parish apprentice, who had been his 'maid of all work' for eight years. Similarly, at the Durham Assizes in 1798, Mary Nicholson, another servant, was found guilty of murdering her master's mother, Elizabeth Atkinson, with poison, albeit by accident. Mary had stolen from her employer and then been tricked by him into admitting the crime. Desirous of revenge, she had poisoned his pudding meat. Her master and two other men fell ill as a result, but only the mother died.[141] More deliberately as to outcome, in 1800, Ann Mead poisoned her employer's infant son with arsenic because his wife was unhappy with her failure to keep the child clean during high summer: "…her mistress called her a slut, and she resolved to spite her".[142]

Poison was also used in many other types of female-perpetrated murder in provincial England. For example, Mary Haddon used it to kill her own mother in 1736.[143] Similarly, Mary Voce used poison to kill her child in 1802. Voce, a native of Leicester, had worked in a mill, before marrying very young. Unfortunately, her husband went for a soldier, apparently against his will, and during his absence she had a child by another man. Learning that her spouse was likely to return, Mary decided to do away with the infant. She eventually succeeded in obtaining some poison from the local overseer of the poor. Having killed her child, she then returned to the same man to ask for financial support for a coffin. Unsurprisingly, he became suspicious and called in a surgeon to investigate. Mary was hanged at Gallows Hill, Nottingham, in March 1802.[144] (George Elliot loosely based the plot of *Adam Bede* on her death).

---

[139] *Public Advertiser*, April 19, 1753. Knapp, Andrew, and Baldwin, William, (1825) *The Newgate Calendar; Comprising Interesting Memoirs of the Most Notorious Characters…*, vol.2, pp.177-178.
[140] *Felix Farley's Bristol Journal*, August 10, 1782.
[141] *Bell's Weekly Messenger*, August 19, 1798.
[142] *The Derby Mercury*, June 26, 1800.
[143] *London Evening Post*, August 10, 1736 - August 12, 1736.
[144] Anon, (1802) *The last dying words and confession of Mary Vice* [sic], p.1.

'Correctional' Violence, Physical Mistreatment and Murder

In the eighteenth century, the use of 'correctional' violence, and the physical mistreatment of inferiors, was commonplace, whether it was directed against apprentices, younger domestic servants, or children.[145] It was considered entirely legitimate, *provided* it was exercised in an appropriate manner against a 'suitable' target. If done improperly, but not in such a way that a fatality was likely to ensue, and a death *did* result, it would normally be deemed to be a case of manslaughter (at most). However, the deliberate use of potentially lethal force in this context was always unacceptable and could well produce a murder indictment if a death followed.[146]

Some forms of correctional violence were not sanctioned in any circumstances. For example, Anne Barnet, a parish-nurse, was indicted at the Surrey Assizes in 1738 for murdering her patient Mary Onner. Mary was in poor health and immobile, because she had lost the use of her legs, which explained why she was receiving the ministrations of the locally funded nurse. Anne apparently lost her temper with Mary, after deciding that she was being "sulky" and deliberately refusing to speak to her. She then beat her about the head and body, as a result of which, it was claimed, Mary "languished" for four days and died. However, the medical evidence suggested that the beating was not the direct cause of her death, which was largely down to existing health issues, and the jury acquitted.[147]

During the course of the eighteenth century there were also significant changes in both legal and social attitudes as to where the dividing line between legitimate chastisement and illegal violence should be drawn, both as to intensity and target. The courts appear to have shown a progressively lower level of tolerance for such behaviour, especially after the middle of the century.[148]

As Barnet's case suggests, women could be the perpetrators of such

---

145 Hurl-Eamon, Jennine (2001) "Domestic Violence Prosecuted: Women Binding Over Their Husbands for Assault at Westminster Quarter Sessions, 1685-1720", p.437.

146 Beville, Robert (1799) *A treatise on the law of homicide, and of larceny at common law*, p.62.

147 Anon, (1738) The Proceedings at the Assizes for the County of Surry, held at Guildford, … On Thursday the 16th, Friday the 17th, Saturday the 18th, Monday the 20th, and Tuesday the 21st March, 1738, p.20.

148 Beattie, John (1985) "Violence and Society in Early-Modern England", pp.50-51.

violence, as well as its victims. Their targets were usually children, adolescents, and young, especially female, servants, as it was normally thought to be wrong for a man to beat a maid.[149] Many women violently abused their home help. For example, Lady Francis Pennoyer appears to have beaten her adolescent and young adult maids in Herefordshire quite regularly, during the middle of the century, even though the legality of such behaviour was increasingly doubtful.[150]

Some female servants, whether driven to extremes or targeting vulnerable employers, responded in kind. In 1755, for example, Mary Sympson, a maid in County Durham, beat her mistress.[151] Others, especially if they were a little older or supported by friends, took legal action against violent employers, including those who were women, before a lethal incident could occur. For example, at the Quarter Sessions for the Lindsey Division of Lincolnshire, servants brought 40 actions against their masters and mistresses between 1740 and 1780. Many of these cases involved female domestics. Thus, a maid prosecuted Betty Thompson, after Thompson pursued her out of her house, threw her to the ground, beat her with her fists, and threatened to murder her. Eventually, the girl got to the sanctuary of a neighbouring residence.[152] Unfortunately, such behaviour could sometimes result in a servant's death, especially where those on the receiving end were inherently vulnerable, as was often the case with parish apprentices.

Parish Apprentices

Parish apprentices were particularly at risk when it came to mistreatment. They were poor children of both genders, usually being bastards or orphans. Once they were no longer infants, often when they were as young as eight or nine, they were 'put out' into the care of 'local' people, though some were sent many miles away from their place of origin. Parishes in Hertfordshire, for example, sometimes advertised for employers in the Metropolitan papers. For a small premium, these people took them into their household and, in *theory*, taught them a trade or skill and good domestic manners. In practice, they were often put to any work that needed doing. For example, from the age of eight, the eventual murderer

[149]Gough, William (1634) *Domesticall Duties*, p.671.
[150] Andrews, William (1899) *Bygone Punishments*, pp.225-226
[151] Morgan, Gwenda and Rushton, Peter (Eds) (2000) *The Justicing Notebook (1750-64) of Edmund Tew,* p.57
[152] Davey, B.J. (1994) *Rural Crime in the Eighteenth Century: North Lincolnshire 1740 – 80*, p.17.

Rebecca Downing had been set to weeding fields and tending cattle. The system was designed to spare parishes the expense and inconvenience of raising these children. By the eighteenth century, it was widely acknowledged that many apprentices were subject to acute mistreatment. They had few people to keep watch over them, were often very young, and sometimes strangers where their employers resided. Parishes were also desperate to save money when 'off-loading' them, often taking minimal care about selecting masters and mistresses as a result.

Of course, most such cases did not end in death, and by the end of the era the authorities were a little more willing to take action against vicious employers than they had been at its start. For example, Elizabeth Hale was tried at the Surrey Quarter Sessions in 1796 for assaulting her two female apprentices, Jane Bray and Sophia Ingram, who were aged eleven and nine respectively. Although initially kind, Hale had quickly started to beat them ferociously, while working them from four in the morning until 10 or 11 pm at night (despite the custom of the trade stipulating a maximum of 12 hours work a day). They had been deprived of food, often dining on just half a dozen potatoes a day. They had also been sworn at and flogged with a rod pickled in brine. If Hale was intoxicated (frequently the case), she would use anything else that came to hand to attack them. Eventually, the parish beadle found the children hiding in the street, late at night, and took them to the Bermondsey workhouse. The parish then paid for Hale's prosecution; this was quite a common phenomenon in such cases by then. She was convicted, fined 3s 4d and imprisoned in the House of Correction for six months on each count.[153]

Nevertheless, many cases of apprentice mistreatment had tragic results. Just as the Brownrigg and Maynard cases became notorious in the eighteenth-century Metropolis, so did that of Elizabeth Branch and her daughter Mary, from Philips Norton in Somerset, after they were hanged in 1740 for murdering their maid. It was claimed that Elizabeth had been noted from childhood for her cruelty. She allegedly made a misery of her husband's life until death released him, and also bullied her servants relentlessly. Mary took after her mother, and had a similarly quick temper. After her spouse died, Elizabeth's reputation became so bad that she could normally only get girls put out by the parish to work for her. Jane Buttersworth was one of them. Eventually, after a prolonged course of mistreatment, Jane was savagely beaten with broomsticks by the two women for being late returning from an errand. She quickly died of her

---

[153] *The Times*, October 13, 1796, p.3

injuries and was buried the same night, her death being reported as due to natural causes.

However, rumours circulated after "neighbours muttered" about what had really happened, and the local coroner ordered that the girl's body be exhumed, so that an inquest could take place. Robert Salmon, a surgeon, found that Butterworth had received several wounds that on their own would have been lethal to the "stoutest" man. Her skull was fractured in at least two places, and the flesh had been beaten off some of her fingers. Bruises covered most of her body, and there had been a great effusion of blood while the girl was still alive. At the subsequent Assizes held at Taunton, in March 1740, Ann Somers, the Branchs' dairymaid, became the principal prosecution witness. Henry Butler, a former servant boy, also gave evidence of the women's vicious behaviour, both towards himself and the deceased girl, on earlier occasions. Once, they had attacked him so ferociously that he had spontaneously defecated through fear, after which they: "…took up my turd, thrust it into my mouth, and made me eat it". When the defendants called good character witnesses, the prosecution was ready to rebut their evidence by calling local people to say that their treatment of servants was notorious. Although legally well represented at trial, both the accused women were found guilty and sentenced to death.[154] Because local people were furiously angry with them, they were taken to the gallows just before daybreak, to prevent a mob interfering with their executions.

There were other, similar, provincial cases. In 1766, Susan Sciffel and her husband, a pair of weavers, were convicted at the Salisbury Assizes of murdering their nine-year-old parish apprentice, Ann Noyes. It was claimed that they had only taken on the girl "for the sake of the premium given with it". They treated her appallingly, depriving the child of food and beating her in a manner that was "too shocking to relate".[155] In 1780, another weaver, Catherine Parker, was executed at Northampton after being convicted of the murder of Thomas Cottingham, also a parish apprentice. Her 30-year-old husband was sought for the same murder but escaped. The lad's death had been occasioned by: "…beating, starving, confining, chaining, imprisoning, and for want of necessary meat, drink,

---

[154] Anon, (1767) *An Appeal to humanity: in an account of the life and cruel actions of Elizabeth Brownrigg…To which is added the Trial of Elizabeth Branch and her Daughter, for the murder of their Servant Maid, &c., pp.27-64; Country Journal or The Craftsman*, April 19, 1740.

[155] *St. James's Chronicle or the British Evening Post*, March 18, 1766 - March 20, 1766.

sustenance, and support".[156] At her execution, Catherine Parker admitted that she had been a "very wicked woman" and rather graciously (if perhaps implausibly) claimed that her husband had not been involved in the crime.[157]

Similarly, if with rather less pre-meditation, Alice Stribling was convicted in 1743 of murdering Elizabeth Tossle, her apprentice maid, at the Exeter Assizes, and executed a few weeks later at Heavytree, just outside the city. Alice was the forty-year-old wife of a respectable farmer from George Nympton, and appears to have struck her maid on the head with a stick. The girl 'languished' for about five hours before dying. Alice was very "sullen" pending her execution.[158] At the gallows she declared that she had never intended to kill her servant.[159]

Such cases were always a matter of degree. Several women found themselves in very similar situations, but had much better outcomes. For example, in 1687, Mary Jenner, from Ninfield in Sussex, thrashed her husband's 17-year-old maid with a horsewhip, as a result of which the young woman "languished" for three days before dying. However, although the coroner's inquest decided from the "ill looks of the deds corps and by the witnesses" that Mary was responsible for the girl's death, the petty jury at Assizes seems to have concluded that she died from natural causes. Mary was acquitted.[160] Similarly, in 1768, it was alleged that Mary Culverhouse, a Wiltshire apprentice employed by James Reynolds, had died through "ill usage and starving" for which his wife was responsible. Even so, Mrs Reynolds was acquitted at the Salisbury Assizes.[161]

Children

Children (other than juvenile servants and apprentices) were also on the receiving end of such violence. It was accepted without question that parents could, quite legally, use reasonable chastisement on their offspring. However, it was not just parents who were behind such acts. Sometimes, relatives and neighbours beat children that were not their own. For example, a northern magistrate: "Granted [a] special warrant against Catherine the wife of William Swan for cruelly beating two of the children

---

[156] *London Evening Post*, February 29, 1780 - March 2, 1780.
[157] *Adams's Weekly Courant*, March 21, 1780.
[158] *London Evening Post*, April 23, 1743 - April 26, 1743.
[159] *Daily Advertiser*, April 26, 1743.
[160] Hunnisett, R.F. (Ed.) (1996) *Sussex coroners' inquests 1603-1688*, p.135.
[161] Hunnisett, R.F. (Ed.) (1981) *Wiltshire Coroners' Bills 1752–1796*, p.34.

of Elinor Southern of Sunderland and threatening her".[162] As this suggests, women were frequently the perpetrators of such correction, especially where smaller infants and girls were involved. The courts were highly reluctant to become involved in these cases, unless the chastisement was extreme.

Several female-perpetrated homicides occurred in this context. Thus, in 1794, Elizabeth Sudry, an infant from Bradford on Avon of less than three years of age, received some "improper correction" from Mary Miny, in whose care she had been placed. She died shortly afterwards. The violence appears to have been prompted by Sudry fouling herself as a result of being ill and "relaxed in her bowels". However, at the coroner's inquest, it transpired that Miny had never previously shown the child anything other than kindness, so that she was acquitted of the "least intention of causing or hastening her death".[163]

Other women were less fortunate. For example, in Warwickshire, in 1778, Mary Knight beat her five-year-old son to death with a stick. She had sent him out to glean in nearby stubble-fields, but been disappointed at how little corn he had brought back. When he cried out under the impact of her blows, she locked him in a pantry, where his older brother later found him dead. Mary then threw the infant's body down a well and warned his sibling to remain silent, threatening that she would murder him too if he talked. She also threw the murder weapon onto the fire. However, neighbours discovered the child's body almost immediately, confronted Knight and recovered her half-burnt stick. Mary was later convicted, largely (and slightly controversially) on the evidence of her eight-year-old son, who was only just old enough to give sworn testimony. It was also shown at trial that she had often threatened to kill her youngest child.[164]

As Knight's case might suggest, for the lower classes the strain of living in a crowded domestic environment, with an uncertain income, could easily lead to sudden violence, especially against minors. This might affect women as well as men. Many such killings occurred spontaneously and were also perhaps indicative of a society in which levels of public exposure to violence were higher, and attendant levels of squeamishness lower, than they are today. Thus, Stephen and Tamar Swain murdered their daughter Ann in Wiltshire, in 1775. Both were sentenced to death at the Salisbury Assizes. At the gallows, their behaviour was: "…hardened

[162] Morgan, Gwenda and Rushton, Peter (Eds) (2000) *The Justicing Notebook (1750-64) of Edmund Tew,* p.52.
[163] Hunnisett, R.F. (Ed.) (1981) *Wiltshire Coroners' Bills 1752–1796*, p.124.
[164] *General Evening Post*, August 25, 1778 - August 27, 1778.

beyond measure, and seemed to be the effect of ignorance".[165] In like manner, Alice Andrews helped Thomas Hurry kill his daughter by "beating and hard usage". She was convicted with him at the Hertford Assizes in 1752, and both were executed.[166] In 1772, Mary Strange was more fortunate before the Salisbury Assizes, when accused of murdering her stepdaughter Sarah Strange by ill treatment and starvation. Although Sarah's body showed many marks of violence, Mary was acquitted.[167]

Equally tragically, Ann Gosling cut the throat of her two-year-old grandson. The boy had been the illegitimate offspring of her daughter, and entrusted to the care of his grandparents. Unfortunately, the child's mother could only provide a shilling a week towards his maintenance, and Ann's husband (the boy's grandfather) had started to complain about his presence, and threaten to have the infant committed to a workhouse. This had driven the already mentally fragile Ann insane (according to her trial verdict), and she decided it was: "...better to send him to heaven than the workhouse".[168]

Murder in the Course of Instrumental Crime

English (and Welsh) women committed very few murders while carrying out other property-related crimes. In this they may have differed *slightly* from contemporary women in lowland Scotland, who appear to have been a little more willing to kill in the course of burglaries and robberies.[169] However, such killings were not entirely unknown, even in provincial England.

In 1736, for example, Elizabeth Thompson was one of a group of 'lewd' women in her mother's disreputable Yarmouth tavern who were accused of murdering a Dutchman. The victim, who appears to have been a sailor, was last seen alive in the public house. His body was later found floating in Yarmouth harbour. The tips of his ears had been cut off to secure his gold earrings. He had a wound under one eye. However, his death appeared to have been occasioned by strangling. Several of the women stood trial. But only Elizabeth was convicted, in part on the evidence of another suspect, and only after the jury had retired for many

---

[165] *Morning Post and Daily Advertiser*, March 28, 1775.
[166] *London Evening Post*, March 7, 1752 - March 10, 1752.
[167] Hunnisett, R.F. (Ed.) (1981) *Wiltshire Coroners' Bills 1752–1796*, p.44.
[168] Anon, (1794) *The trials of Samuel Hammond, for the murder of Ann Avey; and Ann Gosling, for the murder of John Sage,* pp.12-16.
[169] Kilday, Anne-Marie (2007) *Women and Violent Crime in Enlightenment Scotland*, p.50 and p.129.

hours to consider her case.[170] Elizabeth had grown up in what might be termed a deviant sub-culture. She had been "prostituted" by her mother at an early age, and worked in and managed the *Bird in Hand* on her parent's behalf. This establishment was, allegedly: "…one entire scene of all extravagance and vice, swearing, whoring, drinking, cheating, and all the vilest debauchery". There were seldom less than seven or eight 'loose' women in attendance when it was open.[171]

In 1765, Mary Saunders, an 18-year-old who worked as a servant to a widow, Joan Jones, some four miles outside Monmouth (then part of the Oxford Assize circuit rather than the Welsh system), became aware that her employer had £200 hidden in her house. The temptation to get hold of this eventually proved overwhelming. Mary cut the older woman's throat and cracked her skull with a cleaver. Although she then seized the money, a realisation of the enormity of what she had done set in almost immediately, and she rushed into a field and confessed her crime to some local people who were out harvesting. The cash was later found thrown into a hedge.[172]

In 1782, Mary Davies, who kept a small shop in Dorrington, Warwickshire, was found dead in her house by neighbours, after she failed to open up for business one morning. Her brains had been beaten out with a coal-axe. Unsurprisingly, the coroner's inquest brought in a verdict of willful murder, but at this point, immediately after the discovery of Mary's body, it was attributed to a "person or persons unknown". However, Sarah Turner, a habitual criminal who had been to jail on several earlier occasions and whipped at the previous Quarter Sessions, was quickly suspected. Less than a week after the killing she was arrested in Shrewsbury.[173] She was convicted and sentenced to death at that town's Assizes, a few months later.[174]

Other women killed while carrying out burglaries and robberies with men. Jane and Eleanor Clarke, for example, were executed by the Westgate in Newcastle-upon-Tyne with their male accomplice, William Winter, after being convicted of the robbery and murder of Margaret Crozier from the Raw in Northumberland in a sixteen hour trial. Winter appears to have been a career criminal. The Clarkes, who were sisters, were described as "girls" (probably young women); presumably, Winter

---

[170] *Weekly Miscellany (1732),* September 27, 1735.
[171] *Daily Gazetteer (London Edition),* June 22, 1736.
[172] *Lloyd's Evening Post*, September 19-September 21, 1763.
[173] *Craftsman or Say's Weekly Journal*, May 11, 1782.
[174] *Gazetteer and New Daily Advertiser*, July 31, 1782.

was the ringleader.[175]

Conclusion

Eighteenth-century women in the provinces, like those in London, were less likely to resort to violence, and much less likely to have recourse to potentially lethal force than men, the killing of newborn babies apart. This probably reflects a combination of physical, cultural and situational factors. Although women were, on average, not as large or physically strong as men, their smaller representation in offences of serious violence is more readily explicable by contrasts in socially expected behaviour and upbringing.[176] They were less bound by a code of behaviour that required a violent response to provocation and less prone to becoming intoxicated in environments where this was likely to encourage recourse to serious violence, though there were numerous exceptions to both generalisations.

When it came to prosecutions for murder, women were generally favoured during the 1700s, rather than being at any disadvantage. Those on the 'fringes' of killings, especially if the central actors were male, were less likely to be indicted than men, or convicted if they were. More generally, women who came to trial for murder were more likely to be acquitted or (occasionally) found to be insane. Against this, women were also much less likely to become engaged in killings that could be defined as manslaughter than were men. They normally stood trial on a "noose or loose" basis, to use modern American parlance. Where provincial women did kill with premeditation their traditional association with the use of poison was well justified.

---

175 *Lloyd's Evening Post*, August 10, 1792 - August 13, 1792; *Public Advertiser*, August 15, 1792.

176 Beattie, John (1974) "The Criminality of Women in Eighteenth Century England", p.96.

CHAPTER FOUR

INFANTICIDE AND ABORTION

Introduction

This chapter will consider provincial infanticide and abortion during the eighteenth century. However, the latter topic will largely be considered as an alternative to the former, rather than in a wider context or as a subject in its own right. Furthermore, infanticide will be confined to neonaticide, the killing of newborn babies, usually within minutes of their birth, rather than the murder of infants who were more than a few days old and whose existence had been publicly acknowledged (instead of being privately concealed). It will also focus on the deaths of illegitimate babies as this was prosecuted far more frequently than the killing of those born within marriage. For example, in the North of England between 1720 and 1799 almost 200 cases of infanticide were indicted. However, of these, only eight involved women described as married. Of the eight, two were prosecuted as accessories to single women who were accused of infanticide (i.e. it was not their own babies that had been killed). Five of the others had been married but abandoned by their husbands and become pregnant by other men, or were of uncertain marital status.[1] Similarly, Malcolmson found fewer than a dozen cases of infanticide within marriage in his extensive general study of the subject in the eighteenth century. In three of these, the marriage had only barely preceded the child's birth.[2] This pattern was not confined to England, being found in many other parts of Europe. For example, of 29 cases of infanticide that came to trial in eighteenth-century Dubrovnik (in modern Croatia), and in which the family status of the accused is described, only two involved married women, and in one of these her husband was abroad when she fell pregnant by a lover.[3]

---

[1] Jackson, Mark (1996) *New-born child murder*, pp.43-44.
[2] Malcolmson, R.W. (1977) "Infanticide in the Eighteenth Century", pp.187-209.
[3] Lonza, Nella (2002) "Two Souls Lost": Infanticide In The Republic Of Dubrovnik (1667-1808)", p.81.

It seems that suspicious deaths amongst the newborn offspring of married couples were often quietly ignored. In an era of high infant mortality most cases of marital infanticide probably went entirely undetected, being explained as cases of 'overlaying' or domestic accidents. These were genuinely frequent occurrences. For example, in 1732, 133 babies died as a result of being 'overlaid' within the Metropolitan Bills of Mortality alone.[4] Selective neglect, which probably occurred in some pre-industrial agricultural societies that censured neonaticide but lacked effective means of contraception, *may* also have affected a few infants born to the poor within wedlock. This would have been most likely when times were particularly difficult, and there were more productive siblings to be looked after. However, the evidence for such a phenomenon in England is extremely limited.

Provided there was a significant delay between birth and death, and no attempt to hide the baby's arrival, even deaths amongst illegitimate babies were likely to receive minimal scrutiny if they did not show obvious signs of violence. Thus, when Sarah Fustain's three-month-old bastard died in Market Lavington, in 1775, the Wiltshire coroner quickly concluded that she had "accidentally overlain, suffocated and killed" the infant.[5] Of course, very short delays, in which an illegitimate birth had been kept secret, would not be viewed so favourably. For example, Jane Williams, a 22-year-old former servant, executed at Bristol in 1741, had waited for a day or two while considering the very limited options open to her. She rejected theft as a way of supporting herself and her baby, as she was not sufficiently "bold" to embark on such a stratagem and had no previous experience of crime. She also considered suicide and putting the infant on the parish, but was afraid of bureaucracy, the attendant delay it occasioned, and that she would be sent to a Bridewell as a result (though for a 'first offence' this may well not have occurred). Eventually, at the urging of her former lover, she killed her baby. She was convicted and hanged.[6] Unsurprisingly, execution could also follow longer delays if there were clear admissions to the crime. Rebecca Howard was hanged in Norwich in 1797 for drowning her five-week-old baby near Ipswich the previous year, largely because she had been "stung by remorse" after the deed and freely confessed to the coroner.[7]

---

[4] *Grub Street Journal*, December 28, 1732.

[5] Hunnisett, R.F. (Ed.) (1981) *Wiltshire Coroners' Bills 1752–1796*, p.59.

[6] Anon, (1741) *The Reverend Mr. Penrose's Account of the Behaviour, Confession, and last dying words, of the four malefactors executed at St. Michael's Hill at Bristol, on Wednesday the 15th of April, 1741*, p.10.

[7] *True Briton (1793),* September 12, 1796.

Women with unwanted illegitimate babies who were able to pay a small fee could sometimes turn to nefarious wet nurses who would discreetly neglect the infants left in their care until they died.[8] (In many respects, such nurses were simply the lower-end of a wider commercial child-rearing industry). Some went further than this. In 1757, George Burrington claimed that in the Metropolitan area at least there were 'nurses' who would take in such babies for as little as two guineas, and quietly but deliberately kill them. Such: "…monsters throw a spoonful of gin, spirits of wine, or Hungary-Water down a child's throat, which instantly strangles the babe; when the searchers [parish employed women] come to inspect the body, and enquire what distemper caused the death, it is answered, convulsions".[9] Burrington thought this helped to explain why convulsions were such a common cause of death in the Metropolis. There were 102 deaths ascribed to convulsions within the Bills of Mortality in one week alone in August 1744, although not all of these involved infants.[10] Such an option was rather less viable in most parts of provincial England, though probably not entirely absent.

Historically, neonatal infanticide has been found in most societies. Some, such as ancient Sparta and much of the classical world, as well as parts of the early modern Orient, have expressly sanctioned it. Exactly how frequently it occurred in eighteenth-century England is hard to establish. Its victims were necessarily silent and, if newborn, would not be missed by others. Many cases probably went entirely undiscovered, especially in rural areas, while others produced no suspects who could be prosecuted. For a typical example of the latter can be considered a case from early 1772 in which the body of a newborn female baby was found in a pond at Sedghill in Wiltshire. It resulted in the customary verdict (in these situations) of "murder by person or persons unknown". The mother was never traced. In 1794, another Wiltshire coroner recorded the same verdict at an inquest held at Highworth, after considering: "A new-born child: found under some sod and earth in a ground belonging to Queen Laines Farm".[11]

Nevertheless, it seems that only a small minority of unmarried pregnant English women had recourse to such a drastic solution, not least because,

[8] Zunshine, Lisa (2005) *Bastards and Foundlings: Illegitimacy in Eighteenth-Century England*, p.4.

[9] Burrington, George (1757) *An answer to Dr. William Brakenridge's letter concerning the number of inhabitants, within the London bills of mortality*, pp.1-23.

[10] *Penny London Morning Advertiser*, August 1, 1744 - August 3, 1744.

[11] Hunnisett, R.F. (Ed.) (1981) *Wiltshire Coroners' Bills 1752–1796*, p.152 & p.126.

in Europe, the practice had always been strongly deprecated by the Church and in popular moralistic tracts. A study based on the village of Terling in early-modern Essex suggests that it was an exceptional crime, given that at least 61 women there bore one or (rarely) more bastards between 1570 and 1699.[12] This analysis is supported by what appears to have been widespread popular antipathy, especially amongst women, towards those who were suspected of infanticide. Certainly, most magistrates dealt with far more cases of illegitimate babies who were openly born to single mothers than they did of suspicious deaths amongst bastards. For example, between 1767 and 1776 Richard Wyatt, a Surrey J.P., investigated just one suspected case of infanticide but examined many unmarried mothers.

In England, people married late and practiced pre-marital sexual abstinence or restraint to avoid unwanted babies rather than killing them. Where pregnancies did result from intercourse outside marriage, women normally married the genitor or did the best they could as single mothers. In this regard, it should be noted that illegitimacy had few economic consequences and carried *relatively* little social stigma for the children born to parents in 'common law' unions among the rural poor, at least in much of southern and eastern England, even though they were entered as "bastards" on parish registers. The parents had little or no property to pass on, and their offspring do not seem to have been at any obvious disadvantage in the labour market.[13] Numerous eighteenth-century women gave birth to, and cared for, illegitimate babies.

Infanticide was certainly not a predominantly Metropolitan offence. If anything, it was the opposite during the period under consideration. Of the 80 English and Welsh women executed for the crime between 1735 and 1799, 71 were hanged outside the London area, including the very last woman to die for the offence during the century, Elizabeth Lavender, who was executed after the Sussex Assizes in 1799.[14] In 1778 four of the five women executed (for all crimes) in England that year had been convicted of murdering their newborn bastards in the provinces; one each in Gloucester, Leicester, Warwick, and Chester, even though such killings were often easier to conceal in these counties than in a conurbation like London.[15] It also seems that the incidence of infanticide fell with the level of urbanisation found in eighteenth-century Surrey, with the county's

---

[12] Wrightson, Keith and Levine, David (1979) *Poverty and Piety in an English Village Terling, 1525-1700,* p.127.

[13] Zunshine, Lisa (2005) *Bastards and Foundlings: Illegitimacy in Eighteenth-Century England,* p.3

[14] *True Briton (1793)*, July 26, 1799.

[15] www.capitalpunishmentuk.org

populous northern parishes, such as Southwark and Lambeth, returning significantly lower rates of infanticide than its largely rural south, and prosecutions for the crime falling away there much faster during the 1700s.[16]

Infanticide was highly unusual, as it was a very serious crime, that occurred on a fairly regular basis, but which was overwhelmingly carried out by women. With the effective departure of witchcraft from the criminal canon by the early years of the period, this made it unique. Nationally, infanticides that were exposed (inherently much less likely than with an adult killing) would at least double the female homicide rate, and probably increase it rather more than that. Typically, neonatal infanticides made up over half of the homicide cases in Denbighshire where women were the principals between 1660 and 1730. (A total of 79 'normal' homicides, committed by both men and women, and 14 female-perpetrated infanticides were prosecuted in the county during this period).[17] In some areas, it tripled the incidence of prosecuted female killing. For example, 34.8 per cent of all homicide charges in the eighteenth-century North East were brought against women. However, of these, two thirds were for cases of infanticide.[18] Similarly, in the South West, up to two thirds of women accused of a homicide offence between 1735 and 1785 were indicted under the 1624 Act dealing with the killing of illegitimate babies (see below).[19] In Scotland, the inclusion of infanticide would more than triple the amount of female-perpetrated homicides, producing a total of 413 cases between 1720 and 1750, compared to just 116 if 'ordinary' murders are considered on their own.[20] Again, this was not a specifically British phenomenon. At times almost half of all recorded homicides in early to mid eighteenth-century Prussia were of newborn babies and it was the most common single basis for execution.[21]

Male Involvement

[16] Beattie, John (1986) *Crime and the Courts in England 1660-1800,* p.122.

[17] Howard, Sharon (2003) *Crime, Communities And Authority In Early Modern Wales: Denbighshire, 1660-1730*, p.86

[18] Morgan, Gwenda and Rushton, Peter (1998) *Rogues, Thieves and the Rule of Law,* p.112.

[19] Williams, Amy (2000) *The Criminality Of Women In The 18th Century In The South West Of England*, p.200.

[20] Kilday, Anne-Marie (2005) "Women and Crime in Britain, 1700-1850", p.192.

[21] Michalik, Kerstin (2006) "The Development of the Discourse on Infanticide in the Late Eighteenth Century and the New Legal Standardization of the Offense in the Nineteenth Century", p.52

Prosecuted cases of neonatal infanticide usually involved female suspects. Many of the women concerned had been abandoned or disowned by their male partners when (or before) they proved to be pregnant. Nevertheless, men did sometimes assist their partners to kill newborn babies. In August 1735, for example, John Williamson and his late wife's sister were executed for infanticide at Bedford. They had cut their bastard's throat as soon as it was born and buried it in a dunghill.[22] At the Derby Assizes in March 1759, Charles Kirkman was sentenced to death for murdering a newborn baby girl that he had fathered and personally delivered. The mother, Sarah Hall, appears to have been a single woman. Kirkman was hanged the following day.[23] In an extraordinary 'cold case', in the same year, William Horne was convicted and executed for killing the three-day old male baby he had fathered incestuously with his sister, some 35 years earlier. The farmer had put the infant in a bag and then dumped him in a field one freezing winter night. Rumours had swirled around for decades before a family member broke ranks. Witnesses were called at Horne's trial to give evidence of the finding of its body and the coroner's investigation decades earlier.[24]

In a particularly gruesome case from 1728, the Keeper of the Halstead Bridewell in Essex was sentenced to death at the Chelmsford Assizes for murdering his bastard child. He had threatened to whip the baby's mother to death if she did not sleep with him, at which she yielded. She became pregnant and when she was about eight months gone: "…she acquainted the Keeper with it, who order'd his servant to tie her to a post and whip her, and he stood by, till the fellow was weary, and then he whipped her himself till she miscarried, when he took up the infant, in a barbarous manner, and put it into a chamber-pot, and order'd his servant who whipt her, to throw it down the vault [of a latrine]".[25] Presumably, the baby was deemed to have been viable at birth. A few men took even more drastic action to avoid the consequences of fathering an illegitimate baby. For example, at the Gloucester Assizes in 1722, a baker was sentenced to death for poisoning a maid he had impregnated by giving her a cake laced with arsenic.[26]

It is probably safe to say that the help of a male partner who was fit, healthy, and possessed of an equal need to conceal a pregnancy greatly reduced the prospects of discovery for women who committed infanticide

---

[22] *Daily Gazetteer (London Edition)*, August 15, 1735.

[23] *Universal Chronicle or Weekly Gazette*, March 24, 1759 - March 31, 1759.

[24] Anon, (1760) *A Genuine Account of the Life and Trial of William Andrew Horne, Esq.*, 3rd edn., p.8.

[25] *The Weekly Journal; or, British Gazetteer,* March 30, 1728.

[26] *Daily Post,* March 27, 1722.

(and so reduced the number of men who came to court). It is also possible that men were more rarely prosecuted because it was perceived as an inherently 'female' crime, though this does, of course, invite the 'chicken and egg' question as to why this perception might have arisen in the first place. Finally, as men were not covered by the presumption contained in the 1624 Act (see below), prosecuting them would raise a complicated legal difference if they were tried with unmarried women; in theory, one defendant would not require evidence of a live birth while the other would. As a result, the pattern of prosecution probably gives a slightly misleading impression as to the number of men who became actively involved in such crimes. It was almost certainly significantly higher than the figures suggest.

Fornication

Illegitimate births were the result of 'fornication', as sexual intercourse outside marriage was termed. The notion of 'recreational' intercourse for single women was almost entirely absent at this time, although the sexual 'double standard' of the era meant that it was much less criticized in men. As Mary Wollestonecraft noted in 1792, an unchaste man "avoids the shame that pursues the crime in the other sex". As a result, one contemporary observer could define: "...whoredom, to be a woman's giving her person to a man, without any intent of marriage, but either for the mere gratification of lust, or for gain or hire".[27] Nevertheless, in late eighteenth-century England, the average groom was well over 26 years of age when marrying for the first time, and his bride was less than two years younger.[28] Consequently, most people had to wait years between sexual maturity and the arrival of socially sanctioned sexual intercourse. Some, including many servants, serving soldiers, sailors and (in theory) all apprentices, were not in a position to marry even when of appropriate age.[29]

In such a situation, although a reputation for sexual chastity was important to women, it was almost inevitable that fornication would occur with some regularity. Even the most virtuous resolutions would sometimes give way to a human impulse that could "overwhelm all powers of

---

[27] Madan, Martin (1781) *Thelyphthora; or, A Treatise on Female Ruin*, vol.1, p.51.
[28] Hay, Douglas and Rogers, Nicholas (1987) *Eighteenth-century English Society*, pp.44-46.
[29] Macfarlane, Alan (1980) "Illegitimacy and illegitimates in English history", p.71.

reasoning".[30] As one observer noted, when discussing the unmarried sexual relationships of Jenny Butterfield after her deflowering by a brewer at the tender age of fifteen, the young woman was not a vicious wanton: "…let those who have never been tempted, triumph in their celibacy".[31]

In theory, low-level Church Courts, such as that of the Archdeacon, which had its own judge (the 'Official') and registrar, and were popularly termed 'bawdy courts', could still deal with cases of fornication by imposing a penance on the offender. For example, in 1736 a young woman stood in traditional fashion in the porch of Greenwich Church, before divine service, and in the building itself during the celebration, wearing a sheet, carrying a wand in her right hand, and a label on her left arm stating: "I stand here for the sin of fornication".[32] She would also have had a bare head, legs and feet, while penitents normally had to read out or repeat a statement saying that they were sorry for their "detestable sin" and asking for forgiveness from God and the prayers of the congregation.

However, that this case was deemed newsworthy at the time and widely reported is significant; it was unusual, especially that close to the Metropolis. The bawdy courts, although restored in 1660, had never fully recovered from their absence during the Interregnum, and frequently confined themselves to very serious moral lapses, such as the birth of illegitimate children or adultery, rather than focussing on simple fornication. Many were moribund by the middle of the eighteenth century. In theory, failure to perform a Church Court appointed penance would lead to excommunication. Unfortunately, such sanctions were of little value against dissenters, recusants, and those of the unchurched who did not fear exclusion from Anglican sacraments. By the 1750s, most churchwardens were not presenting cases of immorality, especially simple fornication, in the formal reports that they gave in answer to the standard questions asked of them in an Archdeacon's visitation. Many simply replied "omnia bene" or that there was "nothing to present" in their parish.

However, there were a few localised exceptions to this general pattern, where personally diligent churchwardens continued to act against fornication even quite late in the eighteenth century.[33] For example, in 1776, Joseph Hooper was forced to make a public penance in the requisite

---

[30] Anon, (1799) *Thoughts on Means of Alleviating the Miseries attendant upon Common Prostitution*, p.12.

[31] Anon, (1775) *Circumstances of the Death of Mr. Scawen, with Genuine Particulars relative to Miss Jenny Butterfield*, p.11.

[32] *Daily Post*, August 25, 1736.

[33] See Letter to the Editor *Lloyd's Evening Post*, October 20, 1779 - October 22, 1779.

white sheet and wand in Luttons Ambo in Yorkshire for fornication with Ann Scott.[34] Articles of Enquiry about possible ecclesiastical offences were issued until the end of the period and penances were still being imposed in a few places as late as the 1790s.

Nevertheless, such occasional ecclesiastical cases apart, and ignoring the problematic area of prostitution, by about 1750 most forms of consensual heterosexual intercourse outside marriage had drifted beyond the reach of the penal law, in a way that could not have been anticipated even 50 years earlier, though sporadic attempts to re-criminalize some forms of unchastity would linger into the following century.[35] This process was not confined to England. For example, in 1709, at a session of the Scottish North Circuit, held two years after the Act of Union, a pair of judges sitting in Perth (Gilbert Minto and James Erskine) pardoned more than 300 men and women accused of fornication and adultery. This effectively brought about the *de facto* decriminalisation of those crimes (though they were still, of course, punished by the Kirk).[36] Prior to the eighteenth century, the secular authorities throughout Britain had made fitful attempts to enforce laws against illicit consensual sex.

The incidence of 'fornication' in England appears to have expanded during the eighteenth century as sexual attitudes changed to some degree.[37] It would be an exaggeration to suggest, as was sometimes done in the past, that there was a new, widespread, culture of sexual hedonism at this time, perhaps a result of the century being an interstitial period between the Puritanism of the 1600s and the evangelical-dominated years of the early nineteenth century. Nevertheless, total abstinence may have become less common, and various forms of sexual activity that fell short of full intercourse, and a previously widespread recourse to *coitus interruptus*, seem to have been replaced by a new emphasis on sustained penetrative sex.[38]

Certainly, the level of illegitimacy increased greatly during the era.[39] It

---

[34] Hair, Paul (1972) *Before the bawdy court*, p.180.
[35] Dabhoiwala, Faramerz (2012) *The Origins of Sex: A History of the First Sexual Revolution*, pp.77-78.
[36] Levack, Brian (2010) "The Prosecution of Sexual Crimes in Early Eighteenth-Century Scotland", p.172.
[37] Hitchcock, Tim (1997) "'Unlawfully begotten on her body': Illegitimacy and the Parish Poor in St Luke's Chelsea", pp.70-87.
[38] Evans, Tanya (2005) "'Unfortunate Objects': London's Unmarried Mothers in the Eighteenth Century", p.128.
[39] Zunshine, Lisa (2005) *Bastards and Foundlings: Illegitimacy in Eighteenth-Century England,* p.1.

rose from 1.5 per cent of recorded baptisms in 1660 to over five per cent in 1815. The cause of this increase is a matter of considerable debate, although the expansion may, in part, have been assisted by the tighter regulation of marriage, especially after 1753. Even then, some observers had feared that increasing such regulation would merely result in more illegitimacy, and might even be the: "...cause of the murder of many Infants, either after they are born, or by Abortion, before they come to the Time of their Birth".[40]

The growth in illegitimacy was particularly marked in urban areas, but also present in rural locations.[41] For example, and indicative of the more general national trend, albeit influenced by several important local factors, an analysis of six parishes in the Manifold Valley of North Staffordshire suggests that bastardy there rose from 3.5 per cent in the 1750s to the very high level of 9.7 per cent by the 1800s. (There was considerable variation amongst the individual parishes).[42] This, too, was a Europe-wide phenomenon, not a specifically English one. As a result, foundling institutions from Madrid to Moscow (they tended to be an urban phenomenon) saw the number of children put in their care increase dramatically, especially after the middle of the century.[43]

Social Background to Illegitimacy

Regular instances of extra-marital pregnancy resulted when fornication was combined with bad luck, the relatively poor contraception of the era (by definition, previously childless women could not prolong breastfeeding to restrict fertility) and, very importantly, dishonoured promises of betrothal should such an eventuality occur. The last factor was a very common feature of sexual relationships between single people during the period.[44] A typical case was that of Jane Williams who, before her execution for infanticide at Bristol in 1741, blamed the: "…young man who got her with child, under promises of marriage, deluded her to his leud embraces; and when he had gratified his bestial desires, forsook

[40] *Harrop's Manchester Mercury*, October 9, 1753.

[41] Hay, Douglas and Rogers, Nicholas (1987) *Eighteenth-century English Society*, pp.47-48.

[42] See generally, Bromfield, P. (2002) "Incidences and attitudes: a view of bastardy from eighteenth-century rural north Staffordshire, c. 1750–1820", pp.80–98.

[43] Winter, Anne (2010) "Abandoned in Brussels, delivered in Paris: long-distance transports of unwanted children in the eighteenth century", p.233.

[44] Hanway, Jonas (1759) *A Candid historical Account of the Hospital for the Reception of exposed and Deserted Young Children*, p.43.

her".[45] Many of the mothers of illegitimate babies were practising traditional pre-marital sexual and courting customs.[46] They had often agreed to intercourse on an understanding that, at the very least, marriage would ensue if a pregnancy resulted.

Some observers feared that such promises were worthless, and that few men made wives of those who had: "...before wedlock suffered themselves to be debauched by them".[47] However, this is not supported by the statistics. Parish registers indicate that large numbers of women *were* married just before or after they gave birth, when fathers *did* honour these understandings, or were chivvied into doing so by neighbours, clergymen, or local magistrates. For poorer women it was not necessarily true, as some contemporary observers thought, that the: "...man who robs you of your virtue means not to make you his wife".[48]

For example, in 1746, when the J.P. William Hunt managed to get Jane Plank to charge Benjamin Nash with being her soon-to-arrive baby's father, he had both of them arrested and brought before him, after which the "parties consented and were married". He dealt with a similar situation two weeks later, while three months further on again, Israel Middleton was brought before him on a warrant issued at the behest of a parish officer from Market Lavington, accused of impregnating Anne Sutton. He, too, agreed to marry the woman.[49] Parson James Woodforde, the celebrated Norfolk clerical diarist, regretted such marriages, but still conducted them (for a set fee of 10s 6d payable by the parish), although he personally felt that it was a: "...cruel thing that any person should be compelled by law to marry". In January 1787, he noted that a man from Ringland, who had been produced from custody for such a wedding, had hesitated for a long time in his churchyard before going through with the ceremony and marrying the woman he had impregnated.[50]

The same situation applied in the North of England. In 1764, when Margaret Storey, a 40 year-old widow found herself pregnant by the 60

---

[45] Penrose, Reverend (1741) *The Reverend Mr. Penrose's Account of the Behaviour, Confession, and last dying words, of the four malefactors executed at St. Michael's Hill at Bristol, on Wednesday the 15th of April, 1741*, p.10.

[46] Evans, Tanya (2005) "'Unfortunate Objects': London's Unmarried Mothers in the Eighteenth Century", p.136.

[47] Broughton, Thomas (1800) *Serious Advice and Warning to Servants*, p.23.

[48] Anon, (1791) *Advice to Unmarried Women: To recover and Reclaim the Fallen*, p.12.

[49] Crittall, Elizabeth (Ed.) (1982) *The Justicing Notebook of William Hunt, 1744-1749*, p.49 and p.51.

[50] Woodforde, James (1999) *The Diary of a Country Parson, 1758-1802,* at p.198.

year-old widower John Crass, she swore to the identity of the genitor before the Reverend Tew, a County Durham J.P., who issued a warrant against Crass, as a result of which pressure he married her.[51] In many places, such as eighteenth-century Nantwich in Cheshire, there is a very close match between the age of women at marriage and that of those who gave birth to their first illegitimate child. Indeed, over a third of eighteenth-century women gave birth within eight months of marriage. Allowing for miscarriages, it is clear that pregnancy was often the cue for a wedding.[52]

However, in an increasingly mobile society, with much greater population turnover and movement, social pressure to marry could be resisted, even in rural areas, not least by decamping to another village, town or (very commonly) London.[53] Promises and understandings were frequently dishonoured, sometimes because the father had never had any intention of marrying the woman he had impregnated, quite frequently because he did not feel financially secure enough to embark on parenthood when finally put to the test. Most bastard-bearers were not sexually hedonistic teenagers, but young women who had been seduced (if that is not too strong a word) by a man of similar social background.

Of course, some had been taken-in by the proverbial sweet-talking man of a higher social status who: "Having obtained gratification … thinks no more of his promises".[54] In 1700, for example, Mary Butcher from Worcester met a well-to-do man, accepted his "gilded bait", had sexual relations with him, and quickly got pregnant, disposing of her baby in a dunghill after giving birth alone.[55] Nevertheless, such cases were in a definite minority.

This general pattern was found elsewhere in the British Isles. For example, in eighteenth-century Shetland, those indicted for the crime were overwhelmingly young, single women, usually employed in labouring and service occupations. Most had engaged in sexual relations with a man they hoped to marry or, less frequently, had conceived after a fleeting sexual

---

[51] Morgan, Gwenda and Rushton, Peter (Eds) (2000) *The Justicing Notebook (1750-64) of Edmund Tew,* p.191

[52] Hitchcock, Tim (1997) ''Unlawfully begotten on her body': Illegitimacy and the Parish Poor in St Luke's Chelsea", p.71.

[53] Hay, Douglas and Rogers, Nicholas (1987) *Eighteenth-century English Society,* p.48.

[54] Hunter, William (1812) *On the Uncertainty of the Signs of Murder in the Case of Bastard Children,* p.6.

[55] Anon, (1701) *The lamentation of Mary Butcher, now confined in Worcester-City-Goal, on suspicion of murdering her male bastard child, in April last*, p.1.

encounter with an employer, visiting seaman, or work colleague. Typically, in 1699, Margaret Magnusdaughter, a servant, became the first island woman to be convicted of infanticide under Scotland's 1690 Act after being impregnated by her master.[56]

Despite the demands of official morality and its attendant belief that modesty and virtue were the "chief honour of a woman",[57] the absence of virginity in unmarried lower-class females seems to have been viewed as a *relatively* minor sin, at a popular level, in much of eighteenth-century England, provided the woman was not notoriously promiscuous. It was probably not *enormously* uncommon. As one observer cynically noted in 1694: "Yet how many nowadays would be ranked among virgins, who indeed are rank whores".[58] Women could still be valued for other qualities, such as work skills and industry, rather than purely for their reputation for chastity. Indeed, a little higher up the social scale, the properly kept mistress, such as the killer Anne Broderick, was a feature of the period. By contrast, the consequences of giving birth to bastards could be fairly drastic for some poor, single mothers. However, it was not formal legal sanctions that women most feared.

Legal Consequences of Illegitimacy

The simple begetting of illegitimate children was not a secular crime *per se* during the eighteenth century, *provided* the baby could be supported independently of its parish.[59] In theory, in such situations, and as with simple 'fornication' (see above), but rather more commonly, a penance ordered by the judge at an Archdeacon's court and performed in church while wearing a white sheet, *might* have to be carried out, especially in remoter parts of the country and in the earlier decades of the century. For example, in the parish register for Roxby in Lincolnshire it was recorded that Michael Kirby and a widow named Dixon: "...had 2 Bastard Children, one in 1725, ye other in 1727, for which they did publick pennance in our P'ish Church".[60] Almost fifty years later, Sarah Hornblow gave birth to a bastard in Benson, Oxfordshire, in 1772, and received the

---

[56] Abrams, L. (2002) "From demon to victim: the infanticidal mother in Shetland, 1699-1899", pp.182-184.

[57] Broughton, Thomas (1800) *Serious Advice and Warning to Servants*, p.20.

[58] Anon, (1694) *The Ladies Dictionary, Being a General Entertainment for the Fair Sex*, p.127.

[59] Blackstone, William (1769) *Commentaries on the Laws of England*, vol.4, p.65.

[60] Andrews, William (1899) *Bygone Punishments*, p.73.

same religious punishment.[61] As with fornication, if they failed to carry out their penance they could be excommunicated, as happened to Anne Jillman after she gave birth to an illegitimate baby in Lenton near Nottingham in 1753. (She subsequently recanted, performed her penance and was readmitted to the sacraments of the Church).[62] However, there would not be a civil punishment.

Producing bastards that might become a burden to the community was a very different matter, and still an offence that was punishable in the mainstream criminal courts, as it had been since 1576. This could be done under various statutes including, *inter alia*, a Jacobean Act from 1610 (7 James, cap. 4) which allowed "lewd", bastard-bearing, women to be committed to a House of Correction for twelve months for a first 'offence', and punished more severely for subsequent illegitimate births. For example, at the Warwickshire Quarter Sessions in 1677, Anne Kendall was committed to a year in such an institution, for giving birth to an illegitimate baby.[63] This also meant that poor bastard-bearers were punished for their poverty, rather than their immorality, as a: "...rich sinner would not have been the object of legal resentment".[64]

However, by the 1700s, the courts were no longer assiduous about imposing such punishments, even on poor women, unless they were 'repeat' offenders or there was an urgent need to set a local example. Sarah Soames, a single woman from Egham in Surrey, provides an illustration of the former situation. After she gave birth to her third illegitimate child, apparently fathered on this occasion by a journeyman shoemaker who had decamped to London, she was committed by two J.P.s to the county Bridewell for a year.[65] In passing, it can be noted that if it was established that men had fathered numerous bastards who were chargeable to the parish they, too, might be committed to jail. This was quite rare, but occurred with Richard Brown in London in 1744: "...it being his third offence of the like nature".[66]

---

[61] Hair, Paul (1972) *Before the bawdy court*, p.126.

[62] For Jillman's Presentment Bill, Penance and Certificate of Excommunication see University of Nottingham Manuscripts and Special Collections, at AN/PB 313/230, AN/PB 369/12, and AN/E 194.

[63] Ratcliff, S.C. and Johnson, H.C. (1946) *Warwick County Records Volume vii: Quarter Sessions records Easter, 1674, to Easter, 1682,* p.123.

[64] Zouch, Henry (1786) *Hints Respecting the Public Police*, p.15.

[65] Silverthorne, Elizabeth (Ed.) (1978) *The Deposition Book of Richard Wyatt JP, 1767-1776*, p.19.

[66] *Penny London Morning Advertiser*, January 16, 1744 - January 18, 1744.

Nevertheless, parishes were acutely concerned about the cost of supporting illegitimate babies, which would have to be met by local ratepayers. Ideally, they wished to restrict the right to reproduce to those who were capable of supporting their own offspring. This anxiety is evidenced by some of the measures used to avoid such expense. For example, in his diary, Thomas Turner, a churchwarden and overseer of the poor in East Hoathly in Sussex during the 1750s, recorded the large amount of pressure that was put on a pregnant woman from their village not only to marry the genitor of her baby, but to do so in his village of settlement, rather than her own. In other cases, ordinary parishioners in towns and villages, concerned about their rates, would turn away pregnant single women who arrived in their midst.[67] Indeed, providing accommodation for such a woman could be prosecuted as an offence in its own right.

In a revealing case from 1795, two overseers of the poor from Woolwich were tried at the Maidstone Assizes for their callous treatment of a pregnant single pauper who was an entirely legal resident of their own parish. They had refused to admit her to a workhouse when she warned them that she was about to come to term, insisting that she be examined first by local magistrates as to her place of lawful settlement, before being granted such accommodation. When the woman entered labour they hurriedly arranged for her to be carried across the Thames in a boat that dropped her off next to the Tower of London. Ultimately, she was admitted to the Clerkenwell workhouse to give birth, even though this was not her native parish.[68]

Sadly, the drive to economize meant that the mortality rate for infants who 'went on the parish' was quite appalling, as they were often given to poor, neglectful women and quickly died.[69] Others freely spoke of the: "…fatal consequences which too frequently happen from the barbarity of parish nurses".[70] Only a relatively small proportion of these infants reached adulthood.

Nevertheless, despite such parsimony, even the most economical vestry faced considerable expense at a time of rapidly increasing poor rates. As a result, most Justices were primarily concerned with ensuring that the cost of raising an infant was borne by its parents, instead of its parish, rather than with punishing the woman (or man) who had brought it

---

67 Jackson, Mark (1996) *New-born child murder*, p.37

68 *Star*, April 4, 1795.

69 Hanway, Jonas (1759) *A Candid historical Account of the Hospital for the Reception of exposed and Deserted Young Children*, p.21.

70 *Country Journal or The Craftsman*, January 20, 1728.

into the world.[71] Indeed, this constituted a very large part of their 'out of sessions' work, as surviving Justices' notebooks make clear. J.P.s would investigate as soon as it came to their attention that a local single woman was pregnant, perhaps after they received a complaint from a churchwarden or an overseer of the poor, or simply became aware of neighbourhood gossip. One or two pregnant single women even reported themselves to a Justice, though a magistrate's formal powers to compel women to appear before him prior to giving birth were limited.

Poor unmarried women were then pressured to reveal the identities of those who had impregnated them.[72] If a woman refused to answer a magistrate's questions on this subject she could be committed to a House of Correction.[73] Most provided names. An arrest warrant would then be issued to ensure that the prospective father attended the magistrate in his turn, though some did so voluntarily, while others fled rather than appear. Thus, and typically, in 1769, Elizabeth Friend from Chertsey was questioned by Richard Wyatt and duly came up with the name of the man who had impregnated her or, to use the succinct phrase often employed in magistrates' notebooks: "Charges John Bullen labourer".[74]

Occasionally, such an allegation could be hazardous for the woman concerned, even if true (a few lied), after they had given birth. Edward Mangall murdered Elizabeth Johnson at King's Causey, in Yorkshire, in 1689. She had had an illegitimate baby boy and: "…laid him to Mangall's Charge, and required him to Marry her: which he refused at first to do". Later, he lured her to a remote spot and murdered both mother and child with a club.[75]

Once in front of a Justice, if they could not be persuaded to marry (see above), both parents would be required to enter a bond to support their offspring in future and the father would be forced to commit himself to periodic payments and the cost of a midwife at the birth. For example, in the early 1690s a Warwickshire carpenter named Robert Howes had a

---

[71] King, Peter (2004) "The Summary Courts and Social Relations in Eighteenth-Century England", p.152.

[72] Macfarlane, Alan (1980) "Illegitimacy and illegitimates in English history", p.71.

[73] Davey, B.J. (1994) *Rural Crime in the Eighteenth Century: North Lincolnshire 1740 – 80*, p.30.

[74] Silverthorne, Elizabeth (Ed.) (1978) *The Deposition Book of Richard Wyatt JP, 1767-1776*, p.7.

[75] Anon, (1690) *A full and true relation of the examination and confession of W. Barwick and E. Mangall, of two horrid murders …*, pp.1-4.

bastard by his servant Mary Creed. Shortly after giving birth, and unusually, Mary ran off, leaving Howes to deal with their offspring. Although he challenged his paternity, a judgment was made at Quarter Sessions in 1693: "...declaring Howes to be the reputed father". The infant was then put on the parish, and Howes required to pay two shillings a week for its upkeep until it was ten, when (if the child was still alive) he would be required to enter a bond for £40 to indemnify the parish against all future charges, such as the cost of an apprenticeship.[76] Men who refused to find sureties after impregnating women, while being unable or unwilling to marry them, could also be imprisoned, as happened to three men, from different parishes, who were committed to Chelmsford jail by separate Justices over the Christmas period in 1753.[77]

Practical Consequences of Bastard-Bearing

On their own, the small risk of incarceration or being forced to do a church penance, combined with the hostility of local taxpayers and the moral shame of bearing a bastard, provided *some* incentive for pregnancies to be concealed and the resultant babies killed. However, the practical consequences of giving birth to an illegitimate baby were usually a much greater motivation for such behaviour, at least during the eighteenth century.

Most importantly, a very high proportion of those accused of the crime were domestic servants. Public knowledge of their pregnancies would usually result in immediate dismissal. For example, it was claimed that the Essex-born maid Sarah Chandler's journey to the gallows began when she became acquainted with an Irish waiter at a gaming house. She quickly became pregnant by him and so was: "...under the necessity of quitting her service".[78] Furthermore, the women concerned would not receive a character reference and there would be relatively little chance of being taken into service again (though a few women in this situation put their babies out to nurse and successfully sought new positions). In 1805, Mr. Justice Harding, passing a death sentence on Mary Morgan at the Radnorshire Assizes, for murdering her newborn bastard, noted that: "Had it lived, you might have lost your place; you might have lost other places; you might have sunk into poverty as well as into shame; but was this a

[76] Johnson, H.C. (1964) *Warwick County Records, vol.IX: Quarter session records; Easter, 1690 to Michaelmas, 1696*, p.xliii and p.xliv, and p.68.

[77] King, Peter (2006) *Crime and Law in England, 1750-1840,* p.17.

[78] Anon, (1796?) *The True and remarkable life and extraordinary adventures of that unfortunate woman, Sarah Chandler*, pp.2-4.

reason to kill an infant?"[79] Sadly, some women, albeit a minority, thought that it was.

Although it was regularly described as an 'unnatural' and monstrous crime for any mother to commit, many establishment observers also appreciated that it was not entirely surprising if a woman tried to screen herself from public censure by committing a far more dreadful sin than having an illegitimate child.[80] As a Bristol-based cleric, the Reverend Penrose, noted in 1741: "…surely if it was not the apprehension of shame, and the being brought into contempt, thro' the circle of their acquaintance, they [women] would not perpetrate such horrid acts". It was for this reason that Penrose urged the establishment of the equivalent of Thomas Coram's London Foundling Hospital for abandoned children in the West Country city.[81]

Abortion

Some desperate women managed to pre-empt such a situation. Attempting to secure an abortion was always an option for those who were pregnant. Many observers thought they were fairly commonplace, and they also feature in some of the literature from the era.[82] For example, Mary Wollstonecraft's posthumously published (1798) novella *The Wrongs of Woman, or Maria* included a servant girl named 'Jemima', whose seduction by her master was followed by a potion induced abortion (it left her gravely ill). In 1751, Elizabeth Jeffries was to claim that she had had several abortions arranged by an uncle in Essex who had had regular sexual relations with her when she was still a child.[83]

Historically, during the medieval era and at the start of the early modern period, abortion had been punished in the church courts.[84] It had gradually become a matter for the common law forums during and after the Reformation. However, in these courts, abortion was not viewed very

---

[79] *The Hull Packet*, May 7, 1805.

[80] *The Gentleman's Magazine*, 1749, vol.19, p.126.

[81] Penrose, Reverend (1741) *The Reverend Mr. Penrose's Account of the Behaviour, Confession, and last dying words, of the four malefactors executed at St. Michael's Hill at Bristol, on Wednesday the 15th of April, 1741*, p.11.

[82] Defoe, Daniel (1731) *The Generous Projector*, p.10.

[83] See generally, Anon, (1752) *The whole tryal of John Swann, and Elizabeth Jeffries, for the murder of her uncle Mr. Joseph Jeffryey: at Walthamstow ... at the assizes held at Chelmsford in Essex, on Wednesday the 11th of March, 1752.*

[84] Spivack, Carla (2007) "To "Bring Down the Flowers": The Cultural Context of Abortion Law in Early Modern England", p.143.

seriously before a baby 'quickened', supposedly during or (more commonly) after the fourth month of pregnancy. It was considered a 'nefarious' activity, but technically may not even have been illegal outside canon law (the issue was not entirely clear). If it was against the criminal law, it was certainly no more than a low-level misdemeanour, though the courts did not always trouble themselves excessively about the precise boundary for 'quickening'. (Eleanor Beare [see below] may have been punished for aborting a foetus at less than 14 weeks of gestation). Such conduct was only firmly criminalised in 1803. In many cases, herbal 'medicines' sold to regulate a woman's menstrual cycle or to restore it where there had been a "total suppression of the courses" were specifically used to bring about early miscarriage. Certainly, some of them contained ingredients, such as savin, a poisonous species of juniper, that were also found in the era's abortifacients.[85] (Interestingly, exactly the same phenomenon can be seen in eighteenth-century Mexico, although the herbs employed sometimes differed).[86] In any event, as there were no early pregnancy tests during the eighteenth century, policing such behaviour would have been inherently very difficult.

Even post-quickening abortion, although a serious crime, was not a felony, viewed as gravely as infanticide, or prosecuted very frequently. It was usually considered to be a "very heinous misdemeanour" to use William Blackstone's words. As Richard Burn, a cleric, J.P. and legal author noted in 1763, abortion after quickening: "…though a great crime, yet it is not murder nor manslaughter by the law of England, because it [the unborn baby] is not yet in *rerum natura*".[87]

Abortion was not subject to statutory prohibition until Lord Ellenborough's Malicious Shooting or Stabbing Act of 1803 (43 Geo III c. 58). This multi-faceted statute provided that the punishment for a post-quickening abortion was death (subject to reprieve), and otherwise (i.e. if committed before this time) transportation for fourteen years. However, no one appears to have been executed pursuant to the statute except where the mother had died during the process.[88] In 1808, when Thomas Newton was convicted at the Chester Assizes pursuant to the 1803 Act for giving a woman 'medicine' to procure an abortion, he received the more typical

---

[85] Anon (By a Physician), (1739) *The Ladies Physical Directory*, pp.4-5.
[86] Jaffary, Nora E. (2012) "Reconceiving Motherhood: Infanticide and Abortion in Colonial Mexico", pp.8-9.
[87] Burn, Richard (1763) *Ecclesiastical Law*, vol.1, at p.95.
[88] Sauer, R. (1978) "Infanticide and Abortion in Nineteenth-Century Britain", p.84.

"mitigated sentence of three years imprisonment". (He was also fined heavily).[89]

The death penalty for post-quickening abortion was formally abolished by s.6 of the Offences against the Person Act of 1837. (The statute made no distinction between the two forms of abortion). Prior to this time, and throughout the eighteenth century, the key questions for any jurists were, in the words of Michael Ryan's *A Manual of Medical Jurisprudence*: "1. Has there been abortion produced? 2. Is the abortion natural or provoked? 3. Has the foetus quickened?" However, Ryan also cautioned physicians to be "extremely cautious" when making this assessment, as miscarriage/abortion could have many natural causes.[90]

Of course, if a woman died as a result of an abortion that was administered or supervised by another person, the abortionist would be guilty of a serious offence. This was usually murder, despite their lack of intent, because the potion administered (or surgical operation carried out) was: "…not given to cure her of a disease, but unlawfully to destroy her child within her".[91] For example, in 1792, a Tewkesbury carpenter named William Birt was convicted of murder at the Gloucester Assizes after he gave his girlfriend a powder to bring about an abortion. She fell ill immediately after swallowing it and died eleven days later. Although, as the trial judge noted, Birt had not intended to kill her, "malice was implied" in such cases because she died as a result of an illegal act, albeit one to which she was herself an accomplice. Birt committed suicide in jail before he could be executed or reprieved.[92] However, John Winship, a farmer from Monkwearmouth, near Sunderland, was executed and dissected in 1785 for poisoning his maid by administering an abortifacient to her.[93]

Most people, with a little searching, could find a knowledgeable older woman or man who, with basic ingredients supplied by a chemist, such as wormwood (part of the Artemesia genus of plants), pennyroyal (a member of the mint family of herbs), ergot of rye (a fungus), mustard and savin, could "make a medicine which may cause Abortion".[94] Many generally

[89] *The Times,* September 9, 1809, at p.3.
[90] Cooper, Christine M. (2004) "Reading the Politics of Abortion: Mary Wollstonecraft Revisited", p.748.
[91] Burn, Richard (1763) *Ecclesiastical Law*, vol.1, at p.95
[92] *The Times,* August 18, 1791, p.4
[93] *Public Advertiser*, August 2, 1785.
[94] *Fog's Weekly Journal*, August 2, 1729; Spivack, Carla (2007) "To "Bring Down the Flowers": The Cultural Context of Abortion Law in Early Modern England", p.121.

nefarious eighteenth-century women, such as the habitual Yorkshire criminal Mary Bateman, could turn their hand to being abortionists for a fee, and administer "medicines" to terminate pregnancies as a sideline, even if it was not their primary criminal occupation.[95]

For others it was a more specialist career. For example, Jane Hanny, a widow from Trowbridge in Wiltshire, travelled around the county selling pills made up of gunpowder, rust filings, brimstone, liquorice and treacle. Although prescribed for many conditions (they were a type of 'snake-oil'), those who were: "...more wicked than ignorant, had their ends answer'd by making use of them, for they seldom fail'd of procuring abortion". This made them particularly popular with prostitutes and "lewd women". However, and perhaps significantly, it was also noted that Hanny's products were sometimes bought by "sober" females. The law appears to have made little attempt to interfere with her activities prior to her house burning down as a result of the manufacture of the pills.[96]

Other abortionists, like Eleanor Beare, a labourer's wife from Derby, had recourse to physical intervention with a large steel needle or similar implement, usually inserted into the patient's uterus.[97] This method may sometimes have been used after orally ingested abortifacients (the most popular stratagem in the period) had failed. For example, in 1742 in Pomfret, Connecticut, Amasa Sessions arranged for such a "manual operation" after impregnating a local girl, Sarah Grosvenor, and unsuccessfully forcing her to consume "physick".[98]

In 1732, Grace Belfort paid Beare 30s for a surgical abortion. The two women initially got drunk on cider and brandy, presumably to anaesthetise the patient, after which Beare inserted her needle into Grace, who miscarried the following day.[99] When Beare was convicted of this offence, largely on Grace's evidence, it was for a serious misdemeanour, albeit one that her trial judge in Derby described as "barbarous and unnatural". (The Connecticut case 15 years later was also referred to as a "highhanded misdemeanour"). Beare had made a trade of abortion, and when convicted was sentenced to three years' imprisonment and to be pilloried twice on market day in the town. Her crime excited acute popular hostility, suggesting that, although a significant number of contemporary women

---

[95] Anon, (1809) *Extraordinary Life and Character of Mary Bateman, the Yorkshire Witch*, p.9.

[96] *General Evening Post*, March 11, 1735 - March 13, 1735

[97] *The Gentleman's Magazine*, vol.2, August 1732, pp.931-932.

[98] Dayton, Cornelia Hughes (1991) "Taking the Trade: Abortion and Gender Relations in an Eighteenth-Century New England Village", p.19.

[99] Olsen, Kirstin (1999) *Daily Life in 18Th-Century England*, p.51.

may have had tried to have recourse to abortion, it was not necessarily popularly sanctioned. A crowd gathered and pelted Beare mercilessly on both occasions, with rotten eggs, vegetables and, more seriously, stones, so that blood streamed down her face by the time she was returned to prison.[100]

However, abortion was medically a highly uncertain and often very dangerous path. As Beare's trial judge noted, it was: "…attended with the greatest danger to whoever it is practised upon". Even where effective, its results could be physically devastating for the women concerned, as with one of Mary Bateman's clients, who was left emaciated and mortally ill.[101] Throughout the period, numerous women died as a result of such procedures, and many deaths probably went entirely undetected. As a prosecution expert medical witness observed in 1809, 'medicines' powerful enough to procure abortions: "…could not be administered without endangering the life of the female".[102] Thus, when a maid suddenly dropped dead in her chair in 1743, she was examined and found to be heavily pregnant. It was swiftly: "…imagined she had taken medicines to procure abortion, which was the cause of her death".[103] Similarly, at the end of the period, Ann Daws, a servant in a public house in Keynsham, died as a result of a "medicine taken to cause abortion". The coroner's jury heard that the dose had been administered by one Mary Longford and returned a verdict of willful murder. Longford was committed to Shepton jail to await trial.[104]

As some of these cases suggest, abortifacients were as likely to be administered by men as women. In 1775, for example, Joseph Taylor was committed to Derby Jail for having: "…feloniously given poison to Ellen Bamford, for the purpose of procuring abortion, by reason of which she died".[105] Similarly, in 1786, a married farmer from Grazely in Berkshire, was prosecuted by his pregnant (by him) maid, for giving her poisonous 'medicines', and treating her with "barbarity" while attempting to procure

---

[100] Knapp, Andrew and Baldwin, William (1825) *The Newgate Calendar: Comprising Interesting Memoirs of the Most Notorious Characters…*, vol.1, pp.315-316.

[101] Anon, (1809) *Extraordinary Life and Character of Mary Bateman, the Yorkshire Witch*, 9th edn., p.9.

[102] *The Times,* September 9, 1809, at p.3.

[103] *Daily Post*, March 19, 1743.

[104] *Courier and Evening Gazette*, August 1, 1800.

[105] *Adams's Weekly Courant*, November 7, 1775.

an abortion. (The farmer's wife was, apparently, also "very active in this iniquitous affair").[106]

Surgery was probably even more dangerous than 'medicine', at least prior to the 1800s, and many women died as a result. In 1781, Margaret Tinkler was convicted of murdering Jane Parkinson while attempting an abortion that ended in Jane's death. She was reprieved for three months to allow consideration of her case, but ultimately hanged near Durham.[107] Before her death, she told an attendant clergyman that she had only advised the dead woman about *how* to abort her baby, rather than physically performing the operation herself. In Connecticut, almost 40 years earlier, Sarah Grosvenor had struggled against a "malignant fever" for a month after her operation and miscarriage, before dying, despite the ministrations of several physicians. In this case, the man who had carried out the procedure was merely sentenced to a public flogging of 29 lashes.[108]

Dropping

If a foetus did survive to term, many women took the less drastic step (to killing their babies) of 'dropping' the infant in an environment in which it might be found and succoured, or at least handed over to the local authorities. The parish where such a baby was discovered would be forced to take on the financial burden involved in raising it, unless it was adopted. This was especially common in urban areas, particularly the Metropolis, but also occurred, albeit more rarely, in less built-up parts. In Northumberland, for example, one two-week-old baby was found carefully wrapped in a blanket in the entrance to a public house at 9 pm. It was clearly intended that the infant be saved.[109] This was a Europe-wide practice. In the eighteenth-century Republic of Dubrovnik, for example, churches and (to a lesser extent) main roads were popular places for dropping.[110]

---

[106] *Public Advertiser*, April 25, 1786.
[107] *St. James's Chronicle or the British Evening Post*, November 27, 1781 - November 29, 1781.
[108] Dayton, Cornelia Hughes (1991) "Taking the Trade: Abortion and Gender Relations in an Eighteenth-Century New England Village", p.19 and p.21.
[109] Morgan, Gwenda and Rushton, Peter (1998) *Rogues, Thieves and the Rule of Law,* p.114.
[110] Lonza, Nella (2002) "'Two Souls Lost': Infanticide In The Republic Of Dubrovnik (1667-1808)", p.77.

However, outside well-populated areas it was often a dangerous procedure, even with infants, let alone babies. In 1802, Maria Davis and her friend Charlotte Bobbett were convicted of murdering Maria's fifteen-month-old son, Richard. The child had become a burden to Maria, who was a recent widow. The two women decided to abandon Richard, hoping that someone would find and care for him. They left him on Brandon Hill on a cold night in January and he froze to death. Both women were convicted at the Bristol Assizes and executed.[111] Charlotte Turner's son had been more fortunate the previous year. Aged less than four years old, he was abandoned one dark night by a canal in Birmingham, after which his mother returned to her native Yorkshire. However, the child was found and the mother eventually traced. She received one year's imprisonment in the common jail in Warwick. More importantly, a prosperous lady in Birmingham adopted the infant.[112]

Despite such expedients, some women resorted to killing their babies. This was for a variety of reasons, many probably based on simple practicalities, such as personal isolation from sources of assistance, an inability after giving birth to move any significant distance, and the frequent lack of privacy faced by servants living under their masters' roofs.

'Typical' Infanticides

The immediate background to many *prosecuted* cases of neonatal infanticide was very similar. As already indicated, a majority of those suspected of infanticide were domestic maids.[113] Most were motivated by a fear of losing their positions and livelihoods.[114] The great majority of infanticides were committed almost immediately after delivery by a woman who had concealed her pregnancy as best she could, given birth alone, and promptly disposed of the baby's body after killing it or while it was still alive (the same act bringing about both ends). She had then cleaned herself up as much as possible and attempted to return to her normal work as soon as she could. Sometimes, this was within minutes of giving birth. However, a few pregnant women went away from their employments for a few days to have and kill their babies, usually on a

[111] *The Bury and Norwich Post: Or, Suffolk, Norfolk, Essex, and Cambridge Advertiser*, April 21, 1802.
[112] *The Morning Post and Gazetteer*, February 13, 1801.
[113] Malcolmson, R.W. (1977) "Infanticide in the eighteenth century", p.192.
[114] De Mandeville, Bernard (1724) *A Modest Defence of Publick Stews*, p.27.

spurious pretext, such as urgently needing to visit sick relatives.[115] This general pattern was certainly not unique to England. For example, of the 140 infanticide cases that came before the Justiciary Court for South West Scotland between 1750 and 1815, only five involved women who had had accomplices. Only two of the women were married, while over 90 were domestic servants.[116]

In most (if not all) areas, whether urban or rural, the sex of the infant was irrelevant to the mother's decision to kill it.[117] This broadly correlates with evidence for legitimate births in the wider society. For example, in one September week in 1725, 172 male babies and 167 females were christened within the Metropolitan Bills of Mortality.[118] In a February week in 1735, 174 boys and 170 girls went through the same ceremony.[119] Given that the 'natural' ratio at birth is about 105 boys to 100 girls (probably an evolutionary allowance for greater male mortality in early life and a phenomenon that contemporary observers were well aware of),[120] it seems that even if eighteenth-century English families wanted boys, they did not normally get rid of girls.

It is not entirely surprising that many infanticide defendants were servant maids. Domestic service was by far the most common single form of employment for younger single women. They were often socially isolated, at the peak of their fertility and also, perhaps, more ignorant about methods of contraception than slightly older females, and so more likely to get pregnant as a result of 'fornication'. Although eighteenth-century contraception was primitive, it did exist. Animal membrane condoms appeared during the era, though they were very expensive and primarily used to prevent sexually transmitted diseases. Much more pertinently, simple douching after intercourse, using water mixed with vinegar, salt or alcohol, was a commonly used female prophylactic of the time. Very crude caps, some made of beeswax, were also occasionally employed.[121] However, such techniques had to be learnt, over time, from other, perhaps older, women.

---

115 Dickinson, J.P. and Sharpe, James A. (2002) "Infanticide in early modern England: the Court of Great Sessions at Chester, 1650-1800", p.49.

116 Kilday, Anne-Marie (2002) "Maternal Monsters: Murdering Mothers in Eighteenth Century Scotland", pp.162-167.

117 Dickinson, J.P. and Sharpe, James A. (2002) "Infanticide in early modern England: the Court of Great Sessions at Chester, 1650-1800", p.49.

118 *Parker's Penny Post*, September 3, 1725.

119 *Universal Spectator and Weekly Journal*, February 1, 1735.

120 *Guardian*, August 17, 1713.

121 Rees, Sian (2002), *The Floating Brothel*, pp.109-110.

Additionally, maids were regularly exposed to the attentions of men. Although the master (or one of his sons) who impregnated a female servant was a common cultural trope, and it was not without some foundation in reality, many such women had formed a relationship with someone from a similar social background. In 1693, for example, Elizabeth Bibington from Warwickshire was impregnated by a maltster: "…who had carnal knowledge of her in the house of her master". In 1778, even Parson Woodforde's trusted maid 'Sukey' admitted to him that she was pregnant by a local man named simply as Humphrey. She then went before a Norfolk J.P. to "swear to the father of the child she is big with". (Sukey left the cleric's service shortly afterwards, with an extra four shillings and her back pay).[122]

Male domestic staff (i.e. the work colleagues of female servants) posed a particular threat. As Thomas Broughton warned, maids: "…could not avoid conversing with the men servants, and too frequently with such as are lewd and debauched". They needed to be constantly alert to the dangers and temptations that this presented.[123] For example, in Warwickshire, the strangely named Matthew Turrall (she was a woman) became pregnant by William Bloxwich in 1695 after he had: "…carnal knowledge of her in the house of Thomas Harbon, where they both worked as servants".[124]

A combination of these factors meant that it would be natural for a very significant number of infanticide cases to involve female servants. Nevertheless, despite the huge number of maids at work in England at this time, their youth, and the temptations and pressures they were subjected to, it is extremely implausible that young women in domestic service 'got into trouble' at a quite vastly higher rate than the many others who worked on their fathers' smallholdings, in small businesses, or who were widowed at an early age. A crucial variant was privacy and seclusion. It is likely that many instances of neonaticide amongst single women who were not servants, but living alone or with family or friends, went undetected. Occasionally, this is hinted at in the reported cases. For example, in 1735, Sarah Baylis was convicted and executed after the Gloucestershire Assizes for committing two infanticides, in successive years.[125] Clearly, she had initially escaped detection for the first offence.

With the assistance of intimates and a modicum of privacy discovery

---

[122] Woodforde, James (1999) *The Diary of a Country Parson, 1758-1802,* pp.102-104.

[123] Broughton, Thomas (1800) *Serious Advice and Warning to Servants*, p.20.

[124] Johnson, H.C. (1964) *Warwick County Records, vol.IX: Quarter session records; Easter, 1690 to Michaelmas, 1696*, p.xliii and p.xliv, and p.68.

[125] *Country Journal or The Craftsman*, August 23, 1735.

could often be avoided, especially in rural areas. In Cheshire, for example, it seems that close family members sometimes helped a pregnant woman to hide a delivery.[126] Like other aspects of childbirth, this duty would usually fall on female relatives. For example, it was alleged that Elizabeth Archer was assisted by her mother when she killed her newborn bastard by burying it alive in a garden near Burton in Staffordshire. Both women were arrested.[127] Alice Hiscock of Highworth in Wiltshire strangled and suffocated her illegitimate male baby with the assistance of her grandmother in 1765. They were acquitted at the Salisbury Assizes. A similar situation, at the same forum, occurred 15 years later, when Betty Taylor killed her illegitimate baby, again with help from her grandmother. Once more, both women were acquitted.[128] Mary Lamphrey was less fortunate. She was sentenced to death with her daughter, Anne, for assisting the latter to kill her newborn female bastard. Mary was executed in March 1766. However, on the day her mother was hanged, Anne was respited, receiving a free pardon and release in July of the same year.[129] Conversely, Mary Sant stood trial at the Chester Assizes in 1778 with her daughter Sarah, for assisting the latter to kill her bastard, but was acquitted, while Sarah was convicted and executed.[130]

Of course, not all those prosecuted or convicted for infanticide were servants, or even especially young. Some other single women were unlucky. For example, in 1692, Mary Goodenough, a 40-year-old widow with two children, from Bradwell in Oxfordshire, was living in great want. A neighbouring and married baker seduced her, partly by promising her an allowance (if only of his loaves). She fell pregnant, but concealed the fact until she gave birth, which she attempted to hide by pretending to be ill. However, her labour appears to have lasted longer than usual, so that some of her neighbours became suspicious and visited her. They quickly saw from her breasts that she had been pregnant and accused her of giving birth to a child. She admitted this, and directed them to the infant's body, which was wrapped in a blanket at the foot of her bed. She had made no attempt to summon assistance while giving birth. As Zachary Babington noted in 1680, this was: "…contrary to the custome of honest and innocent women (who always desire help in their labour) [and never] chuseth to be

[126] Dickinson, J.P. and Sharpe, James A. (2002) "Infanticide in early modern England: the Court of Great Sessions at Chester, 1650-1800", p.36.
[127] *The British Journal,* 17 June, 1727.
[128] Hunnisett, R.F. (Ed.) (1981) *Wiltshire Coroners' Bills 1752–1796*, p.26 and p.72.
[129] *St. James's Chronicle or the British Evening Post*, July 12, 1766.
[130] *Chester Chronicle Or Commercial Intelligencer*, September 11, 1778.

delivered alone".[131] Ten days later, Goodenough was committed to Oxford castle to await trial at the following Assizes, where she was duly convicted and executed.[132]

Similarly, Elizabeth Waldron was hanged at the age of 35 for murdering her baby, after the Exeter Assizes in March 1782.[133] A contemporary broadsheet suggests that she was the spinster daughter of a rope-maker, with whom she had always lived. She had become pregnant by an exciseman and, it seems, had concealed her pregnancy as far as possible until she came to term. When the baby arrived, Elizabeth was alone and she immediately buried it alive in a dunghill in her father's yard. Unfortunately for her, he returned unexpectedly to the house, and heard it cry. He called a neighbouring woman, who rescued it, and a midwife was sent for, but the baby died a few hours later. Its head was badly bruised and cut. Medical testimony, combined with Waldron's concealment of her pregnancy and failure to provide any clothing for the infant in advance of the birth, led the jury to find her guilty.[134]

In like manner, in 1755, Grace Smith, technically a married woman (her husband had abandoned her almost immediately after their wedding several years earlier), became pregnant by a married man from a nearby parish in Cornwall. Shortly after being delivered, she strangled her infant to "hide her shame".[135] She then threw the corpse into a river, where a man angling near Southill fished it out shortly afterwards. Smith was immediately suspected, something that was indicative of a society in which rumour swirled around, and when examined before the coroner made full admissions (disastrously, given that the 1624 Act [see below] would not apply), acknowledging that the child was hers and had been born alive.[136] She was executed.

Nevertheless, such women were comparative rarities. Significantly, even where the women prosecuted for the crime were not domestic servants they were often employees, living away from their family home in circumstances in which help and privacy were absent. For example, a pregnant Margaret Mantle had travelled to Canterbury from her home in Dover to pick hops. She came to term and "delivered by herself" at her

---

[131] Babington, Zachary (1680) *Advice to grand jurors in cases of blood…*, p.175.

[132] Anon, (1692) *An Account of the Tryal, Condemnation and Execution of Mary Goodenough, at the Assizes held in Oxon, in February 1692*, pp.1-4.

[133] *Whitehall Evening Post (1770)*, March 28, 1782 - March 30, 1782.

[134] Anon, (1782) *Character and dying behaviour of the two murderers, executed at Heavitree gallows, Monday, March 25, 1782*, pp.1-2.

[135] *Public Advertiser*, August 21, 1755.

[136] *Read's Weekly Journal Or British Gazetteer*, July 5, 1755.

lodgings in the cathedral city, and then watched out for an opportunity to "drop the infant down a necessary house, where it was found". She was convicted at Canterbury Sessions, which still had power of general gaol delivery, and executed in December 1754.[137]

The Statistics for Infanticide Prosecutions

When indictment and, even more so, conviction rates for neonaticide are examined, what has been termed a "clear pattern" emerges. The incidence of such offences rose in the early seventeenth century and peaked in the 1650s, remaining at a relatively high level until the 1680s. They then started to fall swiftly, and continued to do so throughout the eighteenth century, which saw a major but uneven (chronologically and geographically) decline from the highs seen during the previous century. It is difficult to identify a pivotal decade for this process, though the years between 1710 and 1750 appear to have been crucial in much of the country. However, its timing and thoroughness seems to have varied considerably from county to county and circuit to circuit.

In Denbighshire, in Wales, for example, the process appears to have set in early. There were eight indictments during the period from 1670 to 1701, of which four resulted in a conviction. However, a fifteen-year gap then followed before the next prosecution took place in 1716, and between then and 1730 there were only four more indictments, none of which led to a guilty verdict. It has also been noted that the most thorough investigation and pre-trial preparation of such cases (detailed depositions etc.) belong to the seventeenth century. Those from the 1710s and 1720s show less conviction, both literally and metaphorically. Sporadic prosecutions continued there, throughout the century, but with much less intent. As in England, attitudes towards Welsh women suspected of the crime were increasingly sympathetic.[138]

In England, two clusters of infanticide cases provide a telling illustration. In April 1740, three women, Johanna Bryant, Dinah Turner, and Ann Cummins were all convicted and executed for *separate* infanticides after the Exeter Assizes. By contrast, Ann Benison and Mary Walker, produced from York Castle to take their trials for two infanticides at the Assizes held in that city in July 1788, were both acquitted.[139] At the

---

137 *Whitehall Evening Post or London Intelligencer*, December 21, 1754 - December 24, 1754.

138 Howard, Sharon (2003) *Crime, Communities And Authority In Early Modern Wales: Denbighshire, 1660-1730*, pp.93-94 & p.44.

139 *World (1787)*, July 14, 1788.

same time, the reprieve rate for those women who were capitally convicted of infanticide also increased significantly (see chapter two).

This decline in convictions and executions was a European-wide phenomenon, although its rate, degree and timing varied greatly from country to country. Thus, in 1740, the Court of Appeal in Prague saw 55 women accused of infanticide and 22 convicted and initially sentenced to death, while only two women were accused of the crime in the four years between 1780 and 1784, and neither was convicted. By contrast, the Paris *Parlement*, one of France's highest courts, saw a more modest fall. There, 100 women were prosecuted for the crime in 1740, 21 of whom were convicted and initially sentenced to death; in 1780, the figures were 45 and 10 respectively.[140]

Pre-trial legal changes and prosecutorial zeal cannot, on their own, fully account for the change in England, as convictions fell significantly faster than prosecutions. For example, on the Northern Circuit (made up of Yorkshire, Cumberland, Westmorland and Northumberland), nearly two hundred cases of suspected neonaticide were brought before the courts between 1720 and 1800, but only six women were convicted and just two were hanged, the last well before the end of the century. This produces a conviction rate of about three per cent (less than a fifth of that found at the Old Bailey at this time).[141] Unlike witchcraft, a decline in convictions did not necessarily prompt a commensurate decline in prosecutions. This suggests that, in this northern part of England at least, local people were still fairly determined to identify those who killed the newborn, and to shame them publicly by initiating prosecutions. It is clear that there was still considerable popular hostility towards those who committed infanticide. Many people, especially women, seem to have gone out of their way to expose such cases.[142]

However, a willingness to convict and execute them on the part of key (male) players in the judicial process was no longer present.[143] It seems that the socially elite judges and middling-order jurors found at Assizes

---

[140] Tinkova, Daniela (2005) "Protéger Ou Punir? Les Voies De La Décriminalisation De L'infanticide En France Et Dans Le Domaine Des Habsbourg (Xviiie-Xixe Siècles)", pp.48-52.

[141] Jackson, Mark (1996) *New-born child murder,* p.3 and p.134, and Jackson, Mark (1994) "Suspicious infant deaths: the statute of 1624 and medical evidence at coroners' inquests", p.70.

[142] Morgan, Gwenda and Rushton, Peter (1998) *Rogues, Thieves and the Rule of Law,* p.117 and p.123.

[143] Roth, Randolph (2001) "Homicide In Early Modern England 1549-1800: The Need For A Quantitative Synthesis", pp.33-67.

were normally sympathetic to infanticide defendants. It was only when the public horror in their localities was matched by official reaction, as occurred in a handful of cases, that the conviction and execution of accused women was likely to come about.[144]

Of course, even if a woman was acquitted, the shame attracted by such a prosecution meant that she might feel obliged to leave her parish, or be sent away by her family, producing a 'result' for the local community. For example, in Cheshire in 1778, it was reported that Mary Sant, acquitted of assisting her daughter commit infanticide, hanged herself after returning home and: "...being received in the neighbourhood with a coolness she did not expect".[145]

When it came to convictions, the Northern Circuit was a fairly extreme illustration, and women from its counties appear to have been slightly favoured compared to those from some other regions. Nevertheless, the Court of Great Sessions in Chester shows the same general pattern, if to a less pronounced degree. Between 1650 and 1699, 72 women were accused of the crime there (in 63 cases), and at least 20 were hanged. In the years from 1700 to 1749 there were 33 defendants, but only four women were hanged (three coming from one Sessions in 1701). Between 1750 and 1800, there were 18 defendants and only three women hanged. The last to be executed, Sarah Sant in 1778, may have been executed during a short-lived local 'panic' about the crime.[146]

Similarly, in Staffordshire, there was less than one prosecution a year on average from 1743 to 1802, and none of the 39 cases resulted in a conviction and death sentence. In Surrey, there appear to have been just three or four trials for infanticide each decade during the eighteenth century, and only one of the 35 cases between 1720 and 1802 resulted in a conviction and execution.[147]

In Wiltshire, the situation during the second half of the eighteenth century was broadly the same. Between 1752 and 1796, the county's two coroners (one for the north and one for the south) investigated about fifty cases of infanticide. (There were separate coroners for some of the county's boroughs, with an overlapping jurisdiction). Very few cases resulted in a conviction, and even fewer in an execution, although in the

[144] Morgan, Gwenda and Rushton, Peter (1998) *Rogues, Thieves and the Rule of Law,* p.117 and p.123.
[145] Jackson, Mark (1996) *New-born child murder,* p.47 and p.3.
[146] Dickinson, J.P. and Sharpe, James A. (2002) "Infanticide in early modern England: the Court of Great Sessions at Chester, 1650-1800", pp.38-39.
[147] King, Peter (2006) *Crime and Law in England, 1750-1840,* p.179.

great majority there was a suspect and often a prosecution.[148] For example, the coroner for North Wiltshire investigated nine cases between December 1752 and December 1762. All but one produced a suspect. However, only one led to an execution, that of Ann Jordan in 1758. Four others went to the Assizes at Salisbury but resulted in acquittals. By 1776, Grace Hedges from Purton could be acquitted at the Salisbury Assizes despite having earlier confessed to killing and burying her illegitimate baby.[149]

In like manner, of the 200 women accused of infanticide *or* child murder (the killing of infants) on the Assizes held for four of the Western Circuit counties between 1735 and 1785 (Devon, Somerset, Cornwall and Dorset), only 29 were convicted and, it seems, just six were executed.[150]

Confirmed provincial executions for infanticide over the last 20 years of the century were particularly rare and have a slight bias towards the southern half of the country. Some eighteen women were hanged for the crime during this period. One woman, Lydia Dickenson, was executed in York in 1784, for the murder of her illegitimate daughter, Martha Dickenson, by drowning her in the River Calder at Clifton-upon-Calder. However, as this is of a named child it is obviously not a neonatal infanticide, but rather the domestic murder of an infant (and so not included in the above total). Of the 18 found guilty of infanticide, one woman was hanged in each of: Worcester, Cambridge, Aylesbury, Buckingham, Taunton, Kennington (Surrey), Gloucester, Horsham, Bridgewater, Maidstone, Norwich, Northampton, Salisbury and Warwick. Two women were executed (at different times) in Shrewsbury and Exeter.[151]

Economic Explanations for Infanticide

Although changing social and cultural attitudes seem to have been behind much of the decline in infanticide prosecutions and, even more so, convictions and executions, it has also been argued that there was a wider economic link between birth rates, premarital pregnancy, age at first

---

[148] Hunnisett, R.F. (Ed.) (1981) *Wiltshire Coroners' Bills 1752–1796*, p.xxi and p.157. Most were apothecaries or surgeons and would travel across the shire, at a set rate of 9d per mile plus a pound an inquest (more for homicides) for most of the period, to investigate suspicious or unexpected deaths.

[149] Hunnisett, R.F. (Ed.) (1981) *Wiltshire Coroners' Bills 1752–1796*, pp.1-21 and p.60.

[150] Williams, Amy (2000) *The Criminality Of Women In The 18th Century In The South West Of England*, p.203.

[151] www.capitalpunishmentuk.org

marriage, abortion, infanticide, and the murder of slightly older children by their parents. This connection might suggest that there was a real, not simply apparent, fall in the number of infanticides. According to this analysis, real wages dropped by more than a third for the poorest 40 per cent of the English population in the late-sixteenth and early-seventeenth centuries (though some economic historians might question this). As a result, young men and women found it harder to marry and raise families. The birth rate and life expectancy dropped, premarital pregnancy rates fell, the age of mothers at first birth rose, fewer women married, and the neonaticide indictment rate jumped fivefold. When real wages rose again in the late-seventeenth and early-eighteenth centuries, the trends reversed, birth and premarital pregnancy rates rose and the neonaticide indictment rate fell to its previous level. Child (rather than baby) murder rates in England also fell. Thus, demographic and economic conditions influenced the incidence of neonaticide and child murder to a considerable extent.[152]

This analysis is unsatisfactory as a full explanation for the phenomenon because it assumes a close and constant link between the incidence of neonatal infanticide and its level of indictment, rather than the latter being heavily influenced by social and cultural factors. Nevertheless, it would, perhaps, be a mistake to dismiss it entirely out of hand. Such factors may have had, at the least, a contributory role to what occurred between 1600 and 1800.

Infanticide and the Law

As already indicated, infanticide fell into the province of the secular (rather than Church) courts during the sixteenth century.[153] Initially, prosecutions faced many difficulties. Most importantly, it was necessary to prove that the baby had been born alive and then been deliberately killed to obtain a conviction. In many cases: "…none for the King could prove the child born alive, and therefore it was impossible to indict and convict her at the common law for murther".[154] The only difference to other types of murder trial was that baby-killing did not permit claims of self-defence or provocation.

Given the surreptitious nature of the act, independent witnesses to such

---

[152] Roth, Randolph (2001) "Homicide In Early Modern England 1549-1800: The Need For A Quantitative Synthesis", pp.33-67. Roth, Randolph (2011) "Biology and the deep history of homicide", pp.535-555.

[153] Hoffer, Peter C. and Hull, N. E. H. (1981) *Murdering Mothers: Infanticide in England and New England 1558-1803,* p.7.

[154] Babington, Zachary (1680) *Advice to grand jurors in cases of blood…*, p.174

crimes were rare, so that, unless there were admissions by the suspect or a badly mutilated corpse, the Crown was usually forced to rely on circumstantial evidence to prove a live birth, something that did not normally find favour with early modern juries. As a lawyer noted when doubting Mary Edmondson's (adult) murder conviction: "Circumstances will not fix a common debt upon a man, much less the dreadful crime of murder".[155] As a result, although the number of infanticide cases heard on the home circuit showed a significant increase during the reign of Queen Elizabeth I, the figures were still very small. In Essex, for example, between 1558 and 1593, there were only 23 indictments, and just 14 in Sussex in the same period.[156]

This led to the passing of a special statute in 1624, after which most unmarried women who were accused of murdering their newborn children were tried under an 'Act to prevent the Destroying and Murthering of Bastard Children' (21 James I, cap. 27). Similar statutes were introduced into the criminal codes of many other European countries during the seventeenth century. They reflected new religious preoccupations and a determination amongst the emerging 'modern' states of the period to control serious deviance within their borders.

The 1624 Act

The wording of the 1624 statute effectively reversed the burden of proof. If newborn, illegitimate, babies were found dead and their mothers had secretly buried them or otherwise concealed their deaths, they would: "...suffer death as in the case of murther, except such mother can make proof by one witness at the last that the child … was born dead".[157] As a result, a woman who hid the death of a newborn bastard was presumed to have murdered it, unless she could prove it had been stillborn by calling a plausible witness.[158] Malice aforethought, the mental state necessary for murder, was assumed in these situations: "…which malice the law implies, although none can prove the child born alive".[159]

The 1624 Act's effects were, initially, very significant, at least in some

---

[155] Anon (By a gentleman of the law), (1759) *The Case of Mary Edmondson*, p.20.

[156] Hoffer, Peter C. and Hull, N. E. H. (1981) *Murdering Mothers: Infanticide in England and New England 1558-1803,* pp.2-30.

[157] Jackson, Mark (1994) "Suspicious infant deaths: the statute of 1624 and medical evidence at coroners' inquests", p.67.

[158] Shapiro, Barbara (1986) "To A Moral Certainty: Theories of Knowledge and Anglo-American Juries 1600-1850", *Hastings Law Journal,* 1986, vol.38, p.156.

[159] Babington, Zachary (1680) *Advice to grand jurors in cases of blood* … p.172.

areas. In the decades immediately after it was introduced, up to forty per cent of women accused of the crime in Essex were found guilty and hanged, and many more prosecutions were brought, these reaching a peak during the Interregnum.[160] Of course, the statute's impact can still be exaggerated. Even in seventeenth-century Cheshire, for example, significant numbers of women (often about half) who were accused of the crime continued to be acquitted, albeit significantly fewer than before its advent. The Act was not usually applied quite as strictly as its wording might suggest.[161] Nevertheless, it had very important consequences for indictment and conviction levels.

An illustration of the statute's operation can be seen in a case from 1674, in which a young woman was executed following trial at the Northampton Assizes. Shortly after taking up a domestic position she was washing items with her mistress when she complained that she was ill, and immediately went up to a: "…Chamber to Lye down, where she was delivered of a Bastard Child, which she pretended was still Born, but however, the Law makes it Death in such case, to go about to conceal it, which she did by wrapping it up in her Apron". She then tried to hide it behind a bedstead. However, her mistress came up to the room and noticed part of the apron; she pulled it out, thinking from its bloodied condition that it needed to be added to the washing, exposing the baby's body.[162]

In theory, the Act remained in force until 1803, so that unmarried English women accused of infanticide during the eighteenth century had to avoid its draconian provisions if they could. As a result, some claimed to have been married but recently widowed, or separated from their still living husbands when they gave birth. Prior to Hardwicke's Marriage Act of 1753 the documentation of marriage was often poor, making such claims easier, especially in a place like London with its fairly large and relatively transient population. It was obviously harder to do this in the more stable parts of provincial England. Nevertheless, such claims were still made outside the Metropolis, and some were entirely valid. In 1740, for example, Ann Powell, a 'live-in' maid in Surrey, who was thought to be a spinster by her employers, was indicted under the 1624 Act for killing

160 Wrightson, Keith (1975) "Infanticide in earlier Seventeenth-Century England", pp.10-21.

161 Walker, Garthine (2003) *Crime, Gender and Social Order in Early Modern England,* pp.151-153.

162 Anon, (1674) *Relation of the most remarkable proceedings at the late assizes at Northampton Conteyning truely and fully, the tryals, confessions, and execution of a most mischievous vvitch, notorious high-way-man, barbarous murderess. ... Who all suffered at Northampton aforesaid, Saturday, August 22, 1674*, pp.1-4.

and burying her baby during the night. She admitted the birth to a fellow servant who shared her bed. However, at trial, this same servant gave evidence that Ann had earlier been married in their local church and that, although working apart from her spouse, he was still living. She was acquitted: "…it appearing that the prisoner was married, and it could not be suppos'd that the child was a bastard".[163]

The 1624 Act in Practice

Although, in many eighteenth-century infanticide trials, it *should* have been extremely difficult to avoid the reach of the 1624 Act, it appears that the statute was frequently being ignored by judges (and so juries) by the end of the 1600s, and largely, though not quite entirely, disregarded after the middle of the following century. This development made a major contribution to the fall in conviction levels. The reversed legal burden contained in the statute was increasingly seen as smacking: "…of severity, in making the concealment of the death almost conclusive evidence of the child's being murdered by the mother".[164] In an important article (posthumously) published in 1784, the distinguished physician, surgeon, anatomist and man-midwife William Hunter was adamant that concealment should amount to no more than a ground of suspicion, since women who were entirely innocent of murder might choose to hide their pregnant condition, before and after birth.[165]

Increasingly sympathetic magistrates, judges and juries also began to accept a range of special, judicially created, defences to the 1624 Act. These were alluded to in 1745 when it was noted that Ann Wooley, from Camberwell, whose illegitimate female baby had been found in a privy, escaped conviction because there were "several circumstances in her favour".[166] Such 'circumstances', or defences, might include what has

---

[163] Anon, (1740) *The Proceedings at the Assizes of Peace, Oyer and Terminer, for the County of Surrey, Held at the Town-Hall of Kingston Upon Thames, in the 14th Year of His Majesty's Reign ... To Which is Added the Genuine Proceedings at the Assizes for the County of Essex*, p.9.

[164] Blackstone, William (1769) *Commentaries on the Laws of England*, vol.4, p.198.

[165] Hunter, William (1784) "On the Uncertainty of the Signs of Murder, in the Case of Bastard Children", pp 266-290.

[166] Anon, (1745) *The Proceedings at the assizes of the peace, oyer and terminer, and general gaol-delivery for the county of Surry, held at Croydon, on Friday the 22d, Saturday the 23d, Monday the 25th, Tuesday the 26th, and Wednesday the 27th Days of March*, p.13.

been termed (probably retrospectively) 'benefit of linen', in which the defendant demonstrated that she had made bed clothes, baby clothes and similar useful items in preparation for a birth, and 'want of help', in which she argued that the infant died despite her manifest efforts to secure assistance. It was also accepted that, if a pregnant single woman had publicly told others of her condition prior to giving birth, the statute would not normally apply.

The presence of such defences was examined increasingly carefully in pre-trial hearings in front of magistrates and coroners, and accorded progressively more significance as the period advanced. For example, when an experienced coroner in the North, George Petch, admitted that neither he nor a constable had confirmed or disproved the claim of Frances Harrison to have had some children's clothes ready for her baby, in her personal box (often a servant's only private space), his note was endorsed: "The greater fools you".[167]

By the middle of the eighteenth century, even if a Justice was made aware of the death of an illegitimate newborn baby, proceedings would not quite *invariably* go further, provided some of these factors were present. For example, it seems that Mary Bailey had taken the vital step of preparing some baby clothes and linen for her child. By 1774, this seems to have been enough to dissuade her examining J.P. from proceeding with the matter and she was discharged, even though, properly speaking, such an issue should have been left to a jury to determine.[168] (The master of the house seems to have had mental health problems, which may also have been a factor in the magistrate's decision).

Even a few inherently more suspicious cases, without such features, do not seem to have survived a Justice's initial examination by the mid-century. In 1754, for example, a newborn male baby was found dead in a ditch in Bristol. His arms had been broken, there was a wound on his belly, and "several other marks of violence". The baby's mother was found and arrested: "…but it appearing on examination that the child was born dead, she was discharged".[169]

The preparation of linen was accorded even more significance at Assizes than it was at the pre-trial hearing. In 1739, Mary Mills was accused of infanticide after a dead baby was found in her personal chest. Fortunately for her, she had (she claimed) made some "provision" for it,

---

[167] Jackson, Mark (1996) *New-born child murder,* p.143.

[168] Silverthorne, Elizabeth (Ed.) (1978) *The Deposition Book of Richard Wyatt JP, 1767-1776*, pp.48-49.

[169] *Whitehall Evening Post or London Intelligencer*, November 7, 1754 – November 9, 1754.

taking baby-clothes to her trial and telling the judge in response to a question specifically on this issue: "My Lord, I did. Here is my childbed linen, it was no secret".[170] Some observers feared that it was easy for such evidence to be deliberately fabricated, in advance of trial, for forensic use.

Defences that effectively amounted to claims of temporary mental disturbance also entered the language of infanticide defendants after the 1730s, as growing numbers of women described themselves as "agitated" or "confused" during the births and deaths of their babies. For example, Mary Mills alleged that: "When I was delivered I knew nothing of the matter, the child dropt from me, and I was taken with a fainting fit and fell down".[171] Such claims attracted growing sympathy, especially towards the end of the period, as the cultural meme spread. William Hunter and other specialist medical observers urged judges and juries to at least consider the defendant's state of mind before convicting, even though insanity was not normally used as a defence in infanticide cases. Hunter argued that the distress and confusion associated with labour could temporarily deprive women of judgment and the ability to act rationally. Having given birth alone, and being: "…quite exhausted they faint away, and become insensible of what is passing; and when they recover a little strength, find that the child, whether stillborn or not, is completely lifeless". Their disturbed condition could also explain why some women then chose to conceal the child's dead body.[172]

Of course, such claims were not necessarily accepted, even at the end of the period. Before her execution for infanticide in Salisbury, in 1775, Elizabeth Aldridge denied that she was guilty, and unavailingly claimed to have been: "…senseless for some time after her delivery, and that when she recovered, she saw the child lying dead by her".[173] Nevertheless, by then, there was far more allowance for such matters than there had been in earlier times. Women could explain and excuse their behaviour without necessarily having to argue that they were fully mad.[174]

---

[170] Anon, (1739) *The Genuine Proceedings at the Assizes on the Home Circuit, Held in March, 1739. ... at Hertford, for the County of Hertford; Chelmsford, for the County of Essex* p.18.

[171] Anon, (1739) *The Genuine Proceedings at the Assizes on the Home Circuit, Held in March, 1739. ... at Hertford, for the County of Hertford; Chelmsford, for the County of Essex* pp.18-19.

[172] Hunter, William (1784) "On the Uncertainty of the Signs of Murder, in the Case of Bastard Children", pp.266-290.

[173] *Morning Post and Daily Advertiser*, March 28, 1775.

[174] Rabin, Dana (2004) *Identity, Crime and Legal Responsibility in Eighteenth-Century England*, pp.95-103.

During the 1700s it seems that the 1624 statute was only expressly mentioned to jurors on relatively (and increasingly) rare occasions, though where it was, it could still affect verdict. By the 1760s, William Blackstone could note that the courts would usually require some sort of evidence that a child was born alive before applying the presumption that a: "…child, whose death is concealed, was therefore killed by it's [sic] parent".[175] For an example of this more relaxed approach, can be considered the case of Elizabeth Ryals, who was accused of murdering her newborn baby in Ecclesall, Yorkshire, in 1770. She was tried under the 1624 statute. Elizabeth claimed that she had given birth to a stillborn baby, wrapped it in an apron, and hidden it in a field. Elizabeth's neighbours and employers were suspicious of her efforts to conceal both her pregnancy and the birth. When a local surgeon testified that the child had probably been born alive, the inquest jury returned a verdict of murder and Elizabeth was sent to trial at the York Assizes. Nevertheless, she was acquitted there by the petty jury.[176] As this case also suggests, in infanticide cases, trial juries at Assizes frequently rejected the verdict returned by the jury at a coroner's inquest.

Like witchcraft prosecutions in the decades prior to the crime's abolition in 1736, the decline in convictions under the 1624 Act largely reflects a transformation in judicial and, via the jury, (relatively) élite social attitudes. Judges were no longer striving for guilty verdicts and juries wanted to be 'charitable' if they could. There was growing sympathy for the plight of women who had been driven to kill illegitimate babies. Of course, much depended on the personal inclinations and beliefs of the judge presiding over the Crown Side at Assizes. Unlike those on the collegiate benches found at the Old Bailey, they normally sat alone, giving greater scope for a conservative or 'old fashioned' judge to resist the eighteenth-century trend and helping to explain occasional 'strict' decisions, even in the latter part of the period.

---

[175] Blackstone, William (1769) *Commentaries on the Laws of England*, vol.4, p.198.

[176] Jackson, Mark (1996) "Infanticide: historical perspectives", p.416.

Repeal of the 1624 Act

There were unavailing attempts in Parliament to abolish the 1624 Act as early as 1772. These got caught up in the wider debate about the role, and desirability, of discretion in the criminal justice system. For example, in 1773, Thomas Lockhart, speaking in the House of Commons, argued that the 1624 Act was of no value because, by then, judges and juries: "...notwithstanding the circumstances are plain, often acquit unfortunate women". It was feared that the statute might even encourage women to lethal action because of its lackadaisical enforcement, when a lesser but strictly implemented punishment would deter them. By contrast, those who supported the Act's continuing existence frequently argued that it allowed the occasional, well-publicised, exemplary trial and conviction, producing a valuable deterrent.[177] Interestingly, in Prussia, the value of deterrence in infanticide cases also began to disappear from public discussion of the crime after the late 1780s, and had almost faded away by the start of the nineteenth century.[178]

In 1803, becoming concerned at the extent to which the (by then) almost routine disregard of the 1624 statute might undermine general respect for the law, Lord Ellenborough, the Lord Chief Justice of the King's Bench, finally introduced a bill to repeal and replace it (amongst several other legal objectives), which passed into law as 'An Act for the further Prevention of malicious shooting, etc' (43 Geo III c 58). The courts subsequently required evidence that a child had been born alive before they could find a woman guilty of murdering it. By then, this was normally the practical reality, and had been for many years. The 1803 statute also created a new offence of concealment of birth (where the birth and death of a baby had been kept secret). This had a maximum penalty of two years imprisonment, and was much more likely to attract convictions. An average of eight people per year were found guilty of the offence between 1810 and 1816. In reality, several (most?) of these probably involved cases of infanticide that would have led to acquittals if charged as such.[179]

---

[177] Jackson, Mark (1996) *New-born child murder* pp.161-163.

[178] Michalik, Kerstin (2006) "The Development of the Discourse on Infanticide in the Late Eighteenth Century and the New Legal Standardization of the Offense in the Nineteenth Century", p.61.

[179] Sauer, R. (1978) "Infanticide and Abortion in Nineteenth-Century Britain", p.82.

Discovery of Infanticide

The initial discovery of prosecuted cases of infanticide most commonly came from a failure to conceal the telltale signs of a baby's birth or its corpse *post mortem*. The last of these posed fewer problems in rural areas; tiny bodies could easily be buried in dunghills, fields and woods, submerged in ponds, lakes and rivers, fed to pigs or even burnt on bonfires. In 1729, for example, Elizabeth Pilcher from Canterbury burnt her illegitimate baby to "prevent a discovery". (She later claimed it had been stillborn and that she was bribed by its father to get rid of the corpse).[180] Even if not burnt, babies' bodies would swiftly be consumed by the ground or water and skeletonised within a few weeks. This was not usually possible in London, and explains the astonishingly high number of Metropolitan cases in which an infant's body was discovered in a privy. However, these were also regularly used in the provinces, especially in towns. For example, in 1761, Ann Nott, the servant to a gentleman living in Worcester, was charged by a Coroner's jury with murdering her male infant after its body was found in the privy of her master's house. Although recovered alive, the baby died from its injuries and exposure shortly afterwards.[181] Nott was convicted and executed after the Assizes held in that city.[182]

As previously noted, if a baby's body was found in a relatively isolated place, locating its mother (and putative killer) could be difficult, if not impossible, especially in rural areas. In other cases, an extensive investigation would first be necessary before its mother could be identified. In 1718, for example, when a newborn baby was found with its throat cut in a ditch in Lambeth, enquiries made a servant who worked in a nearby coffee-shop a prime suspect. She was arrested and a physical examination suggested that she had recently given birth. She admitted this, but claimed that her baby was alive and being nursed in the country. As a result, a man "was sent down to enquire the truth thereof". (In the meantime the suspect unavailingly attempted to kill herself).[183]

In other cases, births came to light after someone was prompted to make enquiries about a sudden loss of weight in the suspected woman. Sometimes this would be after she had gone away for a few days and come back noticeably slimmer. Alternatively, investigations might follow the

---

[180] *Daily Journal*, February 21, 1729.
[181] *Public Advertiser*, October 19, 1761.
[182] *St. James's Chronicle or the British Evening Post*, March 13, 1762 – March 16, 1762.
[183] *Weekly Journal, or, British Gazetteer,* May 10, 1718.

discovery of blood and afterbirth on the floor, soiled linen, or the suspect complaining of the medical problems that might be attendant on an unassisted delivery. Childbirth in even the best of circumstances could be a difficult business during the eighteenth century. However, the mother of an illegitimate baby lacked the "necessary assistance" if she had any sort of emergency, and was devoid of even the help of a kindly neighbour, making such problems more likely.[184] For example, Hannah Miller, from Stannaway in Surrey, was alerted by the strange behaviour of her maid Mary Curtis, and was "confirmed in my suspicion by seeing her bed".[185]

Local women, whether in towns or villages, often appear to have been far more interested and ruthless than men about policing and questioning those suspected of infanticide. They might try to force admissions from them, although most suspects would normally only confess to having given birth and then claim that their baby was stillborn. Sometimes, neighbourhood women would even physically restrain a suspect while a local surgeon examined her, as happened with Mary Robinson in 1791.[186] Over a century earlier, in 1685, a group of Welsh women had demanded that Mary ap Richard "must open the doore & yt they must see her breasts". The leader of the group then: "…takeinge her breasts in her hands drawed out milk".[187] Technically, these incidents probably constituted assaults.

Other cases were rather more subtle. For example, Esther Hall, the wife of a Trinity College (Cambridge) brewer, and her husband helped expose their own niece, Elizabeth Butchill (see above). Elizabeth had lived with them for three years as a college bed-maker. In the small hours one morning Esther heard her niece groan out very loudly, and got up to inquire into its cause. She found Elizabeth complaining of a violent colic and heated some peppermint-water and flannels for her. In the morning, her husband, hearing that a baby's body had been found, immediately suspected Elizabeth, and sent for a surgeon to examine her.

Suspicion could be very drawn out. As Richard Burn noted, if a woman was thought to be carrying a bastard, her neighbours would "keep

---

184 Anon, (1791) *Advice to Unmarried Women: To recover and Reclaim the Fallen*, p.16.

185 Anon, (1740) *The Proceedings at the Assizes of Peace, Oyer and Terminer, for the County of Surrey, Held at the Town-Hall of Kingston Upon Thames, in the 14th Year of His Majesty's Reign ... To Which is Added the Genuine Proceedings at the Assizes for the County of Essex*, p.15.

186 Jackson, Mark (1996) *New-born child murder,* p.68 and p.70.

187 Howard, Sharon (2003) *Crime, Communities And Authority In Early Modern Wales: Denbighshire, 1660-1730*, p.91.

a stricter eye upon her".[188] In Denbighshire, for example, Jane ferch John David became increasingly concerned about the 'condition' of a local woman named Dorothy ferch Thomas. Jane asked her on a number of occasions whether she was pregnant. Dorothy always denied this, but a day came when Jane heard from a neighbour that Dorothy was unwell and, guessing what might have occurred, she immediately went to her house and found her lying in the building's loft. Dorothy claimed that she had a headache, and asked Jane to leave. However, Jane noticed blood on her hands and: "…some other signes that shee did not like of". She went home, but swiftly returned with three other women and carried out a discreet search while talking to the suspect; this revealed that Dorothy was lying next to the body of a newborn child wrapped in a green apron.[189]

In England, most servant girls would have had to hide their pregnancies in an environment that afforded little privacy, partly explaining their high incidence amongst those prosecuted for the offence. Domestic staff usually shared attic rooms, and often beds. Morning sickness might be explained away as a stomach upset. Localised weight gain was harder to account for. However, it has also been noted that a lack of nutrition and the inadequate diets of the period (for many women) meant that pregnancy, especially in its early months, did not necessarily cause the weight gain it is associated with in the modern western world. Moreover, contemporary clothes, especially for poorer people, were often looser than today, making it easier to hide a swelling belly.[190]

When challenged about weight gain, several women alleged that they had a history of putting on fat in particular places. A good illustration of this can be found in the deposition book of the Surrey J.P., Richard Wyatt, who investigated Mary Bailey in 1774. An apprentice apothecary from Brentford had impregnated Mary. Two months later, she took a position as a cook to a prosperous couple in Egham. Her mistress, Margaret Harcourt, and fellow servants, gradually became concerned about her increasing weight and asked her if she was with child, but were assured that it was her "natural shape". Despite this explanation, one servant, at least, was convinced that she was pregnant. Mary later told Wyatt that her baby had been stillborn and that she had wrapped it in a shift and disposed of it in the "necessary house". She then scrubbed her bedchamber and claimed to a colleague that she had been very ill during the night, and voided a great

[188] Jackson, Mark (1996) *New-born child murder*, p.40.

[189] Howard, Sharon (2003) *Crime, Communities And Authority In Early Modern Wales: Denbighshire, 1660-1730*, pp.90-91.

[190] Spivack, Carla (2007) "To "Bring Down the Flowers": The Cultural Context of Abortion Law in Early Modern England", p.125.

deal of blood, so as to explain lingering signs of the birth. Not surprisingly, when she learnt of this, Margaret Harcourt immediately told the local Justice that she suspected that Mary had: "…been delivered of a bastard child and has destroyed it".[191]

Taking Formal Action

As some of these examples suggest, when a woman was suspected of infanticide it was often her neighbours who alerted the authorities. However, occasionally, local people would not pursue matters having become aware of a newborn baby's death. For example, in 1742, in the North of England, Mary Hodgson found the body of an illegitimate baby that had been born to a local villager. She informed neighbouring women, but: "…they agreed to lett it lye where it was". This was much more likely if the mother could plausibly claim it had been stillborn, rather than deliberately killed. Such babies might then be discreetly buried in fields and gardens.[192]

In some parts of eighteenth-century Europe there appears to have been a somewhat greater reluctance amongst local people to report infanticides to the authorities than was normally the case in England. Instead, they might prefer to deal with the perpetrators informally. For example, in one case from eighteenth-century Dubrovnik, where this approach was more common, local people noted that it had been: "…our decision to conceal this case and punish the perpetrator among ourselves".[193] Across the Atlantic, in Spanish colonial Mexico, it seems that many cases of infanticide were quietly ignored altogether during the 1700s, even if neighbours knew about them.[194]

If a baby's death was reported or suspected, a variety of minor officials (including churchwardens and overseers of the poor) might become involved in the ensuing investigation. For example, if its body was discovered in a public place a parish constable could be summoned and would then initiate an enquiry. Thus, when a baby was found dead (and obviously killed) at Britford in Wiltshire, in 1777, the local constable and

---

[191] Silverthorne, Elizabeth (Ed.) (1978) *The Deposition Book of Richard Wyatt JP, 1767-1776*, pp.48-49.

[192] Jackson, Mark (1996) *New-born child murder,* p.50

[193] Lonza, Nella (2002) "Two Souls Lost": Infanticide In The Republic Of Dubrovnik (1667-1808)", p.95.

[194] Jaffary, Nora E. (2012) "Reconceiving Motherhood: Infanticide and Abortion in Colonial Mexico", p.9

bailiff later claimed expenses for "bringing the murderers to justice".[195] The following year, when Sarah Sant's neighbours in Weaverham, Cheshire, became suspicious that she had given birth to and killed an illegitimate baby they also called in the local constable and overseer of the poor to help them search her house (where they found the infant's body hidden in a chest).[196] A magistrate would usually examine any woman who was suspected, and she would always be questioned at the coroner's hearing. (Sometimes, the latter was held so quickly after a body was discovered that the Justice's examination could be abbreviated).

The Coroner

A coroner and his jury would investigate all reported cases of infanticide, just as they would any other form of homicide. They would normally sit very swiftly after the discovery of a body (a corpse was usually necessary for an investigation, and babies' bodies were more easily destroyed than those of adults). They might view a surgeon's autopsy, or hear evidence of its findings, as well as receiving other evidence at their hearing. This inquiry was particularly significant because coroners had the power to commit cases direct to the Assizes, without the matter having to be indicted by that forum's Grand Jury. Of course, the Assizes Grand Jury would consider the case as well, and in most (but not quite all) situations where the coroner had decided there should be a hearing it would also find a 'true bill', so that the defendant would stand trial on both the Coroner's Inquisition and the Grand Jury indictment. Thus, it could be noted in 1773 that Anna Fry, accused at the Salisbury Assizes of killing her male bastard the previous year, was "acquitted of the murder on both the indictment and the inquest".[197] Inevitably, some coroners' juries did not return verdicts that would send suspected women to trial. In these circumstances, a prosecution for the crime following indictment by the Assizes Grand Jury was highly unlikely, though not quite unheard of.

---

[195] Hunnisett, R.F. (Ed.) (1981) *Wiltshire Coroners' Bills 1752–1796*, p.xxi and p.157.

[196] Jackson, Mark (1996) *New-born child murder* p.2

[197] Hunnisett, R.F. (Ed.) (1981) *Wiltshire Coroners' Bills 1752–1796*, p.47.

Securing an Infanticide Conviction

To secure an infanticide conviction after the early years of the eighteenth century it was usually necessary that there be: "...clear proof of the child's being born alive, and having appearances of violence, and that the Jury should be clearly satisfied that the mother intentionally killed the child".[198] This was much the same as the legal burden for normal murder prosecutions. As a result, it was increasingly unusual to see a conviction unless the method used to kill the infant unequivocally indicated murder, the suspect had made explicit admissions to an examining J.P. or someone else deemed to be reliable, or an independent witness had come upon the scene just after a killing occurred (not a common occurrence). These might be supported by circumstantial evidence, but on its own this was rarely enough to secure a conviction.

'Unequivocal' Wounds

One way of proving a deliberate killing was to find wounds on the baby's body that were clearly of human origin, such as cuts inflicted with a blade or, albeit less unequivocally, massive blunt-force trauma. Thus, in a case from Devonshire in 1782, Elizabeth Waldron's baby was found with its head slashed and severe bruising. An examining surgeon suggested that any one of its many wounds could have been fatal. Waldron claimed that the baby's injuries were caused by it being dropped on a stone. In response, the surgeon testified that their position made this impossible, while the clean nature of the cuts proved that they had been inflicted by a knife or other sharp implement. His evidence, combined with Waldron's concealment of her pregnancy and failure to provide any clothing for the infant in advance of its birth, led the jury to find her guilty. She was subsequently executed.[199] Similarly, after the Chester Assizes in 1774, Elizabeth Hyne was hanged for murdering her newborn male bastard: "...which she delivered herself of, and immediately cut its throat, and flung it into a pit".[200] Obviously, a baby could not have had its throat cut by accident.

Even more clear-cut was the case of Mary Morgan, a sixteen-year-old kitchen maid at Maesllwch Castle in Radnorshire, who became pregnant by a local waggoner, before secretly giving birth in the castle in 1804. She

---

[198] OBSP, Trial of Elizabeth Curtis, 15th Sept 1784: t17840915-149.
[199] Anon, (1782) *Character and dying behaviour of the two murderers, executed at Heavitree gallows, Monday, March 25, 1782*, pp.1-2.
[200] *Morning Chronicle and London Advertiser*, September 6, 1774.

was swiftly suspected by the cook and eventually admitted that she had had a baby and then killed it, almost cutting off its head with a penknife. Its body was found hidden under the pillows in Mary's bed. Despite the era (the law had changed the previous year), she was swiftly convicted at the Great Sessions for Radnorshire and executed.[201]

However, in a majority of English cases of infanticide during the eighteenth century the baby's death had been occasioned by smothering, strangling, or drowning. (A higher proportion of infanticides in lowland Scotland appear to evidence throat-slitting and other more obviously 'bloody' methods of killing).[202] These cases were increasingly hard to prove without other incriminating factors. This was in marked contrast to the situation that had prevailed in seventeenth-century Essex (for example) where over half of those accused of killing their babies by these means were convicted.[203] Eighteenth-century juries evinced a growing willingness to accept faintly plausible, if far-fetched, explanations for otherwise suspicious facts. Nevertheless, this still might not be possible if a suspect had made clear admissions, even if the baby's body was unmarked.

Admissions

Clear and unequivocal pre-trial admissions to having committed infanticide were usually enough to secure a conviction, though even this was not quite invariably the case by the very end of the eighteenth century. For example, Elizabeth Butchill made a statement to the Mayor of Cambridge (an *ex officio* Justice for the city) that was later read to her trial jury, in which she confessed that she had given birth to a female child early in the morning, that it had cried for a while after its birth (proving it was alive), and that about twenty minutes later she threw it down a privy hole into the Cam, and buried its placenta in a dunghill near the house in which she resided. Unsurprisingly, she was subsequently convicted and executed, despite a lack of obvious injuries to the corpse.[204] Similarly, Ann Ockford from Gloucestershire, who delivered herself of an illegitimate baby girl that was later found hidden in a coal-hole, with a stone tile pulled

---

[201] *The Hull Packet*, May 7, 1805.

[202] Kilday, Anne-Marie (2007) *Women and Violent Crime in Enlightenment Scotland*, pp.78-79.

[203] Wrightson, Keith (1975) "Infanticide in earlier Seventeenth-Century England", p.15.

[204] *Craftsman or Say's Weekly Journal*, April 1, 1780.

over her body, made clear admissions and was convicted and executed as a result.[205]

As with cases of poisoning, this made the magistrate/coroner's examination of great importance. Many women, nearly always legally unadvised, probably made confessions before their local J.P. or coroner that they later regretted. Indeed, some sympathetic examining surgeons, such as Michael Underwood, actually enjoined women not to say anything personally incriminating to them, something "that would do her hurt", when they carried out their physical investigations.[206]

Indicative of the importance of admissions, in a bizarre case from 1761, Mary Davis confessed to the authorities in Kingston that she had murdered her three-month-old bastard by cutting its throat and then thrown its body into the Thames, saying she had been prompted to turn herself in by remorse, having been "haunted" by the child's face. She signed her admissions to an examining J.P. and was then tried at the Surrey Assizes, almost purely on her confession, no corpse having been located. This was despite extensive searches, although it was claimed that a suspicious bloodstain was found near the alleged murder scene. However, evidence subsequently emerged that Davis was "crazy" and a midwife who examined her in private, during the course of the trial, concluded that she had never been pregnant or given birth in her life. She was acquitted at trial.[207]

Expert Evidence of Infanticide

The use of 'expert' witnesses was comparatively rare in eighteenth-century criminal trials, though it had long been permitted in English courts. However, cases of infanticide (like other murders) were something of an exception to this general rule. Giving birth was a dangerous process, and many children were stillborn for entirely natural reasons. This presented an obvious line of defence to those accused of infanticide, especially as the 1624 Act was marginalised. It also encouraged the Crown to call medical evidence to rebut such a possibility. This type of evidence was usually given in the form of expert testimony from midwives and surgeons or (much less commonly) physicians and apothecaries, who had

---

[205] *Whitehall Evening Post or London Intelligencer*, November 7, 1754 - November 9, 1754.

[206] Trumbach, Randolph (1998) *Sex and the Gender Revolution: Heterosexuality and the Third Gender in Enlightenment London*, vol.1, p.300.

[207] *Lloyd's Evening Post and British Chronicle*, April 3, 1761 - April 6, 1761.

examined either, or both, the defendant and the dead infant's body.[208]

Many eighteenth-century infanticide cases raised two distinct medical questions: firstly, whether a baby had been born rather than miscarried prematurely; and secondly, whether it had survived birth, and then been deliberately killed. The first issue was often addressed by a midwife, who would give evidence about the physical condition of both mother and baby and an opinion as to whether the pregnancy had gone to term or not. For example, were the mother's breasts full of milk or dry?[209] They might also testify about the presence of nails and hair on the baby and its general size, these also being indicative of whether the pregnancy was complete.

Even if gestation was complete, it did not prove that the baby was alive at birth and had then been deliberately killed. If contested, this issue was more likely to come within the remit of a surgeon's expertise. By 1700, a number of tests had been developed and other supposed indicators of a live birth identified. One regular test conducted during infant autopsies, and originating either in seventeenth-century Germany or from a suggestion made by William Harvey in 1628 (or both), was to remove and then attempt to float the baby's lungs in a bowl of water. This was done on the assumption that their buoyancy would be indicative of the presence of air, and thus a sign that the infant had breathed, and so was alive, after birth. The test was also widely used in continental Europe and Scotland.[210] When the surgeon John Coleman gave evidence to the Surrey Assizes in an infanticide case in 1739, he noted that he had opened the baby's body and: "…took out the lungs, and put them in a pail of water and they swam". The trial judge then addressed the jury as to the significance of this finding, observing that it was a test that was frequently carried out in such cases and that: "When the lungs swim, it is suppos'd the child breathed, for the air puffs up the lungs and causes them to swim. If the child had been stillborn, the lungs would have sunk". Nevertheless, and significantly, the defendant was still subsequently acquitted.[211]

This test was often accorded considerable significance by surgeons at the start of the period. However, as the century proceeded, many medical

---

[208] Landsman, Stephen (1998) "One hundred years of rectitude: medical witnesses at the Old Bailey 1717-1817", p.451.

[209] Morgan, Gwenda and Rushton, Peter (1998) *Rogues, Thieves and the Rule of Law,* p.117.

[210] Rizzo, Tracey (2004) "Between Dishonor and Death: infanticides in the *Causes celebres* of eighteenth-century France", p.14.

[211] Anon, (1739) *The Genuine Proceedings at the Assizes on the Home Circuit, Held in March, 1739. ... at Hertford, for the County of Hertford; Chelmsford, for the County of Essex…* p.9.

practitioners, such as William Hunter, became increasingly open about the limitations on their knowledge, sceptical about the value of much medical testimony in infanticide cases, and particularly doubtful about the tests that had been developed to establish whether babies had been born alive. This was particularly marked when it came to the floating lung or 'hydrostatic' test.[212] Carefully observed autopsies established that gas emitted by decomposition could cause a stillborn baby's lungs to float and, conversely, that lung tissue from those born alive could sink.[213] This growth in scepticism was matched in many parts of Western Europe. For example, in Rostock, Professor Christian Eschanbach (1712-1788) urged that autopsies on babies' bodies take place as soon as possible after death, before decay could set in, to prevent 'false positives'.[214]

Such doubts led some doctors to reject the lung test altogether, especially in the Metropolitan area. However, it continued to be accorded significance at some Assizes, and was still occasionally viewed as important, even towards the end of the period. For example, when Elizabeth Butchill (see above) was accused of murdering her newborn baby in 1780, a surgeon named Bond gave evidence that, when he opened up the baby's body, its lungs appeared distended and were lighter than water. This led him to believe that the child was born alive.[215] The discovery of faeces, passed by a newly delivered infant, was also viewed as indicative of a live birth, while clenched fists were thought to be signs of stillbirth.

Infanticide after 1803

Of course, despite legal change in 1803, cases of newborn infanticide continued in the provinces throughout the nineteenth century, even if they did not lead to many formal prosecutions, let alone convictions, and no woman was executed for the crime after 1847. For example, Frederick Lowndes, the Liverpool coroner, carefully analysed the city's inquests on deaths amongst newborn infants between 1869 and 1871. Out of 127 cases, murder verdicts were returned in just 28. The remaining 99 cases were attributed to want of attention (19 instances), being found dead (24 cases), being stillborn (34 examples), with the balance receiving other

---

[212] Hunter, William (1812) *On the Uncertainty of the Signs of Murder*, p.18.
[213] Roth, Randolph (2001) "Homicide In Early Modern England 1549-1800: The Need For A Quantitative Synthesis", pp.33-67.
[214] Häßler, Günther and Häßler, Frank (2011) "Infanticide in Mecklenburg and Western Pomerania: Documents from four centuries (1570—1842)", p.87.
[215] *General Evening Post*, March 16, 1780 - March 18, 1780.

verdicts. Lowndes was sure that such neutral headings covered many instances of newborn child murder. He cited a female author, who had visited Brixton Prison in 1869, to suggest that there was a kind of "sisterhood" amongst women who perpetrated infanticide. Several allegedly passed on techniques for killing babies without trace to their colleagues. In 1873, for example, the mother and grandmother of a newborn baby, along with a female neighbour, were discharged after being accused of its murder. The coroner's jury had returned a verdict of suffocation, but was unable to obtain evidence as to how this occurred. In another case a midwife certified that a child was stillborn, even though its mother admitted it had been born alive. The coroner's beadle stopped the certificate after becoming suspicious, and a post-mortem was carried out. This suggested that the child had "died from exposure and want of attention after birth". Nevertheless, the only outcome to this case was the censuring of the midwife for handing out a false certificate.[216]

Conclusion

Infanticide prosecutions and, very much more markedly, convictions, were in sharp decline by the 1680s and continued to fall throughout the eighteenth century, so that they were a relative rarity by the end of the era, and guilty verdicts were only returned in cases where the evidence was quite unequivocal. This decline was not primarily a matter of incidence, though some real change in infanticide rates due to improving economic conditions may have occurred. Instead, it was largely the result of a transformation in attitudes that produced a marginalising of the 1624 Act and a more general reluctance to convict in all but the most clear-cut cases. Defences were increasingly accepted in situations where guilt would readily have been established in earlier years.

This change can clearly be seen in the trial of Bridget Eley, which was held at the York Assizes, shortly before the formal abolition of the 1624 Act. Bridget was accused of suffocating her newborn bastard in a large tin of powder at Kirkheaton in 1801. A couple of female acquaintances had visited her house shortly after she gave birth, and become suspicious after seeing a large bloodstain on the floor and other incriminating evidence. Many local people assembled outside Eley's home as news of the death spread, a constable arrived, and a midwife and surgeon were summoned to examine the mother and dead baby respectively. Eley claimed that the

---

[216] Archer, John (2000) "Mysterious And Suspicious Deaths: Missing Homicides In North-West England (1850-1900)", pp.45-63.

child had been stillborn. However, one of the two women had heard the cry of a newborn baby when they visited. At trial, Eley was represented by experienced counsel and the witness was forced to concede the: "…cry of a kitten to be similar to that of a child, and might be mistaken for it". The surgeon found no external signs of violence on the baby's body, and could or would not swear that it was born alive. The trial judge advised the jurors that there was no "positive proof" of the child being killed, albeit that there was some "presumptive" evidence. The jury returned a 'not guilty' verdict 15 minutes after retiring. Before he discharged her, the judge: "…admonished the prisoner to amend her life, and be more careful of her conduct in future".[217]

This case reveals many features of 'late' infanticide trials. The suspected woman had effective legal representation, and her lawyer made some telling points in her defence. There was a cautious medical expert, willing to concede the limits of his knowledge, a trial judge who, whatever his (apparent) personal belief, was careful and restrained in his directions to the jury, and twelve jurors who were, it seems, keen to return an acquittal in the absence of the clearest evidence suggesting guilt.

As these facets of the trial also suggest, there had been a growth both in notions of due process and of scepticism about the value of forensic tests for live births. Juries accepted that they would have to give the benefit of the doubt to many guilty women. However, the process reflected more than a growth in legal propriety, as juries acquitted women they must have thought guilty, provided the evidence allowed for a charitable interpretation. As a result, other explanations for the change must be sought. These include a shifting emphasis in the Christianity of the era, which increasingly stressed a more 'rational' religiosity rather than hellfire.[218]

It is also clear that more sympathetic assessments of the character and conduct of infanticide defendants became prevalent during the eighteenth century. They were increasingly seen by juries (if not always by local people) not as wilful murderers but as victims of circumstance and of the "villainy and treachery" of men, motivated by fear and shame, and so deserving of a more compassionate response. As the cleric who ministered to Jane Williams before her execution in Bristol in 1741 noted: "…this poor unfortunate young creature, except the offence for which she suffered, had such a meek and courteous behaviour, that would rather

---

[217] *The Morning Post and Gazetteer*, August 3, 1801.

[218] Dickinson, J.R. and Sharpe, J.A. (2002) "Infanticide in Early Modern England: The Court of Great Sessions at Chester, 1650-1800", p.50.

move pity than contempt".[219] The courts seem to have become more willing to entertain the emotional language of excuse for women placed in this situation.[220] The ground had been laid for infanticide to become a largely 'medical' issue, as it did during the nineteenth century.[221]

Such a change in attitudes was a European wide, not a specifically English, phenomenon, as can be seen from the case of Prussia. After the middle of the century, and under the influence of the Enlightenment and its attendant thinkers, including men such as Cesare Beccaria, Ferdinand Hommel and Voltaire, Prussian society began to look at the social causes of infanticide, rather than viewing it as being purely an exercise in free and malicious will by the women concerned. (Voltaire publicly stated that the execution of one eighteen-year-old for the crime was "unjust"). There was a growing demand that foundling hospitals be established in the German state, like Thomas Coram's hospital in London and the *Maison de la Couche pour les Enfants Trouvés* in Paris. This change in attitude was encouraged by growing Mercantilist sentiment. There was a feeling that both the deaths of babies and the execution of their mothers deprived society of potentially useful members (always a concern in the militarily undermanned state). As a result, Prussia abolished the criminal offence of extra-marital sexual intercourse in 1765, so as to remove some of the shame attendant on giving birth to a bastard. Additionally, the Prussian General Law Code of 1794 guaranteed single women, apart from adulteresses and prostitutes, rights against the men who had impregnated them. For example, any expenditure they incurred before and after the birth, or at the baptism, of their baby could be recovered. Women who had been promised marriage to consent to sexual intercourse had even more financial and other rights.[222]

In England, there is one fairly close comparator, also involving killing, which throws some light on changing attitudes to infanticide. Between 1660 and 1800 the proportion of suicides that were returned *felo de se*, rather than *non compos mentis*, by coroners' juries was utterly transformed. In the first five years of the period, only 6.9 per cent of

---

[219] Penrose, Reverend (1741) *The Reverend Mr. Penrose's Account of the Behaviour, Confession, and last dying words, of the four malefactors executed at St. Michael's Hill at Bristol, on Wednesday the 15th of April, 1741*, p.11.

[220] Rabin, Dana (2004) *Identity, Crime and Legal Responsibility in Eighteenth-Century England*, pp.95-105.

[221] Jackson, Mark (1996) *New-born child murder*, p.128

[222] Michalik, Kerstin (2006) "The Development of the Discourse on Infanticide in the Late Eighteenth Century and the New Legal Standardization of the Offense in the Nineteenth Century", pp.54-55.

suicide verdicts returned by coroners to the Court of King's Bench (one of the requirements of their office) were of *non compos mentis*. By 1714 the number had increased to over 40 per cent. At the end of the eighteenth century, a finding of *felo de se* was largely confined to cases in which the evidence was exceptionally clear-cut and unequivocal, or where the jury disapproved of aspects of the suicide's life. For example, people who had killed themselves while in prison, or who were suspected of other crimes at the time of death, were far more likely to be regarded as self-murderers rather than disturbed.[223] Juries resorted to the fiction of near-universal madness to protect the reputations and property of the dead.[224] Much the same could be said to apply to verdicts in infanticide cases, and was probably influenced, in part, by a similar underlying change in values. Juries proved adept at returning verdicts that avoided the most plausible explanation for a baby's death.

Unlike modern cases of infanticide, which are often associated with *post-partum* depression, those for the eighteenth century tended to be a practical if drastic response to very difficult personal situations. Nevertheless, it should always be remembered that behind the bald facts were numerous personal tragedies. Mary Wollstonecraft, in her *Vindication of the Rights of Women*, suggested that both abortion and infanticide were often the result of women satisfying the sexual demands of dissolute male 'libertines', as a result of which they (the women) became weaker, both mentally and physically, until they did not have sufficient strength to: "…discharge the first duty of a mother; and sacrificing to lasciviousness the parental affection, that ennobles instinct, either destroy the embryo in the womb, or cast it off when born". In 1691, the capitally convicted Mary Goodenough left a poignant letter to her two young children (aged seven and eleven) lamenting the sin that she had committed against: "…that unhappy infant which I took not care to preserve".[225] She probably spoke for many others in the same situation.

[223] MacDonald, Michael (1986) "The Secularization of Suicide in England 1660-1800", p.92.

[224] Houston, R. A. (2012) "Explanations for death by suicide in northern Britain during the long eighteenth century", p.54.

[225] Anon, (1692) *Fair warnings to murderers of infants being an account of the tryal, codemnation [sic] and execution of Mary Goodenough ...* pp.2-4.

CHAPTER FIVE

PROPERTY CRIME

Introduction

This chapter will consider female-perpetrated property crime in provincial England. It will examine its incidence, the methods and motivations of the women who committed such offences, and any gendered differences in their crimes, prosecution, and penal disposal. The emphasis will be on the most common forms of property crime: theft, burglary, housebreaking, robbery, and receiving stolen goods. Taken together, such offences made up the great majority of all indicted crimes, whether committed by men or women, but were especially dominant amongst the latter.

Unlike murder, many minor property crimes were prosecuted at forums other than the Assizes. The most important of these were the Quarter Sessions or (sometimes) their borough equivalents. Throughout the period, these courts would hear most indicted cases of petty theft (under a shilling in value). For example, and typically, at the St. Albans' Quarter Sessions held at Easter 1785, Elizabeth Rush was prosecuted for stealing linen handkerchiefs and socks valued together at 10d. Similarly, in July 1806, Mary Barber was convicted at the same forum for: "…feloniously stealing a wheaten loaf of bread to the value of 10d".[1] However, such courts also frequently heard some lesser, clergyable, cases of grand larceny, especially after the middle of the century, and many prosecutions for receiving stolen goods (which was often only classified as a misdemeanour).[2]

Additionally, there were a number of (usually statutory) misdemeanours, involving the taking of specific types of low-value property, that were tried by magistrates without a jury at all, whether sitting on their own or in groups of two or more at what were termed 'petty sessions'. (These were frequently held in taverns). For example, single Justices could summarily determine and punish the theft of timber from woods, fruit from orchards

---

[1] Dean, David (Ed.) (1991) *St. Albans Quarter Sessions rolls, 1784-1820,* p.5 and p.96.

[2] Dogherty, Thomas (1799) *The Crown Circuit Companion*, vol.1, pp.36-39.

and vegetables from fields.[3] The penalties for such offences were usually very mild, normally being modest fines, the proceeds of which were often used for local purposes rather than being forfeit to the Crown.

Thus, in 1747, the Wiltshire Justice William Hunt convicted two spinsters, Hester and Anne Yates, of "stealing" some posts and rails belonging to a local gentleman, for which he fined them 2s 6d, with a whipping being ordered in lieu of payment. Their convictions were based on the evidence of an independent witness and their own confessions. (Summary offences normally specified the evidence required to secure a finding of guilt). Two years later Jane Gibbs, a widow, was summarily convicted by Hunt on the oath of Anne Street and her own confession for stealing wood and ordered to pay five shillings in damages "or to be whipped". A group of three labourers' wives, arrested for stealing wood on a Wiltshire estate were rather more fortunate in 1746. The same J.P. magnanimously noted that: "…out of regard to their great poverty and their promises of not offending in the like again, I pardoned them".[4]

The number of summary offences gradually increased during the eighteenth century, as Parliament created what has been called a 'bloodless code' by some modern historians, often to encourage the conviction of those suspected of specific forms of theft in situations where essential elements of the felony would otherwise be hard to establish.[5] Women (like men) who were minor thieves might also be diverted from the mainstream criminal justice system by being committed to a Bridewell or House of Correction as vagrants, especially in the first half of the century.

Further complicating matters, many eighteenth-century Justices saw their primary function as preserving the peace in their neighbourhoods, rather than enforcing the strict letter of the criminal law on all occasions.[6] Even where there was a 'victim' and formal complaint, provincial J.P.s often attempted to restore harmony by private arbitration rather than institute proceedings.[7] A frequent feature of such informal determinations was a divorce between legal theory and practice provided this was

---

[3] W., J. (1707) *A Compleat Guide for Justices of the Peace,* pp.10-21.
[4] Crittall, Elizabeth (Ed.) (1982) *The Justicing Notebook of William Hunt, 1744-1749*, p.50, p.83, and p.86.
[5] See generally Smith, Bruce P. (2005) "The Presumption of Innocence and the English Law of theft: 1750-1850", pp.133-173.
[6] Morgan, Gwenda and Rushton, Peter (2003) "The Magistrate, the community and the maintenance of an orderly society in eighteenth-century England", p.56.
[7] *The Gentleman's Magazine*, 1732, vol.2, p.910.

amenable to the parties concerned.[8] Magistrates might discharge a matter having arranged a compromise between the prosecutor and suspect. Although most commonly used to deal with cases of assault and instances of petty theft (under a shilling in value), even cases of clergyable grand larceny (over that amount) could result in an informal settlement. This was especially likely where the victim was reluctant to prosecute, provided his stolen goods were returned or he was financially compensated. It was also common where the allegation arose from a quasi-civil dispute, was between family members and friends, or could be dismissed as a case of youthful high spirits (the eighteenth-century equivalent of stealing garden gnomes).

For an example of this approach can be considered the work of Reverend Edmund Tew, who was the Cambridge-educated and relatively prosperous rector of Bolden, in County Durham. He served as a local J.P. from 1750 until the end of his life in 1770, although he became less active in his final years. (Clerical magistrates were a particular phenomenon of eighteenth-century provincial England). Tew dealt with many minor property offences that were recorded as being "made up". Only about 13 per cent led to a formal prosecution.[9]

Similarly, the magistrate William Hunt was regularly faced with allegations of minor theft in Wiltshire, even if a euphemism, such as the relevant property being "detained", was used to describe the crime. As in County Durham, only the most serious matters would go for trial on indictment. Instead, Hunt would usually reconcile the parties. For example, in 1745, when Anne Davis accused Elizabeth Kyte of "carrying away" three pewter dishes, the Justice recorded: "Upon hearing, they being all near relations, I persuaded an agreement between them, the defendant paying 3s. expenses".[10]

Such resolutions were often highly attractive to both complainants and suspects. The simplest prosecution on indictment could entail significant cost, even where lawyers were not used, although the state provision for reimbursing prosecutors was gradually improved during the century. For example, Ann Taylor claimed and was allowed 7s 4d by the Recorder of St Albans when she successfully prosecuted another woman for petty theft at the town's Quarter Sessions; 2s 4d was paid for the indictment and five

---

[8] Gisborne, Thomas (1794) *An Enquiry into the Duties of men in the Higher and Middle Classes of Society in Great Britain*, p.281.

[9] Morgan, Gwenda and Rushton, Peter (2003) "The Magistrate, the community and the maintenance of an orderly society in eighteenth-century England", p.74.

[10] Crittall, Elizabeth (Ed.) (1982) *The Justicing Notebook of William Hunt, 1744-1749*, p.13, p.38, and p.62.

shillings for "Prosecutors and witnesses loss of time".[11] Nevertheless, informal disposal was very cheap, and also not socially disruptive in what was still usually a face-to-face society. Conversely, from a suspect's perspective, if matters went for trial on indictment the consequences of conviction were uncertain, and sometimes could be very grave. Women featured in many cases of informal resolution.

Of course, this type of settlement required that the parties be willing to accept to such a solution and, perhaps, slightly in awe of their magistrate. Where this was not the case, it might not be viable. For example, in 1747, Elizabeth Coleman, the wife of a carpenter, was arrested pursuant to a warrant issued by William Hunt, for stealing a single sheet from the house of Edward Byng, a gentleman from Pottern in Wiltshire. She was committed to jail and subsequently convicted of theft to the value of 4d at the Salisbury Assizes. She was then sentenced to three months' imprisonment.[12] Clearly, being 'reconciled' was not deemed appropriate in this case, despite the trivial value of the item.

Urbanisation and Female Property Crime

Provincial women were very different to their Metropolitan counterparts when it came to property crimes. As briefly noted in chapter one, women in the late seventeenth and early eighteenth-century capital were notably more prone to offending than most of their contemporaries, and also their own forbears, even those from the mid-seventeenth century. They even made up a narrow majority of those indicted for property crimes in the City of London between 1690 and 1713.[13] It was not just serious offences, prosecuted on indictment, which saw a heavy female involvement in the capital. A similar increase can be seen in the proportion of women committed to the Middlesex and Westminster houses of correction (institutions where vagrancy, prostitution, and petty theft were punished). This rose strongly in the 1690s and remained high during the early eighteenth century. By 1712, women accounted for 57 per cent of all commitments to such institutions for cases of theft and fraud. Similarly, as early as 1691, they made up 59 per cent of those committed to the City's Bridewell prison for the same crimes. This extremely high level of female offending has even been termed a "unique phenomenon" in the history of

[11] Dean, David (Ed.) (1991) *St. Albans Quarter Sessions rolls, 1784-1820,* p.44
[12] Crittall, Elizabeth (Ed.) (1982) *The Justicing Notebook of William Hunt, 1744-1749*, p.61.
[13] Beattie, John (2001) *Policing and Punishment in London, 1660-1750*, p.65.

crime. There has been some debate as to whether it was the result of women committing more offences, an increased propensity to prosecute them, or both. For many, the last possibility appears the most likely.[14] It was also partly the product of war, recruitment removing a large tranche of potential male offenders from Metropolitan society.

The proportion of women involved in crime in the capital then declined slowly (if unevenly) for the remainder of the century to historically more 'normal' levels. Even so, as late as July 1750 there was an all-female execution at Tyburn, in which three "very drunk" women were hanged for forgery, pick-pocketing, and highway robbery.[15] At the end of the century, the proportion of female offenders in the capital was still significantly higher than the national average.

This gender distribution in offending was certainly *not* typical of life outside London. However, there are echoes of it in at least some of the smaller urban areas found in the provinces. Unsurprisingly, Southwark, effectively an extension of the Metropolis into Surrey, also saw high levels of female crime. Indeed, on some assessments 80 per cent of women indicted in the county came from the Borough and its neighbouring urban parts (compared to just two thirds of men).[16] Perhaps more significantly, in eighteenth-century Newcastle, over half (55.1 per cent) of the prosecutions for theft conducted at the city's Quarter Sessions in the years up to 1783 involved female defendants. Similarly, just over half (51.5 per cent) of those prosecuted for property crime in Berwick on Tweed were women.[17] This might suggest, quite strongly, that urbanisation was linked to higher rates of female offending. Supporting this paradigm, Lancashire had a fairly high proportion of female offenders later in the century, as its towns and cities expanded rapidly, while Sussex and Hertfordshire, with the lowest indictment rates for women on the Home Circuit, were also its two most rural counties.

The apparently heavier involvement of urban women in property crime at this time has also been identified in other European cities.[18] In early eighteenth-century Stockholm, for example, women accounted for more than 60 per cent of property offenders, perhaps the highest level anywhere

---

[14] Shoemaker, Robert (2010) "Print and the Female Voice: Representations of Women's Crime in London, 1690–1735", pp.75-76.

[15] *London Evening Post*, July 5, 1750 - July 7, 1750.

[16] Beattie, John (1986) *Crime and the Courts in England 1660-1800,* p.240.

[17] Morgan, Gwenda and Rushton, Peter (1998) *Rogues, Thieves and the Rule of Law,* p.99.

[18] See for example, Kloek, E. (1990) "Criminality and Gender in Leiden's Confessieboken, 1678-1794", p.8.

in Europe (and a challenge to London's uniqueness).[19] Other work suggests that the more urbanized parts of northern France in the second half of the eighteenth century attracted or produced a higher number of women who fell into crime out of economic necessity than more rural, especially Mediterranean parts of the country.[20]

Even so, there were also some interesting differences between the small provincial conurbations with high female crime rates and the Metropolis. For example, the great majority of the women accused in London were single, whereas at Newcastle Quarter Sessions 40 per cent were married (despite *feme covert*) and 20 per cent were widows. However, despite these differences, and a population of little more than 33,000 in 1801, it is probably fair to say that Newcastle, like London, gave women greater freedom and opportunities, including an absence from male and 'patriarchal' constraints. At the same time, it also exposed them to more temptation, risk, and personal pressure to survive. A very high proportion of Metropolitan women were dependant on their own earnings for their livelihoods, whether it came from waged work or letting out rooms.[21] The same probably applied to many female Geordies. (The nickname may originate from city allegiances in the 1745 Jacobite Rebellion). Taken together, these factors probably encouraged female offending in both the capital and Newcastle.[22]

Nevertheless, the notion that outside the phenomenon that was the Metropolis urbanisation *necessarily* translates into more female crime/prosecutions is simplistic, at least below a certain population level. For example, a majority of the small market towns found in late eighteenth-century Essex, such as Halstead and Dunmow, returned lower levels of indicted crime than the county average. The exceptions related to those towns, like Chelmsford, that held a major court, i.e. that had active Borough or Quarter Sessions, where the proportion of indicted females was about 75 per cent higher than the Essex average. Most of these towns were not very different in their social profiles to the others. This suggests that it was local attitudes towards female offenders, and how they were to be disposed of, that largely determined female prosecution rates, rather than their incidence of offending. Where a court was not conveniently

---

[19] Eisner, Manuel (2003) "Long-Term Historical Trends in Violent Crime", p.112.

[20] Feeley, Malcolm and Aviram' Hadar (2010) "Social Historical Studies of Women, Crime, and Courts", p.154.

[21] Laurence, Anne (1996) *Women In England 1500-1760: A Social History*, p.128.

[22] Morgan, Gwenda and Rushton, Peter (1998) *Rogues, Thieves and the Rule of Law,* p.104.

present, it seems that small towns in Essex shared rural traditions about using informal sanctions to deal with female suspects.[23]

More generally, some remote and very rural shires such as Norfolk saw a higher proportion of female prosecutions than several more populous and urbanised counties, and most saw significantly higher levels than the Home Counties. Some sparsely populated Welsh counties also returned a high proportion of female indictments. Additionally, although there may be a link between urbanisation and levels of female offending, it is not a unique association. For example, Cornwall and County Durham were both comparatively un-urbanised counties that also had relatively high female crime rates. As a result, it has been suggested that there might be a further link between a high incidence of female offending and local involvement in mining (tin and coal respectively in the case of these two counties), which industries also employed many women, especially in Cornwall.[24]

The Incidence of Female Property Crime

In *general*, eighteenth-century women outside the Metropolis committed far fewer serious property crimes than men, or at least were prosecuted much less frequently for them than were males. In Essex, for example, only 13 per cent of those indicted at Assizes and Quarter Sessions for property offences between 1740 and 1804 were female, a pattern that was broadly matched elsewhere on the Home Circuit, albeit that this circuit had the lowest proportion of female offenders in England.[25] Thus, in Sussex between 1660 and 1800, women also made up 13 per cent of those who were indicted for property crimes at the two courts. In Surrey, the divergence was less extreme, just under a quarter of offenders being women. However, this is largely explained by the presence of urban parts, such as Southwark, in the north of the county. Women committed almost 30 per cent of offences in these parishes. If the rural parts of the county are considered on their own, a similar total (14.3 per cent) to that found in Sussex and Essex is produced.[26]

Broadly similar, if less extreme, patterns are revealed during this period in counties such as Somerset, Berkshire, and Gloucestershire. The proportion of female indictments rarely went much above 16 per cent,

---

[23] King, Peter (2000) *Crime, Justice and Discretion in England 1740-1820*, pp.198-199.
[24] King, Peter (2006) *Crime and Law in England, 1750-1840,* p.215.
[25] King, Peter (2000) *Crime, Justice and Discretion in England 1740-1820*, pp.196-199.
[26] Beattie, John (1986) *Crime and the Courts in England 1660-1800,* pp.237-238.

although, as already noted, Cornwall and one or two other counties, where as late as the years from 1805 to 1807 25 per cent or more of indictments were of women, are an exception.[27] On a smaller scale, an examination of the Assizes' gaol books from the Western Circuit for the Summer of 1737 suggest that 27 men from the four (of the circuit's six) counties studied were tried for grand larceny, seven for burglary or house breaking, and three for highway robbery, making 37 men in total. By contrast, only three women were tried for grand larceny, and one for burglary (a total of four). Thus, about 11 per cent of those tried for theft and related offences were female.[28]

Nevertheless, it should also be noted that the gender-based figures for prosecution on indictment, especially at Assizes, might be slightly misleading. It seems that at the bottom of the offending pyramid a higher proportion of women were involved in petty thefts that were disposed of informally by magistrates. It is possible that some of these cases would have gone for trial on indictment if committed by men.

General Profile of Female Property Offences

Women tended to steal, rather than rob, a crime that involved the use, or threat, of violence. Additionally, they were less likely to be involved in crimes like burglary (a nocturnal offence committed between sunset and sunrise) and, albeit much less markedly, housebreaking (its diurnal counterpart). There was nothing novel to England in this. Indeed, the pattern in some other countries was more extreme in this regard. For example, of the 240 women prosecuted for property offences at the Armagh Assizes between 1735 and 1795, only two cases involved burglary or housebreaking, and none of them involved robbery. This suggests that Irish women (at least in this area of the country) were, proportionately, much less inclined to commit these types of property crime than were those from England.[29]

[27] King, Peter (2006) *Crime and Law in England, 1750-1840,* pp.202-206.

[28] Williams, Amy (2000) *The Criminality Of Women In The 18th Century In The South West Of England*, pp.89-90.

[29] Garnham, Neil (1996) *Courts, Crime and the Criminal Law in Ireland, 1692-1760*, p.216.

Motivation

Property crime is usually motivated by need or greed. Frequently, a combination of both factors is present at the same time. Those who steal are often poor, denied many of life's luxuries, and desirous of improving the immediate quality of their lives, especially if they can see others around them in a much better situation. Nevertheless, they do not steal purely to keep body and soul together. For example, although servants were regularly involved in theft, they usually received basic food and lodging with their employment and so, by definition, were not destitute. Nevertheless, they were often intimately exposed to significant wealth, while personally living in comparative poverty. As William Godwin (Mary Wollstonecraft's husband) noted, this meant that many of them, or at least those who were not overcome by demoralisation, would inevitably: "…cherish a burning envy in their bosoms, an inextinguishable abhorrence against the injustice of society".[30] This might manifest itself in theft.

Certainly, need was often advanced as mitigation by eighteenth-century women who were accused of stealing small items. How sincerely this was done appears to have depended entirely on the case in question, as most female defendants would have known that it was an effective plea with tribunals, and many such claims were probably entirely spurious. Nevertheless, there is some, albeit very limited, evidence to suggest that female crimes were slightly more likely to be prompted by immediate and pressing need than were those of men.

Most women in waged employment did not earn more than half the income of an equivalently skilled man, and almost none received anything near the same money for doing a similar job. For example, the 16 men who were employed in the Duke of Chandos' garden in 1721 received 1s 2d a day. The two women who were employed in weeding with them earned only 8d.[31] Female pay was often premised on their not being the main breadwinner for their families, even though many women had to adopt this role, having been widowed or abandoned by their partners. The consequences of poverty bore particularly heavily on mothers, who ultimately had to put meals on tables and ensure that their households were clothed and shod.

Between 1660 and 1800, it seems that the number of prosecutions of female thieves did fluctuate with economic conditions to *some* degree,

---

[30] Steedman, Carolyn (2007) "A Boiling Copper and Some Arsenic: Servants, Childcare, and Class Consciousness in Late Eighteenth□Century England", at p.45.

[31] Laurence, Anne (1996) *Women In England 1500-1760: A Social History*, p.118.

although such matters are very difficult to calculate.[32] For example, using the Schumpeter-Gilboy consumer price index for the eighteenth century suggests that there was a close correlation between a sudden spike in prices in the period from 1740 to 1742 and female prosecutions for theft in Devonshire. There was a similar but less pronounced correlation in the same county during price spikes in 1758, 1768 and 1772. However, at other times, such as the mid-1780s, the correlation between high prices and prosecution is almost non-existent.[33] (Similarly, the relationship did not hold for women in London during the same decade).[34] Of course, it is very difficult to distinguish 'crime waves' from 'law enforcement waves' during such periods.

There is also some correlation between typical periods of financial stress in the lives of individual women and their involvement in property crime, again suggesting an economic motivation for their offending, at least to some extent. Thus, the age at which women offended on the Home Circuit during the 1780s peaked at about 20, having risen swiftly from the age of 14. It then fell steadily, if unevenly, until about 36 when, unlike male offenders, it started to rise again to reach a mini-peak at about 39, after which it fell sharply and remained low until a small increase took place amongst women at the end of their forties.[35] An explanation for this pattern can be found in typical female lifecycles.

Crime is, traditionally, disproportionately associated with the young. However, the major early peak in female offending coincides with women leaving home for work and having to become more self-reliant, and then fell with marriage (at the average age of 24). Single women in their early twenties were vulnerable to losing their (often domestic) positions, and might fall into crime to get by in an emergency. Those who were somewhat older, yet still with dependant children on their hands, especially if they had been abandoned by or lost their partners, and some who had been widowed later in life, also figured disproportionately amongst the number of female thieves, at least to a modest extent, explaining the small peaks in criminal involvement amongst women at the end of their thirties and forties.[36] Those poorer females who had earlier

---

[32] Beattie, John (1986) *Crime and the Courts in England*, pp.242-243.

[33] Williams, Amy (2000) *The Criminality Of Women In The 18th Century In The South West Of England*, p.147.

[34] Mackay, Lynn (1999) "Why they stole: women in the Old Bailey, 1779-1789", pp.623-639.

[35] King, Peter (2000) *Crime, Justice and Discretion in England: 1740-1820*, p.202.

[36] King, Peter (1996) "Female offenders, work and life-cycle change in late-eighteenth-century London", in *Continuity and Change*, vol.11, pp.61-90.

made part of their living from prostitution would also have lost much of their income, as their looks faded. Such a pattern was a widespread phenomenon in Western Europe. In eighteenth-century Aberdeen, for example, older female offenders were associated with charges of theft or receiving stolen goods, rather than moral crimes. They were nearly always widowed, and many were probably in severe financial want.[37]

Female Robbery

Robbery involved theft with the use or threat of force. It was considered to be a heinous offence. Highway robbery, the crime's most serious manifestation, had been withdrawn from clergy as early as 1531 (23 Hen viii c.1). This statute did not affect robbery in a "distant field, or footpath". However, all other forms of robbery were withdrawn from clergy in 1692 (3 & 4 W. & M. c. 9).[38] Nevertheless, highway robbery continued to be viewed as the crime's most heinous form. Because robbery necessarily involved the threat of violence, it was widely feared. It excited particular alarm amongst the general public when carried out by a group, especially if accompanied by physical assault, as was frequently the case with bands of footpads.

Relatively few provincial women in England were prosecuted for robbery, especially highway robbery. Nevertheless, they still made up 7.5 per cent of the total for female property offenders indicted on the Home Circuit between the 1780s and the 1820s (the equivalent figure for men was 11.6 per cent).[39] However, few of them were convicted, and even less executed for the crime, whether it was on the highway or not. Acquittal or conviction for a lesser offence (usually theft) was a far more common verdict. Thus, about 33 women went to the gallows for this crime in the Metropolis between 1735 and the end of the century. By contrast, only nine provincial women received such a disposal, and four of those came from a single incident in Surrey. One reason for this was that a large amount of female-perpetrated robbery in the capital was carried out on foot, in what was a very large urban area, all of whose streets were deemed to be highways. There was much less scope for this to occur in the provinces.

Furthermore, several of the women in the nine provincial cases had

---

[37] Jepsen, Theresa Irina Svane (2011) "Wicked Women of 18th Century Aberdeen", pp.19-25.

[38] Blackstone, William (1769) *Commentaries on the Laws of England*, vol.4, p.243.

[39] King, Peter (2006) *Crime and Law in England, 1750-1840,* p.167.

offended, and were executed, with male accomplices. For example, the four women who were hanged after the Surrey Assizes in 1785 died with their three male colleagues. Similarly, in March 1792, Jane Cross was hanged with her accomplice, Thomas Smith, in Northampton. The notion of a woman engaging in such activity on her own was alien to the eighteenth-century mind, especially if conducted on the highway. This can clearly be seen in an incident from 1735, in which a mounted woman, wielding a pistol, stopped a travelling butcher near Romford in Essex, and demanded his money. This was so extraordinary that he: "…being amaz'd at her Behaviour told her, he did not know what she meant". However, at this point (and very significantly) the highwaywoman's armed male companion, who had been hidden from view, came up and explained the situation, forcing the butcher to give her his watch and six guineas.[40]

Nevertheless, a tiny number of women robbed on the provincial highway without male support, albeit nearly always on foot rather than as mounted highwaywomen. Some of them targeted other females. For example, in 1751, Sarah Meredith was convicted at the Maidstone Assizes for highway robbery and executed. Her victim was Sarah Kidder, who was married to a Greenwich naval pensioner. During the robbery, Meredith and another woman, who was later identified as Elizabeth Sparks, threatened to murder Kidder and took nearly all of her clothes, including a gown made of calimanco (a glossy woollen fabric popular in the eighteenth century), a white apron, her cap, stockings, and a handkerchief, as well as her shoes and keys.[41] Sparks was not arrested for some time, and so was not tried with Meredith.[42] Indicative of how seriously Meredith's crime was viewed, although four other people were capitally convicted at the same Assizes, the trial judge reprieved three of them before he moved on. She was one of just two left for execution. (The other was a male horse-thief).[43] Her companion in crime (Sparks) was belatedly convicted for the same offence at the Maidstone Assizes in 1752.[44] Again, the presiding judge did not reprieve her before he left the town and Sparks was hanged on Penenden Heath near Maidstone.[45]

---

[40] *The Gentleman's Magazine*, vol.5, November 1735, p.680.
[41] *Read's Weekly Journal Or British Gazetteer*, August 17, 1751; *St. James's Evening Post*, August 1 - August 3, 1751.
[42] *General Advertiser (1744)*, August 2, 1751.
[43] *London Evening Post*, August 10, 1751 - August 13, 1751.
[44] *London Evening Post,* March 21, 1752 - March 24, 1752.
[45] *Read's Weekly Journal Or British Gazetteer*, March 28, 1752; *General Advertiser (1744)*, April 7, 1752.

A similar crime was tried at the Bristol Assizes in April 1745, when Ann Carrill was capitally convicted of robbing a young girl of her clothes on the highway.[46] In this case, however, Carrill was not subsequently executed. Nine years later, Elizabeth Hind and Ann Brooks were also sentenced to death at the same forum after being convicted of highway robbery in St. Augustine's parish in Bristol.[47] Two servants had heard screams of 'murder' near College Green and hurried to help a young woman who was being stripped (literally) at knifepoint by two female "creatures", who they detained.[48] Elizabeth, an Irish widow, was subsequently executed on St. Michael's Hill in the city. Ann, a single woman, eventually had her death sentence commuted to 14 years' transportation.[49] Away from the highway, in 1727, Elizabeth Hilliard enticed the daughter of Joseph Dix into St. George's Fields and took a gold locket and chain worth three pounds from her neck. She was capitally convicted at the Kingston Assizes but subsequently reprieved.[50]

In the Metropolis, a small but not totally insignificant number of female robbers, acting on foot, without male assistance, robbed adult men. This was quite exceptional in the provinces. Nevertheless, it was not entirely absent. Anne Hutton was capitally convicted at the Monmouth Assizes of highway robbery. She had, apparently, kept the whole county in a "state of apprehension" for several months.[51] Eventually, she was convicted of assaulting Jeremiah Leonard and stealing eight guineas from him.[52] At the Warwick Assizes in 1793 Anne Cooke was convicted of "violently assaulting and robbing" a man named de Mason in Birmingham, with another woman.[53] It is possible that some other women robbed in male attire, and were never even identified as females. One such female, who allegedly robbed numerous times on the highway, was widely celebrated in verse in the late 1600s.[54] However, whatever Lady Katherine Fanshaw *may* have done in the mid-seventeenth century, real examples of

---

46 *Daily Advertiser*, April 16, 1745.
47 *Public Advertiser*, September 17, 1754.
48 Morgan, Gwenda and Rushton, Peter (2004) *Eighteenth-Century Criminal Transportation: The Formation of the Criminal Atlantic*, at p.53.
49 *London Evening Post*, September 28, 1754 - October 1, 1754.
50 *Country Journal or The Craftsman*, August 19, 1727.
51 *London Chronicle*, August 6, 1793 - August 8, 1793.
52 *St. James's Chronicle or the British Evening Post*, July 30, 1793 - August 1, 1793.
53 *Lloyd's Evening Post*, April 12, 1793 - April 15, 1793.
54 Anon, (1690) *The female highway hector: or, An account of a woman, who was lately arraign'd for robbing on the high-way in man's apparel,* pp.1-2.

Wicked Lady-type highwaywomen seem to have been very rare during the 1700s.

In a significant number of the cases of female 'robbery' that went for trial, doubt appears to have arisen over the use of force, an essential element of the offence, allowing conviction for simple theft rather than the more serious crime. For example, in 1740 Margaret Rounce was travelling between Romford and Ilford when she met two women on the highway who lured her into Epping Forest and subsequently ran away with her gown. They were indicted for highway robbery. However, in her evidence at the Essex Assizes, Rounce admitted: "I cannot say they took it by force". As a result, it: "…appearing to the court, that Mrs Rounce was not put in fear, they were acquitted of that part of the indictment, and only found guilty of feloniously stealing".[55] This was a clergyable offence.

Female Burglary and Housebreaking

Burglary was an overwhelmingly male crime, and housebreaking was predominantly, if much less emphatically, masculine. This may have been partly due to the danger of physical confrontation that was inherent in such offences. Both involved breaking into residential premises. The former crime was committed during the hours of night, the latter in the day. Nevertheless, as a proportion of female property cases, burglary and housebreaking were far more important in the provinces than they were in the capital. They made up 17.7 per cent of the total of female property offences on the Home Circuit between the 1780s and the 1820s, compared to just one per cent at the Old Bailey during this time.[56]

Of course, proportionately far fewer women committed such crimes than men, even outside London. In eighteenth-century Surrey, for example, robbery and burglary accounted for about a fifth of men's offences, but only eight per cent of those of women.[57] Women made up only 12.4 per cent of those people indicted for burglary and housebreaking in Essex between 1740 and 1804 (84 out of 669 cases).[58] Furthermore, it appears that diurnal housebreaking, often carried out in empty residential premises, rather than nocturnal burglary, made up a significant part of

---

[55] Anon, (1740) *The Proceedings at the Assizes of Peace, Oyer and Terminer, for the County of Surrey, Held at the Town-Hall of Kingston Upon Thames, in the 14th Year of His Majesty's Reign ... To Which is Added the Genuine Proceedings at the Assizes for the County of Essex*, p.11.

[56] King, Peter (2006) *Crime and Law in England, 1750-1840,* p.167.

[57] Beattie, John (1986) *Crime and the Courts in England 1660-1800*, 1986, p.238.

[58] King, Peter (2000) *Crime, Justice and Discretion in England 1740-1820*, p.196.

these cases. Thus, in Newcastle, women would frequently use their detailed knowledge of other people's daily lives and routines to find criminal opportunities. They would know when local residences were empty, whether short or long-term, facilitating safe entry for housebreakers.[59] For example, divine service could be a dangerous time for churchgoers. Perhaps the Metropolis was simply too busy to allow such opportunities to many women.

Burglary was always an unclergyable offence. However, housebreaking was clergyable where no one was inside the premises during the commission of the crime and the defendant took goods or cash worth less than five shillings.[60] This distinction was indicative of the law's concern about potentially violent confrontations in domestic buildings. For example, in 1727, Mary and Elizabeth Huggins were convicted at the Gloucester Assizes of housebreaking, during which they had forced entry into a woman's (empty) home and stolen cloth, caps, aprons, and three pewter dishes. They were convicted to the value of 4s 6d, burnt in the hand and discharged.[61] However, as with other clergyable property offences, many women were not as lucky as Mary and Elizabeth, especially after the advent of the 1718 Transportation Act. More typically, when Sarah Rogers committed a clergyable housebreaking and was convicted at the Shrewsbury Assizes in 1756, she was sentenced to seven years' transportation to America.[62]

If goods worth more than five shillings were taken, or the house was occupied when entry was made (irrespective of the value of any goods taken), the crime was capital, and several provincial women were both convicted and hanged for it. For example, in 1759, Hannah Thomas, aged just 21, was executed after being convicted at the Winchester Assizes for housebreaking.[63] Two years later, Elizabeth Brooks met the same fate after being found guilty of breaking into a home in Tewkesbury during the day.[64] In 1780, Mary Shelton was capitally convicted at the Bedford

---

[59] Morgan, Gwenda and Rushton, Peter (1998) *Rogues, Thieves and the Rule of Law,* p.107.

[60] Emlyn, Sollom (1736) *Sir Matthew Hale's Historia placitorum coronae: The history of the pleas of the crown*, vol.1, p.547.

[61] *Gloucester Journal*, August 1, 1727.

[62] *Gazetteer and London Daily Advertiser*, August 26, 1756.

[63] *Whitehall Evening Post or London Intelligencer*, April 10, 1759 - April 12, 1759.

[64] *Lloyd's Evening Post and British Chronicle*, March 16, 1761 – March 18, 1761.

Assizes of housebreaking, and also left for execution.[65] Nevertheless, many other women in this situation were more fortunate, and although capitally convicted were reprieved on condition of 14 years' transportation. Only nine of the women who were found guilty of capital housebreaking between 1735 and 1799 appear to have been executed.

As with shoplifting and ordinary cases of larceny, when women broke into houses they were disproportionately likely to steal clothes or domestic items. Typically, in 1742, Sarah Taylor stole two pairs of worsted stockings from the house of William Howard in Godalming, Surrey. (She was only found guilty to the value of 10d).[66] Similarly, in 1787, when Jane Smith broke into the house of Ann Wilks in Great Malvern, while Wilks was out, she stole a petticoat, a cloak, two handkerchiefs and six caps.[67]

Female Theft

When it came to property crime, women were most commonly associated with offences of simple larceny, rather than robbery, burglary, or even housebreaking. Although provincial women may have been more dependent and less isolated than many of their Metropolitan counterparts, and so under less pressure to offend, their involvement in theft was certainly not marginal. For example, in the North East of England (admittedly a special case), between 1718 and 1800, 38 per cent of all accused thieves were female. Most of them were prosecuted at Quarter or Borough Sessions. However, even at the area's Assizes women made up between 20 per cent and 25 per cent of all theft defendants, if counts relating to stolen animals are excluded.[68] Similarly, in Essex, between 1740 and 1804, and taking all courts that indicted for any form of theft in the county, whether Assizes, Quarter Sessions or Borough Sessions (the records of all three forums having been preserved), women made up 19.4 per cent of cases of petty larceny and 12.2 per cent of cases of grand larceny.[69] As late as 1835, over a third of cases of simple theft (even if many were very minor) that were bailed or committed for trial in England

---

[65] *St. James's Chronicle or the British Evening Post*, March 18, 1780 - March 21, 1780.

[66] Anon, (1742) *The Proceedings at the Assizes of Peace, Oyer and Terminer, for the County of Surrey, Held at Kingston Upon Thames, on Friday the 13th, Saturday the 14th, and Monday the 16th Days of August,* p.15.

[67] *World and Fashionable Advertiser*, September 19, 1787.

[68] Morgan, Gwenda and Rushton, Peter (1998) *Rogues, Thieves and the Rule of Law,* p.9.

[69] King, Peter (2000) *Crime, Justice and Discretion in England 1740-1820*, p.196.

involved women. (By comparison, less than five per cent of those accused of burglary and 10 per cent of those accused of housebreaking were female).[70]

When considered as a whole, there were significant differences between what the sexes stole, how they carried out their crimes, and the immediate circumstances in which they offended. Nevertheless, these were normally gender-related rather than gender-specific. Few were unique to either sex. Some types of theft were more popular with men, others with women. For example, although both men and women stole clothes and household goods, the number of females involved in these crimes was proportionately much greater than that for most other types of theft.

Stealing clothing and (even more so) cloth was a quintessentially female offence. Women were more likely to both need and have an intimate knowledge of the value of such items, given that clothes were usually the largest category of household expenditure, while sewing was normally a female skill. Additionally, it seems that many women stole garments for personal use, in what was an increasingly fashion-conscious age and country.[71] In 1782, a visiting German noted that: "Fashion is so generally attended to among the English women, that the poorest maid servant is careful to be in fashion".[72] The 'newer' lightweight fabrics, such as cotton and linen, were especially popular with female thieves. Thus, a total of 43 women were accused of this crime at the Durham Quarter Sessions between 1735 and 1800, compared to just six men. At Quarter Sessions in the North East between 1719 and 1800, clothing was the predominant item stolen by 65.7 per cent of female defendants, compared to just 33.9 per cent of men. For cloth, the figures were 16.3 per cent and 7.5 per cent respectively. (Interestingly, gender proportions for stealing food and drink were almost identical).[73] Similarly, samples of female convictions for property offences taken from the Western Circuit Assizes for selected periods between 1740 and 1784, suggest that the predominant item stolen by women was always clothing, yarn and fabric (even if it was mixed in with other goods of lesser value). It came in ahead of general household goods in each period, making up 41 per cent of the sample in the period from 1740 to 1743, 55 per cent in 1755-1759, and 56 per cent in

---

[70] D'Cruze, Shani and Jackson, Louise A. (2009) *Women, Crime and Justice in England since 1660*, p.33.

[71] Lemire, Beverley (1990) "The Theft of Clothes and Popular Consumerism in Early Modern England", p.264

[72] Moritz, Charles (1797) *Travels in England in 1782*, 2nd edn., p.182.

[73] Morgan, Gwenda and Rushton, Peter (1998) *Rogues, Thieves and the Rule of Law,* pp.100-101.

1780-1784.[74]

There was nothing unique to England in this pattern. It was found in other European countries. Indeed, it can be identified much further afield. Even in eighteenth-century Japan, women were disproportionately involved in the theft of cloth and clothes. Thus, and typically, a woman named Tsuta, who came from Kobinata, was convicted of stealing clothing from a bathhouse there, tattooed (to show her criminal status) and imprisoned for 100 days.[75]

Gender distinctions in appropriation patterns also resulted, in part, from the very different opportunities and responsibilities that males and females experienced in their everyday lives. Women's lives were often more spatially constrained and bound to their immediate neighbourhoods than were those of men. Frequently, they revolved around a single street or a small hamlet, making it much more likely that they would offend close to home. This also meant that women were more likely to be charged with stealing from those they knew. Furthermore, the female 'borrowing networks' of the era, which were an important part of the household economy of many poorer people, could easily go wrong in a number of ways. This encouraged the prosecution of intimates, or at least those who were familiar with each other. Borrowing partners could press theft charges over items that had been lent out and then gone missing or not been returned.[76]

By contrast, men were more likely to travel to, or for, work, and so be away from home when they stole. Some occupations were also predominantly or entirely male. This meant that men were far more likely to commit certain offences at their place of employment. For example, women were inherently unlikely to steal from military stores or docks simply because they did not work in them.

Petty/Minor Theft

Women were heavily associated with small, often opportunistic, thefts, many of which qualified as petty larceny because the proceeds were valued at less than a shilling. In the North East, for example, they frequently stole attractive goods that were easily sold on. They would

---

[74] Williams, Amy (2000) *The Criminality Of Women In The 18th Century In The South West Of England*, p.96.

[75] Wright, Diana (2004) "Female Crime and State Punishment in Early Modern Japan", p.17 and p.27.

[76] Mackay, Lynn (1999) "Why they stole: women in the Old Bailey, 1779-1789", pp.623-639.

often target (and be arrested by) other women, in markets, lodgings, taverns and similar places.[77] There was a huge and ready market for most second-hand goods during the era. Almost any item, including food, could be sold or bartered, if it was not taken for personal consumption, greatly encouraging property crime.

Typically of such cases, in February 1769, Mary Acres, a widow, was employed to work on a regular basis in the house of George Field, a waterman from Chertsey. George may well have been a bachelor as his sister Mary Field paid Acres about 6d a day for the work she carried out. One night his house was entered while he was away, and two brass porridge pots, pewter plate, linen aprons, and various other simple utensils were stolen. The trail initially ran cold. However, a few weeks later Mary Field learnt that some of the items had been sold by Acres to the shop of John Shotten, a Chertsey brazier, for 13d. Field then complained to the local magistrate, Richard Wyatt, accusing Acres of the crime. Acres tried to explain her possession of the items by saying that they had been given to her in lieu of wages, but she was committed to the Kingston House of Correction to await trial at the Surrey Assizes held in Croydon. Acres was found guilty there of stealing goods worth 18s, being clergied, burnt in the hand, and discharged (rather than transported).[78] Some purchasers in Shotten's position probably turned a 'blind eye' to the provenance of tendered goods. However, selling on stolen items was so widespread that others took precautions, questioning sellers about their origins and publicly displaying them so that they could not later be accused of secretive, criminal, behaviour.

Many female thefts were committed without much planning or on the spur of the moment. Typically, female thieves in St. Albans during the late eighteenth century took advantage of chances that suddenly presented themselves to appropriate goods that had been left untended. Thus, in 1797, Elizabeth Prudden, a native of the town, went into a tavern and asked for a quartern of gin (at 9 am!), which she drank and paid for. However, the attendant, Ann Ashdown, was called into another room, briefly leaving Prudden alone. The following morning, Ann missed a pair of patterns (bellows) that had been standing against the kitchen door of the premises, near where Elizabeth had been drinking, and immediately associated her with their disappearance. Ann then went in pursuit of her. (Following the trails of those last seen near missing items was one of the

---

[77] Morgan, Gwenda and Rushton, Peter (1998) *Rogues, Thieves and the Rule of Law,* p.123.

[78] Silverthorne, Elizabeth (Ed.) (1978) *The Deposition Book of Richard Wyatt JP, 1767-1776*, pp.8-9.

most common methods of detection during the period). She found her at a lodging house in the town and accused her of theft. After some hesitation, Elizabeth confessed to stealing the patterns and took Ann to the person who had bought them from her. Elizabeth was prosecuted at Quarter Sessions for petty theft, the patterns being valued at sixpence. She was convicted and sentenced to seven years' Transportation. This was usually the most drastic penalty imposed by Quarter Sessions, and not a 'normal' disposal for cases of petty theft (though entirely legal under the 1718 Act). The early morning consumption of spirits by a female combined with her casual accommodation *may* have encouraged the town's Justices and Recorder to feel that she was a woman that they could usefully be rid of.[79]

Similarly, in 1796, Mary Watson helped herself to a linen sheet worth 8d that was hanging out to dry in a St. Albans' street. Ann Gee saw her take it, and pursued her to the *Rose & Crown* tavern, accompanied by "proper assistance". There, she found Watson still in possession of the sheet. She later prosecuted her to conviction. (Gee's legal costs of 5s 10d were allowed by the Recorder). Elizabeth Stevens was more fortunate in 1790. A maid named Ann Potton had hung up her apron on the door of her master's house. Shortly afterwards, Stevens called; sometime later, Ann missed her garment. Stevens came back to the same premises a few weeks later, with the apron tied around her, something that led Ann to accuse her of theft. However, Stevens claimed that she had bought the apron from a stranger near the town's Market Place three weeks earlier for 9d. The case did not survive scrutiny by the Grand Jury, which returned a verdict of 'no true bill'.[80] Other cases of female theft in St. Albans manifest a little more planning and premeditation, though they were often for relatively small objects.

Even larger scale female thefts frequently had an impulsive quality. For example, Ann Deal was convicted at the Croydon Assizes in 1745 for stealing three guineas while in John Eason's house in Southwark. She was there to nurse his wife's child, and: "…took an opportunity, whilst she was gone to market, to steal the money". She seems to have immediately confessed to the crime in front of a constable and neighbour, after she fell under suspicion.[81]

---

[79] Dean, David (Ed.) (1991) *St. Albans Quarter Sessions rolls, 1784-1820,* pp.43-44.

[80] Dean, David (Ed.) (1991) *St. Albans Quarter Sessions rolls, 1784-1820,* pp.38-39 and p.21.

[81] Anon, (1745) *The Proceedings at the assizes of the peace, oyer and terminer, and general gaol-delivery for the county of Surry, held at Croydon, on Friday the 22d, Saturday the 23d, Monday the 25th, Tuesday the 26th, and Wednesday the 27th*

Female Animal Theft

The theft of animals, particularly 'large' animals, especially horses, was an overwhelmingly male crime. Only highway robbery saw lower levels of female involvement. It has been argued that one reason that cities such as Newcastle and Bristol returned much higher proportions of female defendants than their surrounding areas was that animal theft was largely absent from their courts, necessarily reducing the male component amongst the accused. Indeed, in the North East, the crime has been described as being "almost exclusively" a male preserve.[82]

The Assizes gaol books for four counties of the Western Circuit between 1735 and 1785 produce a similar picture. Of 932 property offences committed by women there, where the stolen items were recorded, only 39 cases involved the theft of sheep (20 carried out with male accomplices), six of horses, while seven others concerned the stealing of fowl (albeit that this was normally a matter for Quarter Sessions).[83]

On the Home Circuit, between the 1780s and the 1820s, almost no women were accused of horse-theft, and only 0.9 per cent of women, compared to 5.6 per cent of men, on trial for property offences at the Assizes held in the Circuit's constituent counties, were accused of stealing sheep or cattle. (Sheep stealing had been withdrawn from benefit of clergy in 1741, with cattle following in 1742).[84] Given that the male total of property offenders on the Circuit for this sample was nine times larger than that for females, the difference in numbers between male and female cattle/sheep thieves is evident.[85] In an extreme case, in Essex, between 1740 and 1804, only one woman was accused of stealing a horse and two of taking sheep, compared to 222 and 264 men respectively for each crime.[86]

Days of March, p.13.

[82] Morgan, Gwenda and Rushton, Peter (2004) *Eighteenth-Century Criminal Transportation: The Formation of the Criminal Atlantic*, p.51.

[83] Williams, Amy (2000) *The Criminality Of Women In The 18th Century In The South West Of England*, p.107.

[84] Beattie, John (1986) *Crime and the Courts in England 1660-1800*, 1986, pp.144-145. The change was prompted by a period of rural distress leading to complaints from farmers and, as a result, a parliamentary committee aimed at addressing the problem. Pigs were not included.

[85] King, Peter (2006) *Crime and Law in England, 1750-1840,* p.167.

[86] King, Peter (2000) *Crime, Justice and Discretion in England 1740-1820*, p.196.

A higher proportion of women accused of stealing animals could usually be found in the lower jury court, because the theft of 'small' creatures, such as hens, rabbits, turkeys, ducks and geese, was normally prosecuted at Quarter Sessions. For example, two men were convicted of stealing "divers chickens" at the Surrey Quarter Sessions in 1768.[87] Elizabeth Dickinson from Hameringham in Lincolnshire provides a female illustration. She kept her eyes open for stray or isolated goslings feeding on local commons, grabbed them, and sold them on (alive) to contacts in neighbouring villages, who appear to have purchased them with no questions asked as to their provenance. Because they grew quickly, it was soon impossible for their original owners to positively indentify them, allowing Elizabeth to continue her nefarious trade for some time.[88]

On a more statistical basis, on 23 occasions between 1735 and 1782, women were tried at the Devon Quarter Sessions for stealing fowl.[89] Similarly, at the County Durham Quarter Sessions between 1735 and 1788 there were 19 cases of female-perpetrated animal theft compared to 86 male ones. (Against this, at the Northumberland Quarter Sessions, between 1719 and 1800, their numbers were tiny, only four women compared to 77 men).[90]

Of course, it is possible that the prosecution level of female animal-theft was artificially kept down, simply because women were not associated with the crime. On the Western Circuit, between 1735 and 1785, only seven females who took part in the theft of sheep as a member of one of the twenty 'gender-mixed' groups of sheep stealers indicted at Assizes were found guilty. The reluctance to convict women in such situations was an extreme illustration of a more general reticence about finding females guilty when they offended with men (evidenced elsewhere in this book). It *may* have led to some initial reluctance even to prosecute them. Posibly, because they did not fit the 'image' of the typical sheep thief, they were ignored or assumed to have been under male pressure to offend, when detained in such groups. This certainly seems to have been the case with Eleanor Langbeere, of Newton St Cyres in Devon, who appears to have escaped prosecution for stealing sheep in 1740, unlike the two men she worked with, despite making admissions to an examining

---

87 *Gazetteer and New Daily Advertiser*, April 22, 1768.

88 Davey, B.J. (1994) *Rural Crime in the Eighteenth Century: North Lincolnshire 1740 – 80*, p.351.

89 Williams, Amy (2000) *The Criminality Of Women In The 18th Century In The South West Of England*, p.121.

90 Morgan, Gwenda and Rushton, Peter (1998) *Rogues, Thieves and the Rule of Law,* pp.99-101.

magistrate. Perhaps because she claimed that one of the pair had proposed marriage to her, she was viewed as having had a subordinate role in the affair.[91] Nevertheless, with this reservation, the low figures for female involvement in such crimes are not surprising.

Looking after large animals was normally a man's job, while dealing in them, especially horses, and particularly at fairs, was nearly always done by men. Some women did not have the riding ability to steal horses, and many could not trade them. A woman trying to sell a horse would also be more likely to attract suspicion. Unsurprisingly, female involvement in horse-theft, especially when conducted in a calculated or quasi-professional manner, was relatively modest.

Nevertheless, it was certainly not entirely absent. In 1729, for example, Jane Bayly and Elizabeth Bing (also known as 'Black Bess') stole two mares from separate stables in Garsington, Oxfordshire, on a Sunday night. They then attempted to sell them on at the St. Albans fair, where (perhaps significantly) they were arrested.[92] Both were capitally convicted at the Oxford Assizes. Jane was reprieved on condition of transportation. Unfortunately, Elizabeth, her co-defendant, had been convicted three years earlier at the same forum and before the same judge (Mr. Justice Price) of an identical crime. On that occasion, she appears to have been kept in Oxford Jail for two years before receiving a royal pardon, then swiftly returning to crime. Unsurprisingly, she was left for execution in 1729.[93] In 1782, it was noted that the septuagenarian Mary Williams, arrested for stealing a silver tankard from a Bristol tavern, had already been twice capitally convicted (and reprieved) for horse-theft.[94]

Only five provincial women were executed between 1735 and 1799 for stealing (large) animals, though the theft of sheep and cattle was clergyable, and so not normally capital, until the early 1740s. To put this into perspective, 22 men were executed in Norfolk alone for animal theft over the same period, 19 of them for stealing horses (with just two for stealing sheep and one for taking cattle). Of course, the great majority of females found guilty of such offences were reprieved. This was especially likely if horses were not involved (usually valued much more highly by the courts than other beasts), and not unlikely if they were, *provided* there was no system to their crimes. For example, Hannah Jones, capitally convicted of

---

[91] Williams, Amy (2000) *The Criminality Of Women In The 18th Century In The South West Of England*, pp.114-115.
[92] *London Evening Post*, March 27, 1729 - March 29, 1729.
[93] *Universal Spectator and Weekly Journal*, July 26, 1729.
[94] *Morning Herald and Daily Advertiser*, August 10, 1782.

stealing a mare at the Shrewsbury Assizes in 1782, was granted clemency.[95] Similarly, at the Salisbury Assizes in 1775, three women who had killed and stolen two sheep were sentenced to death, but all were reprieved before the trial judge left the city.[96] In like manner, Sarah Harper was reprieved at the Gloucester Assizes in 1785, as was Margaret Palmer at the Shrewsbury Assizes in 1796, after they were capitally convicted of stealing sheep.[97] Against this, many men convicted of sheep and cattle theft were also reprieved, even if proportionately fewer of them received such clemency than women. It was especially likely where, as was the case with many females, it was thought that the sheep had been taken for personal consumption.

The five cases of animal-theft that led to female hangings between 1735 and 1799 were quite exceptional, having seriously aggravating features. For example, Elizabeth Rumbelow, who was aged 63 at the time of her execution in 1783, had spent her life in Bampton in Devonshire. Her trade was spinning, but being "unsatisfied with the gains of honest industry" she began to pilfer. At one point, she was even whipped for one of her many petty thefts in the small town. Her daughter and another young woman, Elizabeth Rowland, lived with her. Rowland had earlier been apprenticed to a butcher (an interesting illustration of female work-involvement towards the end of the eighteenth century), and being "expert in the business" appears to have led the others into sheep stealing. Neighbouring farmers began to lose animals and soon suspected Rumbelow because of her previous history. They decided to search her house (apparently without a warrant) and discovered a large quantity of mutton inside. They then took the group before a J.P. for examination. Perhaps foolishly, the women quickly admitted stealing seven sheep. Rumbelow and Rowland would lead an animal home while the former's daughter kept watch to ensure that the coast was clear. Once there, Rowland would use her skills to butcher it. Most of the animal was used. Its fat was melted down for sale. The meat was salted, the wool carded and spun. The entrails were then buried in their yard and its skin burnt. All three women were charged on one specimen count. The daughter was acquitted, but Rumbelow and Rowland were convicted of the capital offence. Rowland, who was only 21, was reprieved, although she seems to have been a prime mover in the affair. Rumbelow, as an "old offender", and one who had (allegedly) corrupted her daughter, was hanged.[98]

---

[95] *Felix Farley's Bristol Journal*, August 3, 1782.
[96] *Morning Post and Daily Advertiser*, March 28, 1775.
[97] *The Times*, July 21, 1785, p.3. *True Briton (1793)*, March 26, 1796.
[98] *Felix Farley's Bristol Journal*, September 6, 1783.

In 1797, Diana Davies became the only other woman to hang for sheep stealing during the eighteenth century, when she was executed at Presteigne in Wales. She appears to have stolen the sheep from a Shropshire farmer, who was the prosecutor, with the assistance of her son. She was also accused of stealing another sheep, belonging to Richard Jones, from Llanfair Waterdine, but this charge was not proceeded with after she was convicted on the first count. Again, there was evidence of both 'system' and multiple offences, explaining the result.[99] Nevertheless, she was not the last woman to die for the crime. In August 1801, Ann Baker was executed at Oakham in Rutland, along with a man named John Exton, for stealing and killing sheep.[100]

It seems that no women were executed for cattle theft during the century. However, three provincial women were hanged for stealing horses between 1735 and 1799: two in England and one in Wales. Thus, Martha Allen went to the gallows in Devonshire in 1740. Similarly, Mary Morgan was executed for the crime at Gloucester in 1785.[101] She had three previous convictions for similar offences, which explains her fate.[102] Catherine Lloyd, executed at Cardigan in Wales in 1791, became the last woman in the century to die for the crime. Again, she was no opportunist thief. She had: "…made a practice of stealing horses in the counties of Caermarthen and Cardigan for several years, which she used to drive to Yorkshire, and other counties".[103] Like Morgan, she was also a "very old offender".[104]

Women, Theft and 'Social' Crime

The notion of social crime has been used to describe behaviour that is defined as criminal by the authorities but which is carried out as a conscious challenge to the prevailing social and political order. In this respect, eighteenth–century women appear to have taken an important role in food riots, aimed at forcing a lowering in the price of staples. Exactly how significant their contribution was is a matter of considerable debate. Nevertheless, it seems that their involvement in purchasing supplies for

---

[99] National Library of Wales, Records for the Court of Great Sessions, File number 4/531/7, Docs 3-5.
[100] *The Bury and Norwich Post: Or, Suffolk, Norfolk, Essex, and Cambridge Advertiser*, August 12, 1801.
[101] *General Evening Post*, July 19, 1785 - July 21, 1785.
[102] *The Times*, July 21, 1785, p.3.
[103] *St. James's Chronicle or the British Evening Post*, May 3, 1791 - May 5, 1791.
[104] *Whitehall Evening Post (1770)*, May 7, 1791 - May 10, 1791.

their families made them particularly sensitive to price rises and a deterioration in quality.[105]

Some riots were even led by, or predominantly made up of, women, who might seize bread, flour, and grain before distributing it amongst the crowd for what was deemed a 'fair' price. Wagons carrying grain to places where a higher price could be secured might also be blockaded. For example, a woman appears to have been the ringleader of a very small food riot aimed specifically against one speculating individual, Samuel Booton, that took place on a market day at Tenbury Wells, Worcestershire, in 1814. Booton, a labourer from Knighton-on-Teme, had already bought 170lb of butter, before attempting to buy 30s worth of eggs and a further quantity of butter. Word quickly got around that he was buying up large quantities of dairy products, something that would drive up local prices. While Booton was purchasing his eggs, a local woman, Sarah Shepherd, warned him that if he bought them they would be broken and that he would also not be allowed to carry his butter away. Sarah then led a crowd against him; they grabbed the butter and eggs and smashed them in their containers. Booton had to flee, although he later returned to serve an arrest warrant on Shepherd.[106]

However, the concept of 'social crime' has also been used more broadly to refer to conventional crime that received a degree of community support. Obviously, this included overwhelmingly male offences such as poaching and smuggling. Nevertheless, the eighteenth century also witnessed the 'criminalisation' of what had previously been accepted work-related perquisites and customs. For example, the taking of discarded materials by employees in manufacturing, the construction industry, or in the docks, was sometimes redefined as theft. Again, many of these were predominantly male employments.

Nevertheless, it seems that many pilfering servants, including numerous maids, did not view taking small amounts of tea, sugar, and other foodstuffs as theft.[107] Instead, they regarded them as legitimate perquisites of their employment.[108] This led some observers to warn of the slippery slope that might follow from such appropriations. Grace Force, from

---

[105] Archer, John (2000) *Social Unrest and Popular Protest in England, 1780-1840*, pp.34-36.

[106] Maynard, John (2005) *The Agricultural Labourer in Worcestershire: Responses to Economic Change and Social Dislocation 1790-1841*, pp.151-152.

[107] Moreton, Andrew (Daniel Defoe) (1725) *Every-Body's Business is No-Body's Business*, pp.7-9.

[108] Hill, Bridget (1996) *Servants: English Domestics in the Eighteenth Century*, pp.45-46.

Dorset, fell to the bottom of this slope in the early 1780s. In 1782 she admitted to a local J.P. that she had embezzled a very large quantity of dairy products from her employer over the previous three years. She had used cheese, cream, and butter taken from work to pay local women for goods and services, such as providing her with cider or helping her wash her master's clothes.[109]

Gleaning was one area where women did become heavily (and almost uniquely) involved in openly resisting the erosion of what had long been treated as a traditional rural right, and its redefinition in certain circumstances as theft. It was an important source of food for poor labouring families. By ancient customary right, in many (but not all) areas of England, the poor could gather uncut or fallen grain left in the fields after the harvest, to supplement their incomes. A good gleaner could often recover four shillings and sixpence worth of corn from two average acres (one good, one bad) of arable harvested crops.[110] In some poor families it was a vital supplement to their incomes, at a time, just after the harvest, when work was often scarce. It has been estimated that it made up between 2.7 per cent and well over 10 per cent of the annual family income of labouring families in traditional gleaning areas. The practice was an ancient one and appeared to be based on scriptural authority (such as the injunctions in Leviticus and the story of Ruth gleaning in the fields of Boaz). Sometimes, a parish sexton would even ring a church bell in the morning and evening to tell gleaners when they could begin and end work, ensuring fairness between them when it came to access to fresh fields. It was especially important in the grain-growing areas of East Anglia, and was overwhelmingly carried out by women and their attendant children. Adult male gleaners (often elderly men) usually made up less than a tenth of those engaged in the activity.[111]

In the late eighteenth century, many prosperous farmers became increasingly resistant to the practice. In part, this was because it provided cover for the theft of already harvested wheat (unquestionably stealing). In 1807, for example, William Day, a nailer from Bromsgrove in Worcestershire, was walking in the early evening when he saw a sheaf of wheat fly over a nearby hedge. Several women who had been 'gleaning' in an adjacent field then hid it behind a haystack. Day reported them to the owner of the wheat field, who subsequently found several more sheaves

---

[109] Williams, Amy (2000) *The Criminality Of Women In The 18th Century In The South West Of England*, p.110.

[110] *World (1787)*, September 2, 1790.

[111] King, Peter (1991) "Customary rights and women's earnings: the importance of gleaning to the rural labouring poor, 1750-1850", pp.462-463.

missing from his field. The women were prosecuted, convicted and fined at the Worcester Quarter Sessions. (It should also, perhaps, be noted that 1807 was not a year of dearth).[112] In the case of barley, farmers also began to value the fallen grain lost to gleaning, as it provided valuable animal feed. As a result, they started to use legal sanctions to attack gleaners' rights.[113] Ultimately, in *Steel v Houghton et Uxor,* in 1788, the Court of Common Pleas considered a gleaning case originating from the Suffolk parish of Timworth. After lengthy deliberations, the judges concluded by a majority (Mr. Justice Gould supported the gleaners) that no one had a right at common law to glean in the harvest field. It was an indulgence, an act of charity, not a legal entitlement. The 1788 case established an important legal precedent, ultimately being referred to in the law reports as the "great case of gleaning".[114] However, gleaning was never redefined by parliament as a criminal offence.

In the short to medium term, *Steel v Houghton* had very little effect on gleaning, which continued unabated and would do so until well into the following century. This engendered conflicts between farmers and female gleaners. The former would try to force the women out of their fields, sometimes twisting their arms behind their backs and frog-marching them off, throwing them to the ground, beating them, or accusing them of theft. However, the women would often fight back by accusing the farmers of assault before local magistrates. They enjoyed some success in this. One woman even brought an action against a farmer for petty theft after he seized her bag. Usually, the farmers would be forced into a settlement, endorsed by a magistrate, in which they paid costs and a small sum in damages to the women.[115] None of the gleaners were ever successfully prosecuted for theft. The law had changed faster than social attitudes.

Shoplifting

Women were heavily associated with shoplifting. This was most obviously the case in the Metropolis, with its advanced retail industry and numerous

---

[112] Maynard, John (2005) *The Agricultural Labourer in Worcestershire: Responses to Economic Change and Social Dislocation 1790-1841,* pp.151-152.

[113] King, Peter (1989), "Gleaners, Farmers and the Failure of Legal Sanctions in England 1750-1850", pp.116-150.

[114] King, Peter (1992), "Legal Change, Customary Right, and Social Conflict in Late Eighteenth-Century England: The Origins of the Great Gleaning case of 1788", pp.1-31.

[115] King, Peter (1989), "Gleaners, Farmers and the Failure of Legal Sanctions in England 1750-1850", pp.118-125.

well-stocked shops; women made up a majority of those formally prosecuted for the offence at the Old Bailey. However, many provincial shoplifters were also female. Typically, and for example, in 1758, Elizabeth Hinde had Mary Tapsell committed to Maidstone Jail, claiming that Mary, a married woman, had stolen four pieces of lawn (a kind of fine linen) from her shop in Milton in North West Kent.[116]

Female shoplifters used a variety of techniques. Some manifest a considerable degree of professionalism. Many were well dressed, to reduce suspicion. They would sometimes work in pairs, one distracting the shopkeeper, perhaps by haggling over an item, while the other concealed goods about her person. A few (not many) operated in larger female gangs. For example, in Wrexham, Denbighshire, in 1710, four women worked together to steal from a mercer's shop. Three of them went in, one then haggled over the price of a handkerchief with the shopkeeper, while the others took items from his shop window which they passed on to the fourth woman, who had remained outside the premises. This woman immediately "conveyed the same away under her mantle". More typically, a decade later, in the same town, a Scottish pedlar watched as two women stole from a neighbouring market stall. One of them spread a piece of cloth over some silk handkerchiefs that were on display, after which the other picked up the parcel and hid it under her mantle, while walking swiftly away.[117]

As these cases suggest, women's frequently voluminous clothes provided considerable scope for concealment. Typical female shoplifters would have several large pockets: "...but that which stands her principally instead, is her gown or petticoat, is tuckt up before, that it will contain any thing without falling out".[118] Some experienced thieves could hide goods under their petticoats, between their thighs, and as they left a shop: "...walk very well without putting their hands to hold it".[119]

Other crimes of this nature were purely opportunistic, and committed on the spur of the moment by the women concerned. Some simply secreted items that came readily to hand when a shopkeeper was not looking. The wonderfully named Dorothy Vile stole a gold watch worth ten guineas in this manner from the shop of a Mr. Jordan, who was a

---

116 *Whitehall Evening Post or London Intelligencer*, January 21, 1758.

117 Howard, Sharon (2003) *Crime, Communities And Authority In Early Modern Wales: Denbighshire, 1660-1730*, p.127.

118 Anon, (1694) *The Ladies Dictionary, Being a General Entertainment for the Fair Sex*, p.447.

119 Anon, (1786) *The Whole Art of Thieving and Defrauding Discovered*, p.4.

goldsmith in Bristol High Street.[120] Vile was a servant who had gone into the premises simply to have one of her employer's silver spoons marked, and seeing three valuable watches lying on the counter had succumbed to temptation and hidden one of them in her stays before leaving. Unfortunately for her, Jordan had missed it immediately and: "...dogg'd her into her master's house, where it was found upon her".[121] Vile was capitally convicted at the Bristol Assizes in April 1745, but not, it seems, subsequently executed (the lack of premeditation would have encouraged a reprieve).

The phenomenon of well-to-do older women apparently impulsively taking items from shops, which has been well evidenced in the modern era, also seems to have been present in the eighteenth century, though most such cases probably did not come to trial. One exception occurred at the Somerset Assizes in 1800, when Mrs Jane Leigh Perrot (who was also Jane Austen's aunt) was accused of stealing from a haberdasher's shop in Bath. She had been stopped outside the premises and found in possession of a card of ribbon. The shop assistants were firm in their evidence. The matter was prosecuted by counsel, who produced a detailed plan of the shop's interior for use at the hearing. Nevertheless, Mrs Perrot was also legally represented. Her barrister called several women to say that they too had sometimes been given items they had not purchased by assistants from the same shop. This, together with Mrs Perrot's excellent character witnesses, people of the "first respectability", such as Lord Baybrooke, and a sympathetic trial judge, secured an acquittal.[122] (This 'type' of theft was not confined to shoplifting. Twenty years later, when a respectable and elderly woman from the same city brought a libel action against a local vicar who had accused her of stealing a pound note from a collection plate she also blamed absent-mindedness). Such cases were to contribute to the development of the nineteenth-century concept of kleptomania, something that came to be seen as a specifically female mental malady.[123] By 1819, a House of Commons committee could note that a significant number of shoplifters were not: "...regular traders in thieving, but are persons in better circumstances, particularly the women".[124]

---

[120] *Daily Advertiser*, April 16, 1745.

[121] *Daily Gazetteer (London Edition)*, February 5, 1745.

[122] *The Derby Mercury*, April 10, 1800; Pinchard, John (Attorney) (1800) *The Trial of Jane Leigh Perrot, wife of James Leigh Perrot*, pp.40-42.

[123] D'Cruze, Shani and Jackson, Louise (2009) *Women, Crime and Justice in England since 1660*, p.38.

[124] Whitlock, Tammy C. (2005) *Crime, Gender and Consumer Culture in Nineteenth-century England*, p.140 and p.133.

'Shoplifting Act' of 1699

The 'Shoplifting Act' of 1699 made the offence of "privately stealing" goods worth five or more shillings from retail premises a capital offence by removing it from benefit of clergy, although it had to be prosecuted under an appropriately worded indictment (or it would be simple grand larceny). However, successful prosecutions under the statute appear to have been very rare, whether in London or the provinces.[125] In *theory*, the crime could be capital until 1832, although no one had been executed for it for a least a decade by then.

Frequently, of course, no formal action at all was taken against detained shoplifters. Instead, some form of summary justice, such as a beating, might be inflicted. Alternatively, and perhaps far more commonly with women, the victim would accept financial payment in lieu of prosecution, even if this was theoretically illegal (compounding a felony). If shopkeepers did choose to have recourse to prosecution by indictment, they might bring proceedings for petty theft if the goods were worth less than a shilling, or he was prepared to say they were below this value to moderate the consequences of conviction. Alternatively, he might prosecute for simple grand larceny, over one shilling but less than five in value or, if more than five shillings, without alleging that the technical requirements of the 1699 Act had been made out.

Even when prosecutions were brought under the Shoplifting Act, they would often result in acquittals or (very commonly) convictions for the lesser offences of petty or grand larceny. Thus, in 1736, after Elizabeth Dey stole some cambric (a valuable lightweight plain weave cloth) from a shop in Norwich, she was burnt in the hand, having been convicted of a clergyable felony (i.e. larceny over one shilling in value but not within the 1699 Act).[126] In 1739, Mary Mills was even more fortunate. She was indicted at the Surrey Assizes for "privately stealing" four yards of printed cotton from the shop of Mary Willoughby. Although convicted, she was only found guilty to the value of 10d. Thus, not only was she not convicted under the 1699 Act indictment originally charged, but she even escaped being found guilty of clergyable grand larceny.

It became increasingly easy to return such verdicts because the technical requirements for an offence to be made out under the 1699 Act were interpreted progressively more strictly by the courts as the century

[125] Whitlock, Tammy C. (2005) *Crime, Gender and Consumer Culture in Nineteenth-century England*, p.130.
[126] *Daily Gazetteer (London Edition)*, August 31, 1736.

advanced.[127] In the Metropolitan area, of 294 cases indicted under the statute at the Old Bailey during the 1730s, only 11 resulted in convictions for the full offence, and these were often subject to post-conviction reprieves. By the latter part of the century, the tiny number of prosecutions under the 1699 Act that produced both convictions and executions usually had specially aggravating features.[128]

Exactly the same situation applied in provincial England. On the relatively few occasions that convictions were secured under the 1699 statute, a reprieve was likely to follow, especially after the early years of the century. Thus, in 1736, a woman who was capitally convicted at the Warwick Assizes for shoplifting in Birmingham, in the course of which she had taken fully £40 worth of goods, was reprieved on condition of transportation.[129] Rather more strangely, when Anne Smart was convicted under the 1699 Act at the Reading Assizes in 1744, she was sentenced to death and then immediately reprieved, not on condition of transportation but with the requirement that she be burnt in the hand (and discharged).[130] In 1782, Anne Smith, having been found guilty of shoplifting at the Shrewsbury Assizes was also reprieved, albeit with some delay.[131] More typically, when Sarah Wright and Sarah Thompson were capitally convicted of shoplifting before the Surrey Assizes in 1797, they were reprieved almost as a matter of course by the trial judge, before he moved on to the next town on the circuit.[132]

As a result, it appears that only two, possibly three, women were executed for shoplifting in provincial England in the years between 1735 and 1799 (three more were hanged in the Metropolis during the same period).[133] The first of these cases, from 1779, is instructive. Sarah Jones was found guilty under the 1699 Act of stealing 28 yards of chintz calico from the shop of a linen-draper in Chester. Female shoplifters who stole cloth were often older than the typical offender.[134] This was certainly the case with Sarah, who was fully sixty years of age. The likely reasons for her unusually draconian punishment were alluded to in a statement that

---

[127] Palk, Deirdre (2006) *Gender, Crime and Judicial Discretion: 1780-1830,* p.70.
[128] See for example, OBSP, Trial of Mary Jones, 11 September 1771:t17710911-32. Marks, Alfred (1908) *Tyburn Tree its History and Annals*, pp.255-257.
[129] *London Spy Revived*, August 30, 1736.
[130] *Country Journal or The Craftsman*, March 10, 1744.
[131] *Felix Farley's Bristol Journal*, August 3, 1782.
[132] *True Briton (1793),* March 30, 1797.
[133] www.capitalpunishmentuk.org
[134] Palk, Deirdre (2006) *Gender, Crime and Judicial Discretion*, p.39 and pp.57-59.

she made shortly before execution. She attributed her fall to an unfortunate connection she had made over the previous three years with a "dangerous set of shoplifters".[135] The combination of a comparatively high value item and 'professionalism' in the venture appears to explain the result.

The second case, from 1784, is less obviously explicable. Vicaria Owen was convicted at the Shrewsbury Assizes and hanged for stealing a piece of printed linen, valued at five shillings, from George Crump, a mercer in the town.[136] This was only just within the limit of the 1699 Act, although the suspension of transportation (often a condition of reprieve) during the American Revolutionary War *may* have contributed to the decision. Doubtless, if a detailed investigation were possible it would reveal other aggravating factors.

Pick-pocketing

Legally, picking pockets, like shoplifting, was a particular type of theft, one that involved "privately" (secretly) stealing from another's person goods that were worth more than a shilling. This was a longstanding capital offence as, unlike most other forms of grand larceny at this value, it had been put beyond the reach of benefit of clergy in 1566 (8 Elizabeth, c.4). As with shoplifting, it required a specially worded indictment. Picking pockets of goods below a shilling in value remained petty theft and thus not capital under any circumstances. Additionally, openly 'snatching' goods worth more than 12d from the person might not qualify, as it was not done secretly. As the century advanced, and as with shoplifting, the technical requirements for the offence, especially the meaning of "privately", came to be interpreted increasingly strictly, reducing its scope.[137] For example, in 1743, at the Bristol Assizes, Elizabeth Harris was indicted for picking John Dove's pocket of a purse containing 35 pounds. However, a special verdict was returned for consideration by the 12 Westminster judges, a: "…point of law arising concerning privately stealing". This was because Dove admitted in questioning at trial that he had "felt the money go from him".[138] In 1808, the offence was redefined to include any theft from the person, but no longer attracted a death penalty. Of course, it was always open to eighteenth-century prosecutors who had been the victims of such crimes to indict for petty theft or simple grand

---

[135] *Chester Chronicle and General Advertiser*, October 8, 1779.

[136] *Whitehall Evening Post (1770)*, March 20, 1784 - March 23, 1784; *St. James's Chronicle or the British Evening Post*, March 30, 1784 - April 1, 1784.

[137] Palk, Deirdre (2006) *Gender, Crime and Judicial Discretion*, pp.69-70.

[138] *Daily Post*, May 3, 1743.

larceny (a clergyable offence), and for juries to convict of such lesser offences, even if a capital charge had initially been brought.

Like shoplifters, many pickpockets were female. Again, this was particularly marked in the Metropolis. For example, between 1780 and 1808, just over half of those who stood trial for the crime at the Old Bailey were women.[139] Their victims tended to be men. In part, this was because more men were abroad and carrying valuable objects or cash. More significantly, a great many cases involved prostitutes or 'loose women' stealing from their (often intoxicated) clients or 'pick-ups'. The commoditisation of sex, and the relative informality with which it often occurred, at variance with 'normal' practice in many rural areas, provided the background for much urban crime. This was less common in provincial England, although prostitution was often widespread outside the capital.

Nevertheless, even in the provinces, pick-pocketing was a crime with a heavy female involvement, relative to men, although the per capita numbers involved were fairly small in absolute terms when compared to the capital. Thus, 38 women were convicted of either shoplifting or picking pockets from a sample taken from the Home Circuit between 1782 and 1827, compared to 49 men.[140] This made it one of the relatively few property crimes in which provincial women participated with roughly equal frequency to men. One reason may have been physical; women were more likely to have small hands and the proverbial 'light touch'.

A few women exhibited a high degree of professionalism in this form of crime. Again, this was most marked in the Metropolis, which produced the master pickpocket, Jenny Diver (executed in 1740). However, a few similar women operated in the provinces. For example, Mary Grey was a professional pickpocket for many years before her death in 1804. She was a Scottish woman by origin, and also known as 'Scots Maggy' as a result. Mary was, apparently, universally admitted by law officers to be the "most expert pickpocket" in England. She specialized in race meetings, but took advantage of any other opportunities that presented themselves, from Cornwall to Northumberland. On one occasion, she stole a valuable gold watch from the Mayoress of Bath during divine service at a church in that city. Grey was a small woman who, like many top-level pickpockets, normally dressed in a "very genteel style". She abandoned her husband to live with a male companion and fellow pickpocket for several years, had several children studying in boarding schools, and often associated with specialist gangs. She had been tried on capital charges several times during

---

[139] Palk, Deirdre (2006) *Gender, Crime and Judicial Discretion*, p.69.

[140] King, Peter (2006) *Crime and Law in England, 1750-1840,* p.174. The source does not distinguish between the two types of crime.

her career, but was always acquitted.[141] Some other women were also extremely audacious. In 1790, Jane Stephenson, an "old offender", was caught picking pockets in court, during a murder trial held in the Newcastle Moot Hall! She had taken a handkerchief valued at 6d (below the capital level and so merely petty theft). Stephenson was immediately put on trial at the same forum, convicted, and sentenced to seven years transportation (a relatively unusual disposal for petty theft).[142]

Even if found guilty of the full offence, many women were reprieved from execution. For example, Jane Tinsley was capitally convicted at the Kingston Assizes in 1727 of picking the pocket of Edward Hollis of a guinea and a Moidore (a Portuguese gold coin) but subsequently reprieved.[143] At the Bristol Assizes in April 1745, Elizabeth Symes was capitally convicted after she picked Maurice Fitzgerald's pocket of eight guineas.[144] Again, she was not subsequently executed. Only five women were hanged for picking pockets outside London after 1735 (along with just two in the Metropolitan area), the last being Susanna Guise, who was executed at Worcester in December 1762.

Details of some of these crimes are hard to come by. However, as with shoplifting, it is safe to say that, by then, those that resulted in execution were normally accompanied by particularly aggravating features. For example, in 1736, Elizabeth Gilham, convicted at the Surrey Assizes of picking Daniel Kootes's pockets of a "considerable sum" of money, was executed at Kingston on Thames.[145] Unlike Jane Tinsley's relatively modest total nine years earlier, Gilham had taken several foreign gold coins (her victim may have been Dutch) worth over £17, and this proved (literally) fatal.

Theft by Female Servants

Female servants (like male ones) had ready access to other people's valuables and, usually, knowledge of their whereabouts. Sometimes, they even had responsibility for their security (ensuring that doors were locked and windows fastened at night etc.). This explains the importance placed by many employers on character and references. Turnover of domestic

---

[141] *The Ipswich Journal*, December 22, 1804; *Caledonian Mercury*, December 24, 1804.

[142] Redfern, Barry (2003) *Shadow of the Gallows: Crime and Criminal Justice in and Around Newcastle Upon Tyne in the Eighteenth Century,* p.23.

[143] *Country Journal or The Craftsman*, August 19, 1727.

[144] *Daily Advertiser*, April 16, 1745.

[145] *London Spy Revived*, August 30, 1736.

staff was much slower in provincial England than it was in the capital, encouraging a greater degree of security in this regard. Nevertheless, servant-perpetrated crimes were a regular feature of the era, even in the remotest parts. They were such obvious suspects that they would often guard their employers' property jealously against external threats, partly though loyalty, but also for fear that they would be blamed if items went missing. In 1711, when Mary Evans caught a woman taking a pan from her master's house in Denbighshire she confronted the thief, because otherwise: "…she knew her master would question nobody but her [Evans] for it".[146]

As the majority of 'indoor' servants were female, it is unsurprising that women should figure prominently in such crimes. For example, towards the end of the century, Sarah Chandler took a position with a jeweller and was left in charge of his house. The attendant temptation proved too acute and, with the assistance of her paramour, she stole diamonds worth the enormous sum of £1,600. Initially, she managed to escape the law (unlike her lover), dressing in men's apparel to do so. However, she was eventually caught in a raid carried out by Bow Street officers during the early hours of the morning.[147] Sarah was subsequently executed.

As in the capital, servants who were prosecuted for theft were more likely to have been taken on fairly recently. For example, 18-year-old Ann Robson had been in her master's employment for just a week before being committed to Morpeth jail, accused of stealing a bundle of clothes from his house.[148] Nevertheless, the risk from servants did not end when they left their employment. Mary Cooper came back to burgle the large residence in Surrey where she had been a maid, earlier in her life, something that gave her the "advantage of knowing the house better".[149]

---

[146] Howard, Sharon (2004) "Investigating responses to theft in early modern Wales: communities, thieves and the courts", p.417.

[147] Anon, (1796?) *The True and remarkable life and extraordinary adventures of that unfortunate woman, Sarah Chandler*, pp.2-4.

[148] Morgan, Gwenda and Rushton, Peter (1998) *Rogues, Thieves and the Rule of Law,* p.108.

[149] Anon, (1740) *The Proceedings at the Assizes of Peace, Oyer and Terminer, for the County of Surrey, Held at the Town-Hall of Kingston Upon Thames, in the 14th Year of His Majesty's Reign ... To Which is Added the Genuine Proceedings at the Assizes for the County of Essex*, p.4.

The 1713 Act

Theft, as opposed to forced entry via burglary or housebreaking, from domestic premises ('stealing from a dwelling house') of goods worth more than 40s was withdrawn from clergy, and so made a capital crime, by statute in 1713 (12 Ann, c.7). This Act was, in part, specifically passed to deal with "ill-disposed servants". There was particular concern that domestic staff might allow criminals into their employers' homes, or provide them with intelligence about valuables where they worked.[150] There had been a cluster of such cases in the years immediately prior to the advent of the new statute. For example, Grace Tripp, a native of Lincolnshire, had procured a position in the London house of Lord Torrington. She became romantically connected with a man named Peters, who persuaded her to assist him in robbing her master's house. She let Peters in one night when everyone, apart from an unfortunate housekeeper, was out of London. The housekeeper came down as Tripp and Peters were packing up the family plate, at which point Peters cut her throat while Tripp held a candle to light him. The pair then searched the pockets of the dead woman for money before escaping. Both were caught a few days later. Although he was the actual killer, Peters was admitted as a Crown witness, to ensure that the treacherous Tripp was convicted and, at the age of nineteen, executed in March 1710.[151]

Of even greater concern, from a legal perspective, was the case that seems to have prompted the introduction of the 1713 statute. Jane Roberts and her male friend John Daley had been accused of burglary from the house of Sarah Cross, where Roberts worked as a maid. While her mistress was out one night, Roberts answered Daley's knock at the front door. Daley and another man then entered and proceeded to bind and gag two other servants before ransacking the premises and stealing more than £30 of silverware and other valuables. When examined by the Lord Mayor, Roberts claimed that Daley "made love to her, and drew her in".[152] However, although they were accused of the unclergyable (and so capital) crime of burglary, both were acquitted of this count and found guilty of the lesser offence of simple grand larceny, for which they were duly clergied, branded and released (the case occurred before the advent of the 1718 Transportation Act). The fact that Roberts had invited the men into the

---

[150] Humfrey, Paula (1998) "Female Servants and Women's Criminality in Early Eighteenth-Century London", p.74.

[151] Rayner, J. L. and Crook, G. T. (Eds) (1926) *The Complete Newgate Calendar*, vol.II, pp.213-214.

[152] OBSP, Trial of Jane Roberts, 25 February 1713: s17130225-1.

house raised a doubt about whether it was legally a burglary. The 1713 Act would have allowed her to be executed. Of course, the statute covered all thefts to this value from a dwelling house, not just those perpetrated by servants. If, for example, a female (or male) hawker was invited into a house and, while left unattended, took goods to this sum, she would also be guilty of the capital felony.

Despite the popular fear of corruption by male lovers, most maids who stole acted alone and on their own initiative, sometimes taking advantage of sudden opportunity, at others planning their crimes carefully in advance. For example, in one notorious case, a maid who had nursed a dying Hampshire farmer on her own for some time, became aware of his hidden cache of £100 in cash. She stole it shortly after he expired. Unfortunately for her, he had identified both the money and where it was hidden in his will. When it was not found, the maid was quickly suspected and the money discovered in her trunk. She swore to her innocence and asked that the Almighty strike her down if she was lying. He duly complied and she dropped dead on the spot! (Perhaps from a stroke or heart attack brought on by stress).[153]

Both the victims/prosecutors of this type of theft, and the juries that tried the female servants accused of them, seem to have been fairly benign towards erring maids, especially as they were provided with food and accommodation (if at a rather basic level) as part of their employment and so could not argue that that they acted out of pressing need. Indeed, some employers did not take any formal action at all, other than dismissing them from their positions or, even more leniently, making them pay them back by deducting money from their wages. In 1770, for example, a newspaper correspondent from Leigh in Lancashire, decrying the widespread availability of the death penalty for property crimes, noted that he had once had valuable items stolen by his maid. However, fearful that she might pay for her crime with her life, he "bore the loss" and took no formal action against the girl.[154] Of course, such forbearance was not unique to England. In early-modern Germany, servant maids who stole were also frequently dealt with by dismissal or a reduction in salary, and the authorities only rarely became involved.[155]

In this context, and as with some other crimes, any suggestion that an employer had negotiated with his servant to compromise a matter was

---

[153] Anon, (nd) *The Hampshire Tragedy: Shewing how a Servant Maid first robbed her master, and was afterwards struck dead for telling a lie*, pp.7-8.
[154] *Lloyd's Evening Post*, August 17, 1770 - August 20, 1770.
[155] Rublack, Ulinka (1998) *The Crimes of Women in Early Modern Germany*, p.99.

likely to be fatal to a subsequent prosecution. Thus, in 1740, Sarah Cathew was prosecuted at the Surrey Assizes in Kingston for stealing 20 shillings and several shirts and tablecloths from her employer Henry Salter. She admitted taking the cash and items, and spending the money, to both Salter and an examining J.P. However, at trial, Cathew was acquitted after she called witnesses to say that Salter had agreed to "make the matter up" for five pounds 10 shillings, this money to be paid off at a shilling a week from her wages. Taking formal action also raised the possibility of embarrassing defences being advanced by female defendants. Several maids, like Mary Floodgate at the same Assizes, claimed that they had been given allegedly stolen items as presents by their employers or, even worse, in exchange for sexual favours: "He gave me the sheets and things to let him lie with me".[156] Even if maids were put on trial, juries frequently indulged in 'pious perjury' to down-value stolen goods below the strategic levels at which offences committed ceased to be petty thefts (a shilling) or, alternatively, became unclergyable and thus capital felonies (40 shillings).

Why were jurors so indulgent to domestic servants, especially if they were female? The simple answer must be that they did not view such crimes as being terribly serious. Thefts by maids were usually committed stealthily, and normally involved no potential risk of violence to their employers. (Where this was not the case, as with Grace Tripp, the judicial process could be ruthless). Such cases also provided obvious suspects, who could be pursued, as goods and maids often disappeared at the same time, especially if items of major value were taken.

Normally, jurors seem to have felt that transportation, branding and discharge, flogging, or a short spell of imprisonment, rather than execution, met the demands of justice. Many of the women sentenced to be transported to America (and later Australia) were household servants prosecuted for theft from (and by) their employers. For example, in 1725, 18 out of 26 transported thieves (69 per cent), who were known to be servants, had been employed by, and stolen from, their prosecutors.[157] Similarly, by far the most common profession amongst women in the First Fleet to Australia, one held by 61 of them, was that of domestic servant.[158]

---

[156] Anon, (1740) *The Proceedings at the Assizes of Peace, Oyer and Terminer, for the County of Surrey, Held at the Town-Hall of Kingston Upon Thames, in the 14th Year of His Majesty's Reign ... To Which is Added the Genuine Proceedings at the Assizes for the County of Essex*, p.10

[157] Lodine-Chaffey, Jennifer (2010) "From Newgate to the New World: A Study of London's Transported Female Convicts, 1718-1775", at www.earlyamerica.com/review.

[158] Ferguson, Reay (2008) *Female Felons of the First Fleet*, p.106.

Those few female servants who were capitally convicted and executed would usually have done something to aggravate their crime, such as stealing quite exceptional amounts of money or refusing to co-operate with the authorities after arrest.[159] For example, in 1768, Martha Green, a twenty-year-old servant, was hanged after stealing from her mistress's house in Suffolk. Not only was this a gross breach of trust (like all such cases) but items of great value, including a large diamond ring and a hair-ring set with garnets, had been taken. Several other pieces of jewellery and some fine clothes were also stolen.[160] So grave was her offence that Sir John Fielding, in the Bow Street Police Office in London, had issued a public advertisement offering five guineas for Green's capture and describing her appearance.[161] Significantly, Thomas Thorpe, who had been capitally convicted of housebreaking at the same Assizes, was reprieved, unlike Green.

In like manner, in 1799, Sarah Lloyd, a young maid (possibly only 19 and certainly not more than 22) working for a woman in Hadleigh, Suffolk, let her lover, Joseph Clark, into her employer's home. The pair took some jewellery and set the building on fire, albeit that the blaze was quickly extinguished. Both Sarah and Joseph were arrested and charged, but ultimately only Sarah was convicted of stealing goods in a dwelling house to the value of more than 40 shillings, when tried at the Assizes held in Bury St. Edmunds. Although this was, theoretically, a capital offence, by the end of the eighteenth century it almost never resulted in execution. Nevertheless, Lloyd was condemned to death and the trial judge did not recommend a reprieve. A local magistrate organized a petition calling for her to be spared. However, the Home Secretary, the Duke of Portland, rejected it. The arson combined with the breach of trust were seen as aggravating factors, particularly as it seems that the property had been set on fire in several places, allegedly with combustible material being placed under a staircase, and it was claimed that there had been a deliberate attempt to kill Lloyd's employer.[162] Although Sarah had not been convicted of arson, she was duly executed.[163]

---

[159] Humfrey, Paula (1998) "Female Servants and Women's Criminality in Early Eighteenth-Century London", pp.74-75.

[160] *Public Advertiser,* August 3, 1768.

[161] *Public Advertiser*, June 28, 1768.

[162] *The Times*, April 11, 1800, p.3.

[163] *The Ipswich Journal*, April 26, 1800.

Receivers

As early as the medieval period, women had been disproportionately associated with receiving and disposing of stolen goods. As late as 1840, well over a fifth of all prosecuted cases of receiving involved women.[164] However, the eighteenth century saw an especially heavy female involvement in this crime, particularly in urban areas. In the Metropolis, they made up almost half of those indicted for the offence. Similarly, the *Hibernian Journal* reported women as defendants in 34 out of 57 cases of receiving stolen property in late eighteenth-century Dublin.[165]

In the (English) provinces female involvement in receiving was slightly more modest, but still important. Some of the women concerned were widows, supplementing otherwise meagre incomes.[166] Perhaps significantly, a contemporary observer, discussing the typical buyer of stolen goods, referred to "him or her".[167] Little or no behaviour that fell outside gendered 'expectations' for females, or that was viewed as uncharacteristic of women, was required in the crime's commission. A combination of female employments and family economic responsibilities, such as managing their home's budget and purchasing provisions also provided women with both the cover needed for receiving and knowledge of the value of household items. This allowed them to avoid drawing excessive suspicion to their nefarious side-trade if they turned to this form of crime, as well as encouraging success in its commission.[168]

An Act of 1691 made those who received stolen goods while knowing them to be stolen accessories to a felony, and thus theoretically liable to a death sentence. However, despite further statutes reinforcing this Act in 1702 and 1706, prosecutions for such a capital crime were normally only possible if someone else had been or was (at the same time) convicted of the original theft. This made them quite rare. Even where they did take place, it was very difficult to secure convictions. For example, after Richard Milliard pleaded guilty at the Kingston Assizes to stealing a bed, bolster, and rug, Diana Cooper was indicted for feloniously receiving the

---

164 D'Cruze, Shani and Jackson, Louise (2009) *Women, Crime and Justice in England since 1660*, p.33.
165 Henry, Brian (1993) *Dublin Hanged: Crime, Law Enforcement and Punishment in Late 18th-century Dublin*, p.57.
166 Golby, J. M. and Purdue, A. W. (1999) *The Civilisation of the Crowd: Popular Culture in England 1750-1900*, p.141.
167 Anon (Lover of his country), (1752) *Villain'y Unmask'd* … p.8
168 Callahan, Kathy (2012) "On the Receiving End: Women and Stolen Goods in London 1783-1815", at p.119.

same items. A prosecution witness, Ann Bridle, stated that Cooper had paid less than half their true value, and had had earlier contact with Milliard. However, in her own evidence, the defendant merely stated that she traded as a broker, gave what she thought was the worth of various items offered to her, and: "…had not the least suspicion of their being stolen". She called a good character witness and was acquitted.[169]

Some cases did not even come to trial. In 1709, Margaret Edwards swiftly confessed that she had stolen a sheet when examined by a J.P. She also claimed that she had taken it to Ursula Fowler in Wrexham who paid her for it with drink, as she had done on other occasions with stolen items. Ursula denied this, and claimed that Margaret's claim was motivated by malice stemming from an earlier physical conflict between the two women after a heated argument. Margaret was convicted and whipped for petty theft. However, Ursula's indictment was thrown out by the Grand Jury. (Petty theft could not have accessories). In a similar case from the same town, involving the theft of two sheets, Rebecca Wood, though bound over to appear in court, was ultimately not even indicted, even though the thief, Jane Locker, was convicted.[170]

At its higher end, competent exponents of this nefarious trade would have access to workmen who could erase marks (the numbers on watches etc.) and alter the appearance of valuable fenced goods, so that they could be sold "publickly in Town and Country" without risk.[171] It also made it very difficult to bring successful prosecutions for receiving if identification was in issue, as was frequently the case, and something that the courts were usually very strict about.

Even if a guilty verdict was secured and a death sentence passed on a woman convicted of feloniously receiving stolen goods it was very likely to result in a reprieve. Inevitably, there were a few exceptions to this general pattern. For example, 45-year-old Grace Bootle was executed at Ilchester in 1787 for receiving property from her burglar son, John, knowing it to have been stolen.[172] However, Jane Maugham, from the North East, was more fortunate, and much more typical. Mary Grainger had pleaded guilty to grand larceny (rather than an offence under the 1699 Act) after stealing four pounds' worth of ribbons, linen, and cotton from a

---

[169] Anon, (1739) *The Genuine Proceedings at the Assizes on the Home Circuit, Held in March, 1739. ... at Hertford, for the County of Hertford; Chelmsford, for the County of Essex,* p.15

[170] Howard, Sharon (2003) *Crime, Communities And Authority In Early Modern Wales: Denbighshire, 1660-1730*, pp.129-130.

[171] Anon (Lover of his country), (1752) *Villain'y Unmask'd* … p.8

[172] *The Times*, August 24, 1787, p.4.

female shopkeeper. She was clergied, branded and released. Some of the goods were found in Jane Maugham's house (she was a married woman but issues of coverture do not appear to have arisen at trial) and she was convicted of "receiving such stolen goods, knowing them to be so". She was ultimately transported for 14 years, presumably, given the length of time involved, having been reprieved from a capital conviction at Assizes.[173] Welthian Jones received the same result at the Bristol Assizes in 1743, after being convicted of receiving the 33 guineas stolen by her daughter Ann (who was capitally convicted at the same sessions) from the desk of a glazier.[174] Indeed, transportation for 14 years appears to have been the almost standard punishment for felonious receiving for much of the century.

Many cases of receiving were still prosecuted as misdemeanours. Even then, it was often difficult to secure a conviction, as it was still necessary to prove that the receiver knew or believed the goods to have been stolen, something that was inherently difficult in a world in which second-hand goods were widely traded and nearly always had a ready market. Thus, in Denbighshire, at the start of the period, those women who were accused of the crime would strongly deny the allegation, and the courts would normally accept their denials.[175] Nevertheless, a few convictions were secured for the lesser form of the crime. For example, in 1787, at the Worcestershire Assizes, two related women, Hester and Sarah Stone, were sentenced to two years' imprisonment for receiving stolen goods.[176]

It was regularly claimed that receivers were the primary cause of much property crime in England. Certainly, some female retailer-receivers, such as the shopkeeper Jane Rogers, actively encouraged other women to supply them with stolen items. In 1738, Rogers confessed to a Plymouth magistrate that she had urged Elizabeth Woone to provide her with saleable goods by "gett[ing] into peoples windows and gett[ing] some things and to bring them to her". Woone was later paid a penny for a stolen shirt and went on to carry out other thefts on behalf of Rogers.[177] More commonly, it seems that female receivers simply turned a 'blind

---

173 Morgan, Gwenda and Rushton, Peter (Eds) (2000) *The Justicing Notebook (1750-64) of Edmund Tew,* p.181.

174 *Daily Post*, May 3, 1743.

175 Howard, Sharon (2004) "Investigating responses to theft in early modern Wales: communities, thieves and the courts", p.422.

176 *The Times*, March 21, 1787, p.3.

177 Williams, Amy (2000) *The Criminality Of Women In The 18th Century In The South West Of England*, p.135.

eye' to the provenance of extremely suspicious goods that were brought to them.

Trial and Disposal

As discussed in chapter two, women accused of property crimes were more likely than their male counterparts to receive favourable outcomes from the criminal litigation process, whether in the form of outright acquittals or being convicted of lesser offences than those initially charged. If convicted, women were also often treated more leniently than men. Many who were found guilty of capital offences, such as Sarah Starr, who was sentenced to death at the Salisbury Assize for stealing two snuffboxes and some clothes from a house in Bradford (Wiltshire), were reprieved before the judge left the Assizes town.[178] For understandable reasons, women were also much less likely to be swept up in the the crime/prosecution surges and draconian penal regimes that often followed large-scale post-war demobilisations of young men, such as that which occurred in the 1780s.

Conclusion

Whatever might have been the case in earlier eras, there does not appear to have been a predominantly or specifically 'female' culture of dishonest activity, separate to that of men, in most of provincial England during the 1700s. Typically, in Durham during the 1750s and 1760s, purely female networks of thieves and receivers were normally limited in both their nature and size, and were usually relatively short-lived.[179] Female property crimes were widespread but often opportunistic and as a result frequently involved items of small to middling value. Women might work with partners (who were often female) but did not usually operate in large gangs. They were only rarely involved in robberies and burglaries, offences that normally involved the possibility of serious violence. This helps to explain why female thieves were more likely to be seen as a nuisance rather than a menace than their male counterparts. These factors helped secure favourable results for those women who were accused of property offences, even for those whose crimes were, on an objective basis, quite serious.

---

178 *Morning Post and Daily Advertiser*, March 28, 1775.

179 Morgan, Gwenda and Rushton, Peter (1998) *Rogues, Thieves and the Rule of Law,* p.112.

CHAPTER SIX

ARSON AND COINING

Introduction

The most 'important' female crimes, when judged by a combination of incidence and gravity, have been considered in the preceding chapters of this book. However, to put them into a slightly broader context, this chapter will consider two rather more recondite, less frequently prosecuted, but very serious offences: arson and coining. The former was more significant amongst provincial, especially rural, rather than Metropolitan women; the latter was the opposite.

Arson

A significant proportion of the women who were hanged during the eighteenth century had been sentenced to death for arson. It was the fourth most common cause of female execution between 1735 and 1799, when 16 of the roughly 323 women definitely executed in England and Wales (about five per cent of the total) died for the crime.[1] This is particularly significant, because arson was both very difficult to prosecute successfully and a crime where it was often difficult even to identify a suspect. The 'dark figure' of unrecorded early modern arson is probably very high.[2] For example, in 1780, a range of buildings burnt down as a result of a fire that broke out at Downton Mews in the Oxford Road. No one was arrested although: "It was supposed to have been [done] wilfully, as no light had been in the premises since the night before".[3] At about the same time, fire broke out in a blacksmith's shop and spread to adjacent houses in Yelverton in Staffordshire, causing very considerable destruction, and the

---

[1] www.capitalpunishmentuk.org.

[2] Capp, Bernard (2000) "Arson, Threats of Arson, and Incivility in Early Modern England", p.198.

[3] *Craftsman or Say's Weekly Journal*, April 1, 1780.

deaths of many horses. Again, although a suspect was not forthcoming: "It was supposed to be wilfully set on fire".[4]

However, when it came to female execution, arson was a disproportionately and overwhelmingly provincial, rather than Metropolitan, offence. Of the sixteen women, only one met her death at Tyburn. Indeed, 17-year-old Betty Limpany was one of the last women to be executed during the eighteenth century. She was accused of burning down her master's house at Kentisbeare in Devon, where she had worked as a maid, and hanged in April 1799.[5] Cases of female-perpetrated arson were certainly not absent from the Metropolis. Indeed, there had been a cluster of trials there involving women at the end of the seventeenth century, and several executions had ensued, including two from a group of four women who were capitally convicted in 1690 for trying to burn their way out of Newgate by setting fire to a prison door.[6] However, during the eighteenth century, only three or four women appear to have been capitally convicted for the crime in the city, and these cases were normally subject to reprieve, only one or two women actually being executed. As will be seen, there were reasons for the rural bias in female executions.

Arson was defined at common law as the malicious burning of the dwelling house of another person. Burning down your own house was merely a serious misdemeanour. Dwelling meant a place of residence. A structure did not become a residence until it had been lived in, and ceased to be so if it was abandoned long-term. However, it was not confined to the main building: "…not only the bare dwelling house, but all outhouses that are parcel thereof, though not contiguous thereto, nor under the same roof, as barns and stables, may be the subject of arson".[7] Such arson was not a clergyable offence.

The position of some other buildings was slightly more ambiguous. At the start of the eighteenth century, setting fire to non-residential buildings was still a clergyable offence. This was changed by statute, including some of the provisions in the 'Black Act' of 1723, which provided that burning certain work-buildings and hay or straw-stacks would also be a capital offence. The precise scope of these changes provided a loophole for Sarah Taylor. She was convicted at the Rochester Assizes in 1759 of setting fire to her master's paper-mill. However, she was legally represented at her hearing, and her counsel successfully moved an arrest of judgment just as the death sentence was about to be passed on her, as a

[4] *Gazetteer and New Daily Advertiser*, March 17, 1780.
[5] *Star*, April 1, 1799.
[6] OBSP, Trial of Constance Wainright et al, 10th December 1690: t16901210-34.
[7] Blackstone, William (1769) *Commentaries on the Laws of England*, vol.4, p.221.

result of a: "…doubt [about] whether a Paper-mill was included in the Act of Parliament; and therefore sentence is respited till next Assizes".[8] Presumably, this point was then referred to the 12 Westminster judges for consideration. Taylor was not subsequently executed.

The common law had always viewed arson exceptionally seriously. According to Blackstone, it was an offence of: "…very great malignity, and much more pernicious to the public than simple theft". It produced terror, confusion, and even death, as well as great damage to property, making it a crime with a double aspect. It could also spread to affect people who were completely unknown to the incendiary, and not intended as his or her victims.[9] In a society with minimal protection against fire, and in which wood and thatch were widely used building materials, especially in rural areas, it could cause enormous financial and personal loss. Draconian penalties were a response to the fear that this evinced. For example, in 1727, Jane Thomas was convicted at the Bristol Assizes of setting fire to a house and, it seems, not only hanged at Ivelchester but subsequently anatomized.[10] Indeed, even threats to commit arson were frequently prosecuted when combined with an assault. Thus, Mary Pine was tried at the Devon Quarter Sessions for threatening to fire the town of Hambury in 1766.[11]

Four main categories of arson can be identified. Amongst them were acts of revenge; these were frequently committed by servants against their masters, and sometimes by neighbours or other associates of the victim; as will be seen, they were especially common with women. Another common form of the crime was the use of fire to cover the commission of property crimes, whether by stealing items in the mayhem that normally occurred while rescue and recovery operations were underway (goods being thrown into the street from a blazing building etc.), to hide an offence that had already been committed, on the basis that it would be assumed that the stolen item had been lost in the fire, or to divert attention while a theft was effected. Insurance frauds constituted a third major category, whereby insured premises were set on fire with a view to claiming on the relevant policy. Insurance was a rapidly growing eighteenth-century industry, but this type of offence affected relatively few women, who did not normally take out such policies, particularly in rural areas. Fourthly, arson was sometimes prompted by a political motive, as with the firing of Newgate

---

[8] *Universal Chronicle or Weekly Gazette*, March 24, 1759 - March 31, 1759.

[9] Blackstone, William (1765) *Commentaries on the Laws of England*, vol.3, p.220.

[10] *Mist's Weekly Journal*, May 6, 1727.

[11] Williams, Amy (2000) *The Criminality Of Women In The 18th Century In The South West Of England*, p.163.

prison during the Gordon riots of 1780 or, more commonly, the periodic outbreaks of rick-burning in rural areas. These were often an indicator of wider popular unrest. For example, in late 1766, during an acute shortage of grain, farmers were targeted in several parts of England, presumably because it was felt that they were hoarding wheat and barley and so artificially driving up prices. In October of that year, two barns of grain were destroyed at Wellington in Shropshire. Grain stored in Kettering in Northamptonshire was burnt on Guy Fawkes Night the following month. This event was greeted with cheers and dancing by a watching crowd. Most such cases did not come to court. Thus, it has been noted that between 1795 and 1820, very few instances of arson reached the Assizes when compared to the relatively large number reported in local newspapers.[12]

Although politically motivated cases of arson were often perpetrated by men, some women also became involved in these crimes. In 1791, for example, a woman attempted to fire the house of a Mr. Hutton in Birmingham, during a disturbance occasioned by meetings in sympathy with the French Revolution. Other rioters held her back, out of a fear that the conflagration would spread to houses whose owners were not their intended targets.[13] Supplementing these four main categories, and of lesser significance statistically, were cases occasioned by mental disturbance, depression or outright insanity.

Occasionally, more than one motivation was present at the same time. For an example can be considered a Metropolitan arson case from 1687. Mary Benson had been employed by Benjamin Peak as a servant, but learnt that she was about to be replaced. Indeed, Peak had, rather unwisely, already recruited her successor. This was too much for Mary, who stole diamonds and silver to a considerable value and then set fire to the premises, both to cover her crime and to exact revenge. However, her replacement spotted the blaze, and quenched it. Mary fled but was later captured, convicted, and sentenced to death.[14]

As this case suggests, servants featured heavily in cases of arson. Unsurprisingly, given the number of female domestic staff employed, some perpetrators were women. Despite this, the great majority of convicted arsonists were male. Elizabeth Sedgwick, executed in 1787, has

---

[12] Maynard, John (2005) *The Agricultural Labourer in Worcestershire: Responses to Economic Change and Social Dislocation 1790-1841,* p.142.
[13] Anon, (1791) *An Authentic Account of the riots in Birmingham on the 14th, 15th, 16th, and 17th Days of July 1791*, p.9.
[14] OBSP, Trial of Mary Benson, August 31st, 1687: t16870831-1

even been referred to as a "rare female incendiary".[15] However, this probably understates female involvement in the crime. Many cases of arson for gain came to light because of the financial aspect of the crime; arsonists were found in possession of stolen goods etc. Those motivated by revenge were much harder to identify and convict, unless caught red-handed, yet this was probably the most common form of the crime amongst women. Many capitally convicted female arsonists in the provinces were, or had been, domestic maids who were possessed of a desire to hurt a current or former employer. It is likely that numerous similar cases went entirely undetected, being put down to accident or as arson committed by an unknown person.

The case of Mary Adams, who set fire to a large farm near Bawburgh in Norfolk in early 1791, provides a good example of a female-perpetrated arson that was motivated by revenge. She appears to have been a former servant who had been discharged by the farmer in acrimonious circumstances some three weeks earlier, and had been overheard threatening reprisals. It was a well-planned crime. She lit multiple fires on his premises with a flint and striker, so that hayricks, a pigsty, stables, and several barns all went up in flames and burned to the ground. In the blaze, many animals were also killed, including six horses that were each worth £30, along with assorted pigs, cows, and poultry. Adams was swiftly suspected, pursued, and arrested, still in possession of her flint. Her companion, who seems not to have taken an active role in what had occurred, became a prosecution witness for the Crown. Adams was convicted and met her death with "great firmness and resolution". (Her case was not helped when it transpired that she was also a bigamist).[16] She was certainly not alone. Thus, in 1787, Mary Welkin was executed in Coventry for maliciously setting fire to the *Golden Horse* public house, which was also the dwelling of a Mr Crosby (presumably her former employer).[17] Seventeen-year-old Joan Stone was hanged in Devon in 1794 for setting fire to her master's house and barn, both of which were "consumed" by the flames.[18]

In one of the most extreme cases, Elizabeth Osborne was executed in 1813 after being convicted of arson at the Cornish Assizes in Bodmin. She had nursed a grudge against a local farmer, John Lobb, for three years

---

[15] McLynn, Frank (1989) *Crime and punishment in eighteenth-century England*, p.85.
[16] *Morning Chronicle,* January 3, 1791; *Evening Mail*, April 13, 1791 - April 15, 1791.
[17] *Coventry Mercury,* April 11, 1787.
[18] *Exeter Flying Post*, April 10, 1794.

after being dismissed from her position as an apprentice maid, and had publicly vented "expressions of malice toward him". She eventually fired a mow (a pile of sheaves in a barn) of his wheat, one night, hoping that that the financial damage inflicted would mean that he would be forced to "eat barley bread as well as herself". (This was inferior to wheaten loaves). She had then carefully spread the fire using a flint and striker. Afterwards, she had freely and publicly boasted of what she had done, and her trial largely revolved around her mental condition. Unfortunately, none of the witnesses or her jailer (who had observed her carefully during her incarceration pending trial) were willing to suggest that she was anything but sane, even if she had a foul temper.[19]

Elizabeth Tarrant was another servant prompted to commit arson by a wish for revenge, but this time it seems it was the desire of others to take reprisals against her master, Edward Clerke, who was also an active Wiltshire J.P. He had made dangerous enemies as a result. Tarrant was executed after being convicted at the Salisbury Assizes of setting fire to Clerke's house. It may not have been the first time. He had had several haystacks and ricks burnt down on earlier occasions. Before her execution, Tarrant admitted that she had been induced to commit her crime by some "old offenders" whose prosecutions Clerke had earlier supervised.[20]

However, although much less common, there were a few cases of female-perpetrated arson that were committed for personal gain and which also resulted in convictions. For example, seventeen-year-old Susannah Minton had been a servant at Paul Gwatkin's farm near Kilpeck in Herefordshire. She stole a large number of caps, linen sleeves, and other items, after setting fire to a barn, so as to distract his family. She was executed at Hereford in September 1786.

One reason for the heavily provincial, indeed rural, orientation of female executions for arson after 1735 is that the crime, to be successfully carried out, and to occasion large-scale damage (and so little chance of a post-conviction reprieve), required a degree of privacy and, in an era with far fewer accelerants (such as petrol) readily to hand, access to easily combustible material, such as hay or straw. Igniting these materials was often an aspect of female perpetrated fires that produced an execution. Thus, in 1783, Martha Brown was tried, convicted and hanged at the Chester Assizes after setting fire to a haystack with six bays full of corn and hay, all of which were consumed in the blaze.[21] In like manner, Sarah

---

[19] *Royal Cornwall Gazette, Falmouth Packet & Plymouth Journal*, August 28, 1813.

[20] *St. James's Evening Post*, April 7, 1747 - April 9, 1747.

[21] *Felix Farley's Bristol Journal*, May 3, 1783.

Cave was executed after the Bedford Assizes for deliberately setting fire to some haulm (stems or stalks of grain used for litter or thatching) belonging to her master. The blaze then spread to several ricks, which were also destroyed.[22] Similarly, Ann Catchpole was convicted, and executed, at Bury St Edmunds for igniting a straw-stack, while Ann Giles was hanged after she set fire to a barn at Speenhamland near Reading.[23]

Of course, many prosecuted female-perpetrated cases of arson did not result in convictions, not least because it was such a hard crime to prove. Even cases that did produce guilty verdicts did not necessarily result in executions. Thirty-six women were tried for arson in four counties on the Western Circuit between 1735 and 1785. Of these, just 12 were found guilty. Eight of these women were subsequently reprieved after being capitally convicted, while one was sentenced to transportation and another incarcerated for six months (presumably for a still clergyable form of arson). In 1746, Mary Daley, who was just seventeen, even managed to get her former master, whose property she had set fire to, to intercede on her behalf in favour of transportation rather than death.[24]

Coining/Currency Offences

Women were (comparatively) heavily involved in coining offences. This serious crime involved counterfeiting or adulterating silver and gold English money. In some of its manifestations, it was classified as treason. However, until statutory change in 1741 (15 Geo.2 c.28), the counterfeiting of small-value domestic copper coins, such as halfpennies, was merely a misdemeanour, for which a sentence of imprisonment might be imposed on conviction. Counterfeiting foreign gold and silver coins did not normally constitute treason, though a serious offence was committed when they were 'passed'.

Some of the techniques used in coining cases were extremely sophisticated. Amongst them was the mass production of moulded 'silver' sixpences, shillings and half-crowns out of base metal. For example, in 1713, Barbara Spencer, Alice Hall and Elizabeth Bray, from Bishopsgate in the City of London, were prosecuted at the Old Bailey for counterfeiting. They had made a fire in Bray and Hall's room, locked the door, made

---

[22] *General Evening Post*, August 16, 1783 - August 19, 1783.

[23] *Bingley's Journal Or Universal Gazette (1771)*, March 30, 1771 - April 6, 1771; *Lloyd's Evening Post and British Chronicle*, February 20, 1761 - February 23, 1761; *London Evening Post*, March 7, 1761 - March 10, 1761.

[24] Williams, Amy (2000) *The Criminality Of Women In The 18th Century In The South West Of England*, p.164.

moulds, melted what appears to have been pewter, and then poured it into them. Having done this they cast 40 counterfeit shillings in a single day. Their landlord later found a ladle and file hidden in a cupboard on the premises.[25]

Other techniques were a little more basic. In 1797, the septuagenarian Rebecca Dunn was executed for colouring copper coins with silver after the Surrey Assizes.[26] (She was hanged, as burning for the crime having been abolished seven years earlier, although still drawn to the gallows on a sledge).[27] Some forms of coining were exceptionally simple. Amongst the most popular of these was clipping, which entailed removing slivers of precious metal, whether gold or silver, from the edges of good coins, so that they could be accumulated and then melted down into bullion for resale. For example, in 1728, 30 pieces of gold were found in a drawer in the house of Joseph Hyans, most of which had been cut and filed, so that three ounces of gold dust was also discovered.[28] Skilled clippers might take up to two shillings from a 'good' guinea, usually using a pair of scissors, before smoothing the edges, restoring the milling with a file, and returning the coin into circulation.

Although some of the women involved in this crime were married and working with their husbands, many, like Spencer and her friends, acted on their own or with other females, a mother and daughter combination being fairly common. For example, it was noted of one such pairing that: "While the mother cast the coins, her daughter 'cut off the tails with a pair of scissars, scraped the edges round with a knife, and then filed them". The coins were then coloured to look old by shaking them about in wheat, meal, or crumbled Cheshire cheese. Commonly, coiners would then 'put off' such bad money by using it to buy things such as: "…smallcoal, tape, thread, or any odd trifle to get change".[29]

Nevertheless, as these cases also suggest, female coining had a very strong Metropolitan bias. Almost half (46 per cent) of those tried at the Old Bailey for such offences were women.[30] Apart from Rebecca Dunn, it seems that all of the rest of the (eight) women executed for coining during the 65 years after 1735 were burned or hanged in the Metropolitan area,

---

[25] OBSP, Trial of Barbara Spencer et al, 25th May 1721: t17210525-56.

[26] *Morning Post and Fashionable World*, August 22, 1797.

[27] *St. James's Chronicle or the British Evening Post*, August 19, 1797 - August 22, 1797.

[28] *Weekly Journal, or the British Gazetteer,* August 10, 1728.

[29] OBSP, Trial of Elizabeth Wright et al, 5th December 1733: t17331205-65

[30] Tosney, Nicholas (2007), "Women and 'False Coining' in Early Modern London", p.104.

although Ann Lucas, who was capitally convicted of coining at the Summer Assizes at Kingston in 1781, would have been burned had she not successfully pleaded her belly.[31]

The Metropolitan bias towards coining was encouraged by the crime's need for an anonymous environment. The Act for Preventing Counterfeiting and Clipping of 1695 had provided a reward of £40 for those who apprehended and prosecuted coining offenders to conviction. Additionally, coiners who gave information leading to the conviction of two of their accomplices were offered a free pardon, and informing on those possessing or selling clippings from coins was also encouraged by granting them half the fine levied on the accused after conviction.[32] In small communities it was hard to keep secrets from neighbours or to avoid erstwhile criminal colleagues out to save their own necks.

However, some Metropolitan-based women passed their counterfeit coins in the provinces, if only because country people were less alert to fake money, blurring the dividing line between town and country. For example, Ann St Lawrence, giving evidence for the prosecution against her two female accomplices in a coining case from 1733, noted that half-crowns were easier to pass in rural areas, because people there were "not so sharp as those in London". On one occasion she had made a profit of six pounds by buying necklaces and other peddler's wares, selling them while on a trip around Oxford and Banbury, and giving fake money as change for the good specie that had been tendered by her customers.[33]

Additionally, although direct female involvement in provincial coining was more muted than in the capital, several women were found amongst hundreds of people from around Halifax who, when facing a recession in the textile industry during the 1760s and 1770s, used their work skills to counterfeit British and Spanish coins.[34] An extensive manhunt produced a series of trials and many of the coiners were imprisoned or sentenced to hang at York's Tyburn. However, high-level female involvement appears to have been quite small. Although Betty Crossley, the wife of a spinner, who was accused of paying to have clipped coins 'put off', was amongst the major suspects it seems that no females were executed.[35] Nevertheless,

---

[31] *Morning Post and Daily Advertiser*, August 3, 1781.

[32] Tosney, Nicholas (2007) "Women and 'False Coining' in Early Modern London", p.106.

[33] OBSP, Trial of Elizabeth Wright et al, 5th December 1733: t17331205-65

[34] McLynn, Frank (1989) *Crime and punishment in eighteenth-century England*, p.167.

[35] Styles, John (1980) "'Our Traitorous Money Makers': the Yorkshire Coiners and the Law, 1760-1783", pp.202-203.

it is likely that (as with many other crimes) the willingness of law enforcement agencies and the courts to ignore married women in premises where such activities were conducted, even if it was likely that they had had some involvement in their husbands' activities, contributed to such a male-dominated profile, even though, where coining constituted high treason, coverture had no formal application. A woman in such a situation: "…cannot, as in ordinary cases, be considered as acting under the influence of her husband".[36]

Even so, in 1806, Sarah Herring was executed at Horsemonger Lane in Surrey after being convicted at the county's Assizes, along with her husband, for coining. They had carried on the trade for a long period from their house in St. George's in the Fields. A search of their residence revealed a full set of coining instruments, punches, *aqua fortis* and a very large number of forged silver coins.[37] In like manner, in August 1809, Susan Grant was executed for coining after the Warwick Assizes.

Deliberately uttering ('passing on') forged money that had been made by others was sometimes just a misdemeanour. Thus, Bridget Caines received 12 months' imprisonment at the Surrey Assizes in 1797 for "selling and uttering counterfeit money".[38] If someone unintentionally passed on counterfeit money, the recipient could insist on payment in good currency, while a magistrate could confiscate the fakes, so that the loss was borne by the person who had tendered them.

Conclusion

Arson and coining were very different offences, though both required great secrecy, albeit for different lengths of time. One was often motivated by fierce passion, and the chance to get back at resented employers. The other was calculated, and prompted by a desire for gain. Although they made up only a small minority of female perpetrated crimes in eighteenth-century England, they are indicative of the sheer breadth and versatility of women's offences at this time and the huge range of motivations behind their crimes. There were few offences in which they were entirely absent, even if there were many in which they produced only a modest showing.

---

[36] *The Times,* January 26, 1805, p.3.
[37] *The Morning Post*, March 29, 1806.
[38] *True Briton (1793),* March 30, 1797.

CHAPTER SEVEN

GENERAL CONCLUSION

Much can be learnt from a study of provincial women, crime and justice during the eighteenth century, not least because it casts considerable light on the era's wider society and legal process. Additionally, and as with their Metropolitan counterparts, studying women's crimes can tell modern observers a great deal about their broader lives and concerns at this time. However, in their turn, such studies provide almost as much information about the preoccupations of modern historians. Depending on their stance, academics might search for signs of female agency or passivity, oppression or rebellion.

One thing that does quickly become apparent is that the London area was not typical of the rest of England. The late seventeenth and early eighteenth-century female 'crime wave' that seems to have occurred in the capital was not replicated elsewhere in the country, though there were echoes of it in several major provincial cities and mining areas. With some qualifications, the 'traditional' portrayal of female offending in provincial England during this period, which suggests that women committed fewer offences than men, *especially* those that were, or were perceived to be, grave crimes, and that their transgressions were usually treated less severely by the criminal justice system, appears to be borne out by much of the available evidence. Of course, the incidence of formal prosecution, let alone conviction, was not a true reflection of the real rate of female offending. However, although official figures probably underestimated the number of offences perpetrated by women to a greater extent than they did for their male equivalents, especially when they 'worked' with men, it was not significant enough to change the validity of this generalisation.

This does not mean that provincial women were less criminally minded; it does mean that they were less inclined to break the law, particularly when it came to the most serious offences. This book has explored the possible reasons for this phenomenon. Partly, it was to do with innate physical factors, especially when it came to crimes of violence. In part, it can also be explained by the degree of (male) control to which women were subject, the reduced opportunities for crime in their quotidian lives, and that they were, perhaps, socialized into different roles, and to be submissive to the law's demands to a greater degree than their male counterparts. All of these factors probably played some role in the process, but exactly how much relative to each other is nearly impossible to estimate, particularly given the passage of time. Some, such as the level of male control and the presence of criminal opportunities for women are inextricably intertwined. Thus, it seems that female offending fell sharply with marriage. Was this because: women were under closer supervision; their lives were more circumscribed and their employments (and resulting criminal opportunities) more limited than previously; they were under less economic pressure when supported by a male breadwinner; that the legal doctrine of *feme covert* and, even more significantly, the social attitudes towards married women who offended in the company of their husbands deterred prosecutions; or, perhaps most likely, a combination of all of the above?

Some modern academics seem to view lower levels of female offending as a badge of shame, rather than being creditable, something that would have astonished eighteenth-century observers. It is taken to be indicative of a lack of female agency. Such observers are often keen to lay the 'myth' of female passivity by stressing women's deviance. In part, this is a natural reaction to an apparently strange alliance of past and present, and of diametrically opposed views as to how the world should be ordered. Early feminists often explained female offending by asserting that the women concerned were the victims of their circumstances, and so not fully responsible for their actions. In like manner, some representatives of the patriarchal society that was eighteenth-century England viewed females as essentially powerless and marginal, and so not to be taken quite as 'seriously' as their male counterparts.

Nevertheless, the modern pre-occupation is not entirely surprising. A long school of criminologists, from Luke Owen Pike in the late nineteenth century to Otto Pollack in the 1930s, have effectively equated female agency with crime. As a result, they also feared that changes in the position of women in modern society, which gave them more power or influence, or saw a reduction in controls and limitations on them, would inevitably produce more female crime.[1] Additionally, it might be expected that increased criminal opportunities would be presented to women as they entered the commercial labour force in unprecedented numbers, further driving up their offending rates. These factors have encouraged female

[1] Lacey, Nicola (2007) *From Moll Flanders to Tess of the D'Urbervilles: Women, Autonomy and Criminal Responsibility in Eighteenth and Nineteenth Century England,* p.28.

deviance to be seen as an indicator of emancipation. However, although there have been enormous changes in the position of women over the last 50 years, the increase in female crime, though real, has been more modest than might have been expected. It is possible that crime is not the right field to search for female agency during the eighteenth century, and that other areas, such as female-run businesses, would provide better, and certainly more constructive, examples.

Nevertheless, even accepting that female-perpetrated crime was a significantly smaller phenomenon than its male counterpart, especially in the provinces, it is also clear from the evidence explored in this book that it was not a minor issue in eighteenth-century England. It was both widespread and a thorough nuisance. Women were behind a very significant minority of lesser to middle ranking thefts and frauds. They also played an important role in facilitating all property crimes via their heavy involvement in receiving stolen goods. Furthermore, they committed a large number of low to medium level assaults, albeit that they often attacked other women when doing so.

Even so, female crime was not viewed as seriously by the era's criminal justice system as this level of involvement might seem to demand. Women were often treated *relatively* leniently as a result. However, this was not a matter of simple ignorance on the part of those involved in the eighteenth-century criminal justice process. The majority of the system's components, that is, nearly all of its judges, most of its J.P.s, and many of the jurors who sat in judgment on women, were intelligent, educated, and informed men, who would have been well aware of the reality of crime in their society. They treated many of the women being processed through the system in a *fairly* benign manner, even though they must have known that their numbers were not nugatory. This was not the result of simple prejudice, 'chivalry', or a respect for womanhood.

To the eighteenth-century mind, 'crime' was not a monolithic concept. As all criminologists appreciate, crime and the fear of crime are different, and not always logically linked, phenomena. As already noted, some (perhaps many) misdemeanours were viewed in a very different way to felonies during the eighteenth century. For example, until very late in the era, assaults were often considered as quasi-civil matters, and numerous prosecutions for the offence were primarily aimed at securing compensation for the victim, rather than the punishment of the perpetrator.[2]

[2] See generally, Landau, Norma (1999) "Indictment for Fun and Profit: A Prosecutor's Reward at Eighteenth-Century Quarter Sessions", pp.507-536.

However, the process went further than this. Within the category of 'felony' there was another major eighteenth-century distinction. This was not the *de jure* separation of felonies into clergyable and unclergyable offences, although, of course, such a division existed. It was a *de facto* division between those felonies that excited real alarm amongst the public, including male judges, jurors and magistrates, and the rest, which were primarily viewed as serious irritants. A distinguished historian of the period has noted that highway robbery epitomized crime in the eighteenth century. Indeed, its prevalence was often considered to be a gauge of crime in any given locality.[3] Nevertheless, robbery was not quite unique in this status. Murder, burglary and, albeit to a smaller extent, housebreaking in occupied premises, were also viewed very seriously. These were crimes that necessitated, or had the potential for producing, violent confrontation. They were the offences for which the vast majority of English hangings took place. When contemporary observers spoke of a 'crime problem' it was these offences that they normally had in mind. They were also crimes for which women posted very low totals, especially when acting on their own, and where forensic lenience towards females was most clearly manifest. The two phenomena were linked.

As already noted, the eighteenth century was wedded to the notion of progressively deteriorating criminal careers. Minor sins, like Sabbath-breaking and drunkenness, led on to more serious offences, such as larceny, before culminating in robbery and murder. This was sometimes given a religious basis, especially early in the period. In 1712, for example, the Newgate Ordinary reminded Elizabeth Chivers, a woman of over 30 and of good reputation until the last year of her life, of this danger. Chivers had suddenly killed her three-month-old illegitimate baby, after having it baptized, and despite being supported by the married father of the child (her former employer) by drowning it in a Hackney Pond. The cleric took the opportunity to show her how: "…cunningly the Devil had dealt with her; how he generally brings those who suffer themselves to be tempted by him, from one Sin to another; and how therefore we should be aware of his sleights, and keep as great distance from any sin as possible".[4] However, such an analysis was also supported by those with a much more secular outlook on life. For example, in 1792, the Home Secretary warned Parliament that rogues "reached the gallows by degrees". They started as youthful pickpockets, used the proceeds of their

---

[3] Landau, Norma (2010) "Gauging crime in late eighteenth-century London", pp.396-417.

[4] Ordinary's Account, 1st August 1712: OA17120801

crimes to buy a horse, and then took to robbery on the highway.[5] This theme was so widely alluded to that it formed the basis for the life of Hogarth's 'Idle Apprentice' in his series of prints from 1747.

The notion of progressive moral deterioration had very important implications for the criminal justice system. It was thought that early intervention via firm criminal sanctions might prevent offenders' careers progressing from drunkenness to capital offences.[6] At the same time, draconian sentences would deter others from following in their footsteps. Nevertheless, such considerations were primarily relevant to men. Women did not rob on the highway, very rarely burgled or broke into occupied houses, and only occasionally committed murder. It has been noted that nineteenth-century observers made numerous connections between masculinity and crime, so that it was on male offenders that late Victorian courts focused their full disciplinary powers.[7] However, such an analysis was already well evidenced in the previous century.

Significantly, grave 'female' felonies did not elicit public anxiety. Infanticide was almost certainly the most serious individual crime that women committed in numbers during the period, allowing for the many cases that went entirely undetected. However, it was not directed towards the wider society and had only been effectively criminalised (in the secular courts) over the previous two centuries. It was not viewed like other crimes of violence. As has been seen, it was not an offence that occasioned much concern to the well-to-do men who sat on eighteenth-century juries, hence the numerous acquittals, even in apparently strong cases. The other grave 'female' crime in existence at the start of the period, witchcraft, ceased to be an offence a third of the way into the century, and was believed to exist by very few educated men even in 1700. It elicited even less male anxiety in the political nation than did infanticide.

An awareness of the low female involvement in what were perceived to be the most heinous crimes influenced the way in which female crime generally was viewed. It also meant that, when women came before the courts, judges and jurors appreciated that there was less need to set an example or 'interrupt' their progression to more serious crimes by being quick to convict or harsh when sentencing. As a result, offences like robbery were also the crimes for which females were most likely to

---

[5] Anon (By a Friend to the Constitution), (1800) *Observations on the Duty and Power of Juries, as established by the Laws of England*, 5th edn., p.448.

[6] Grant, F. (1701) *A Vindication of Informers of the Breaches of the Laws Against Prophaness and Immorality*, pp.6-7.

[7] Godfrey, Barry et al (2005) "Explaining Gendered Sentencing Patterns for Violent Men and Women in the Late-Victorian and Edwardian Period", p.714.

receive favourable results in court. Conversely, larceny, whether petty or grand, the crime that women committed most frequently, and where their offending totals was closest to those of men, was also the one for which their forensic outcomes differed least from those of males. Again, the two phenomena were linked.

Nevertheless, even for routine thefts, *some* indulgence towards females was shown, if to a much more modest degree than for robbery or burglary. It seems that male decision-makers in the criminal justice process tacitly accepted that part of the price paid for the subordination of women in their society was that females, who were often greatly economically disadvantaged in an increasingly commercial and mobile world, were likely to commit minor, opportunistic offences, if only to survive or to help provide for their families and children. There was a growing recognition that, for females at least, and in the words of Defoe's anti-heroine, Moll Flanders, when discussing her first descent into crime: "…a time of distress is a time of dreadful temptation, and all the strength to resist is taken away; poverty presses, the soul is made desperate by distress, and what can be done?" In this situation, an element of chivalry, or at least understanding, probably did come into play. In the words of John Wilkes, it was generally acknowledged that the state of womankind was: "…more destitute and defenceless than that of man; but this is amply compensated for, by man's thinking it incumbent upon him to become upon every occasion her protector".[8]

As a result of a combination of these different factors, women were often treated more leniently by the eighteenth-century justice system than their crimes properly warranted on an objective basis or than their exact male equivalents, though the extent of this leniency varied greatly. Overall, they were less likely to be prosecuted, indicted, convicted, hanged, or transported. Of course, it was always a matter of degree. By modern standards women were often on the receiving end of exceptionally draconian punishment. Additionally, where women committed crimes that appeared to threaten the social order or which showed considerable premeditation the English judicial system could be as ruthless as it was with men. Those female offenders who could not be contained within benign gender-stereotypes were viewed as capable of extreme immorality and treated accordingly.[9] Female poisoners, for example, evinced particular fear because their crimes occurred on a fairly regular basis, were extremely serious (especially for men), very hard to detect, and almost

[8] Wilkes, John (1764) *An Essay on Woman*, p.17.

[9] Parker, George (1781) *A View of Society and Manners in High and Low Life*, p.90.

impossible to protect against. Accordingly, women were often convicted and executed for such crimes on a weaker than normal evidential basis. More generally, "lewd women" were still sometimes feared as "ravenous harpies" and the "merciless destroyers of soul and body", although such a portrayal was less common at the end of the period that at its start.[10]

Finally, it should always be remembered that, although this book is about female offenders, when it came to crime, eighteenth-century women were usually more sinned against than sinners. Only women could be raped or sexually assaulted (probably very under-prosecuted crimes) and far more females than males were the victims of severe domestic violence. Women were also much more at risk of some rather less obvious crimes. For example, it seems that widows were quite disproportionately the victims of domestic burglaries.[11] That is, however, another story, for another book.

---

[10] Broughton, Thomas (1800) *Serious Advice and Warning to Servants*, p.14.
[11] Laurence, Anne (1996) *Women In England 1500-1760: A Social History*, p.262.

BIBLIOGRAPHY

Modern Secondary Sources (post-1850)

Abrams, L. (2002) "From demon to victim: the infanticidal mother in Shetland, 1699-1899", at pp.180-203 in Brown, Y.G. and Ferguson, R. (Eds) *Twisted Sisters: Women, Crime and Deviance in Scotland since 1400*, East Linton: Tuckwell Press.

Andrews, William (1899) *Bygone Punishments*, London: William Andrews & Co.

Anon, (2002) *Taking Stock: What do we know about interpersonal violence?*, The ESRC Violence Research Programme, London.

Archer, John (2000) *Social Unrest and Popular Protest in England, 1780-1840*, Cambridge: CUP.

Archer, John E. (2008) "Mysterious and Suspicious Deaths: Missing Homicides in North-West England (1850-1900)", in *Crime, History & Societies*, vol.12, no.1, pp.45-63.

Baker, John (1973) "Criminal Justice at Newgate 1616-1627", in *The Irish Jurist*, vol. 8, pp.307-322.

—. (1998) "The Three Languages of the Common Law", in *McGill Law Journal*, vol.43, pp.5–24.

Beattie, John (1974) "The Criminality of Women in Eighteenth Century England", *Journal of Social History*, vol.8/4, pp.80-116.

—. (1985) "Violence and Society in Early-Modern England", at pp.36-60 in Doob, A. et al (Eds), *Perspectives in Criminal law. Essays in Honour of John Edwards*, Ontario: Aurora.

—. (1986) *Crime and the Courts in England 1660-1800,* Oxford: OUP.

—. (1995) "'Hard Pressed to Make Ends Meet': Women and Crime in Augustan London", at pp.103-115 in *Women and History,* Firth, Valerie (Ed.), Toronto.

—. (2001) *Policing and Punishment in London, 1660-1750*, Oxford: OUP.

Bell, Suzanne (2008) *Crime and circumstance: investigating the history of forensic science*, Westport: Greenwood Press.

Bellamy, John G. (1998) *The Criminal Trial in Later Medieval England: Felony Before the Courts From Edward I to the Sixteenth Century*, Toronto: University of Toronto Press.

Borsay, Peter (Ed.) (1990) *The eighteenth-century town: a reader in English urban history, 1688-1820*, London: Longman.

Bromfield, P. (2002) "Incidences and attitudes: a view of bastardy from eighteenth-century rural north Staffordshire, c. 1750–1820", *Midland History*, vol.27, pp.80–98.

Burney, Ian (2006) *Poison, Detection, and the Victorian Imagination,* Manchester: Manchester University Press.

Callahan, Kathy (2012) "On the Receiving End: Women and Stolen Goods in London 1783-1815", in *The London Journal,* vol.37, no.2, pp.106-121.

Campbell, Anne et al (2001) "Women and crime. An Evolutionary Approach", in *Aggression and Violent Behaviour*, vol.6, issue 5, pp.481-497.

Campbell, Charles (2001) *The Intolerable Hulks: British Shipboard Confinement 1776-1857,* 3rd edn., Tucson: Fenestra Books.

Campbell, Ruth (1984) "Sentence of Death by Burning for Women", in *Journal of Legal History*, vol.5, pp.44-48.

Capp, Bernard (1996) "Separate Domains? Women and Authority in Early Modern England", at pp.117-145 in *The Experience of Authority in Early Modern England*, Griffiths, P. et al (Eds), Basingstoke: MacMillan.

Capp, Bernard (1999) "The Double Standard Revisited: Plebeian Women and Male Sexual Reputation in Early Modern England", in *Past and Present*, no.162, pp.70-100.

—. (2000) "Arson, Threats of Arson, and Incivility in Early Modern England", in Burke, Peter et al (Eds), *Civil Histories*, Oxford: OUP.

Castan, Nicole (1993) "Criminals", at pp.475-488 in Davis, Natalie (Ed.) *A History of Women in the West: Renaissance and Enlightenment Paradoxes* vol.3, Harvard: Harvard University Press.

Caswell, Marisha Christine (2012) *Married Women, Crime, And Questions Of Liability In England, 1640-1760*, PhD Thesis, Queen's University, Ontario, Canada.

Clayton, Mary (2008) "The Life and Crimes of Charlotte Walker, Prostitute and Pickpocket", in *The London Journal*, vol.33, no.1, pp.3-19.

Coldham, Peter Wilson (1992) *Emigrants in chains: a social history of forced emigration to the Americas of felons, destitute children, political and religious non-conformists, vagabonds, beggars and other undesirables, 1607-1776*, Baltimore: Genealogical Publishing.

Cooper, Christine M. (2004) "Reading the Politics of Abortion: Mary Wollstonecraft Revisited", in *Eighteenth-Century Fiction*, vol.16: issue

4, pp.736-782.

Cornett, Judy M. (1997) "Hoodwink'd by custom: The exclusion of women from juries in Eighteenth-Century English Law and Literature", in *William and Mary Journal of Women and the Law*, vol.4, pp.18-28.

Cotton, J. (2003) "Homicide", at pp.1-23, in Flood-Page, C. and Taylor, J. (Eds), *Crime in England and Wales 2001/2002: Supplementary Volume*, London: Home Office.

Dabhoiwala, Faramerz (2012) *The Origins of Sex: A History of the First Sexual Revolution*, Oxford: OUP.

Davey, B.J. (1994) *Rural Crime in the Eighteenth Century: North Lincolnshire 1740 – 80*, Hull: Hull University Press.

Davies, Andrew (1999) "'These viragoes are no less cruel than the lads': young women, gangs and violence in late Victorian Manchester and Salford", in *British Journal of Criminology*, vol.39(1), pp.72-89.

Davies, Owen (1999) "Witchcraft: The Spell that Didn't Break", *History Today*, vol. 49(8), pp.7-13.

—. (1999) *Witchcraft, Magic and Culture, 1736-1951,* Manchester: Manchester University Press.

Dayton, Cornelia Hughes (1991) "Taking the Trade: Abortion and Gender Relations in an Eighteenth-Century New England Village", in *The William and Mary Quarterly*, vol.48, no.1, pp.19-49.

D'Cruze, Shani and Jackson, Louise (2009) *Women, Crime and Justice in England since 1660*, Basingstoke: Palgrave Macmillan.

Dean, Trevor (2001) *Crime in Medieval Europe 1200-1550*, Harlow: Longman.

Devereaux, Simon (2005) "The Abolition of the Burning of Women in England Reconsidered", in *Crime, History & Societies*, vol.9, no.2, pp.73-98.

Dickinson, J.P. and Sharpe, James A. (2002) "Infanticide in early modern England: the Court of Great Sessions at Chester, 1650-1800", at pp.35-51, in Jackson, Mark (Ed.), *Infanticide: Historical Perspectives on Child Murder and Concealment, 1550-2000*, Aldershot: Ashgate.

Dolan, Frances E. (2003) "Battered women, petty traitors, and the legacy of coverture", in *Feminist Studies,* vol.29, no.2, pp.249-277.

Durston, Gregory (2007) *Victims and Viragos: Metropolitan Women, Crime and the Eighteenth-Century Justice System,* Ipswich: Abramis.

Dyndor, Zoe (2008) "Death Recorded: Capital Punishment and the Press in Northampton, 1780–1834", in *Midland History*, vol.33, no.2, pp.179–195.

Eigen, Joel (1998) "Criminal Lunacy in Early Modern England Did Gender Make a Difference?", in *International Journal of Law and Psychiatry*, vol.21, no.4, pp.409–419.

Eisner, Manuel (2001) "Modernization, Self-control and Lethal violence", in *British Journal of Criminology*, vol.41, pp.618-638.

—. (2003) "Long-Term Historical Trends in Violent Crime", in *Crime and Justice; A Review of Research*, vol.30, pp.83–142.

Elias, Norbert (1982) *The Civilising Process*, vols.1 and 2, Oxford: Blackwells.

Evans, Tanya (2005) "'Unfortunate Objects': London's Unmarried Mothers in the Eighteenth Century", in *Gender & History*, vol.17, no.1, pp.127-153.

Feeley, Malcolm and Little, Deborah (1991) "The Vanishing Female: The Decline of Women in the Criminal Process, 1687-1912", in *Law and Society Review*, vol.25, no.4, pp.719-757.

Feeley, Malcolm (1994) "The decline of women in the criminal process; a comparative history", in *Criminal Justice History*, vol.15, pp.235-274.

Feeley, Malcolm and Aviram, Hadar (2010) "Social Historical Studies of Women, Crime, and Courts", in *Annual Review of Law and Social Science,* vol.6, pp.151-171.

Ferguson, Reay (2008) *Female Felons of the First Fleet*, Trafford Publishing.

Forbes, Thomas R. (1977) "Inquests into London and Middlesex Homicides, 1673-1782", in *Yale Journal of Biology and Medicine*, vol.50, pp.207-220.

—. (1982/3) "Deadly Parents: Child Homicide in Eighteenth-and Nineteenth-Century England" in *Journal of the History of Medicine and Allied Sciences*, vol.41, pp.175-199.

—. (1988), "A jury of matrons", *Medical History*, vol.32(1), pp.23–33.

Foyster, Elizabeth (2005) *Marital Violence: An English Family History, 1660-1857*, Cambridge: CUP.

Galloway Brown, Yvonne and Ferguson, Rona (Eds) (2002) *Twisted Sisters: Women, Crime, and Deviance in Scotland Since 1400*, East Linton: Tuckwell Press.

Garland, David (1990) *Punishment and Modern Society: A Study in Social Theory,* Oxford: Clarendon.

Garnham, Neil (1996), *Courts, Crime and the Criminal Law in Ireland, 1692-1760*, Dublin: Irish Academic Press.

Gatrell, V.A.C. (1996) *The Hanging Tree: Execution and the English People 1770-1868*, Oxford: OUP.

Goddard, K. S. (2004) "A Case of Injustice? The Trial of John Bellingham", in *American Journal of Legal History*, vol. 46, no.1, pp.1-25.

Godfrey, Barry and Lawrence, Paul (2005) *Crime and Justice: 1750-1950*, Collompton: Willan Publishing.

Godfrey, Barry et al (2005) "Explaining Gendered Sentencing Patterns for Violent Men and Women in the Late-Victorian and Edwardian Period", in *British Journal of Criminology*, vol.45, pp.696-720.

Golby, J.M. and Purdue, A.W. (1999) *The Civilisation of the Crowd: Popular Culture in England 1750-1900*, Stroud: Sutton Publishing.

Gottlieb, Gabriele (2005) *Theater Of Death: Capital Punishment In Early America, 1750-1800*, PhD Thesis, University of Pittsburgh.

Gowing, Laura (1997) "Secret Birth and Infanticide in Seventeenth-Century England", in *Past and Present*, vol.156, pp.157-187.

Häßler, Günther and Häßler, Frank (2011) "Infanticide in Mecklenburg and Western Pomerania: Documents from four centuries (1570—1842)", in *History of Psychiatry*, vol.22(1), pp.75-92.

Hair, Paul (1972) *Before the bawdy court: selections from church court and other records relating to the correction of moral offences in England, Scotland, and New England, 1300-1800*, London: Elek.

Hanawalt, Barbara (1974) "The Female Felon in Fourteenth-Century England", in *Viator*, vol.5, pp.253–268.

Harrison, John G., (1998) "Women and the Branks in Stirling, c.1600 to c.1730", in *Journal of Scottish Historical Studies*, vol.18 (2), pp.114 - 124.

Hay, Douglas and Rogers, Nicholas (1987) *Eighteenth-century English Society*, Oxford: OUP.

Hay, Douglas (2010) "Hanging and the English Judges: The Judicial Politics of Retention and Abolition", at pp.129-165 in Garland, David et al (Eds), *America's Death Penalty: Between Past and Present,* New York: New York University Press.

Henry, Brian (1993), *Dublin Hanged: Crime, Law Enforcement and Punishment in Late 18th-century Dublin*, Dublin: Irish Academic Press.

Hill, Bridget (1996) *Servants: English Domestics in the Eighteenth Century,* Oxford: Clarendon Press.

Hillier, Bevis (2003) "The Mysterious Case of Elizabeth Canning", in *History Today*, vol.53, issue 3, pp.47-53.

Hindle, Steve (2003) "Crime and Popular Protest" at pp.130-147 in Coward, B. (Ed.) *A Companion to Stuart Britain,* Oxford: Blackwells.

Hitchcock, Tim (1997) ''Unlawfully begotten on her body': Illegitimacy and the Parish Poor in St Luke's Chelsea", at pp.70-87 in King, Peter et al (Eds) *Chronicling Poverty: The Voices and Strategies of the English Poor, 1640-1840,* Basingstoke and London: Macmillan.

Houston, R. A. (2012) "Explanations for death by suicide in northern Britain during the long eighteenth century", in *History of Psychiatry*, vol.23(1), pp.52-64.

Hoffer, Peter C. and Hull, N. E. H. (1981) *Murdering Mothers: Infanticide in England and New England 1558-1803,* New York: New York University Press.

Howard, Sharon (2003), *Crime, Communities And Authority In Early Modern Wales: Denbighshire, 1660-1730,* PhD Thesis, University of Wales, Aberystwyth.

—. (2004) "Investigating responses to theft in early modern Wales: communities, thieves and the courts", *Continuity and Change*, vol.19 (3), pp.409–430.

Humfrey, Paula (1998) "Female Servants and Women's Criminality in Early Eighteenth-Century London", at pp.58-84 in Smith, G.T. et al (Eds), *Criminal Justice in the Old World and the New,* Toronto: University of Toronto Press.

Hunnisett, R.F. (Ed.) (1981) *Wiltshire Coroners' Bills 1752–1796*, Devizes: Wiltshire Record Society.

Hurl-Eamon, Jennine (2001) "Domestic Violence Prosecuted: Women Binding Over Their Husbands for Assault at Westminster Quarter Sessions, 1685-1720", in *Journal of Family History*, vol.26, no.4, pp.435-454.

—. (2005) *Gender and Petty Violence in London, 1680-1720*, Columbus: Ohio State University Press.

Ingram, Martin J. (1994) "'Scolding Women Cucked or Washed": A Crisis in Gender Relations in Early Modern England", at pp.48-80, in Kermode, J.L. & Walker, Garthine (Eds), *Women, Crime and the Courts in Early Modern England*, London: UCL Press.

Jackson, Mark (1994) "Suspicious infant deaths: the statute of 1624 and medical evidence at coroners' inquests" at pp.64-86 in Clark, M. and Crawford, C. (Eds), *Legal Medicine in History*, Cambridge: CUP.

—. (1996) "Infanticide: Historical Perspectives", in *New Law Journal*, vol.146, p.416.

—. (1996) *New-born child murder: women, illegitimacy and the courts in eighteenth-century England*, Manchester: Manchester University Press.

Jackson, Mark (Ed.) (2001) *Infanticide: Historical Perspectives on Child Murder and its Concealment, 1500-2000*, Aldershot: Ashgate.

Jaffary, Nora E. (2012) "Reconceiving Motherhood: Infanticide and Abortion in Colonial Mexico", in *Journal of Family History,* vol.37, no.1, pp.3-22.

Jepsen, Theresa Irina Svane (2011), "Wicked Women of 18th Century Aberdeen", in *Women's History Magazine,* issue 66, pp.19-25.

Kesselring, Krista (2006) "Detecting 'Death Disguised'", in *History Today*, vol.56, issue 4, pp.26-28.

Kilday, Anne-Marie (2002) "Maternal Monsters: Murdering Mothers in Eighteenth Century Scotland", in Brown, Y. and Ferguson, R. (Eds), *Twisted Sisters: Women, Crime and Deviance in Scotland Since 1400,* Farnham: Ashgate.

—. (2005) "Women and Crime in Britain, 1700-1850", at pp.174-193 in Barker, H. and Chalus, E. (Eds), *Women's History: Britain, 1700-1850*, London: Routledge.

—. (2007), *Women and Violent Crime in Enlightenment Scotland*, Woodbridge: Boydell Press/Royal Historical Society.

King, Peter (1989) "Gleaners, Farmers and the Failure of Legal Sanctions in England 1750-1850", *Past & Present,* no.125, pp.116-150.

—. (1991) "Customary rights and women's earnings: the importance of gleaning to the rural labouring poor, 1750-1850", in *The Economic History Review*, vol.44, issue 3, pp.461–476.

—. (1992), "Legal Change, Customary Right, and Social Conflict in Late Eighteenth-Century England: The Origins of the Great Gleaning case of 1788", in *Law and History Review*, vol.10, issue 1, pp.1-31.

—. (1996) "Punishing Assault: The Transformation of Attitudes in the English Courts", in *Journal of Interdisciplinary History,* vol.27, no.1, pp.43-74.

—. (1996) "Female offenders, work and life-cycle change in late-eighteenth-century London", in *Continuity and Change*, vol.11, pp.61-90.

—. (1998) "The rise of juvenile delinquency in England 1780-1840: changing patterns of perception and prosecution", in *Past and Present*, vol.160, pp.116-166.

—. (1999) "Gender, crime and justice in late eighteenth-and early nineteenth-century England", at pp.44-74 in Arnot, M. et al (Eds), *Gender and Crime in Modern Europe*, London: UCL Press.

—. (2000) *Crime, Justice and Discretion in England: 1740-1820*, Oxford: OUP.

—. (2004) "The Summary Courts and Social Relations in Eighteenth-Century England" in *Past & Present*, no.183, pp.125-173.

—. (2006) *Crime and Law in England, 1750-1840: Remaking Justice from the Margins,* Cambridge: CUP.
—. (2007) "Newspaper reporting and attitudes to crime and justice in late-eighteenth-and early-nineteenth-century London", in *Continuity and Change*, vol.22, issue 1, pp 73-112.
Kloek, E. (1990) "Criminality and Gender in Leiden's Confessieboken, 1678-1794", in *Criminal Justice History*, vol.11, pp.1-29.
Komlos, John (Ed.) (1994) *Stature, Living Standards, and Economic Development*, Chicago: Chicago University Press.
Lacey, Nicola (2007) *From Moll Flanders to Tess of the D'Urbervilles: Women, Autonomy and Criminal Responsibility in Eighteenth and Nineteenth Century England,* London: LSE Law, Society and Economy Working Papers.
Lacour, Eva (2001) "Faces of violence Revisited. A Typology of Violence in Early Modern Germany", in *Journal of Social History,* vol.34, no.3, pp.649-667.
Landau, Norma (1998) "Appearance at the Quarter Sessions of Eighteenth-Century Middlesex", in *London Journal,* vol.23, pp.30-51.
—. (1999) "Indictment for Fun and Profit: A Prosecutor's Reward at Eighteenth-Century Quarter Sessions", *Law and History Review,* vol.17, no.3, pp.507-536.
—. (2010) "Gauging crime in late eighteenth-century London", *Social History*, vol.35, no.4, pp.396-417.
Landsman, Stephen (1998) "One hundred years of rectitude: medical witnesses at the Old Bailey 1717-1817", in *Law and History Review*, vol.16, pp.445-494
Langbein, John (1978) "The Criminal Trial Before the Lawyers", in *The University of Chicago Law Review*, vol.45, pp.263-316.
—. (2003) *The Origins of Adversary Criminal Trial*, Oxford: OUP.
Langford, Paul (2000) *Eighteenth-Century Britain: a Very Short Introduction*, Oxford: OUP.
Laurence, Anne (1996), *Women In England 1500-1760: A Social History*, London: Weidenfeld and Nicolson.
Lemire, Beverley (1990) "The Theft of Clothes and Popular Consumerism in Early Modern England", in *Journal of Social History*, vol.24, pp.255-276.
Lemmings, David (2011) *Law and Government in England during the Long Eighteenth Century: From Consent to Command,* Basingstoke: Palgrave Macmillan.

Levack, Brian (2010) "The Prosecution of Sexual Crimes in Early Eighteenth-Century Scotland", in *Scottish Historical Review*, vol.89 (2), pp.172-193.

Linebough, Peter (1991) *The London Hanged: Crime and Civil Society in the Eighteenth Century*, Harmondsworth: Penguin.

Lodine-Chaffey, Jennifer (2010) "From Newgate to the New World: A Study of London's Transported Female Convicts, 1718-1775", *Early American Review*, vol.ix, no.2, at www.earlyamerica.com/review.

Lonza, Nella (2002) "Two Souls Lost": Infanticide In The Republic Of Dubrovnik (1667-1808)", *Dubrovnik Annals,* vol.6, pp.67-107.

MacDonald, Michael (1986) "The Secularization of Suicide in England 1660-1800", in *Past & Present*, no.111, pp.50-100.

Macfarlane, Alan (1992) "Illegitimacy and illegitimates in English history", at p.82 in Laslett, P, Oosterveen, K. and Smith, R. (Eds), *Bastardy and its Comparative History,* London: Arnold & Co.

Mackay, Lynn (1999) "Why they stole: women in the Old Bailey, 1779-1789", in *Journal of Social History*, vol.32, pp.623-639.

Malcolmson, R.W. (1977) "Infanticide in the eighteenth century", at pp.187-209 in Cockburn, J.S. (Ed.), *Crime in England 1550-1800*, London: Methuen.

Marks, Alfred (1908) *Tyburn Tree its History and Annals*, London: Brown, Langham & Co.

Maynard, John (2005) *The Agricultural Labourer in Worcestershire: Responses to Economic Change and Social Dislocation 1790-1841,* PhD thesis, Coventry University.

McKenzie, Andrea (2005) "'This Death Some Strong and Stout Hearted Man Doth Choose': The Practice of Peine Forte et Dure in Seventeenth and Eighteenth-Century England", in *Law and History Review*, vol.23, no.2, pp.279-314.

McLynn, Frank (1989) *Crime and punishment in eighteenth-century England*, London: Routledge.

Melling, Elizabeth (Ed.) (1969) *Crime and Punishment, Kentish Sources VI,* Maidstone: Kent County Council.

Mercer, E.D. and Goodacre, K. (1965) *Guide to the Middlesex sessions Records, 1549-1884,* London: Greater London Record Office.

Michalik, Kerstin (2006) "The Development of the Discourse on Infanticide in the Late Eighteenth Century and the New Legal Standardization of the Offense in the Nineteenth Century", at pp.51-71 in Gleixner, Ulrike (2006) *Gender in Transition: Discourse and Practice in German-speaking Europe 1750-1830*, Ann Arbor: The University of Michigan Press.

Miles, Caroline (2012) "Intoxication and Homicide: A Context-Specific Approach", *British Journal of Criminology,* vol.52(5), pp.870-888.

Mitchell, Stephen (2000) "Witchcraft Persecutions in the Post-Craze Era: The Case of Ann Izzard of Great Paxton, 1808", *Western Folklore,* vol.59, no.3/4, pp.304-328.

Monkkonen, Eric (1991) "Bound for America: A Profile of British Convicts Transported to the Colonies, 1718-1775", in Monkkonen, Eric (Ed.) *Crime and Justice in American History*, vol.1.

Morgan, Gwenda and Rushton, Peter (1998) *Rogues, Thieves and the Rule of Law: The Problem of Law Enforcement in Northeast England,* London: University College London Press.

Morgan, Gwenda and Rushton, Peter (Eds) (2000) *The Justicing Notebook (1750-64) of Edmund Tew, Rector of Boldon*, vol.205, Woodbridge: Boydell for the Surtees Society.

Morgan, Gwenda and Rushton, Peter (2003) "The Magistrate, the Community and the Maintenance of an Orderly Society in Eighteenth-century England", in *Historical Research*, vol.76, pp.54-77.

Morgan, Gwenda and Rushton, Peter (2003), "Running Away and Returning Home: The Fate of English Convicts in the Colonies", in *Crime, Histoire et Societes*, vol.7, pp.61-80.

Morgan, Gwenda and Rushton, Peter (2004), *Eighteenth-Century Criminal Transportation: The Formation of the Criminal Atlantic*, Basingstoke: Palgrave Macmillan.

Morgan, Gwenda and Rushton, Peter (2005) "Visible Bodies: Power, Subordination and Identity in the Eighteenth-Century Atlantic World", in *Journal of Social History*, vol.39, no.1, pp.39-64.

Morris, N. and Rothman, D. J. (Eds) (1995) *The Oxford History of the Prison*, Oxford: OUP.

Muchembled, Robert (2012) *A History of Violence: From the End of the Middle Ages to the Present*, London: Polity Press.

Nixon, Cheryl L. (2011), *The Orphan in Eighteenth-Century Law and Literature: Estate, Blood, and Body*, Farnham: Ashgate.

Oldham, James (1985) "On Pleading the Belly: A History of the Jury of Matrons", in *Criminal Justice History,* vol.6, pp.1-64.

—. (1987) "Law Reporting in the London Newspapers, 1756-1786", in *The American Journal of Legal History*, vol.31, no.3, pp.177-206.

—. (2011) "Informal Lawmaking in England by the Twelve Judges in the Late Eighteenth and Early Nineteenth Centuries", in *Law & History Review,* vol.29, pp.181-220.

Olsen, Kirstin (1999) *Daily Life in 18Th-Century England*, London: Greenwood Press.

Palk, Deidre (2006) *Gender, Crime and Judicial Discretion: 1780-1830,* Woodbridge: Boydell Press.

Phillips, Jim, and May, Allyson N. (2002) "Female Criminality in 18th-Century Halifax", *Acadiensis*, vol.XXXI, no.2, pp.38-71.

Pike, Luke Owen (1876) *A History of Crime in England*, vol.2, London: Smith Elder & Co.

Porter, Roy (1991) *English Society in the 18th Century*, London: Penguin.

Pugh, R.B. and Crittall, Elizabeth (Eds) (1953) *The Victoria History Of The Counties Of England: A History Of Wiltshire*; vol.7, London: The University Institute Of Historical Research.

Rabin, Dana (2003) "Searching for the Self in Eighteenth-Century English Criminal Trials, 1730-1800", in *Eighteenth-Century Life*, vol.27, no.1, pp.85-106.

—. (2004), *Identity, Crime and Legal Responsibility in Eighteenth-Century England*, Basingstoke: Palgrave Macmillan

Redfern, Barry (2003) *Shadow of the Gallows: Crime and Criminal Justice in and Around Newcastle Upon Tyne in the Eighteenth Century,* Newcastle: Tyne Bridge Publishing.

Rees, Sian (2002), *The Floating Brothel: The Extraordinary True Story of an Eighteenth-Century Ship and Its Cargo of Female Convicts,* London: Headline Review.

Rizzo, Tracey (2004) "Between Dishonor and Death: infanticides in the *Causes celebres* of eighteenth-century France", in *Women's History Review,* vol.13, no.1, pp.5-21.

Roth, Randolph (2001) "Homicide In Early Modern England 1549-1800: The Need For A Quantitative Synthesis", in *Crime, History & Societies*, vol.5, no.21, pp.33-67.

—. (2011) "Biology and the deep history of homicide", in *British Journal of Criminology*, vol.51(3), pp.535-555.

Rowe, G. S. (1988) "Femes Covert and Criminal Prosecution in Eighteenth-Century Pennsylvania", in *The American Journal of Legal History,* vol.32, no.2, pp.138-156.

Rublack, Ulinka (1998) *The Crimes of Women in Early Modern Germany*, Oxford, Oxford University Press,

Ruff, Julius (2001) *Violence in Early Modern Europe 1500-1800*, Cambridge: CUP.

Sauer, R. (1978) "Infanticide and Abortion in Nineteenth-Century Britain", in *Population Studies*, vol.32, no.1, pp. 81-93.

Saxton, Kirsten T. (2009) *Narratives of Women and Murder in England, 1680-1760,* Farnham: Ashgate.

Shapiro, Barbara (1986) "To a Moral Certainty: Theories of Knowledge and Anglo-American Juries 1600-1850", in *Hastings Law Journal,* vol.38, pp.153-194.

Sharpe, James (1981) "Domestic Homicide in Early Modern England", in *Historical Journal*, vol.24, pp.29-48.

Shaw, A.G.L. (1977) *Convicts and the Colonies: A Study of Penal Transportation from Great Britain and Ireland to Australia and Other Parts of the British Empire,* Melbourne: Melbourne University Press.

Shoemaker, Robert (1991) *Prosecution and Punishment: Petty Crime and the Law in London and Rural Middlesex, c. 1660-1725,* Cambridge: CUP.

—. (1998) *Gender in English Society 1650-1850: The Emergence of Separate Spheres?* London: Longman.

—. (2001) "Male Honour and the decline of public violence in eighteenth-century London", in *Social History*, vol.26, no.2, pp.190-208.

—. (2004) *The London Mob: Violence and Disorder in Eighteenth-Century England,* London: Hambledon and London.

—. (2010) "Print and the Female Voice: Representations of Women's Crime in London, 1690–1735", in *Gender & History*, vol.22, no.1, pp.75–91.

Smith, Bruce P. (2005) "The Presumption of Innocence and the English Law of theft: 1750-1850", in *Law and History Review*, vol.23, no.1, pp.133-173.

Smith, M.G. (1982) "Pastoral Discipline and the Church Courts: the Hexham Court 1680-1730", *Borthwick Papers*, no.62, York.

Snell, Esther (2007) "Changing Discourses of Crime: Representations of Criminality in the Eighteenth-Century Newspaper Press", in *Continuity and Change*, vol.22, issue 1, pp.13-47.

—. (2005) "Representations of Criminality and Victimisation in Provincial Newspapers: The Kentish Post 1717 to 1768", in *Southern History*, vol.27, pp.48-75.

Spivack, Carla (2007) "To "Bring Down the Flowers": The Cultural Context of Abortion Law in Early Modern England", in *William & Mary Journal of Women and the Law*, vol.14, issue 1, pp.107-151.

Steedman, Carolyn (2007) "A Boiling Copper and Some Arsenic: Servants, Childcare, and Class Consciousness in Late Eighteenth Century England", in *Critical Inquiry*, vol.34, no.1, pp. 36-77.

Steinbach, Susie (2004*), Women in England 1760-1914*, London: Weidenfeld & Nicolson.

Steffensmeier, Darrel and Allan, Emilie (1996) "Gender and Crime: Toward a Gendered Theory of Female Offending", in *Annual Review of Sociology*, vol.22, pp.459-487.

Stone, Lawrence (1985) "Debate: The History of Violence in England, A Rejoinder" in *Past & Present*, vol.108, pp.214-216.

Styles, John (1980), "'Our Traitorous Money Makers': the Yorkshire Coiners and the Law, 1760-1783", at pp.172-249 in Styles, J. and Brewer, J. (Eds) *An Ungovernable People. The English and their Law in the Seventeenth- and Eighteenth-Centuries.* London: Hutchinson.

Symonds, Deborah A. (2006) *Notorious Murders, Black Lanterns, & Moveable Goods: The Transformation of Edinburgh's Underworld in the Early Nineteenth Century*, Akron, Ohio: The University of Akron Press.

Tickell, Shelley (2010) "The prevention of shoplifting in eighteenth-century London", in *Journal of Historical Research in Marketing*, vol.2, issue 3, pp.300-313.

Tinkova, Daniela (2005) "Protéger Ou Punir? Les Voies De La Décriminalisation De L'infanticide En France Et Dans Le Domaine Des Habsbourg (Xviiie-Xixe Siècles)", in *Crime, History & Societies*, vol.9, no.2, pp.43-72.

Tosney, Nicholas (2007) "Women and 'False Coining' in Early Modern London", in *The London Journal*, vol.32, no.2, pp.103-123.

Trumbach, Randolph (1998) *Sex and the Gender Revolution: Heterosexuality and the Third Gender in Enlightenment London*, vol.1, Chicago: University of Chicago Press.

Twyford, A. W., and Griffiths, Arthur (1880) *Records Of York Castle: Fortress, Court House, And Prison*, London.

Ulbricht, Otto (1988) "Infanticide in eighteenth-century Germany" at p.111 in *The German Underworld,* Evans, R.J. (Ed.), London: Routledge.

Walker, Garthine (1994) "Women, theft and the world of Stolen Goods", at pp.81-105, in *Women, Crime and the Courts in Early Modern England,* Kermode, J. et al (Eds) London: UCL Press.

—. (2003) *Crime, Gender and Social Order in Early Modern England,* Cambridge: CUP.

Walker, Nigel (1969) *Crime and Insanity in England*, vol.1, Edinburgh: Edinburgh University Press.

Warner, Jessica and Ivis, Frank (1999) "'Damn You, You Informing Bitch.' Vox Populi and the Unmaking of the Gin Act of 1736", in *Journal of Social History*, vol.33, no.2, pp. 299-330.

Warner, Jessica and Ivis, Frank (2000) "Gin and Gender in Early Eighteenth-century London", in *Eighteenth-Century Life,* vol.24, pp.85-105.

—. (2003) *Craze: Gin and Debauchery in an Age of Reason*, London: Profile Books.

Warner, Jessica, and Lunny, Allyson (2003) "Marital Violence In A Martial Town: Husbands And Wives In Early Modern Portsmouth, 1653-1781", in *Journal of Family History*, vol.28, no.2, pp.258-276.

Warner, Jessica et al (2005) "Women Behaving Badly: Gender and Aggression in a Military Town, 1653–1781", in *Sex Roles: A Journal of Research*, vol.52, numbers 5-6, pp.289-298.

Warner, Jessica (2008) "Men and Women Fighting Side By Side: Examples From an English Town, 1653-1781", in *Journal of Family History*, vol.33, pp.156-172.

Watson, Katherine D. (2004) *Poisoned Lives: English Poisoners and Their Victims*, London: Hambledon and London.

Whitlock, Tammy C. (2005) *Crime, Gender and Consumer Culture in Nineteenth-century England*, Aldershot: Ashgate Publishing.

Wiener, Martin J. (1999) "Judges v Jurors: Courtroom Tensions in Murder Trials and the Law of Criminal Responsibility in Nineteenth-Century England", in *Law and History Review*, vol.17, no.3, pp.467-506.

—. (2001) "Alice Arden to Bill Sikes: Changing Nightmares of Intimate Violence in England, 1558-1869", in *Journal of British Studies*, vol.40, pp.184-212.

—. (2004) *Men of Blood: Violence, Manliness, and Criminal Justice in Victorian England,* New York: CUP.

Williams, Amy (2000) *The Criminality Of Women In The 18th Century In The South West Of England*, PhD Thesis, University of Plymouth.

Willis, J. (2005) "Transportation versus Imprisonment in Eighteenth-and Nineteenth-Century Britain", in *Law & Society Review*, vol.39, issue 1, pp.171-210.

Winter, Anne (2010) "Abandoned in Brussels, delivered in Paris: long-distance transports of unwanted children in the eighteenth century", *Journal of Family History,* vol.35(3), pp.232-248.

Wright, Diana (2004) "Female Crime and State Punishment in Early Modern Japan", in *Journal of Women's History*, vol.16, no.3, pp.10-29.

Wrightson, Keith (1975) "Infanticide in earlier Seventeenth-Century England", in *Local Population Studies*, vol.15, pp.10-21.

Wrightson, Keith and Levine, David (1979) *Poverty and Piety in an English Village Terling, 1525-1700,* Oxford: Clarendon Press.

Wrigley, E.A. (1967) "A simple model of London's Importance in Changing English Society and Economy 1650-1750", in *Past and Present*, no.37, pp.44-70.

Zedner, Lucia (1991) *Women, Crime and Custody in Victorian England*, Oxford: OUP.

Zunshine, Lisa (2005) *Bastards and Foundlings: Illegitimacy in Eighteenth-Century England,* Columbus: Ohio State University Press.

Pre-1850 Sources (even if published after that date)

Aikin, Lucy (1810) *Epistles on Women, Exemplifying Their Character and Condition,* London: Printed for J. Johnson and Co.

Anon, (1632) *The Laws Resolutions of Womens Rights: or, the Lawes Provision for Women*, London: John More.

Anon, (1681) *The True narrative of the confession and execution of the prisoners at Kingstone-upon-Thames, on Wednesday the 16th of this instant March, 1681*, London.

Anon, (1682) *An Account of the tryal and examination of Joan Buts, for being a common witch and inchantress, before the Right Honourable Sir Francis Pemberton, Lord Chief Justice, at the assizes holden for the burrough of Southward and county of Surrey, on Monday, March 27, 1682*, London.

Anon, (1659) *The Caterpillars of this Nation Anatomised,* London.

Anon, (1670) *Inquest after blood, being a relation of the several inquisitions of all that have died by any violent death in the city of London, and borough of Southwark commencing from Jan. 1, 1669, to the conclusion of the last sessions holden at the Old Baily, Feb. 21, and the assizes for Surrey, March 1, with some remarkable observations*, London.

Anon, (1674) *Relation of the most remarkable proceedings at the late assizes at Northampton Conteyning truely and fully, the tryals, confessions, and execution of a most mischievous witch, notorious high-way-man, barbarous murderess. ... Who all suffered at Northampton aforesaid, Saturday, August 22, 1674*, London.

Anon, (1681) *The True narrative of the confession and execution of the prisoners at Kingstone-upon-Thames, on Wednesday the 16th of this instant March, 1681*, London.

Anon, (1682) *An Account of the tryal and examination of Joan Buts, for being a common witch and inchantress,* London.

Anon, (1687) *A Full and true account of a most barbarous and bloody murther, committed by Esther Ives, with the assistance of John Noyse a cooper; on the body of William Ives, her husband, at Rumsey in Hampshire, on the fifth day of February 1686,* London: Printed for P. Brooksby.

Anon, (1687) *The poysoners rewarded, or, The most barbarous of murthers, directed and published…*, London

Anon, (1690) *The female highway hector: or, An account of a woman, who was lately arraign'd for robbing on the high-way in man's apparel,* London: Printed for C. Bates.

Anon, (1690) *A full and true relation of the examination and confession of W. Barwick and E. Mangall, of two horrid murders …,* London.

Anon, (1692) *Fair warnings to murderers of infants being an account of the tryal, codemnation [sic] and execution of Mary Goodenough at the assizes held in Oxon in February, 1691/2 together with the advice sent by her to her children, in a letter sign'd by her own hand the night before she was executed,* London: Printed for Jonathan Robinson.

Anon, (1694) *The Ladies Dictionary, Being a General Entertainment for the Fair Sex*, London: Printed for John Dunton.

Anon, (1699) *Concealed Murther Revealed*, London: Printed for William Aldredge.

Anon, (1701) *The lamentation of Mary Butcher, now confined in Worcester-City-Goal, on suspicion of murdering her male bastard child, in April last*, London.

Anon, (1703) *The tryals of Haagen Swendsen, Sarah Baynton, John Hartwell and John Spurr: for feloniously stealing Mrs Pleasant Rawlins, a virgin and heiress of a considerable fortune*, London.

Anon, (1705) *The Northamptonshire Witches*, London.

Anon, (1706) *Serious admonitions to youth, in a short account of the life, trial, condemnation and execution of Mrs Mary Channing, who, for poisoning her husband, was burnt at Dorchester in the county of Dorset on Thursday, March the 21st 1706*, London: printed for Ben Bragg.

Anon, (1712) *A Full Confutation of Witchcraft,* London.

Anon, (1713) *A Full Account of the Case of John Sayer*, 2nd edn., London.

Anon, (1732) *A Treatise of Feme Coverts or the Lady's Law,* London: Printed for R. Nott.

Anon (A female author), (1735) "The Hardships of the English Laws in Relation to Wives", in Jones, V. (Ed.), *Women in the Eighteenth Century*, London.

Anon, (1738) *Baron and Feme: A treatise of Law and Equity Concerning Husbands and Wives*, 3rd edn., London: R. Nott.

Anon, (1738) *The Proceedings at the Assizes for the County of Surry [sic], held at Guildford, ... On Thursday the 16th, Friday the 17th, Saturday the 18th, Monday the 20th, and Tuesday the 21st March, 1738,* London

Anon, (1738) *A Full, True, and Genuine Account of the Uncommon Behaviour of Mr. Gill Smith, ... Likewise the Confession, Behaviour, and Dying Words, of Anne Goodson, who was burnt for the murder of her husband*, Southwark.

Anon, (1739) *The Genuine Proceedings at the Assizes on the Home Circuit, Held in March, 1739. ... at Hertford, for the County of Hertford; Chelmsford, for the County of Essex …* London.

Anon (By a Physician), (1739) *The Ladies Physical Directory*, 7th edn., London.

Anon, (1740) *The Proceedings at the Assizes of Peace, Oyer and Terminer, for the County of Surrey, Held at the Town-Hall of Kingston Upon Thames, in the 14th Year of His Majesty's Reign ... To Which is Added the Genuine Proceedings at the Assizes for the County of Essex*, London: Sold by J. Standen.

Anon, (1740) *A Dialogue Between A Married Lady and a Maid*, London.

Anon, (1742) *The Proceedings at the Assizes of Peace, Oyer and Terminer, for the County of Surrey, Held at Kingston Upon Thames, on Friday the 13th, Saturday the 14th, and Monday the 16th Days of August. In the 16th Year of His Majesty's Reign,* London: Printed for C. Crouch.

Anon, (1745) *The Proceedings at the assizes of the peace, oyer and terminer, and general gaol-delivery for the county of Surry, held at Croydon, on Friday the 22d, Saturday the 23d, Monday the 25th, Tuesday the 26th, and Wednesday the 27th Days of March*, London.

Anon, (1747) *The Art of Governing a Wife*, London: J. Robinson.

Anon, (1750) *The Female Soldier; Or, The Surprising Life and Adventures of Hannah Snell*, London.

Anon, (1752) *The Tryal of Mary Blandy, Spinster; For the Murder of her Father, Francis Blandy, Gent.*, London.

Anon, (1752) *The whole tryal of John Swann, and Elizabeth Jeffries, for the murder of her uncle Mr. Joseph Jeffryes : at Walthamstow ... at the assizes held at Chelmsford in Essex, on Wednesday the 11th of March, 1752,* London.

Anon (Lover of his country), (1752) *Villain'y Unmask'd …* London: Printed for W. Owen.

Anon ('Mira'), (1756) *The Wife*, London.

Anon ('A clergyman of the City of London'), (1758) *Friendly Advice to the Fair Sex*, London: printed for G. Kearsly.

Anon (By a gentleman of the law), (1759) *The Case of Mary Edmondson*, London.

Anon, (1760) *A Genuine Account of the Life and Trial of William Andrew Horne, Esq.,* 3rd edn., London.

Anon (By a Lover of Justice), (1760) *An Answer to the Pamphlet Wrote by the Juryman, Touching the Death of Ann Sharp*, London.

Anon, (1762) *God's Revenge Against Murder!*, London.

Anon, (1763) *The genuine trial of Margery Beddingfield and Richard Ringe, ... for petty treason and murder committed on John Beddingfield, ... Carefully taken in court, by an eminent shorthand writer*, London.

Anon, (1767) *An Appeal to humanity: in an account of the life and cruel actions of Elizabeth Brownrigg ... To which is added the Trial of Elizabeth Branch and her Daughter, for the murder of their Servant Maid, &c.*, London.

Anon, (1769) *A Collection of Tracts, Relating to the Crimes, Examination, Trial, Sentence and Execution of Sussanah Lott and Benjamin Buss, for Poisoning Mr. Lott*, Canterbury.

Anon, (1772) *The Complete Parish Officer,* London.

Anon, (1775) *Circumstances of the Death of Mr. Scawen, with Genuine Particulars relative to Miss Jenny Butterfield*, London.

Anon, (1775) *The Trial of Jane Butterfield for the Wilful Murder of William Scawen, Esq*. London.

Anon, (1777) *The Laws Respecting Women*, London: Printed for J. Johnson.

Anon, (1782) *Character and dying behaviour of the two murderers, executed at Heavitree gallows, Monday, March 25, 1782*. Exeter: Printed by E. Brice.

Anon, (1786) *An Authentic Narrative of the Most Remarkable Adventures, and Curious Intrigues, Exhibited in the Life of Miss Fanny Davies*, London.

Anon, (1786) *The Whole Art of Thieving and Defrauding Discovered*, London.

Anon, (1791) *An Authentic Account of the riots in Birmingham on the 14th, 15th, 16th, and 17th Days of July 1791*, London.

Anon, (1791) *Advice to Unmarried Women: To recover and Reclaim the Fallen*, London.

Anon, (1792) *The Evils of Adultery and Prostitution*, London.

Anon, (1794) *The trials of Samuel Hammond, for the murder of Ann Avey; and Ann Gosling, for the murder of John Sage. At the Lent Assizes, at Bury St. Edmund's, in the county of Suffolk*, Newmarket.

Anon, (1795) *The Trial of Mrs. Mary Reed, Upon the Charge of Poisoning Her Husband, At Berkeley, in Gloucestershire, in April, 1794,* London.

Anon, (1796?) *The True and remarkable life and extraordinary adventures of that unfortunate woman, Sarah Chandler*, Newcastle.

Anon, (1798) *The Young and Thoughtless Criminal*, London.

Anon, (1798) *The Female Aegis; or, The Duties of Women from Childhood to Old Age and in most Situations of Life, Exemplified*, London.

Anon, (1799) *Reports from Select Committees, Respecting The Arts-Masters and Apprentices of Bridewell Hospital*, London.

Anon, (1799) *Thoughts on Means of Alleviating the Miseries attendant upon Common Prostitution*, London: Printed for T. Cadell.

Anon, (1802) *The last dying words and confession of Mary Vice [sic], who were executed on Nottingham Gallows, on Tuesday the 17th day of March, for the willful murder of her child by poison*, Leicester.

Anon, (1809) *Extraordinary Life and Character of Mary Bateman, the Yorkshire Witch*, 9th Edn., Leeds.

Anon, (1840) *A Concise View of the Origin and Progress of the British Ladies: Society for Promoting the Reformation of Female Prisoners*, London: Hatchard & Co.

Anon, (nd) *The Hampshire Tragedy: Shewing how a Servant Maid first robbed her master, and was afterwards struck dead for telling a lie*, London.

Babington, Zachary (1677) *Advise to Grand Jurors in Cases of Blood*, London: Printed for John Amery.

—. (1680) *Advice to Grand Jurors in Cases of Blood*, London.

Bacon, Sir Francis (1906) "On Judicature", *The Essays,* London: J M Dent.

—. (1641) *Cases of Treason*, London: printed by the Assignes of John More.

Baldwin, R. (1776) *Considerations on some laws relating to the office of Coroner*, Newcastle: printed for T. Saint.

Beville, Robert (1799) *A treatise on the law of homicide, and of larceny at common law*, London.

Bingham, Peregrine (1816) *The Law of Infancy and Coverture*, London: Butterworth & Son.

Blackerby, Samuel (1715) *The Justice of Peace His Companion*, 3rd edn., London.

Blackstone, William (1765-9) *Commentaries on the Laws of England*, Oxford: Clarendon Press, vols 1-4.

Blandy, Mary (1752) *Genuine letters that pass'd between Miss Blandy and Miss Jeffries, before and after conviction*, London.

Bohun, Edmund (1693) *The Justice of Peace: His Calling and Qualifications,* London.

Broughton, Thomas (1800), *Serious Advice and Warning to Servants*, 6th Edn., London.

Brown, John (1757) *An Estimate of the Manners and Principles of the Times*, London.

Brown, Thomas (1705) *A Legacy for the Ladies Or, Characters of the Women of the Age…*, London.

Brydall, J. (1700) *Non compos mentis: or, The law relating to natural fools, mad-folks, and lunatick persons*, London.

Burn, Richard (1763), *Ecclesiastical Law*, vol.1, London: Printed by Woodfall.

Burrington, George (1757) *An answer to Dr. William Brakenridge's letter concerning the number of inhabitants, within the London bills of mortality*, London.

Chitty, J. (1816) *A Practical Treatise on the Criminal Law,* vol.1, London.

Coke, Sir Edward (1644) *Institutes of the Lawes of England, Part Three, Concerning High Treason, and other Pleas of the Crown and Criminal causes*, London: W. Lee.

Cooke, George Alexander (1802), *The modern British traveller: or, Tourist's pocket directory. Huntingdon*, London: C. Cooke.

Crittall, Elizabeth (1982) *The Justicing Notebook of William Hunt, 1744-1749*, Wiltshire Record Society: Devizes.

D'Archenholz, Johann Wilhelm (1791) *A Picture of England*, Dublin.

Dean, David (Ed.) (1991), *St. Albans Quarter Sessions rolls, 1784-1820: A calendar of rolls of the General Court of Quarter Sessions for the borough of St. Albans*, Hertford: Hertfordshire Record Society.

De Mandeville, Bernard (1724) *A Modest Defence of Publick Stews*, London: Printed for A. Moore.

Defoe, Daniel (1697) *An Essay Upon Projects,* London: Printed by R.R. for Thomas Cockerill.

—. (1731) *The Generous Projector*, London: Printed for A. Dodd.

Dogherty, Thomas (1799) *The Crown Circuit Companion*, vol.1, London: Printed for E. and R. Brooke.

Downright, Sir D. (1768) *The Bastard Child, or a Feast for the Church-wardens,* London.

Farr, Samuel (1788) *Elements of Medical Jurisprudence*, London: printed for T. Becket.

Gilbert, Humphrey (1760) *The Law of Evidence,* 2nd edn., London: Printed by Catherine Lintot.

Giles, William (1771) *A Treatise on Marriage*, London.

Gisborne, Thomas (1797) *An Enquiry into the Duties of the Female Sex*, London.

Gough, William (1634) *Domesticall Duties*, London.

Grant, F. (1701) *A Vindication of Informers of the Breaches of the Laws Against Prophaness and Immorality*, London.

Gurney, Joseph (1819) *Notes on a visit made to some of the prisons in Scotland and the north of England*, London.

Hale, Mathew (1736) *History of the Pleas of the Crown*, Book 1, London: Printed by E. & R. Nut.

Hanway, Jonas (1758) *A Plan for establishing a Charity-House or Charity Houses for the reception of repenting prostitutes*, London.

Hanway, Jonas (1759) *A Candid historical Account of the Hospital for the Reception of exposed and Deserted Young Children*, London.

Hanway, Jonas (1789) *Advice from Farmer Trueman to his Daughter*, 2nd edn., Edinburgh.

Hawkins, William (1724) *A Treatise of the Pleas of the Crown*, Book 1, 2nd Edn., London.

Hayward, Arthur (Ed.) (1927) *Lives of the Most Remarkable Criminals: Who have been Condemned and Executed for Murder, the Highway, Housebreaking, Street Robberies, Coining or other offences. Collected from Original Papers and Authentic Memoirs, 1735*, London: Routledge & Sons.

Howard, John (1777) *Account of the Present State of the Prisons, Houses of Correction, and Hospitals in London and Westminster,* London.

Hunnisett, R.F. (Ed.) (1981) *Wiltshire Coroners' Bills 1752–1796*, Devizes: Wiltshire Record Society.

Hunnisett, R.F. (Ed.), (1996) *Sussex coroners' inquests 1603-1688*, London: PRO Publications.

Hunter, William (1812) *On the Uncertainty of the Signs of Murder in the Case of Bastard Children*, London: printed for J Callow (first published 1784).

—. (1784) "On the Uncertainty of the Signs of Murder, in the Case of Bastard Children", *Medical Observations and Inquiries*, vol.6, pp.266-290

Hyde, Edward (1803) *A Treatise of the Pleas of the Crown*, vol.1, London: printed by A. Strahan, London.

Johnson, Captain Charles (1742) *A General and True History of the Lives and Actions of the most Famous Highwaymen, Murders, Street-Robbers etc*., Birmingham.

Johnson, H.C. (1964) *Warwick County Records, vol.IX: Quarter session records; Easter, 1690 to Michaelmas, 1696*, Warwick: Warwick County Records

Knapp, Andrew and Baldwin, William (1825) *The Newgate Calendar; Comprising Interesting Memoirs of the Most Notorious Characters…*vols. 1 & 2, London: J. Robins and Co.

Madan, Martin (1781) *Thelyphthora; or, A Treatise on Female Ruin*, vol.1, London.

Misson, Henri (1719) *Memoirs and Observations in his Travels over England*, London.

Moreton, Andrew (Daniel Defoe) (1725) *Every-Body's Business is No-Body's Business*, London.

Morgan, Gwenda and Rushton, Peter (Eds) (2000) *The Justicing Notebook (1750-64) of Edmund Tew, Rector of Boldon*, vol 205, Woodbridge: Boydell for the Surtees Society.

Moritz, Charles (1797) *Travels in England in 1782*, 2nd edn., London.

Parker, George (1781) *A View of Society and Manners in High and Low Life*, London.

Penrose, Reverend (1741), *The Reverend Mr. Penrose's Account of the Behaviour, Confession, and last dying words, of the four malefactors executed at St. Michael's Hill at Bristol, on Wednesday the 15th of April, 1741*, Bristol.

Pinchard, John (Attorney) (1800), *The Trial of Jane Leigh Perrot, wife of James Leigh Perrot*, Taunton.

Quarrell, W. H. and More, Margaret (Eds) (1934) *London in 1710 From the Travels of Zacharias Conrad Von Uffenbach*, London: Faber & Faber Ltd.

Quick, John (1676) *Hell open'd, or, The infernal sin of murther punished being a true relation of the poysoning of a whole family in Plymouth,* ... London.

Ratcliff, S.C. and Johnson, H.C. (1946) *Warwick County Records Volume vii: Quarter Sessions records Easter, 1674, to Easter, 1682,* Warwick: Stephens.

Rayner, J. L. and Crook, G. T. (Eds) (1926) *The Complete Newgate Calendar*, vols 1- 4, London: Privately printed for the Navarre Society.

Shakesheff, Tim (2003) *Rural Conflict, Crime and Protest: Herefordshire 1800-1860*, Woodbridge: Boydell Press.

Silverthorne, Elizabeth (Ed.) (1978) *The Deposition Book of Richard Wyatt JP, 1767-1776*, Abinger: Surrey Record Society.

Smith, Alexander (1719) *A Compleat history of the lives and robberies of the most notorious highwaymen ... for above an hundred years past,* vol.2, London: Briscoe.

Stubbs, W. and Talmarsh, G. (1749) *The Crown circuit companion: containing the practice of the assises on the Crown side, and of the courts of general and general quarter sessions of the peace*, London.

Swetman, Joseph (1733) *The Arraignment of Lewde, Idle, Froward and Unconstant Women,* London.

Van Muyden, Madame (Trans and Ed.) (1902) *A foreign View of England in the reigns of George I and George II,* London: John Murray.

W., J. (1707) *A Compleat Guide for Justices of the Peace,* London.

Wenderborn, Frederick Augustus (1791) *A View of England Towards the Close of the 18th Century*, vol.1, Dublin: Printed for P. Wogan.

Wilkes, Reverend Wettenhall (1751) *A Letter of Genteel and Moral Advice to a Young Lady*, London.

Wilkes, John (1764) *An Essay on Woman*, London.

Wollestonecraft, Mary (1792) *Vindication of the Rights of Women,* 2nd edn., London.

Woodforde, James (1999) *The Diary of a Country Parson, 1758-1802,* Norwich: The Canterbury Press.

Zouch, Henry (1786) *Hints Respecting the Public Police*, London.

Contemporary Journals and Newspapers Cited

Adams's Weekly Courant,
Applebee's Original Weekly Journal,
Bath Chronicle,
Bedfordshire Mercury and Huntingdon Express,
Bell's Weekly Messenger,
Bingley's Journal,
Caledonian Mercury,
Chester Chronicle and General Advertiser,
Chester Chronicle Or Commercial Intelligencer,
Country Journal or The Craftsman,
Courier and Evening Gazette,
Coventry Mercury,
Craftsman or Say's Weekly Journal,
Daily Advertiser,
Daily Gazetteer,

Daily Post,
English Chronicle or Universal Evening Post,
English Post,
Evening Post,
Exeter Flying Post,
Felix Farley's Bristol Journal,
Fog's Weekly Journal,
Gazetteer and London Daily Advertiser,
Gazetteer and New Daily Advertiser,
General Advertiser,
General Evening Post,
Gloucester Journal,
Grub-street Journal,
Guardian,
Harrop's Manchester Mercury,
Hull Packet,
Lloyd's Evening Post and British Chronicle,
Lloyd's Evening Post,
London and Country Journal,
London Chronicle,
London Daily Post and General Advertiser,
London Evening Post,
London Packet or New Lloyd's Evening Post,
London Post,
London Spy Revived,
Mist's Weekly Journal,
Morning Chronicle and London Advertiser,
Morning Herald and Daily Advertiser,
Morning Post and Daily Advertiser,
Morning Post and Fashionable World,
Old England or The National Gazette,
Old Whig or The Consistent Protestant,
Oracle and Daily Advertiser,
Parker's Penny Post,
Penny London Morning Advertiser,
Post Man and the Historical Account,
Public Advertiser,
Read's Weekly Journal Or British Gazetteer,
Royal Cornwall Gazette, Falmouth Packet & Plymouth Journal,
St. James's Chronicle or the British Evening Post,
St. James's Evening Post,

Star,
Sun,
Telegraph,
The British Journal,
The Bury and Norwich Post: Or, Suffolk, Norfolk, Essex, and Cambridge Advertiser,
The Daily Journal,
The Derby Mercury,
The Flying Post,
The Gentleman's Magazine,
The Ipswich Journal,
The London Chronicle or Universal Evening Post,
The London Journal,
The Middlesex Journal,
The Morning Post and Gazetteer,
The Morning Post,
The Post-Boy,
The Spectator,
The Tatler,
The Times,
Trewman's Exeter Flying Post,
True Briton (1793),
Universal Chronicle or Weekly Gazette,
Universal Spectator and Weekly Journal,
Weekly Journal, or The British Gazetteer,
Weekly Miscellany (1732),
Whitehall Evening Post (1770),
World and Fashionable Advertiser,

INDEX